Teaching with The Norton Anthology of English Literature

SEVENTH EDITION

A Guide for Instructors

THE EDITORS

M. H. Abrams, General Editor
CLASS OF 1916 PROFESSOR OF ENGLISH EMERITUS,
CORNELL UNIVERSITY

Stephen Greenblatt, Associate General Editor
COGAN UNIVERSITY PROFESSOR OF THE HUMANITIES, HARVARD UNIVERSITY

E. Talbot Donaldson
LATE OF INDIANA UNIVERSITY

Alfred David
PROFESSOR OF ENGLISH EMERITUS, INDIANA UNIVERSITY

Hallett Smith
LATE OF THE HUNTINGTON LIBRARY

Barbara K. Lewalski
WILLIAM R. KENAN PROFESSOR OF ENGLISH AND OF HISTORY
AND LITERATURE, HARVARD UNIVERSITY

Robert M. Adams
LATE OF THE UNIVERSITY OF CALIFORNIA AT LOS ANGELES

George M. Logan
JAMES CAPPON PROFESSOR OF ENGLISH, QUEEN'S UNIVERSITY

Samuel Holt Monk
LATE OF THE UNIVERSITY OF MINNESOTA

Lawrence Lipking
PROFESSOR OF ENGLISH AND CHESTER D. TRIPP PROFESSOR OF
HUMANITIES, NORTHWESTERN UNIVERSITY

Jack Stillinger
CENTER FOR ADVANCED STUDY PROFESSOR OF ENGLISH,
UNIVERSITY OF ILLINOIS

George H. Ford
LATE OF THE UNIVERSITY OF ROCHESTER

Carol T. Christ
PROFESSOR OF ENGLISH, UNIVERSITY OF CALIFORNIA AT BERKELEY

David Daiches
FORMER DIRECTOR OF THE INSTITUTE FOR ADVANCED STUDIES,
UNIVERSITY OF EDINBURGH

Jon Stallworthy
PROFESSOR OF ENGLISH LITERATURE, OXFORD UNIVERSITY

Teaching with The Norton Anthology of English Literature

SEVENTH EDITION

A Guide for Instructors

Alfred David
INDIANA UNIVERSITY

Kelly Hurley
UNIVERSITY OF COLORADO, BOULDER

Philip Schwyzer
OXFORD UNIVERSITY

W. W. NORTON & COMPANY
New York • London

COVER ART: (front) The Ditchley portrait of Elizabeth I (ca. 1592), by Marcus Gheeraerts. Reproduced by courtesy of the National Portrait Gallery, London. (back) Detail from *Swan Upping at Cookham* (1914–19), by Stanley Spencer. Tate Gallery, London. Photo: Tate Gallery, London/Art Resource.

ISBN 0-393-97514-2 (pbk.)

W. W. Norton & Company, Inc., 500 Fifth Avenue, New York, N.Y. 10110
www.wwnorton.com

W. W. Norton & Company Ltd., Castle House, 75/76 Wells Street,
London W1T 3QT

3 4 5 6 7 8 9 0

Contents

Expanded Table of Contents

This table of contents lists, alphabetically by author or, where there is no author, by title, the *NAEL* works discussed in chapters 2–8 of the Guide.

PREFACE

A Brief Guide to the Guide

The purpose of this Guide is to assist instructors in formulating and applying different approaches to teaching with *The Norton Anthology of English Literature* (*NAEL*), Seventh Edition. While *NAEL*, together with its Web site and Online Archive, provides as wide a selection of texts as possible for teachers to choose from in order to design their own courses, perhaps the greatest challenge for instructors is to decide which texts to teach. This challenge is made all the more difficult by increased possibilities of readings to be assigned, for, as the twentieth century has come to a close, the ground to be covered has kept expanding. Not only are new contemporary writers—British and Anglophone—to be included: "rediscovered" writers in earlier periods are of great interest to teachers and students. Furthermore, whereas the New Criticism once taught that close reading of literary texts required us to dismiss extraneous biographical and historical data and to focus on their formal qualities, the New Historicism teaches that close reading also involves historicizing such works with reference to other kinds of texts. Both kinds of reading are desirable.

Although *NAEL* has been attacked in some quarters for presuming to establish a "canon," in other quarters for replacing "classics" with noncanonical works, the contents of the Seventh Edition bear out John Guillory's argument against the distinction between "canonical" and "noncanonical" works. A literary canon exists only in the abstract: "What does have a concrete location as a list . . . is not the canon but the syllabus, the list of works one reads in a given class, or the curriculum, the list of works one reads in a program of study. When teachers believe they have in some way challenged or overthrown the canon and its evaluative principles, what they have always really done is devise or revise a particular syllabus, as it is only through the syllabus that they have access to the imaginary list which is the canon."[1]

The business of the Guide, then, is not only to provide ideas for teaching particular selections but also to suggest some of the many possibilities of organizing those selections into a coherent syllabus. Chapter 1 provides an introduction to the teaching aids (e.g., maps, timelines, appendixes) in the anthology and on the Web, pointing out innovations in the Seventh Edition. Chapters 2–8 discuss ways for organizing and teaching a relatively traditional historical survey. Within those chapters, works are grouped under broad historical and generic topics. An Expanded Table of Contents has been provided (pp. ix–xix), which lists the titles of the works discussed under those topics. Where they might be helpful, we have inserted cross-references to related selections on the Web site and Audio Companion that accompany *NAEL*. In addition, we run, at the end of each of these seven chapters, brief contents lists for Norton Topics Online, the Norton Online Archive, and the NAEL Audio CD. Chapter 9 gives examples of how two or more periods or the entire course could be structured around a single theme or topic. The availability of the Seventh Edition in six separate period volumes makes it possible to use one or more of these volumes in custom-designed period courses. Chapter 10 gives samples of examination questions, paper topics, and study questions. An appendix discusses special problems in teaching lyric poetry and drama.

For the convenience of instructors who will be teaching from only one volume of the two-volume edition, we have supplied the volume and page numbers for quotations and other specific references to works; there are numerous cross-references between the two volumes. The pagination of the splits is the same as in the two-volume edition except for the appendices and index, which are paginated A1–A72.

Acknowledgments

This Guide has been a collaborative effort from start to finish. Alfred David wrote the opening chapter, the chapter on the Middle Ages, the chapter "Making Up Courses," and Appendix B; he also read and commented on the complete manuscript and, in collaboration with George Logan, Barbara Lewalski, Lawrence Lipking, and Jack Stillinger, made revisions and additions in Chapters 3–6. Philip Schwyzer wrote the chapters on the Sixteenth Century, the Early Seventeenth Century, and the Restoration and Eighteenth Century. Kelly Hurley wrote the chapters on the Romantic Period, the Victorian Age, and the Twentieth Century. The *NAEL* Editors commented on the chapters for their respective periods

1. John Guillory, *Cultural Capital: The Problem of Literary Canon Formation* (Chicago: The University of Chicago Press, 1993), p. 30.

and contributed to Chapter 10, "Examinations, Paper Topics, and Assignments." The late John Benedict wrote the section of "The Staging of the NAEL Plays" in Appendix A. The Guide authors thank Katherine Eggert (University of Colorado at Boulder) for co-authoring the course syllabi included on the Web site and, at Norton, Julia Reidhead and Marian Johnson, for their efforts coordinating the project.

CHAPTER 1

Introducing *The Norton Anthology of English Literature,* Seventh Edition

The levels of preparation and motivation of students who take general survey or period courses in English literature will vary within every class and from one school to the next. Every student, however, requires a great deal of linguistic, historical, and cultural information to work with texts created for vastly different audiences in the remote past. The *Norton Anthology of English Literature* (*NAEL*) is designed to supply much of that information; you should call your students' attention to the help available between the covers of each volume of *NAEL* and online at www.wwnorton.com/nael and www.wwnorton.com/nael/NOA and encourage them to use it. This chapter provides a quick guide to those resources.

1. New in *NAEL7* is "The Persistence of English," Geoffrey Nunberg's excellent short essay on the history of the language that begins with the question "What exactly do we mean when we talk about the 'English language' in the first place?" The essay traces the historical origins, changes, and diffusion of English and demonstrates that what one means by "English" depends on political as well as on linguistic considerations.

2. The maps inside the covers of both volumes have been revised to reflect a greater political sensitivity, evident throughout the Seventh Edition, to the national identities of Wales, Scotland, and Ireland in English history and literature. A modified version of the same map (among other things, it shows the county divisions), entitled "The British Isles in the 19th and 20th Centuries," is printed inside the front cover of Volume 2. These maps can be used in conjunction with a valuable new appendix in both volumes, "Geographic Nomenclature: England, Great Britain, The

United Kingdom," which explains the historical origins of these place-names—a source of confusion to many American readers.

A revised map of "London from Chaucer to Johnson" is printed inside the back cover of Volume 1. ("London in the 19th and 20th Centuries," formerly inside the back cover of Volume 2, now faces the appendix "Geographic Nomenclature.") A new map inside the front cover of Volume 2, "The British Empire ca. 1913," charts the spread of the English language and the settings of works by the Commonwealth and postcolonial writers newly represented in the Seventh Edition. There are plenty of occasions to consult these maps to help develop a sense of regional differences; find one's way around the British Isles, the coast of France, the city of London, and the British Empire; locate birthplaces, battlefields, churches, and theaters; and trace the routes of pilgrimages and other journeys.

3. As the maps provide a sense of geography, the new Timelines in the Seventh Edition provide a sense of chronology for important texts in their historical and cultural contexts. The Timeline for each period follows the period introduction.

4. All of the period introductions and many of the headnotes and footnotes have been revised for *NAEL7*. If you have used the anthology before, you will probably want to look them over. Students, a few of whom might be tempted to ignore small print, should be told that the headnotes and footnotes are extremely helpful. Although the period introductions are not easy for students to assimilate on a first reading, when most of the authors and texts referred to are still just names, these introductions can be assigned in parts and might mean more to students once they have read the selections assigned. You might also recommend students reread them before exams.

5. On the model of the section "Victorian Issues" in previous editions, the Seventh Edition contains clusters that provide literary, historical, intellectual, and social backgrounds for every period. The Guide chapters on individual periods suggest how these clusters can be used to illuminate the many ways in which literary texts respond to and are influenced by events, ideologies, and controversies of their own day. In the Table of Contents, these clusters are set off by headings. Volume 1 includes "Legendary Histories of Britain" and "Celtic Contexts" (Middle Ages); "Literature of the Sacred" and "The Wider World" (Sixteenth Century); "The Science of Self and World" and "Voices of War" (Early Seventeenth Century); "Debating Women: Arguments in Verse" and "Slavery and Freedom" (Restoration and Eighteenth Century). Volume 2 includes "The French Revolution and the 'Spirit of the Age' " (Romantic Period); "Light Verse," "Victorian Issues," and "The Nineties" (Victorian Age); and "The Rise and Fall of Empire," "Voices from World War I," and "Voices from World War II" (Twentieth Century).

6. Appendices.

A. "Poems in Process," introduced in the Third Edition of *NAEL*, contains drafts of poems by Milton, Pope, Johnson, and Gray (Volume 1); Blake, Wordsworth, Byron, Shelley, Keats, Tennyson, Hopkins, Yeats, and Lawrence (Volume 2). When you teach any of these poems, referring students to the poets' earlier drafts can dispel the impression that anthology pieces exist in a timeless form on the printed page. These drafts can also serve as topics for exercises or papers on the topic "What could account for the revisions made in earlier drafts or, in some cases, subsequent printings of the poem?" E.g., why did Pope change "He hangs between, uncertain where to rest" (1.2894) to "He hangs between, in doubt, to act or rest" (1.2561)? Write an interpretation of *Leda and the Swan* (2.2110), making use of the successive drafts (2.2875–77), especially the earlier title and different versions of the first line.

B. "Selected Bibliographies" are updated in each edition and are, of course, expanded to include authors appearing for the first time.

C. "Geographic Nomenclature." See above, the discussion of maps.

D. "British Money" will help students understand the value of sums mentioned in various texts in the arcane system of pounds, shillings, and pence. It gives colloquial terms for particular notes or coins (guinea, quid, bob, tanner, farthing, copper) and discusses the decimal system instituted in 1971. However, because of centuries of ongoing inflation, one can at best estimate the actual value of goods, services, and fortunes. Specific examples, cited from life and literature, do give us a relative idea. Thus, if we should want to know, what it would have cost a "gentleman . . . to give ten shillings for the carcass of a good fat child" in 1729 (Swift, *A Modest Proposal*, 1.2476), it helps to know that Lady Booby's servant Joseph Andrews, in Henry Fielding's novel of 1742, received wages of £8 annually. According to a price list in Blake's 1827 letter to George Cumberland (2.90), Blake would have had to sell 195 copies of "*Songs of Inn. & Exp*," any one of which would fetch millions today, in order to achieve the annual income of Mr. Bennet in *Pride and Prejudice*, 1813.

E. "The British Baronage" explains the origins and the past and present-day significance of titles and honors. It also gives the proper forms for addressing male and female royalty and different degrees of nobility. There are some revisions in the Seventh Edition, e.g., we learn that honors, though still conferred by the monarch, are now decided by the government in power and have been democratized to include rock stars and actors. The list of "Royal Lines of England and Great Britain" from Egbert, king of Wessex (802–839), to Elizabeth II (1952–) remains unchanged.

F. "Religions in England" helps readers thread their way through the historical divisions between the Roman Catholic Church and the different denominations within the Protestant faith; between the degrees of "high" and "low" in the Church of England; and among the proliferation of dissenting sects in the seventeenth century. Formerly limited to Christian sects, the new version now refers to Judaic, Islamic, and Hindu presence in the British Isles.

G. "Poetic Forms and Literary Terminology." This appendix, also revised for the Seventh Edition, provides students with a handy reference guide to the vocabulary of versification, figurative language, literary and philosophical schools, literary genres, and literary criticism. Refer students to this appendix, especially for writing about poetry.

7. Web Resources

A. Norton Topics Online (www.wwnorton.com/nael). In addition to the special topic clusters reprinted in the anthology, each period has been supplemented by three online thematic groupings of texts and images, cross-referenced to selections in the anthology. The online topics are preceded by an overview, accompanied by pop-up annotations and links, and followed by questions inviting students to think about and explore the topics in connection with texts in the anthology. Tables of contents for Topics Online are provided at the end of the Guide chapter on each period; specific suggestions for using them are included throughout the Guide.

B. Norton Online Archive (www.wwnorton.com/nael/NOA). With each edition of *NAEL*, the limitations of space make it necessary to drop some texts in order to include new ones. The Internet, however, makes it possible to keep these older texts available online. An archive of over 150 texts from the Sixth Edition of *NAEL*, ranging from the Middle Ages to the early Victorian period, can be downloaded for your classes.

8. Audio Companion. In response to numerous requests from instructors who use the Audio Companion accompanying the anthology, we are making an expanded version available without charge to students purchasing new copies of *The Norton Anthology of English Literature*, Seventh Edition, The Major Authors. The two compact disks offer readings by the authors of the works represented in the anthology, readings of poems in Old and Middle English and in English dialects, and performances of poems written to be set to music. New to the Audio Companion, Disk 1, are a generous sampling of Seamus Heaney's reading of *Beowulf*, *The Battle of Maldon* read by R. D. Fulk, and additional Chaucer selections read by V. A. Kolve. Recordings of the poets Robert Graves, Ted Hughes, Eavan Boland, and Thom Gunn reading their work have been added to Disk 2. A list of selections on the Audio Companion is appended to the chapter on each of the periods.

CHAPTER 2

The Middle Ages to ca. 1485

Language and Literature

Academic study of English and other national literatures did not begin until the nineteenth century when an intense interest developed in the history and structure of the "modern" languages—English, German, and French and the other Romance languages. They were called modern to distinguish them from the ancient languages, Latin and Greek, which had for centuries served as the cornerstone of education for men in the church and the upper classes. This movement led to the founding of older American academic journals such as *Modern Philology* and *The Journal of English and Germanic Philology* as well as The Modern Language Association. At first, such studies were primarily philological and focused on earlier forms of the Germanic and Romance languages as these had been preserved in medieval literature. English departments taught "English language and literature." In the middle twentieth century, undergraduates at Oxford were still required to read *Beowulf* in the original, and until quite recently Old and Middle English were required subjects for most graduate students in English. Gradually, English studies became weighted far more in favor of literature than of language.

As a result, the history of English and American literature has been divorced from the history of the English language, which is now taught mainly as a separate subject. Many of our students are not even aware that the language they speak is Germanic, implanted in the fifth century on the southern part of the island called Great Britain by pagan invaders from the delta of the river Elbe. Subsequently, English underwent the influence of other languages and evolved over fifteen centuries into the principal literary language of the British Isles, the United States, and Canada and of writers from every corner of what used to be called the British Empire. A sense of how the language developed adds a great deal to the study of the history and the spread of English literature and is essential to a proper understanding of its origins in the Middle Ages.

A good place to start is Geoffrey Nunberg's essay, new in this edition of *NAEL*, "The Persistence of English." Nunberg asks "a basic question: what exactly do we mean when we talk about 'the English language' in the first place?" For the Middle Ages he provides a concise history of its origins: "The Emergence of the English Language." For our purposes, we might rephrase his basic question: "What exactly do we mean when we talk about 'English literature'?" An answer is in part the purpose of the new division of the Middle Ages into three periods instead of, as in former editions, "Old English Literature" and "Middle English Literature." As Nunberg points out, "the determination that English began with the Anglo-Saxon period was not generally accepted until the nineteenth century" and that "this point of view . . . has led to the addition of Anglo-Saxon works to the canon of English literature." Whether one thinks of *Beowulf* as an Anglo-Saxon or as an Old English poem does not matter. Yet to say that the poem belongs to "Anglo-Saxon England" recognizes its kinship with Germanic literature on the Continent and in Scandinavia and its geographic boundaries in that part of the United Kingdom, which is still designated as England. The period following the Conquest has here been designated "Anglo-Norman England." England was now ruled by an aristocracy speaking the Anglo-Norman dialect of Old French, in which several of the most important works of medieval French survive. Literature in the Celtic languages coexisted with French, Early Middle English, and Latin literature, and all of these contributed to the forms of "Middle English Literature in the Fourteenth and Fifteenth Centuries," the third subperiod into which the Middle Ages has been divided for this edition. Thus the selections translated from Early Middle English, French, Celtic, and Latin illustrate the international character of the literature that bridges the centuries between Anglo-Saxon England and the age of Chaucer, whom Dryden looked back on as the "father of English poetry" (1.2121). Perhaps the question of what we mean when talk about English literature admits more than one answer. If we mean to include under that heading everything from the earliest literary works written in England to the most recent works written in English in Great Britain, Ireland, the Americas, Africa, and Asia, then Anglo-Saxon or Old English poetry and prose certainly belong to that tradition. If we mean what fifteenth-century writers, like the "Scottish Chaucerian" Robert Henryson (1.439), or Sidney (1.909), or Dryden considered to be English literature, the tradition begins late in the fourteenth century with Chaucer whom they esteemed for having made the English vernacular worthy of comparison with Latin, French, and Italian literature.

Although half of the works in this period are necessarily provided in translation, instructors may at least show their students two specimens of Old English poetry (1.24–25 and 1.104). The new translation of *Beowulf* by Seamus Heaney gives students an excellent idea of the structure and movement of Old English alliterative verse. Heaney reads several passages on the Audio Companion. The Companion also has a reading of the first stanza of *Sir Gawain and the Green Knight*, printed in Middle English with interlinear translation (1.157–58), which provides an example of the Middle English alliterative long line. Marie Borroff's translation of *Gawain* and E. T. Donaldson's of *Piers Plowman* re-create Middle English alliterative meter. The selections from Chaucer, the lyrics, and the drama introduce students to late Middle English verse in a normalized text. Several Chaucer passages can also be heard on the Audio Companion. The selections from Julian of Norwich, Margery Kempe, and Sir Thomas Malory render Middle English prose in modernized spelling. Some suggestions for teaching Chaucer's Middle English are given below.

Christian and Pagan Traditions in Anglo-Saxon England

The Conversion

Except for a runic alphabet, the Germanic peoples did not acquire the art of writing until after their conversion to Christianity, which for England began in 597 with a mission sent by Pope Gregory the Great to the southeastern kingdom of Kent (1.3). We owe most of our knowledge of that conversion to Bede's Latin *An Ecclesiastical History of the English People*, which also provides our first written record of an English poem, Cædmon's *Hymn*, in the chapter from which the first selection in *NAEL* has been translated. Bede, an English monk, tells the story, traditional in his monastery, of how an illiterate cowherd, tending the monks' cattle, was miraculously granted the gift of poetry. Religious works—biblical narratives, saints' lives, allegories, homilies, and sermons—make up the great majority of works that have been preserved from the Anglo-Saxon and, indeed, from the entire medieval period. The predominance of religious writings is natural enough, because the earliest manuscripts were inevitably produced and preserved by the Church. Yet Christianity did not do away with preliterate traditions of Germanic poetry but rather preempted these for its own purposes (1.5). A good way, therefore, to approach the literature of Anglo-Saxon England is to discuss the ways in which the poetic forms and themes of the Germanic invaders were also "converted" to the service of Christian poetry.

Alliterative Verse

The most fundamental element of pagan Germanic verse that was applied to Christian subjects was its metrical form. The headnote to Bede's account of Cædmon's *Hymn* discusses the concept of oral-formulaic poetry. Through the use of traditional poetic formulas, cast in meters such as the Homeric Greek hexameter and the Anglo-Saxon alliterative line, professional singers of tales were able to improvise performances of long narrative poems. Cædmon's *Hymn* provides instructors and their students with a relatively simple text to demonstrate how an oral-formulaic poem works and enables them to read a few lines in Old English. A splendid performance of the *Hymn*, accompanied by a harp reconstructed from instruments probably used by Anglo-Saxon bards, is available on the Audio Companion. Although Seamus Heaney's translation of *Beowulf* does not consistently observe the strict rules governing the meter of Old English poetry (see 1.19), many of his lines can serve as good examples of the relation of metrical stress and alliteration:

> The *fórtunes* of wár *fávored* Hróthgar (line 64)
> the híghest in the *lánd*, would *lénd* advice (line 172)
> and *find* *fríendship* in the *Fáther's* embráce (line 188)

Heaney's reading on the Audio Companion will also introduce students to the rhythms of alliterative verse. Ask your students to look up *alliteration* in the appendix "Poetic Forms and Literary Terminology" (1.2947), where they will also find iambic pentameter lines in later English poetry that have a beat and movement like those in Old English alliterative poetry. Alliteration comes more naturally to Germanic verse because in Germanic languages stress normally falls on the initial syllable. Many traditional English expressions made up of alliterative doublets will already be familiar to students. For example, "laid down the law" and "safe and sound" occur in Heaney's translation.

Heroic Poetry

In the year 797, the English scholar Alcuin, whom the emperor Charlemagne had recruited to run his palace school, wrote a letter to the bishop of Lindisfarne, a great monastery off the northeast coast of England, in which he asks the rhetorical question, "Quid Hinieldus cum Christo?" (What has Ingeld to do with Christ?). Ing was a Germanic deity (in *Beowulf* the Danes are twice referred to as "friends of Ing"), and Ingeld is king of the Heatho-Bards (*Beowulf*, 1.76, lines 2032–69), the tribe involved in a feud with the Danes that will probably result, though we can only infer this, in the burning of Heorot. In Alcuin's question, "Ingeld" stands for "heroic poetry," which, Alcuin has learned, was being recited to the monks. One is reminded of the third line of *Beowulf*: "We have *heard* of those princes' heroic campaigns." For Alcuin, the answer to his question is, of course, "Nothing whatsoever!" For us, as students of Anglo-Saxon literature, the actual answer is, "A good deal."

Our knowledge of pagan Germanic mythology and heroic literature is limited and comes to us through archaeology and through literary sources like *Beowulf* in which the pagan world of a distant past has already been filtered through the imagination of Christian authors. Alcuin's letter shows that the *Beowulf* poet could certainly have heard oral poems—perhaps even in a monastic dining hall. He adopted the verse form and probably much of his narrative material from oral poems. *Beowulf* contains representations of bards performing poems in the mead hall; but few scholars today believe that the long work, which survives in the unique manuscript that has come down to us, is a transcription of a poem that was ever performed extempore by one or more oral poets.

Perhaps the way to answer Alcuin's question is not to start with *Beowulf* itself but rather with a much shorter and very late Anglo-Saxon poem, *The Battle of Maldon*—for several reasons. First, *Maldon* (1.103) has the length, texture, and feel of a genuine oral poem that someone copied down. Even the accident that the beginning and end are missing contributes to its rough-hewn character. We know that *Maldon* commemorates an actual historical event, and there are records of its hero, Earl Birhtnoth, and of his tomb in Ely Cathedral. Thus we can see how history could be transformed and preserved as epic poetry, how one of the cities on the archaeological site of Troy could become the Troy of Homer's *Iliad*. Second, *Maldon* creates for us a picture of how some five centuries before this battle, the Christian Britons must have been cut down by the fierce pagan ancestors of Earl Birhtnoth and his men. The poet stresses the "heathen" character of the Viking "slaughter-wolves" and the Christian faith of Birhtnoth, who prays in dying that the "fiends of hell" not be given power over his soul as the heathens have over his body. Third and most important, the speeches of the earl's men, especially the famous lines of Bihrtwold (printed in Old English with interlinear translation in the headnote), eloquently demonstrate how "the aristocratic heroic and kinship values of Germanic society continued to inspire both clergy and laity in the Christian era" (1.4). The Christian warriors of Maldon live up to the heroic code: retainers are obliged to avenge their lord or die in the attempt. The *Beowulf* poet treats that code with much greater complexity. Students may enjoy discussing a question much debated by scholars. Was Birhtnoth's permission to let the Vikings cross the causeway "overconfidence" (Old English *ofermod*) or was it good military strategy to risk a battle to destroy the invaders rather than to allow them to sail along the coast and attack a less well defended beachhead?

The poem that most clearly illustrates the "conversion" of the heroic to the Christian is *The Dream of the Rood* (1.26), which can be taught as a unit alongside *The Battle of Maldon*. Christ is portrayed as a "young Hero," the Crucifixion as a "great struggle," the personified Cross as a loyal retainer who "must stand fast" with his lord and undergoes death and burial with him (1.27). But, like its lord, the Cross is ultimately resurrected in glory and holds out that promise to the weary and sin-stained dreamer who is instructed to "tell men of this vision." The language and motifs of the heroic ethic are applied to teaching the new doctrine whose lesson is to suffer and endure rather than to take vengeance. Yet the poem ends on a note of triumph with a reference to the Harrowing of

Hell as a warlike rescue mission in which the souls of the patriarchs and prophets are liberated from captivity by the Devil. (Christ's descent into Hell is a part of medieval Christian doctrine, based on apocryphal sources, which students need to have explained.) The last words, "þær his eþel wæs" (where his homeland was), touch on an important allegorical theme in Old English and later Christian literature (e.g., Chaucer's poem *Truth*, 1.315, lines 17–21), poignantly elaborated in *The Wanderer* (1.99). We are all wanderers on earth, separated from our true Lord, and exiled from our native land, which is in Heaven.

Beowulf is the oldest and finest example of Germanic heroic literature. Its poet was an antiquarian, fascinated by the artifacts, customs, and beliefs of his pagan ancestors, which he re-created with solemn magnificence. The ship burial of Shield, the eponymous founder of the Danish dynasty (lines 26–52) was vividly documented by the discovery of an early Anglo-Saxon king's funeral ship at Sutton Hoo in East Anglia in the 1930s. If images of the Sutton Hoo treasure, now housed in the British Museum, can be obtained, they make splendid illustrations for the opening of *Beowulf* (try your art department's slide library). Like the *Odyssey*, *Beowulf* is an exciting adventure story with fights against monsters. Its hero personifies the values of the distant heroic world at its best. But the Christian poet, though he admires those values, represents them as limited and ultimately, like Beowulf himself, doomed. Notably, the religion of these peoples, although pagan, is not basically polytheistic. Hrothgar's *scop* sings a creation hymn reminiscent of Cædmon's, and characters, while they sometimes speak of a deterministic *Wyrd* or Fate (e.g., lines 455, 573), have a concept of a just ruler of all things (e.g., lines 1724–26). Yet the values of the characters are governed by the duty of blood vengeance. The Danes' troubles at the hands of the Grendel family are expressed in the language of a feud. The horror of Grendel's assaults is magnified by the fact that they are incapable of killing the monster or exacting compensation from him; Grendel's mother takes revenge for her son by slaughtering Hrothgar's most beloved retainer. The poet's treatment of the feud ethic is clearest in the "digressions." These include the scattered reminiscences of the wars between the Swedes and the Geats, which, after Beowulf's death, forebode the annihilation of the Geats by the vengeance of their traditional enemies; the Finnsburg episode about the feud of the Danes with the Frisians and Jutes; and the allusions to the feud between the Danes and the Heatho-Bards. The feud mentality is graphically portrayed in Beowulf's speech about a political marriage, contracted to make peace, between Hrothgar's daughter and the Heatho-Bard king Ingeld, whose father has been slain in a feud with the Danes (lines 2020–69). Beowulf foresees how the feud is likely to break out afresh at the wedding banquet when a bitter old warrior will egg on a young man to take blood vengeance on some Dane in the wedding party wearing plundered Heatho-Bard trophies. The Christian poet's allusion to the flames that will destroy the great hall Heorot and the description of the funeral fires that consume the corpses at Finnsburg and finally Beowulf's body (lines 1107–25, 3143–47) foreshadow the apocalyptic fire that awaits the world and all heroic endeavor. The earliest English epic is also the first to question the warrior code.

The transitoriness of the world and the human condition are also expressed in the Old English lyrics called elegies of which *The Wanderer* is an outstanding example. Heroic poems most often treat the deeds of a band of warriors, whether in victory or defeat, but another theme of heroic poetry is that of exile in which a hero is outlawed or banished from the community of warriors. Sigemund, whose adventures are referred to in one of the inset songs in *Beowulf* (lines 883–96), is such a hero. The isolation of the narrators and the bleak landscapes and seascapes of *The Wanderer* and *The Wife's Lament* focus on the inner world of the exile where all men and women are searching for a new lord or the one from whom they are separated.

Romance

History and Romance

On the origins of "romance" in Anglo-Norman England, see 1.7–8. As explained there the word originally referred to works written in the French vernacular. In particular, it appeared in the titles of several long twelfth-century French poems that today we might think of as "historical romances" but which their original readers or listeners probably regarded as ancient histories, retold not in Latin but in their native language as poetry. The French *Roman de Troie* was translated into Latin prose as the *Historia Destructionis Troiae* (History of the destruction of Troy), which ironically came to be considered the scholarly original from which the *Roman* had been translated. Wace's *Roman de Brut* (1.118) is a very free adaptation of Geoffrey of Monmouth's Latin prose *History of the Kings of Britain*. Most people continued to regard Geoffrey's work as authentic history until the seventeenth century. Through intermediate English works such as Holinshed's *Chronicles* it provided materials for Shakespeare and Spenser. There is no clear-cut way to sort out epic, history, and romance in early English literature. Even the *Peterborough Chronicle*, which for the most part soberly records contemporary events, contains flashes of poetry and marvelous tales. What starts out as the English chronicler's eulogy of the dead William the Conqueror modulates into moralizing doggerel rhyme condemning the greed and violence of the late king, as the wicked king Heremod is twice denounced in *Beowulf* (lines 900–14, 1709–22). Sinister sightings and sounds of the mythical Wild Hunt signal the arrival of an unscrupulous French cleric who has gotten the king to make him abbot of Peterborough. Some of the machines with which evil barons tortured prisoners in their dungeons are like gruesome devices writers of Gothic horror stories employed in later fiction.

In the twelfth century, Arthurian literature evolved out of a mixing of history and romance in narratives that catered to the tastes and ambitions of the French barons who ruled England in the twelfth century (1.115). Historically, "Arthurian Britain" was the Roman province Britannia whose people fought against the Anglo-Saxon invaders after the legions had been withdrawn in the fifth century. After they had been conquered, the Britons told stories in which their defeat was turned into the overthrow of a legendary kingdom whose greatest ruler had been on the verge of conquering Rome itself before he was betrayed at home. The three selections from Geoffrey of Monmouth, Wace, and Layamon trace that kingdom from a prophecy of its foundation by descendants of the survivors of Troy, to its zenith, to the beginning of its downfall, and finally, to a myth of its future restoration. One can already see in these brief selections the paradigm of medieval tragedies of Fortune, the rise and fall of princes, which anticipates the cyclical themes that students will encounter in *Sir Gawain and the Green Knight* and in Malory's *Morte Darthur*.

Real kings invoked the legendary Arthur to further their own policies. The last line of Layamon's *Brut* tells of Merlin's prophecy that "Arthur once again would come to aid the English" (1.126), showing that the legendary king of the Britons had become a national hero of the very people whose ancestors he had fought against. Later kings of England invoked the Arthurian legend for their own political purposes. See the selection from Adam Murimuth's *Chronicle* under "King Arthur" on the *NAEL* Web site for Edward III's proposal to reestablish an order of knights of the Round Table; also for the image of an oak round table, eighteen feet in diameter, probably made for Edward I around 1255. Henry VIII had the table painted with heraldic insignia to assert the Tudor claims of Arthurian ancestry. Thus a succession of English kings presented themselves as reviving a chivalry that had flourished in the days of King Arthur.

The "romance" elements in Latin, French, and English literature owe a great deal to Celtic stories of love and magic. Geoffrey of Monmouth claimed to have translated his *History* from an ancient Welsh book, which probably never existed (1.115), but he unquestionably obtained much of his material from Welsh oral tradition. The *Exile of the Sons of Uisliu* (1.142), from Old Irish, and the story of *Lludd and Lleuelys* (1.150), from Middle Welsh, are examples of the rich Celtic literature that influenced medieval romance. The former tale became a favorite of the Celtic Revival at the end of the nineteenth century (2.1910). Derdriu is a tragic heroine, an Irish Helen whose passion for "a game young bull" (1.145), for whose love she rejects an old royal one, brings about a great war between Ulster and Connaught. The Welsh tale is about the rescue of Britain from three "plagues": an alien people with supernatural powers of hearing, a pair of fighting dragons, and a powerful sorcerer.

Chivalric Romance

In France during the latter half of the twelfth century, King Arthur's court became the center for the most characteristic form of romance associated with the Middle Ages, the romance of chivalry (1.7–8). Its protagonist is a knight who typically rides out alone in search of adventures or on a quest, which is often a rescue mission on behalf of a fellow knight or lady in distress. Worthy knights are praised and wicked knights condemned by the standards of a moral code and a code of manners called chivalry. The word designates the honorable deeds and behavior of a knight (*chevalier, caballero, Ritter*), especially in war and tournaments on his *cheval* (horse). A knight's adventures serve not only as tests of his strength and courage but of his character and courtliness. Nobility, wealth, good looks, and military prowess are qualities with which the romance hero is often endowed by birth, although in some romances a knight from the lower nobility and humble means rises to high rank through feats of arms and a great marriage (1.9). In the most interesting romances, a knight, though nobly born, achieves true chivalry through overcoming his shortcomings and failures in the course of his adventures. Truth, religious faith, loyalty, and humility are the most important qualities in which a knight is tested. The best romances, therefore, focus not just on the hero's brave deeds but also on his psychology and his relationships with his fellow knights, with women, and with God.

Inevitably, the illustrious reputation of Arthurian chivalry was not always viewed with complete seriousness. In Marie de France's *Lanval* (1.127), Arthur is introduced as "the brave and courtly king" and his knights are the best "in all the world." Your students can have a good time discussing how Marie's dry wit proceeds to undercut this conventional estimate of Arthur and his court. Arthur neglects the foreign knight Lanval and turns out to be an uxorious husband trying to pacify his queen, who plays the part of Potiphar's wife (Genesis 39.7–23). Disorder in his kingdom is not so much caused by ravaging Scots and Picts (lines 7–8) as by petty jealousies within Camelot itself; the knights are not portrayed in war or in tournaments but in well-bred social activities and in a comical trial by jury that keeps getting interrupted. In this romance, it is not the knight who rescues the lady, but the lady who rescues the knight, who is last seen riding off seated behind her on her "milkwhite horse."

The motif of the fairy bride and the inversion of gender roles in romance also figure in the *Wife of Bath's Tale* (1.253), which may be compared with *Lanval*. This story, too, is set "In th'olde dayes of the King Arthour" (line 863). The humor is broader than in *Lanval*; and Chaucer adds another dimension by telling the tale from the point of view of the Wife, who cleverly manipulates her tale much as she has told the pilgrims she manipulated her husbands. Could one compare Marie's and the Wife's points of view toward romance? How successful is Chaucer in creating the point of view of his female narrator? Can we detect him manipulating the Wife of Bath, even as she manipulates the characters in her tale?

Sir Gawain and the Green Knight

The poet of *Sir Gawain and the Green Knight*, writing late in the fourteenth century in the northwest of Britain, takes stock of a romance tradition that was already three hundred years old in his time. He begins where Geoffrey of Monmouth did with Aeneas, framing his poem at the beginning and end with references to "the books of Brutus' deeds" (1.158–57, lines 1–26, and 1.210, line 2523). Although the poet evokes the legendary history of Britain, he also clearly recognizes his story as what we have come to call "romance" by calling it an "adventure," "a marvel," one of Arthur's "wonders," "a tale of derring-do." Yet, in another way, he sets his story in the fourteenth century through his elaborate descriptions of contemporary costume, armor, and architecture. The moral questions it raises about the meaning of chivalry are also pertinent to the age in which he was living.

The military value of the heavily armored knight on horseback was declining in the late fourteenth century because of the tactical use of the longbow and the introduction of gunpowder. Nevertheless, although the actual usefulness of the knight on the battlefield was diminishing, the cult of chivalry was celebrated more spectacularly than ever in heraldry, ceremony, and spectacle. Edward III and his people were passionately fond of tournaments and pageantry. He did not carry out his plan of founding a new order of the Round Table, but he did establish the Order of the Garter, which remains the highest honor the English monarchy can bestow. When Arthur's knights adopt the green girdle as their badge of honor, either the poet himself or the scribe was reminded of the motto of the Garter, "Hony Soyt Qui Mal Pense" (1.210, line 231 and n. 2), which is inscribed below the text in the unique manuscript of the poem.

In the New Year's Day celebration at Arthur's court, at the beginning of the story, the poet observes the gay entertainment of the youthful court—the jousting, the dancing, the laughter, exchange of gifts, and the games—with an amused eye, much as Marie de France had viewed the knights and ladies celebrating Saint John's Day (1.131–32, lines 213–46). The Green Knight mocks that scene when he playfully asks the king to grant him a "game," which challenges the court's reputation for chivalry. Gawain's "adventure" is, therefore, a test not only of his own knighthood but of the court and, in a larger sense, of the worth of chivalry itself. The essence of chivalry is supposedly truth, as proclaimed by the pentangle on Gawain's shield. In fourteenth-century English, *truth* meant not simply truthfulness but "troth," or fidelity (1.157). Very much aware of that, Gawain is anxious to demonstrate his fidelity by keeping what he thinks will be his fatal appointment at the Green Chapel. But as it turns out, his "troth" will be tested in ways he does not expect. The poet passes cursorily over Gawain's adventures on the way to keep his appointment on New Year's Day, but he makes us feel Gawain's isolation and the winter hardship, not just of the knight sleeping in his armor but of the birds, "That peeped most piteously for pain of the cold" (line 747). On Christmas morning, the action shifts from the winter wilderness to the bedroom, where the hero thinks he is defending himself against the advances of the lady; she counters his resistance by mockingly questioning his reputation for gallantry. Can this be the Gawain she has heard so much about? When Gawain comes to face what he believed all along to be the real test, he does not realize, nor do most readers, that the real test is already over and that he has, at least partly, failed it. But Gawain will be absolved, and the failure will bring him to true humility instead of a false modesty that he professed in accepting the Green Knight's challenge. Instead of actually dying under the Green Knight's ax, Gawain is, in a sense, reborn—with a new awareness of his vulnerability to pride and self-deception, which he now recognizes as a potential pitfall of the chivalry to which he aspired.

While taking a nostalgic and critical look at Arthurian romance, the *Gawain* poet is also mindful of an even older tradition: Germanic epic. Not only did this poet and his audience respond to the alliterative beat of the verse (though the line had been greatly modified since Anglo-Saxon times), they must still have understood many archaic words that belonged to the poetic diction of the *Beowulf* poet. The effect of the vocabulary is, of course, lost in translation, but a look at the Middle English of the opening stanza (1.157–58) gives a fair sample of this poet's word-hoard, which you may want to pause over briefly with your students. In line 1, "Sege" (siege), "assaut" (assault), "sesed" (ceased) are French loan words; in line 2, "borgh" (city, -burgh), "brittened" (crumbled), "brondes" (brands), "askes" (ashes) are Germanic. The form of "askes" is Scandinavian, reflecting the influence of Danish settlement in the north of England, as do "tulk" (man), "biges" (builds), "bonkkes" (banks), "wrake" (revenge), "blunder" (strife), "skete" (swiftly), and "skyfted" (shifted). (Compare these with the list of Scandinavian loan words near the bottom of 1.xlix). In part, the archaisms of the poem can be attributed to its regional dialect. But it is also reasonable to assume that the *Gawain* poet, like the *Beowulf* poet, was fond of old and obscure words and deliberately played with the greatly increased lexicon that English, by the end of the fourteenth century, had acquired through Scandinavian, French, and Latin borrowings.

Like the *Beowulf* poet, the *Gawain* poet was an antiquarian in regard to language and style. Unlike *Beowulf, Sir Gawain and the Green Knight* does not dress up its warriors in ancient armor. Its characters do not hold pre-Christian beliefs, although some critics have seen vestiges of primitive fertility cults in the Green Knight. A comparison between these works helps bring out the cultural gap between Germanic epic and medieval romance. The *Beowulf* poet can still imagine and sympathize with a deeply flawed heroic society that is nevertheless capable of brave and generous actions worthy of being remembered with admiration, love, and compassion. But it is a bleak world threatened within and without by forces of evil. Even the lighter moments in *Beowulf* have their dark underside. While Heorot celebrates Beowulf's victory over Grendel with feasting and the singing of heroic lays, we can sense tensions that will eventually bring the great hall down in flames. The treasure Beowulf wins from the dragon, which he is eager to view as he lies dying, cannot save him or his people. It will be returned to the earth "as useless to men now as it ever was" (1.99, line 3168). There is plenty of irony in *Beowulf* but hardly any humor. The tone remains elevated and somber throughout. In contrast, the romance is filled with genuine comedy. The gaiety of the New Year's celebration at Camelot is hardly heroic and is abruptly silenced by the appearance of the Green Knight. There is a threatening air in his speech and appearance, but there is also a grotesque humor when he holds up his severed head "and it lifted up its lids" (1.167, line 446). In the Christmas celebration at the castle, one may sense a slight queasiness when the traditional boar's head is carried in (line 1616) if one happens to think of Sir Gawain's bargain with the Green Knight and the one with his boisterous host returning from the boar hunt. The entire poem is "a Christmas game" (line 283), which in the end turns out to proclaim the serious Christmas message of hope, mercy, and joy:

> In the old days of Arthur this happening befell; . . .
> Many such, ere we were born,
> Have befallen here, ere this.
> May He that was crowned with thorn
> Bring all men to His bliss! (lines 2522–30)

Romantic Love

In the second of the bedroom scenes in *Sir Gawain and the Green Knight*, the lady teasingly reproaches Gawain for his reluctance to make love to her as a knight is supposed to do:

> And name what knight you will, they are noblest esteemed
> For loyal faith in love, in life as in story;
> For to tell the tribulations of these true hearts,
> Why, 'tis the very title and text of their deeds,
> How bold knights for beauty have braved many a foe,
> Suffered heavy sorrows out of secret love. (lines 1512–17)

The *Gawain* poet's original audience might well have shared the lady's surprise at her knight's coyness if they had read about Gawain's amorous adventures in the thirteenth-century French prose romances, which were to become the sources of Sir Thomas Malory's *Morte Darthur*. In Malory, when the recently slain Gawain appears to Arthur in a dream to warn his uncle not to engage Mordred in battle, he is accompanied by "a number of fair ladies" for whom he has done battle "in righteous quarrels" (1.430). In Tennyson's *Idylls of the King*, Sir Bedivere, in the same context, makes Gawain's reputation as a philanderer more explicit: "Light was

Gawain in life, and light in death / Is Gawain, for the ghost is as the man" (2.1295, lines 56–57). In contrast, the young Gawain appears virginal in the anonymous English poet's romance. His only lady seems to be Mary, whose image is painted on the inside of his pentangle shield. The poet probably intended the surprise; in any case, Gawain's maneuvers to counter the lady's advances are part of the comedy.

Romantic love between a man and a woman is absent from Anglo-Saxon literature. The closest one comes to love between man and woman is *The Wife's Lament* (1.102), which is not about romantic love but about the pain of exile and the separation of wife and husband on account of feuds and hatreds that are never explained. Romantic love is rightly said to be the staple of medieval romance—according to one distinguished critic, the Middle Ages invented it or, more precisely, that form of romantic love that one historian of medieval French romance called "amour courtois," translated into English as "courtly love."

In theory courtly love has been seen as the other side of the coin of medieval antifeminism. Scholars have used the term to designate a set of literary conventions that supposedly idealizes women and makes them into objects of worship. The lady is wooed, usually at a distance, by a knight who fights in her honor, calls himself her "servant," and suffers insomnia, anorexia, pallor, chills and fever, and other symptoms that, he insists, will be his death if he does not obtain her "mercy." The relationship between the knight and the lady is an inversion of the relationship between the lord and vassal under feudalism. Because aristocratic women were married off for rank and property, and husbands enjoyed total authority over their wives, it has been argued that courtly love was incompatible with marriage and thus necessarily clandestine.

Courtly or Petrarchan love in both medieval and sixteenth-century literature revolves around the ideal love for a seemingly unattainable object. In one typical conceit, the lady is a distant star; the lover, the storm-tossed ship that tries to steer by the star. The one straightforward example of this kind of love in *NAEL*'s Middle Ages is *Troilus's Song*, printed with Chaucer's lyrics (1.314). Actually these stanzas are taken from the great romance *Troilus and Criseyde*, where they are said to have been composed by Troilus to describe his conflicting emotions after he falls in love with Criseyde. In the fifteenth century it was printed in some manuscripts as a separate love poem. The poem is a translation of one of the sonnets in Petrarch's famous sonnet sequence, which inspired the sixteenth-century sonnets by Wyatt, Surrey, Sidney, Spenser, Shakespeare, and others. The last line of *Troilus's Song*, "For hoot of cold, for cold of hoot I die," employs that most conventional of lovers' clichés that he will die of unrequited love.

This is the trope employed by hende Nicholas in *The Miller's Tale* (1.239, lines 172–73) and in Chaucer's parody of the lover's complaint in *Complaint to His Purse* (1.316). Chaucer almost always treats courtly love tongue-in-cheek. The wooing of both Nicholas and Absolon satirizes the typical language and gestures of courtly lovers, and of course Alison whom they are pursuing is not a lady. She warns Nicholas that he must be "ful derne" (very secret) in this affair. The treatment of romantic love and lovers in *Lanval* and *The Wife of Bath's Tale* in which the ladies take the initiative and the lovers are passive or "daungerous" (see 1.257, n. 8), as in *Gawain*, is also satirical. Popular love songs like *Alison* and *My Lief Is Faren in Londe* (1.351 and 352) use the motif of unrequited, distant, or betrayed love. These poems are short, but in conventional romances the woes of long-suffering lovers often run on for hundreds of lines.

The one totally serious affair in the medieval section of *NAEL* is that of Lancelot and Guinevere, the most famous pair of lovers in medieval literature. Their liaison first appears in Chrétien de Troye's unfinished romance *Lancelot* and was greatly elaborated in the French prose romances of the thirteenth century. Reading of Lancelot's and Guinevere's first kiss, Francesca tells Dante in the *Inferno,* she and her brother-in-law Paolo looked at one another, and "That day we read no further." Malory omits the tale of the first kiss (an image of that scene from a French *Lancelot* manuscript is available on the *NAEL* Web site)—for him the love of Lancelot and Guinevere is a given on which he ultimately blames the destruction of the Round Table.

As Malory treats the affair, it is remarkably free of romantic longing and passion. He is far more interested in the dangers that Lancelot undergoes rescuing the queen from perilous situations than he is in their trysts. Malory opens the last book of *Morte Darthur* with a conventional reference to spring as the season "when every lusty heart flourisheth" (1.421)—the same topos that begins *The Canterbury Tales.* Here, however, the coming of spring sets up a tragic irony: "so this season it befell in the month of May a great anger and unhap that stinted not till the flower of chivalry of all the world was destroyed and slain." Warned by his nephew, Sir Bors, of the risks of visiting the queen on the night they are betrayed. Lancelot replies that the queen has sent for him and he will "not be so much a coward" (1.423) as to refuse her invitation. When they are together, Malory professes not to know "whether they were abed or at other manner of disports" (1.424).

The most passionate declarations of their love take place after the end of the affair, when she has become a nun and he a priest. A vision instructs Lancelot that, for remission of his sins, he must hasten to Guinevere's convent, where he will find her dead, and that he must bury her beside King Arthur. He learns from the nuns that she had known of his coming and had prayed aloud as though making a public confession, "I beseech Almighty God that I may never have power to see Sir Lancelot with my worldly eyes." Seeing her face in death, Sir Lancelot "wept not greatly, but sighed. . . . And when she was put in the earth Sir Lancelot swooned and lay long still" (1.435–36). Reproached by a hermit that he is displeasing God by such excessive grief, Lancelot replies that his sorrow is not "for any rejoicing of sin" but for his fault and pride. The measure of his repentance is also the measure of his love for both Guinevere and Arthur. Thereafter, Lancelot barely takes nourishment and shrivels away until he is dead. Malory goes so far as to imply that he has become a saint, for the head of the monastery has a vision of Lancelot being taken into heaven by angels, and his body gives off a sweet odor. His nephew Sir Bors, his brother Sir Ector, and two other knights go to the Holy Land where they fight many battles against the infidels, "and there they died upon a Good Friday for God's sake" (2.438).

This final reference to the crusades is a reminder that romance and religion are never far apart in medieval literature. Although in a different key, *Sir Gawain and the Green Knight* also concludes with confession and repentance. The breaking up of the Round Table is already foreshadowed in the French prose romances and in Malory by the Quest for the Holy Grail, which is the only one in which Lancelot fails absolutely. On chivalry as an order, like a religious order, and its social and religious obligations, see the selections from William Caxton's translation of Ramón Lull's *Book of the Order of Chivalry* at the *NAEL* Web site under "Medieval Estates and Orders." Chaucer's *Troilus and Criseyde* ends with Troilus's ghost condemning "the blinde lust, the which that may not laste"; and the narrator advises the young people in his audience to set their hearts on the love of Christ instead of "worldly vanitee" that "passeth soone as flowres faire." In the *Retraction*, which follows *The Canterbury Tales* (1.313), the author asks Christ to forgive him for his writings of "worldly vanitees" and prays for grace "of verray penitence, confession, and satisfaccion."

Varieties of Religious Experience

Literature and the Medieval Church

Many students who come to the literature from a secularized environment have very little knowledge of the Church in the Middle Ages or, for that matter, of the Bible. The literature of the period often assumes some familiarity with the history, doctrines, hierarchy, religious orders, rituals, sacraments, holidays, and many other aspects of medieval religion. Of course, the teaching of the period need not be limited to supplying arcane information, much of which is provided in the notes. In many ways the literature itself continues to teach modern readers about religion, as it was originally intended to teach both clergy and lay readers during the Middle Ages.

The dominant and pervasive role of religion need not be introduced as doctrinaire or monolithic. There were many different kinds of faith and worship, and the literature shows how the Church was changing over the many centuries in this period. In the best literature, students may feel a tension between the religious and secular aims of both medieval authors and their characters: for example, in the Christian poet's admiration for Beowulf's heroism and his compassion for the good pagans who possess no knowledge of the redemption; in the Wife of Bath's lament, "Allas, allas, that ever love was sinne!" (1.267, line 620); in Sir Gawain's reluctant acceptance of the green girdle so that he may live; and in Lancelot's joining a religious order after the fellowship of good knights as been destroyed. To explain the purpose and institutions of monastic life, excerpts of *The Rule of St. Benedict* have been included among the selections under "Medieval Estates and Orders" on the Web site.

"And pilgrimes were they alle"

The allegorical trope of life as a pilgrimage has already been mentioned in connection with *The Dream of the Rood* (1.26), *The Wanderer* (1.99), and Chaucer's ballade *Truth* (1.315). Both clerics and laypeople went on pilgrimages throughout the Middle Ages, but by the end of the fourteenth century, pilgrimages had become such a popular and, to a considerable degree, commercial institution that they were condemned by reformers. An example of that is *Piers Plowman Shows the Way to Saint Truth*. Inspired by a revivalist sermon preached by Repentance,

> A thousand men then thronged together,
> Cried upward to Christ and to his clean mother
> To have grace to go to Truth—God grant that they might!
> But there was no one so wise as to know the way thither,
> But they blundered forth like beasts over banks and hills
> Till they met a man, many hours later,
> Appareled like a pagan in pilgrims' manner. (1.325, lines 510–14)

The man bears the pilgrim's traditional staff, bowl, and bag, but his costume is absurdly decorated with souvenirs acquired from the different shrines he has visited so that instead of a Christian he resembles a "pagan" (Middle English *paynim*, usually referring to a Saracen). Asked if he has ever heard of a saint called Truth, this professional pilgrim is at a loss. At this point Piers Plowman makes his entry into the poem and gives the seekers after Truth allegorical directions that lead through the Ten Commandments and fundamental Christian and moral doctrine. Offered pay by the pilgrims, Piers says, "I wouldn't take a farthing's fee for Saint Thomas's shrine" (line 358).

You could use this passage to introduce the idea of pilgrimage and to point out the very mixed characters and motivations among the "sondry folk, by aventure yfalle / In felaweshipe, and pilgrimes were they alle" (1.216, lines 25–26), gathered at the Tabard Inn to seek "Saint Thomas's shrine." Less obviously than Langland, Chaucer, too, is satirizing the profane aspects of his pilgrims in *The General Prologue* and throughout *The Canterbury Tales*, but that is not to say that the secularism and realism of his work excludes a religious and allegorical level. Both as a whole and in its individual prologues and tales, the poem exhibits the tension between the spiritual and the worldly, which was referred to above, and so does Langland's.

The famous opening passage of *The General Prologue* draws all of nature together in the great annual movement of physical and spiritual rebirth. The portraits in the rest of the *Prologue*, the tales, and the links between them display the pilgrims in all their variety—their quarrels, their vanities, their desires, and their faiths. The metaphor of the pilgrimage of life is reinforced by the fact that several of the pilgrims are characterized as travelers—the Knight by his crusades; the Wife of Bath by her "wandring by the waye" in the course of her multiple marriages and pilgrimages; the Pardoner by his itinerant preaching. Chaucer's tongue-in-cheek apology in the *Miller's Prologue* for the "harlotrye" of the fabliaux (1.237, lines 63–78) promises that the tales will contain enough of "moralitee and holinesse." He amply keeps that promise, although the length of those tales has kept them out of *NAEL*. In *The Parson's Prologue*, Chaucer makes the allegorical implications of the Canterbury pilgrimage explicit when the Parson offers to show the pilgrims "the way in this viage / Of thilke parfit glorious pilgrimage / That highte Jerusalem celestial" (1.312, lines 49–51). One loses sight of the latter pilgrimage but is reminded of it from time to time. One such instance comes in *The Epilogue to The Pardoner's Tale*. The Pardoner has mocked the pilgrims and the religious goal of their pilgrimage—to be healed by seeking the relics of Saint Thomas at the shrine in Canterbury—and has, in turn, been mocked and silenced by the Host and laughed at by the company. The Knight steps in to restore peace and harmony and soothingly begs the Pardoner and the Host to exchange the kiss of brotherhood: "Anoon they kiste and riden forth hir waye" (1.296, line 680).

Religious Visions and Allegory

The dream vision was a genre of both love and religious poetry. The significance of dreams—whether they were prophetic or phantasmal—was, of course, a topic of lively interest and debate for medieval people and for the rooster and hen in Chaucer's *Nun's Priest's Tale*. Chaucer's first three narrative poems were love visions (1.211–12). *The Dream of the Rood* is the earliest English vision poem in which religious doctrine is cast in the form of a dream. The dreamer in that work describes himself as "stained with sins, wounded with wrongdoings . . . afflicted with sorrows" (1.26–27), and the effect of his dream is to give him renewed "hope of life" (1.28). That is also the pattern of *Piers Plowman*, the full title of which in W. W. Skeat's edition is *The Vision of William Concerning Piers the Plowman*.

Piers Plowman is structured as a series of visions dreamed by the narrator who calls himself "Will" (see 1.317) and who represents the author-narrator William Langland. Willfulness is a prominent trait of the dreamer and, we may suppose, of the poet who made the dreamer his alter ego. The best introduction to the dreamer-poet is in the last of the selections, the seemingly autobiographical passage (1.346–49) from the C-text of *Piers Plowman*. It is legitimate to interpret Will's dialogue with

Conscience and Reason in this passage, added in the final version of the work, as Langland's personal confession and apology for his life. Will has just woken up from his vision of the Confessions of the Seven Deadly Sins and describes himself as living in a rundown part of London among "lollers" (1.346, nn. 4 and 5). The derogatory term *lollard* for a lazy person, a drifter would soon be applied to a religious sect, followers of John Wycliffe, who were persecuted by the Church and some of whom were burned at the stake as heretics in the fifteenth century (see the headnote to *The Man of Law's Epilogue*, 1.252). Although Langland was orthodox in his Christian doctrine and had probably died before *lollard* came to mean "heretic," he was a much fiercer and far more blunt critic of venality and corruption in church and state than Chaucer. For "Piers Plowman" as a catchword in the Uprising of 1381, see Henry Knighton's *Chronicle*, under "Medieval Estates and Orders," on the *NAEL* Web site.

The Field of Folk has interesting parallels with Chaucer's *Prologue* (in particular, compare the portrait of Chaucer's Pardoner and *The Pardoner's Prologue* with 1.320–21, lines 66–86; see also Langland's scathing indictment of lawyers (1.321, lines 211–15). Langland's *Confessions of the Seven Deadly Sins* (represented here by Envy and Gluttony) is sharp and entertaining satire, as is the search for Saint Truth, mentioned above. In the earlier parts of the poem the satire is primarily social and political: the unjust division of society into rich and poor and the corruption of greedy officials. The simple and utopian solution, allegorized in *The Plowing of Piers's Half-Acre* (1.328–35), is that everyone should go to work, but Langland acknowledges the naívetě of such a solution. The knight cannot enforce order (as he does in *The Epilogue* to Chaucer's *Pardoner's Tale*), and the wasters and loafers quickly relapse into their old ways. The only true authority is exercised by Hunger, in whom Langland gives a powerful personification of famines repeatedly suffered by medieval people.

Frustrated with social injustice, the dreamer turns inward, and the poem centers on a question that the dreamer had asked Lady Holy Church in the first passus, "How I may save my soul." The answer takes him through dream conversations with a series of interlocutors, some of which personify functions of his own psyche such as Thought and Intelligence. Like the dreamer of the *Rood*, he grows "weary of the world." For Will, too, the answer to his many questions comes with a dream vision of the Crucifixion and the Harrowing of Hell, which is the doctrinal and emotional climax of the poem and, for many readers, the single most moving piece of Middle English religious poetry.

The images of romance blend with those of the Bible. The dreamer's vision of Christ's entry into Jerusalem "As is the nature of a knight that draws near to be dubbed" (1.336, line 13), like *The Dream of the Rood*, allegorizes the Crucifixion as a battle, only here the imagery is that of a tournament in which the prize is humanity's salvation. Christ rides to the combat barefoot, armed only in the flesh of His incarnation, to win His spurs in a joust with the Devil, who claims his entitlement to all human souls by right of the sin of Adam and Eve. As in medieval drama, Hell is portrayed as a castle, from which the Christ-knight liberates the imprisoned souls of the saved. As knights in romance tournaments sometimes conceal their identities, so Christ's humanity also serves as a disguise. The disguise here is a trick to catch the Devil, justified by the Devil's trick in disguising himself as a serpent to betray Adam and Eve into sin. The dreamer asks Faith "what all this affair meant, / And who was to joust in Jerusalem" (1.336, lines 19–20). The speaker in William Herebert's lyric (1.352) asks what amounts to the same question—"What is he, this lordling, that cometh from the fight"—of the Christ-knight returning in blood-red garment from battle, and the Knight himself answers, "Ich it am . . . / Champioun to helen mankinde in fight." For the same romance image of Christ as the champion of a lady, with yet another twist, see *Ancrene Riwle* (1.153).

The Cult of the Virgin and Affective Piety

Medieval literature, as is often remarked, reveals two diametrically opposed stereotypes of women: one represented by Eve, who caused the Fall, and the other by Mary, sometimes referred to as the second Eve (as Christ is the second Adam), who bore humanity's Savior. The Latin *Ave*, the angel's salutation to Mary in the Annunciation, it was noted at that time, is *Eva* spelled backward; and as the Fall was associated with Eve's sexuality, so salvation was associated with Mary's virginity. The cult of the Virgin developed at the same time as the cult of chivalry. In Nativity scenes in art and the drama, Mary appears as a simple maiden in a medieval version of pastoral. In the final scene of *The Second Shepherds' Play* (1.391), she speaks kindly to the shepherds after they make their humble but symbolic offerings to the Christ Child, which "lies full cold" (line 1078) in the stable. She also presents a majestic figure as "the high Queen of heaven (1.172, line 647). One of the "five fives" symbolized by Sir Gawain's pentangle are her five joys and therefore, says the poet, her image is fittingly portrayed on the inside of Gawain's shield (1.172, lines 646–49). Gawain is in "Great peril . . . / Should Mary forget her knight" (lines 1768–69).

The cult of the Virgin in the late Middle Ages is especially associated with highly emotional expressions of religious feeling. Poetry, drama, and art depicted the physical torment of Christ on the cross and the grief of Mary with a vividness meant to generate powerful feelings of empathy in readers and spectators. When Margery Kempe visited Mount Calvary, she could visualize "in her ghostly sight the mourning of our Lady, of St. John and of Mary Magdalene" (1.373). She falls to the ground, spreads her arms, writhes, and cries out loudly. This is the first of her chronic outbursts of violent weeping that alienate her fellow pilgrims and others for the rest of her life. In the Passion plays and in the lyric *Ye That Pasen by the Weye* (1.353), Christ on the Cross asks the spectators to pause and contemplate his wounds. In the four-line lyric *Sunset on Calvary* (1.353), the feeling is all the stronger for being greatly compressed. In this poem, the sympathy of the natural world for its Creator is conveyed by the sun setting behind the wood (the woods in the background but also the wood of the Cross). However, the setting sun also holds the promise of its rising and, therefore, of the Resurrection, which is one of the joys of the Virgin. Affective piety was not always or primarily expressed through an outpouring of grief. It could also be an expression of joy as it is in the *Shepherds' Play* when the Angel sings the *Gloria in excelsis* and as in lyrics like *I Sing of a Maiden* and *Adam Lay Bound* (1.353–54), which celebrate the Mother of Christ in vernacular song.

The Mystery Plays

The religious drama was another vehicle for suddenly turning distress and sorrow into gladness, and comedy into solemnity and awe. There is no better example of this than *The Second Shepherds' Play*. One must remember that the plays were performed as part of the celebration of major religious feasts, Corpus Christi and Whitsuntide, when the weather was most likely to be at its best. The shepherds make their entrances complaining of the bitter cold, the insolence of "these gentlery-men" (1.393, line 26) who exploit them, and the miseries of married men. Their sour mood is at odds with the holiday season, and although one can sympathize with much of their grumbling, it also has its comic side. The ingenious comic plot of the false Nativity, with much slapstick like the tossing of Mak in a blanket, consumes 80 percent of the play. Then the Angel sings, and the mood magically changes. You and your students have undoubtedly seen the annual Christmas special *Charlie Brown's Christmas*, which has the same tonal structure. Charlie Brown is trying to organize the children to rehearse the school Christmas play, but they pay no attention to him, preoccupied with their usual activities. All is comic noise and confusion until Linus begins to read from the text, "And there were in the same country shepherds abiding in the field, keeping watch over their flock by night."

The play *Noah's Flood* is printed first in the anthology, following biblical order, although it is actually a much later play. Its authors lack the sophistication of the Wakefield Master, but the play works in a similar way. The recalcitrance of Noah's wife and her quarrel with her husband acts out the impending storm on the family level. This was clearly a cherished comic scene, as indicated by the allusion to it in *The Miller's Tale* (1.245, lines 430–32). Noah's sending of the dove, the symbol of peace and the Holy Spirit, and God's setting of the rainbow in the sky as a sign of His promise, which will be fulfilled in the Nativity and Resurrection plays, conforms with the typological meaning and emotional structure of the cycle plays.

Everyman is a late and not very typical example of medieval morality plays, which are generally full of slapstick comedy with clowns personifying vices. In moralities the theme of salvation is played out not, as in the mystery cycles, as the history of the world from the Creation to Judgment Day, but as an allegory of the day of judgment that comes in the life of every human being. Death makes a chilling appearance in the first scene. There is comedy in the way Everyman's kindred and friend abandon him, but the last part of the play is serious didacticism. The personification allegory enacts the steps every man must take to gain salvation. First he must gain Knowledge, which leads him to Confession. When Everyman performs penance by scourging himself, Good Deeds, which had been too feeble to rise, is finally able to get on its feet and accompany Everyman to the grave while his personal qualities desert him one by one. The doctrine of the play is interesting inasmuch as it insists that not grace alone but some good works, however faint, are essential to obtain salvation.

Women and the Religious Life

Although only men could become priests, from early Christian times the convent was an option for women, though mainly women of the aristocracy, who chose to lead a spiritual life. The Abbess Hilda founded the community at Whitby where she presided over both monks and nuns (see 1.24, n. 1). The miracle of Cædmon's gift is first reported to her, and she gives the orders for testing whether it comes from God. The most likely candidate for the authorship of the lays of Marie de France is Marie, abbess of Shaftesbury, who was a half-sister of Henry II. Instead of the communal life of the convent, women might also decide to become recluses like the three well-born sisters for whom the *Ancrene Riwle* was written in the early thirteenth century. The author tells us in a preface addressed to the sisters (an abridged text of the preface is available on the Web site) that the rule was written at their request. The selection from *Ancrene Riwle* (1.153–55) again illustrates the mutual influence of the forms of medieval religion and romance. The anchoress's cell is by no means safe from the temptations of the world but is like a castle besieged by enemies. That metaphor generates the author's allegory of the Christ-knight who comes to the defense of a lady who dwells in a "castle of clay" (i.e., the body). Like the proud mistresses in romances, the lady is hard of heart and rejects the love of the knight who fights for her and finally dies for her sake. The parable concludes with an allegory of the crucifix as a shield raised in our defense.

The life of Julian of Norwich was changed by a mystical vision that came to her during an illness from which she believed herself to be dying. The priest attending her places a crucifix before her eyes. Suddenly the room turns dark except for the crucifix, from which blood begins to flow copiously beneath the crown of thorns. Julian spent the rest of her life meditating on this vision and developing a mystical theology that is startlingly original. The minute detail in which she describes the drops of blood and a round object like a hazelnut, which Christ is holding, has its counterpart in the precise reasoning by which she discriminates the persons and functions of the Trinity, in particular the role of Jesus as mother.

Julian's *Showings* survives in several manuscripts and was known to T. S. Eliot, who quoted her in *Four Quartets* (see 1.361, n. 1). *The Book of Margery Kempe* (1.367) survived in a single manuscript that was not recovered until the 1930s. Kempe's vision of Jesus, who appears to comfort her after she has suffered a nervous breakdown, is quite different from Julian's. Kempe sees Christ as "most beauteous" and "most amiable," dressed in a mantle of purple silk and sitting on the side of her bed. He addresses her as "Daughter," reproaches her for having forsaken him, then ascends slowly until he disappears in the heavens. Unlike Julian, whose interpretation of her vision is original but who lived the accepted life of a religious recluse, Kempe's religious opinions are fairly conventional, but the life she lived was radically different. She was controversial, and—as she tells us—she aroused intense hostility among both churchmen and laymen, although many, most notably Julian of Norwich, supported her. Kempe is remarkable for her struggle to make herself independent and to lead a holy life in the world rather than in a convent or anchorage. She is constantly negotiating her freedom—with her husband, freedom from continuing to have sexual relations with him and to go on pilgrimage to Jerusalem; with the archbishop of York, freedom to speak her conscience. These arguments she wins by a combination of courage and cunning. Late in her life, she negotiates with God not to be burdened with the nursing of her old husband, who has become senile and incontinent, so that she may not be interrupted in her prayers and other religious observances. This time she does not get her way. She accepts the Lord's will "that thou be free to help him at his need in my name" (1.378). And she resigns herself to her husband's care, reflecting,

> how she in her young age had full many delectable thoughts, fleshly lusts, and inordinate loves to his person [body]. And therefore she was glad to be punished with the same person and took it much the more easily and served him and helped him, . . . as she would 'a done Christ himself. (1.379)

Anticlerical Satire

The previous sections have looked at different ways in which the literature of the Middle Ages expressed Christian doctrine and faith. In the case of Will, the dreamer in Langland's poem, the search for social justice comes to be replaced by a search for hope, faith, and love, a quest temporarily fulfilled by the dreamer's vision in Passus 18. In the final passus of *Piers Plowman*, however, "Unity," the poet's allegorical name for the church of his own time, remains under attack from without by the forces of Anti-Christ and from within by Friar Flatterer. Langland's *Prologue* and the earlier steps of his poem, which deal with the marriage of Lady Meed (see 1.317–18), participate in a genre of writing that modern scholars call "estates satire." On the classification of society into "estates," i.e., classes and professions, see "Medieval Estates and Orders" on the *NAEL* Web site, where you find will find examples of estates satire from two works by Chaucer's contemporary John Gower. *The General Prologue* to *The Canterbury Tales*, although its narrative structure, style, and irony are very different from Gower's, has affinities with estates satire; comparison with Gower and with Langland provides a literary context for Chaucer's prologue to pilgrimage and helps bring out its special qualities. Estates satire is aimed at all estates and professions—barons, knights, lawyers, doctors, merchants, etc.—but much of its sharpest criticism targets those who abuse the Church—bishops, priests, monks, nuns, friars, and laymen employed by the Church, such as summoners and pardoners.

In Chaucer's *Prologue*, three portraits—those of the Knight, the Parson, and the Plowman—establish a standard; when measured against it, all the others fall short in varying degrees. Some critics have argued, on the basis of what actually happened on the Crusades in which the Knight participated, that Chaucer is also satirizing him as a mercenary. On the other hand, it is possible to think that Chaucer viewed the Crusades, just as Malory still did a hundred years later, as righteous wars in contrast with the French wars or the Wars of the Roses—wars among Christians in which Chaucer and Malory had actually participated. In any case, no one has ever questioned the true perfection of the Parson and his brother, the Plowman.

The lady Prioress is certainly not guilty of serious abuses of her office. The satire is mild and based mainly on her ladylike qualities, such as her impeccable table manners, which are not necessarily attributes that make her an ideal Mother Superior of a convent. It has been pointed out that a few phrases in the portrait—"simple and coy," "yën greye as glas," "mouth . . . softe and reed"—are conventional features of heroines in medieval romances. She bends a few rules, for example, by keeping pet dogs, which she spoils by feeding them the finest bread, perhaps even by leaving her convent to go on a pilgrimage at all. A delicate ambiguity hovers around her spirituality. Does the *Amor* engraved on her brooch emblematize spiritual love, as she intends, or does Chaucer hint at her attachment to worldly things—objects like the gold brooch attached to her rosary?

In the portraits of the Monk and the Friar, which, with the portrait of the Prioress, make up a group portrait of the regular clergy, i.e., those subject to a *regula* or rule, the abuses become increasingly serious and the satire increasingly sharp. As a huntsman and inspector of monastic properties, the portly monk is hardly ever in his monastery, and he condemns the rule of Saint Augustine, bidding a monk to stay in the cloister, as out of date. "How shall the world be served?" he asks rhetorically (1.219, line 187). Are monks supposed to be serving the world, and how is *this* monk serving it?

Several double-entendres about the Monk's hunting hint broadly that he does not keep his vow of chastity. In the case of the Friar, his seemingly charitable arrangements for many a marriage of young women "at his owene cost" thinly disguise that these women were victims of his seductions (1.220, lines 212–13). He can well afford to do so because the income from his licensed begging for charity exceeded what he turned over to his house. His worst abuse is that of the sacrament of confession, which he in effect sells to its consumers in return for a healthy donation.

The Summoner and Pardoner are laymen employed by the Church. The one is a corrupt bailiff who hauls persons before an ecclesiastical court for morals offenses if they do not buy him off; the other sells pardons and indulgences (as well as doing a brisk business peddling fake relics) to obtain forgiveness for sins from the heavenly judge. It was the institution of pardons and indulgences that perhaps more than any other abuse of religion provided ammunition for the Protestant Reformation. As one may see by reading Langland, Gower, and other contemporaries of Chaucer, his criticism of the Church was neither bold nor harsh, and he was certainly no reformer. Students will have no difficulty responding to his irony. What is more difficult to convey to them—and reading just a little bit of Gower makes this easier—is an appreciation of the special qualities of Chaucer's irony: its artfulness, humor, sympathy, and avoidance of a judgmental righteousness. Chaucer the pilgrim narrator presents *all* his fellow pilgrims, not just the good Parson, Plowman, and Knight, as the most wonderful group of people in the world; each is in some respect the best of his or her kind. The narrator's lack of discrimination invites readers to discover for themselves that most of the pilgrims are flawed and that several are, indeed, rascals who are admired chiefly for their consummate charlatanism. Yet the resulting irony need not cancel out the effect of the narrator's delight in and affection for the pilgrims. By reserving judgment, Chaucer leaves critics and students free to disagree about the effect of individual portraits. In many cases there is a delicate balance between satire and sympathy that, depending on the reader, could tilt either way.

The Pardoner's Prologue, *Tale*, and *Epilogue* dramatize the deep despair at sin and longing for absolution. The Pardoner's shameless confession—that he is guilty of the very sin he practices by preaching against it, always on the same text "*Radix malorum est cupiditas*"—can be construed as both an outrageous insult to the other pilgrims and as a plea to be accepted as one of them. The sermon with its exemplum of the three men who set out to slay death is a tour de force. The exemplum brings to mind another text of Saint Paul's: "The wages of sin is death." Cynically, the Pardoner's peroration holds out to the sinners in his congregations the promise contained in the other half of Paul's text: "but the gift of God is eternal life through Jesus Christ" (Romans 6.23). The Pardoner tells them, "I you assoile by myn heigh power— / Ye that wol offre—as clene and eek as cleer / As ye were born" (1.295, lines, 625–27). Thus he asks his listeners to pay him for God's gift. But in the dramatic context of the pilgrimage to Canterbury, the Pardoner's corruption and perversion of the gift of grace does not deny its efficacy. Perhaps it is even affirmed through the

Knight's making peace between the Host and the Pardoner. In this quiet and understated ending of this fragment, the Pardoner is pardoned, and the search for Saint Truth continues.

Antifeminism

Just as one ought to strike a balance in teaching and responding to anticlericalism in medieval literature, one needs to put medieval antifeminism into perspective. The Middle Ages inherited an antifeminist tradition from the ancients, and the ideal of sexual purity intensified that bias. Even sexual intercourse between husband and wife was doctrinally considered sinful except for the purpose of producing children. Such attitudes did not prevent the idealization of love in romance; however, they did nothing to discourage the prejudice that women, and wives in particular were on the whole promiscuous, luxury-loving, extravagant, loose-tongued, proud, quarrelsome, deceitful, domineering, and guilty of every other vice or annoying disposition men could think of. After Sir Gawain learns from the Green Knight how he has been taken in by the lady, he tries to comfort himself with a bitter catalog of men who have been betrayed by women, starting with Adam (1.207, lines 2415–28). It is a temporary lapse of courtesy, which may be forgiven because Gawain eventually accepts the blame as his own. Still, it is the enchantress Morgan le Faye, King Arthur's aunt and half-sister, not the Green Knight himself, who gets credited with the plot against Camelot. The Wife of Bath's fifth husband has an anthology of antifeminist literature, which includes most of Chaucer's sources for the *Wife of Bath's Prologue*. The most important of these is Saint Jerome's *Epistle against Jovinian* (see the headnote 1.253). Relevant excerpts from the latter can be found in a useful volume, *Chaucer: Sources and Backgrounds*, edited by R. P. Miller. Excerpts from the speech of the Old Woman, a character in Jean de Meun's part of the *Romance of the Rose* who was a model for the Wife of Bath, may be found on the Web site.

The Wife of Bath is already a controversial character on the pilgrimage. She is mocked and patronized in her *Prologue* by the Pardoner and the Friar. The Clerk dedicates an ironic envoy to her at the end of his tale. A character in *The Merchant's Tale* cites her as an authority on the miseries of getting married. She has been interpreted somewhat literally by some modern scholars as an incarnation of the sins of the flesh and the scourge of husbands. Perhaps the more common tendency today is to regard her as a proto-feminist heroine, who is fighting against and, to a degree, triumphing over a patriarchal system that disposes of women as chattel. You and your students can argue for or against either of these views in class, or you may prefer the position that Chaucer is, as so often, trying to have it both ways. However, it is difficult not to sympathize with the resentment the Wife feels toward the men she married and the clerks who wrote diatribes demonizing women and difficult not to admire her courage, her with, her staying-power, and her love of life. In the fantasy world of her tale, the Wife of Bath enjoys settling a few scores. In the real world, Margery Kempe suffered clerkly antifeminism at the hands of the bishop of York's men, and like the Wife of Bath, she knew how to defend herself by telling a good story.

The Nun's Priest tells a tale about a household that consists entirely of females with one exception: the rooster Chauntecleer. Chauntecleer rules the roost, that is to say, his seven hens who are "his sustres and his paramours." His favorite wife is "faire damoisele Pertelote." Chauntecleer and Pertelote have a few romance trappings—Chauntecleer's colors and martial bearing have chivalric associations; Pertelote's sententious words on what all women desire (1.298–99, lines 92–97) suggest that she, like Sir Bertilak's lady, has read romances. But the argument that she has with Chauntecleer, in which she puts down the epic and tragic intimations he sees in his dream by diagnosing its cause as indigestion, makes her sound more like the Wife of Bath arguing with one of her husbands. In putting Pertelote down, Chauntecleer behaves like a clerk, overwhelming her with a long string of authorities on dream lore. But though he silences her, he succumbs to her charms. He cannot resist, however, a jest at her intellectual inferiority that she won't understand without a footnote. He quotes a Latin maxim, *Mulier est hominis confusio* (1.304, line 344), which might be said to sum up the antifeminist gospel, and mistranslates it to flatter her:

> Madame, the sentence of this Latin is,
> "Womman is mannes joye and al his blis." (lines 344–46)

He pays for his arrogance with a close call.

In moralizing his fable, the Nun's Priest, who is the Prioress's confessor but her social inferior, momentarily strays into the standard antifeminist narrative:

> Wommenes conseils been ful ofte colde,
> Wommanes conseil broughte us first to wo,
> And made Adam fro Paradis to go,
> Ther as he was ful merye and wel at ese.

Then he quickly recovers:

> But for I noot to whom it might displese
> If I conseil of wommen wolde blame,
> Passe over, for I saide it in my game—
> Rede auctours where they trete of swich matere,
> And what they sayn of wommen ye may heere—
> Thise been the cokkes wordes and nat mine:
> I can noon harm of no womman divine. (lines 436–46)

Antifeminism is just one of the many kinds of medieval writing that Chaucer plays with in *The Nun's Priest's Tale*. Others include dream lore, philosophy, epic, proverbs, scriptural exegesis, bestiaries, and, of course, fables. The narrator almost buries the tale under sententious commentary that parodies the habit of medieval preachers and poets to find multiple meanings and morals in everything. Parody does not exclude affection for the works that are being parodied. Part of the tale's charm lies in Chaucer's delight in the pretentious kinds of language he is taking off. There is some danger that students will find some of the parody more tedious than amusing. The verses quoted above about "wommenes conseil," for which the priest disclaims all responsibility, are plain enough. Other passages, like the priest's musings about predestination (lines 414–31)—whether Chauntecleer's fate is a case of simple or conditional necessity—may be harder to digest. Tell your students that if they cannot "bulte it to the bren," like the priest they "need nat han to do of swich matere."

Whoever enjoys *The Nun's Priest's Tale* will also take pleasure in the imitation written about a century later by Robert Henryson. Henryson's works, especially his *Testament of Cressid*, which is a sequel to Chaucer's *Troilus and Criseyde*, testify that by the end of the fifteenth century a literary canon, of which Chaucer was revered as its progenitor, was now established in England. Few of Chaucer's many followers captured his spirit, especially his humor, as successfully as Henryson. Henryson is more overtly a moralist than Chaucer, and the *Moralitas* (1.444) at the end of the fable spells out its lesson with more gravity. But he shares Chaucer's gift for endowing his animals with human speech. An original twist in his version of the fable is the introduction of speeches individualizing three of Chauntecleer's wives after the fox makes off with him in which they voice their different opinions about the rooster as a husband and lover. Each wife represents an antifeminist stereotype, and one of them is clearly a sister of the Wife of Bath. The fable is short, and if you assign the *Nun's Priest's Tale*, your students will probably appreciate Henryson and the challenge of wrestling with his Scots dialect after Chaucer's by then familiar Southeast Midland.

Teaching Chaucer in Middle English

Some users of *NAEL* prefer to teach Chaucer in translation because they believe there is not adequate time to teach Chaucer in Middle English. Others, however, believe that students stand to gain greater pleasure and knowledge by encountering even a limited number of the selections in *NAEL* in the original rather than by reading more of his works in translation. Students love to hear Chaucer read aloud; even if the instructor is not a specialist, it is well worth the effort to master a few passages to read to the class. When time is limited, the choice of tales is difficult. Because *The General Prologue* is perhaps the most formidable of the selections, since it requires so many annotations, you may wish to abridge the number of portraits you assign. The Knight and Squire and the three pilgrims in religious orders (Prioress, Monk, Friar, see pp. 23–24 on this sequence) make a good start. After that, many portraits could be sacrificed. One might cover the Parson and Plowman, the Wife of Bath, the Miller and Reeve, and the Summoner and Pardoner. The choice of tales depends on the taste of the instructor. Even if you omit some of the tales, however, ask your students to read the headnotes to get some sense of the growth of *The Canterbury Tales* as Chaucer revised it and discovered new possibilities in the form he had invented. *The Man of Law's Epilogue* has been included partly because of the theory that it once belonged to a stage when the Man of Law told a tale in prose (probably *The Tale of Melibee*), and the Wife of Bath told the fabliau that eventually became *The Shipman's Tale*.

A systematic presentation of Middle English is available on 1.14–18. One can always refer back to it; but to start with, students are probably just as well off coping with the glosses and notes and listening to the NAEL Audio Companion. You can obtain recordings of the Chaucer selections in *NAEL* in Middle English from The Chaucer Studio, Department of English, Brigham Young University, Provo, UT 84602-6218, at a moderate price. You may request a printed catalog or view the catalog at http://English.byu.edu/Chaucer/.

A few general points about the principal differences from Modern English can be helpful.

Phonology

1. Pronounce the long vowels the way you would in modern European languages—Spanish, French, Italian, German.
2. Pronounce consonants that have become silent, such as the *g* in *g-nat*; the *k* in *k-night*; the *l* in *fol-k*.
3. In combination with the vowels *a, o, u, gh* had the sound of *ch* in the name of the German composer *Bach*; in combination with *e* and *i, gh* had the sound of *ch*, in the German noun *Licht* (light). If you have trouble with those sounds, you can leave them silent as in modern *thought* and *lit* (past participle of the verb *to light*), or they can be pronounced with the sound of *k*, in which case Middle English *nought* (not) sounds like *knocked* and Middle English *light*, like *licked*, pronounced at the back of the throat.
4. Pronounce *-e* as an unstressed syllable at the end of words, *unless* it would spoil the meter. This is more easily said than done. Obviously this is something one learns to do instinctively after one develops a feeling for the proper number of syllables in the line. The final *-e* is normally suppressed before words beginning with a vowel or *h*.

Grammar

1. The second personal singular pronoun is *thou* (nominative), *thee* (objective). The second person plural pronoun is *ye* (nominative),

you (objective). In Middle English the singular forms of address are familiar as in Spanish and French *tu*, German *Du*; the plural forms are formal as in *usted*, *vous*, *Sie*. In Chaucer the social distinction between these forms is often important in dialogue. For example, in *The Miller's Prologue* the Host addresses the lordly Monk as *ye*, but the churlish Miller as *thou* (1.236, lines 10, 27). Chauntecleer and Pertelote, being an aristocratic couple, address one another as *ye* and *you*.

2. The third person singular feminine form (*her*) is *hir*(*e*), *her*(*e*).
3. The third person plural possessive form (*their*) is like the feminine singular *hir*.
4. The third person plural objective form (*them*) is *hem*.
5. A few nouns form their plural with *-n*, most frequently *yën* (eyes).
6. The ending *-st* in verbs is a sign of the second person singular. The ending *-th* is usually a sign of the present tense, third person singular, but it also occurs in all persons of the present tense plural and in the plural imperative. In the indicative, these endings remain standard in Shakespeare and in the King James translation of the Bible.
7. The plurals of verbs in the third persons and the infinitive may end in *-n*.
8. The prefix *y-* often marks the past participle. In later periods, the prefix was used (especially by Edmund Spenser) to give the style an archaic effect.
9. Sentence structure is much more flexible than it is in Modern English. One will often find the subject or verb at the end of a sentence.

Students gain a good deal of confidence from having read some Chaucer in the original and are thereby better prepared for the language of Spenser, Shakespeare, and Milton, which presents difficulties of another order.

Contents: Norton Topics Online, The Middle Ages
www.wwnorton.com/nael

Contents: Norton Online Archive, The Middle Ages
www.wwnorton.com/nael/NOA

Contents: NAEL Audio Companion, The Middle Ages

- Caedmon's Hymn
  - Read by J. B. Bessinger, Jr.
- Beowulf
  - Translated and read by Seamus Heaney
    - Prologue, Building of Heorot, arrival of Grendel, lines 1–98
    - The Fight with Grendel, lines 710–823
    - The Last Survivor's Speech, lines 2241b–70a
    - Beowulf's Funeral, lines 3137–82
- The Battle of Maldon
  - Read by Robert Fulk
    - Birhtwold's Speech
- Geoffrey Chaucer
  - The Canterbury Tales
    - General Prologue, lines 1–18
      - Read by J. B. Bessinger, Jr.
    - General Prologue, portrait of the miller, lines 547–68
      - Read by Alfred David
    - The Miller's Prologue
      - Read by V. A. Kolve
    - The Miller's Tale, lines 163–98
      - Read by Alfred David
    - The Man of Law's Epilogue
      - Read by V. A. Kolve
    - The Wife of Bath's Prologue, lines 1–29
      - Read by Marie Borroff
    - The Pardoner's Tale, lines 428–61
      - Read by Alfred David
    - The Nun's Priest's Tale, lines 337–66
      - Read by Alfred David
- Middle English Lyric
  - The Cuckoo Song ("Sumer is ycomen in")
    - Performed by the Hilliard Ensemble

CHAPTER 3

The Sixteenth Century 1485–1603

Introducing Sixteenth-Century Literature

Knowing where to begin in teaching the sixteenth century can be puzzling because the century seems to "begin" so many times. Where do we locate the break, if indeed there really *is* one, that marks the end of the Middle Ages and the start of something new? Should we begin at the chronological beginning of the century, emphasizing what is already nonmedieval in the works of John Skelton and (especially) Sir Thomas More? Should we point to the profound and traumatic impact of the Reformation? When we consider how much of the century's remarkable literary achievement was packed into the second half of the reign of Elizabeth (four-fifths of the pages in this section of *NAEL* are devoted to literature written after 1580), the question of when this century really gets going as a new literary period looks even trickier.

Because the first period break in *NAEL* comes with the sixteenth century, you might begin with a discussion of the problems of literary and historical periodization. The general introductions to each period do, of course, explain most of the new departures, but inevitably the beginnings and ends of periods overlap to some degree; and some important authors straddle the two. Skelton was born in 1460. As a young man, More seriously considered becoming a monk. It should not be surprising, therefore, that the Utopians are especially impressed "that Christ encouraged his disciples to practice community of goods, and that among the truest Christians, the practice still prevails" (1.517). More wrote this only twenty years before three monks were "hanged, drawn, and quartered" for refusing to swear the oath of supremacy, which declared Henry VIII "Supreme Head of the Church of England" (1.475), and More's execution followed in the next year. Such radical change helps explain period divisions in an anthology but also explains why the English people in the sixteenth century and through the first part of the seventeenth were deeply divided, and how these divisions profoundly affected the history and literature of those periods.

Without subjecting your students to an account of the border wars between medievalists and early modernists, you might explain to your class that there are two different terms for what seems to have begun in the sixteenth century: "the Renaissance" and "the Early Modern Period." The term *Renaissance*, which was first used in the nineteenth century (as in Walter Pater's *The Renaissance* [2.1636]), draws attention to the period's conscious break with medieval culture. It applies to the revival of Greek and Roman culture that began in Italy during the fourteenth century and spread to England in the late fifteenth and the sixteenth centuries. Because the term means "rebirth," it implies that classical learning in the Middle Ages had become moribund. Of course, the Middle Ages, and especially its monastic institutions, had in fact preserved and transformed much of the Latin culture it inherited. Few medieval scholars, on the other hand, knew any Greek; and many of the key Greek texts and some by Latin authors had not been available to them. The revival of Greek and the addition of new (old) texts to the classical canon (especially the editing and translating of the Greek New Testament) had enormous influence. Sidney regarded himself as a pioneer in a new age of English literature. His *Defense of Poesy* makes a display of the author's familiarity with Greek and Latin literature; with condescending praise, he wonders that Chaucer "in *that misty age* could see so clearly" while "we in *this clear age* go so stumblingly after him" (1.949; emphasis added).

The more recent term, *Early Modern Period*, is borrowed from linguistics, where it is used to distinguish the language, which had undergone "the Great Vowel Shift," from Middle English. From the point of view of students, the language still presents many problems; but in the sixteenth century there are no longer difficult texts, like *Sir Gawain and the Green Knight*, that need to be translated, and something like standard English begins to emerge in printing practices. But the term Early Modern is also used to refer to historical and cultural changes in the sixteenth century to emphasize ways in which some of the seeds of the modern world were sown—seeds of such phenomena as the market economy, the individual subject, and the centralized state. Whereas the idea of the Renaissance attunes our ears to the new, sometimes brashly confident tone characteristic of the era, the notion of early modernity draws our attention instead to tensions, ambiguities, and conflicts between residual and emergent ideologies.

Isabella Whitney's *Will and Testament* (1.606), for example, is a uniquely early example of publication by a woman of satirical verses. The poem is based on the double meaning of *leave*. Whitney is leaving London, presumably because she can no longer afford it; but she "leaves," as in a will, the city and its expensive tradesmen the good things she is "leaving" behind. Thus the poem can be read almost like a tour guide to shopping in sixteenth-century London. The "testament" was, in fact, a medieval genre (for example Henryson's *Testament of Cressid* and François Villon's *Testament*); Whitney's is a testament with a difference: a poem about women, money, and consumerism.

The extraordinary revolution in literature that took place after 1580 did not come in response to any decisive historical event. It is instead best understood as resulting from the confluence of many different currents (humanism, Protestantism, the Italian Renaissance, the exploration of the New World, the decline of magic, the centralization of state power, etc.) in the minds of writers attuned to their culture. Spenser, Marlowe, and Shakespeare could not have been as innovative as they were had they not been masters of a kind of cultural alchemy. In their works, disparate materials—some new, some old—were blended together and transformed into gold. Thus *The Faerie Queene*, a work unprecedented in English literature, is at the same time deliberately old-fashioned: an allegorical romance employing an archaic vocabulary. Marlowe's *Doctor Faustus* applies the conventions of the medieval morality play to a topical story. And the story of King Lear is at once timeless and exquisitely contemporary, as old as a fable and as up-to-date as a court case of 1603.

Where to begin? You could start with one or two poems by John Skelton, the first author in this section, the language of which students might find hard to differentiate from Middle English. *Mannerly Margery* and *Lullay, lullay* are both mildly bawdy. *The Tunning of Elinour Rumming* is a rollicking satire of an alewife who adulterates her brew (in this excerpt with chicken shit). Much of the effect depends on the tumbling rhythms (known as "Skeltonics").

To make a point about periodization, however, you may want to leap ahead and compare a famous later sixteenth-century text with a predecessor. Marlowe's *Doctor Faustus,* a play to which students almost always respond favorably, can be instructively paired with the late medieval morality play *Everyman*. Reading *Faustus* lets students take advantage of supplementary texts on the Norton Web site contemporary with the play (excerpts from Marlowe's source, *The Damnable Life and Deserved Death of Doctor John Faustus*; a pamphlet detailing a witch hunt that involved the torture and execution of a Doctor Fian, accused of making a pact with the devil). *Everyman* was written around 1500, and we don't know how or for what sort of audience it was originally performed. Although there is some satire, it is a very serious play, lacking the bawdy humor that characterizes *Mankind*, a morality that one can tell from internal evidence was performed by strolling players, probably in places like the courtyards of inns. Marlowe's drama was performed on a professional stage like the London playhouse pictured on 1.2962. *Everyman* is written in loosely structured four-stress lines rhyming in couplets, or *abab*. The comic scenes in *Faustus* are in prose, but for the most part it was written in the strongly marked blank verse that Jonson dubbed "Marlowe's mighty line" (1.1415, line 30), which was especially declaimed by the great actor Edward Alleyn and which paved the way for Shakespeare's drama.

The characters in *Everyman*, including the title character, are all personifications in a continued allegory. In most respects Faustus is anything but an "everyman." In the opening scene he is already the most learned man in the world, having mastered all the arts and sciences but one, the forbidden art of black magic for which he makes his pact with the devil. Yet Faustus is also like Everyman inasmuch as he must eventually make his reckoning with God, and in this, as the least educated groundling watching Marlowe's play would realize, Faustus remains stubbornly ignorant of the essential knowledge that Knowledge gives to Everyman at the end of that play. The whole point of *Everyman* is to teach him and thereby the audience the doctrine of Confession and Penance, which brings him to salvation, the standard conclusion of the morality play. Throughout Marlowe's play, Faustus is repenting his bargain but is afraid of breaking it. For the first audience of *Faustus*, there must have been suspense as the final scene proceeded. The speech of the Old Man in the B Text, printed on page 1.1025, seems to encourage the hope that Faustus will, after all, pronounce the saving words. Like Everyman, Faustus desperately begs for time, "A year, a month, a week, a natural day" (1.1022, line 64). The stage effect of the striking clock emphasizes the urgency. Even if one already knows the outcome, the trap door opening with smoke pouring from it comes as a shock. The old morality play has turned magnificently into a new tragedy.

In another respect the study of *Doctor Faustus* differs from that of *Everyman* and most other medieval texts. We know nothing about the author of the latter except what can be deduced from the text itself. With many sixteenth-century writers, although records are scarce, enough documentary evidence is available to encourage biographical interpretations. But what little evidence there is must be used with caution, particularly in the case of Marlowe. Early in the twentieth century the sensational details about his death were discovered (1.970–71); these and testimony against Marlowe implied that he had been employed in the queen's secret service. The comments on Marlowe by the government spy Richard Baines and the Puritan Thomas Beard (among the documents provided on the Web site) have been used to suggest that characters like Tamburlaine and Faustus are projections of Marlowe's own radical skepticism and his hunger for knowledge and new experience.

Cultural Currents

The English Reformation

Teaching the themes and conflicts of the English Reformation to students today means starting more or less from scratch. Many will be unclear even on the nature of the division between Catholicism and Protestantism, let alone the finer points of Calvinism, Lutheranism, and the Anglican compromise. The task of conveying so much information may seem both daunting and a waste of valuable class time, but it is vital, especially if you are planning to cover book 1 of *The Faerie Queene*. The Seventh Edition of *NAEL* includes a new section, "The Literature of the Sacred" (1.538–61), consisting of short selections from Tyndale, Calvin, Foxe, Hooker, and others, which provides a basis for exploring the most important debates and outcomes of the Reformation. These selections illustrate the point that the Reformation was not a single event, but rather a series of ruptures and conflicts on every level of society. It brought England into conflict with most of the Continent and the English language into conflict with Latin; it pitted the north of the country against the south, men against women, and individual men and women against the authority of church and state. "The Literature of the Sacred" also emphasizes the crucial role played by literature and literary problems in the events of the Reformation. One of the central conflicts was over who should be allowed to read a certain book, and in what language. Rebels and martyrs on both sides expressed their faith and their defiance in poetry and songs. (Additional texts and commentary are available at Norton Topics Online under "Dissent, Doubt, and Spiritual Violence in the Reformation.") Above all, the Reformation proved to people of all faiths the extraordinary power of the English language when allied with a relatively new invention, the printing press.

The introduction to the section "The English Bible" (1.539) describes the controversy surrounding the translation of the Bible into the vernacular in the Reformation era. In the preface to his translation of the Pentateuch (included on the Web site), William Tyndale recalled the opposition he encountered from church authorities in England. Tyndale recognized that this was in essence a debate over the rights and duties of textual interpretation; in the context of a literature course, his words have a resonance that goes beyond the question of biblical translation:

> A thousand books had they liefer to be put forth against their abominable doings and doctrine, than that the scripture should come to light. For as long as they may keep that down, they will so darken the right way with the mist of their sophistry, . . . and with wresting the scripture unto their own purpose clean contrary unto the process, order, and meaning of the text, and so delude them in descanting upon it with allegories, and amaze them expounding it in many senses before the unlearned lay people (when it hath but one simple literal sense whose light the owls cannot abide), that though thou feel in thine heart and art sure how that all is false that they say, yet couldest thou not solve their subtle riddles.

Protestant reformers like Tyndale were not the first to contemplate the translation of the Bible into the English tongue. The project had previously been undertaken by, among others, John Wycliffe, the fourteenth-century religious reformer who was claimed by later Protestants as a forerunner. But Tyndale and his fellows had an unprecedented advantage in the printing press, which made it almost impossible for the authorities to suppress unwelcome texts and the ideas they contained. Students will be both entertained and instructed by a telling anecdote from Hall's chronicle (also on the Web site), which reveals how print made traditional methods of censorship such as book burning suddenly and comically obsolete. Hall reports how a confederate of Tyndale's happily assisted the bishop of London in buying up copies of the English Bible to burn them. Later, when questioned by Thomas More as to how Tyndale continued to finance his publishing operations, the confederate cheerfully replied: "it is the Bishop of London that hath holpen us, for he hath bestowed among us a great deal of money in New Testaments to burn them, and that hath and yet is our only succour and comfort." Print did not, of course, make literature impervious to censorship, but it gave censored texts a much better chance of surviving, as well as allowing uncensored texts an opportunity to reach tens of thousands of new readers. It was for these reasons that John Foxe, himself the author of one of the most frequently printed books of the century, declared "that either the pope must abolish knowledge and printing, or printing at length will root him out."

The four different versions of 1 Corinthians 13 (1.540–42) illustrate what was at stake in the debate over translating the Bible and will also allow you to open up a discussion of the problems inherent in the task of translation. No language precisely matches another in the sense and connotation of every word. Variant translations are thus inevitable, and in periods of ideological strife are apt to become a focal point of conflict. This is the case with Tyndale's controversial choice of "love" instead of "charity" in 1 Corinthians 13 (1.541), and also with his translation of Latin *ecclesia* (a loan word from the Greek for "assembly") as "congregation" rather than as "church." (Such instances drove Thomas More to complain that Tyndale, by his own stated principles as a translator, might as well translate the word "world" as "football.")

In addition to introducing important issues relating to the eucharist, lay preaching, and individual conscience, *The First Examination of Anne Askew* (1.548) is not without literary interest and dramatic force. One of the most important woman writers of the sixteenth century, Askew struggled and succeeded in making her voice heard through preaching during her life and in print after her death. Like her predecessor Margery Kempe (1.374) and her successor Anna Trapnell (1.1743), she was bold and sometimes witty in answering the religious authorities, who accused her of heresy. Askew was less fortunate in her fate than Kempe and Trapnell, but like them she left a record of her examination, which survived her. She may in addition have been the author of the ballad "I Am a Woman Poor and Blind" (Web site, *A Ballad of Anne Askew*), which remained widely popular for at least a century after her death. Students could be assigned a comparison of Askew's account with Kempe's and/or Trapnell's, noting similarities and differences in their responses to interrogation. Alternatively, they might compare the authorial voice in *The First Examination of Anne Askew* with that in "I Am a Woman Poor and Blind." What signs suggest that these are or are not the work of the same hand? What aspects of Askew's beliefs and her sufferings are emphasized in each?

It is important to convey that opponents of the English Reformation included not only lofty figures like Thomas More but thousands of ordinary people of all social classes, appalled by changes that included the dissolution of monasteries and abbeys and the seizure of church property. The *Homily Against Disobedience*, sternly instructing the faithful that "all sins possible to be committed against God or man be contained in rebellion" (1.557), serves as a reminder that resistance to the Reformation was not swiftly snuffed out. That its inclusion in the *Book of Homilies* followed the Northern Rebellion of 1569 is also a reminder of the link between religious and regional tensions: in the middle decades of the century a string of rebellions pitted the north and west of England against London and the southeast, as well as Catholics against Protestants. The First and greatest of these was the Pilgrimage of Grace (1536–37); the Web site contains several remarkable documents of the Pilgrimage, including the *Pilgrims' Oath* and *A Song for the Pilgrims of Grace* (reminiscent of Skelton):

> Alack, alack!
> For the Church sake,
> Poor commons wake,
> And no marvel!
> For clear it is,
> The decay of this,
> How the poor shall miss
> No tongue can tell.

Like the *Homily Against Disobedience*, these rebel texts purport to uphold sacred values against those who would desecrate or deny them; they can be instructively compared in terms of the vocabulary, rhetoric, and imagery they have in common, though coming from opposite sides of the religious divide.

The Wider World

English men and women of the sixteenth century experienced an unprecedented increase in knowledge of the world beyond Europe, especially that "New World" reached by Christopher Columbus in 1492. The goal of the great sixteenth-century voyages was, in the words of Sir Walter Ralegh, "To seek new worlds for gold, for praise, for glory." Poets and other writers were inevitably attracted both by the glory of the enterprise and by the opportunity to imagine other worlds. Yet perhaps the most profound effect of the voyages of discovery was that they allowed—even forced—the English to look at their own society in startlingly new ways.

In addition to providing fascinating records of the encounter between the New World and the Old, texts like Ralegh's *Discovery of the large, rich, and beautiful Empire of Guiana* (1.885) and the selections gathered in the new section, "The Wider World" (1.889–906), are important texts in the history of English autoethnography.

As indicated by the discussion "The English and Otherness" (1.477) in the Introduction to the period, the English in the sixteenth century became practiced in defining themselves by what they were not. Travel books, sermons, political speeches, civic pageants, public exhibitions, and theatrical spectacles of otherness all testify to the prevalence of this sort of negative self-definition. In particular, many English writers used descriptions of foreign lands as a means of commenting on affairs at home. Rife as they sometimes are with racism and xenophobia, sixteenth-century travelers' tales often manage to leave the impression that other societies may be better—wiser, more just, or more noble—than English society.

The wellspring of this tradition is Thomas More's *Utopia* (1.506), inspired by Amerigo Vespucci's accounts of the New World discoveries. *Utopia* inaugurates a tradition of self-reflective travel writing whereby descriptions of the farthest-flung corners of the globe could reveal new and sometimes uncomfortable truths about the English themselves. In book 1 of *Utopia*, the returned traveler Raphael Hythloday counters More's suggestion that he "devote . . . time and energy to public affairs . . . by joining the council of some great prince" (1.509) with sarcastic remarks about kings and their counselors and with a devastating critique of European society and government. Pointing up the greed, arrogance, ignorance, and cruelty that riddle societies such as England's, Hythloday asserts that only through the abolition of private property and the introduction of common ownership can society be made just. In book 2, Hythloday describes the imaginary commonwealth of Utopia (More coined the name from Greek for "no place"), which he claims has solved the problems that so beset England and every other European nation.

The state of Utopia, almost all readers will feel, is not without problems of its own. The state punishes crime with slavery, repeated adultery with death, and oversees almost every aspect of its citizens' lives. Some students may, in fact, respond to Utopia as though it were a darkly ironic dystopia. Some of the unsettling ambiguities may be intentional humor. For example, should we take seriously the Utopian practice of having bride and groom inspect one another naked before the wedding to reveal any defects (1.515)? Hythloday thinks it foolish, though the Utopians, for their part, are "amazed" at the folly of Europeans in disallowing this custom. More may be remembering a passage in *The Wife of Bath's Prologue* in which she claims that her old husbands complain that men have the right to inspect every article or animal before they purchase it, except for a wife (1.260, lines 288–98). It may also be relevant that Plato, whose *Republic* is the great model for More's ideal commonwealth, in all seriousness commends a similar practice in *Laws VI*. Whatever one thinks of Utopian customs, they force readers to think about the customs of their own country. *Utopia* might lead to a creative assignment for your students: "In the style of More, write about a Utopian solution (serious or comic) for something you find wrong with our society."

If the description of an imaginary New World society like Utopia was one way to critique English social values and practices, another was to describe natives of the recently discovered New World as "noble savages" inhabiting a Paradise or primitive "Golden Age." Michael Drayton in his *Ode. To the Virginia Voyage* praises Virginia as "Earth's only paradise" (1.968, line 24) and describes its inhabitants as those to whom "the golden age / Still nature's laws doth give" (1.969, lines 37–38). Similarly, Arthur Barlowe describes the people of Virginia as "most gentle, loving, and faithful, void of guile and treason, and such as live after the manner of the golden age" (1.900). These ideal descriptions of New World peoples did not of course prevent the English from seeking to conquer and exploit them—even as Drayton praises the native way of life, he exhorts the English voyagers to "Let cannons roar" (1.969, line 53).

The notion that humanity once experienced an age of innocence and plenty is common to many cultures. The Renaissance dream of the earthly paradise drew both on the Eden of Genesis and on Ovid's description of the Golden Age. The relevant passage from Arthur Golding's translation of Ovid's *Metamorphoses* (1.600) can be compared with passages from Ralegh's *Discovery*, Amadas and Barlowe's *Voyage* (1.897), Drayton's *Ode*, and (looking ahead), Marvell's *Bermudas* (1.1686), all of which discover features of the Golden Age in the New World. (Another interesting text for purposes of comparison is Nashe's description of the Roman "summer banqueting house" in *The Unfortunate Traveler*, where "there was no winter, but a perpetual spring, as Ovid saith" [1.1206].) As More's *Utopia* criticizes the English, so Ovid's description of the Golden Age entails a sharp critique of civilized Roman norms:

> There was no fear of punishment, there was no threatening law
> In brazen tables nailèd up, to keep the folk in awe.
> There was no man would crouch or creep to judge with cap in hand,
> They livèd safe without a judge, in every realm and land.
> (1.601, lines 105–8)

A dark irony is involved in the use of Ovid's Golden Age as a model for travelers' descriptions of newly discovered lands. One of the central features of the Golden Age according to Ovid was that people never undertook sea voyages: "The lofty pinetree was not hewn from mountains where it stood, / In seeking strange and foreign lands, to rove upon the flood" (lines 109–10). If Europeans rediscover the Golden Age by voyaging, it is also such voyaging that must bring the Golden Age to an end.

Perhaps the most profound exploration of the idea of the "noble savage"—a human being uncorrupted by civilization, whose natural dignity and virtue were superior to anything in what we call "developed" societies—is the essay *Of Cannibals* by the French nobleman Michel de Montaigne: "I find (as far as I have been informed), there is nothing in that nation that is either barbarous or savage, unless men call that barbarism which is not common to them." (The Web site has an excerpt from the Elizabethan translation by John Florio.) A possible assignment would be to compare the qualities that Montaigne finds admirable in the Brazilians with qualities that Barlowe describes in the Virginians and with those that characterize the people of Ovid's Golden Age.

A notable feature in many accounts of first encounters between Europeans and New World peoples is the sense of wonder experienced on both sides. Both peoples found themselves suddenly exposed to utterly strange, sometimes incomprehensible, societies and ways of life. The Europeans, of course, relied to a large extent on pre-existing stereotypes (the noble or ignoble savage), and often saw just what they expected to see. Nevertheless, such preconceptions were liable to be overturned, for example, when the Eskimo in the account of Frobisher's voyage indignantly denies the charge of cannibalism (1.894).

The English often had equally strong preconceptions regarding the way the natives would perceive them. The author of the account of Drake's voyage is convinced that the Ohlone people of California worshiped the English as gods and interprets their unfamiliar rituals as "sacrifices"; he is equally convinced that the native "king" has granted Queen Elizabeth title to the whole country. Similar assumptions are in play in Thomas Hariot's *Brief and true report of the new-found land of Virginia* (1.901), which is among the most complex, ambiguous, and unsettling of Elizabethan travel narratives. Hariot reports with satisfaction that the Algonkians regarded the English as favored by God, and that their priests "through conversing with us . . . were brought into great doubts" (1.903–4) about their own religion. But this incitement to doubt worked both ways: Hariot's observations have severe implications for European beliefs as well. For instance, his description of how the Algonkian priests control the "common and simple sort of people" (1.903) with false tales of torments after death in a place called Popogusso raises unsettling questions about the Christians' belief in hell.

The New World encounter allowed the English to re-examine their Old World culture with fresh eyes. While Hariot invites the reader to enter into daring speculations about religion, the account of Frobisher's voyage makes us think anew about practices of representation. The Eskimo captive taken on board ship first mistakes a painting of another Eskimo, captured the previous year, for a living being and then concludes (so the writer imagines) that the English are magicians who can "make men live and die at our pleasure" (1.894). This fablelike anecdote projects onto the New World savage a set of ideas about representation, artifice, and magic that are in fact pervasive through English Renaissance literature. You will be able to refer back to the story of the Eskimo and the portrait on a number of occasions, for instance when discussing Doctor Faustus's conjuring of Alexander and his paramour (1.1014) or Hero's floral veil "Whose workmanship both man and beast deceives" (*Hero and Leander*, 1.972, line 20).

Sex, Poetry, and Power

If it was entirely an accident that English poets discovered Francis Petrarch's love poetry shortly before the beginning of a half-century of female rule, it was an accident with profound consequences for English literature. The existence of a reigning queen—especially a virgin queen whose marital intentions were a matter of anxiety—unquestionably heightened the fascination of courtiers and poets with the Petrarchan themes of the power of eros and the erotics of power.

The lives and works of the first two Petrarchan poets in English, Sir Thomas Wyatt and Henry Howard, earl of Surrey, belong to the reign of Elizabeth's father. Wyatt's sonnet *The long love that in my thought doth harbor* (1.527) and Surrey's *Love, that doth reign and live within my thought* (1.571) are based on the same original, Petrarch's Sonnet 140. Because it is a good idea to provide students with a modern, literal translation to compare with the freer translations of Wyatt and Surrey, we include translations of Sonnets 140, 189, and 190, from *Petrarch's Lyric Poems*, translated and edited by Robert Durling (Harvard University Press, 1976), at the end of this chapter (pp. 57–58). A comparison between these two translations reveals much about the differences between Wyatt and Surrey as English poets, as well as about how the Petrarchan spirit entered into English literature. Wyatt, in his knotty and vigorous style, and Surrey, with his smoother and more regular verses, portray the lover as the victim of both an intemperate passion and an ideal but cruelly indifferent mistress. The lover is exalted and suffers by turns, is tossed between hope and despair. Wyatt's path-breaking work is less typical of the English Petrarchan tradition in that the poet's despair and bitterness tend to predominate, a feature also seen in original poems like *They flee from me* (1.529). Later sonneteers, like Petrarch himself, cling more stubbornly to the hope of transcendence.

Certain attitudes about class and gender underlie much sixteenth-century love poetry. Lust in a woman is a base instinct signifying low birth and breeding. Courtly women are naturally chaste and may yield sexually only out of compassion for the lover's suffering and for his loyal service. Lust in courtly men is natural but should be repressed. These romance conventions received a quasi-philosophical rationalization in the Platonism, grafted onto the Petrarchan tradition in the centuries following Petrarch's death. Physical beauty, which we experience through the senses, is only a limited manifestation of a higher spiritual or divine beauty, which exists in the soul and which we experience in the mind. This notion, derived from Plato by fifteenth-century Florentine Neoplatonic philosophers, became enormously influential in the sixteenth century through its popularization by Castiglione's *The Courtier* (1528), translated into English by Sir Thomas Hoby (1561). According to the theory of the "Ladder of Love," expounded in the last book of *The Courtier* (1.579), a man's falling in love with a woman through the senses ought to be a step on a stair ascending to the higher spiritual love, which no longer seeks sexual gratification. Laura, the ideal mistress of Petrarch's sequence, beckons the poet to aspire to heavenly love; the poet's sufferings, which, along with the lady's beauty, are the principal subjects of most Petrarchan sonnets, result from the difficulties the poet has keeping his lust under control. The sonnet mistress is distant and ethereal, as indicated by her names. Petrarch's Laura signifies fame or immortality, associated with the nymph Daphne who was turned into the laurel tree to save her from being raped by Apollo. Every sonnet mistress has attributes similar to those of Petrarch's ideal figure, even when the sonnets are addressed to a real woman (as Sidney's were to his married cousin Penelope Devereux Rich) and she is given a symbolic name. In Sidney's sequence she is Stella (star) to his Astrophil (star lover); she is Daniel's Delia (a name for the goddess Diana); she is Drayton's Idea. Elizabethan sonnets, then, are most often not based on an actual romantic relationship, and you may need to convince students that this does not disqualify them from being poems of genuine beauty and psychological complexity. Assigning your students an explication of a sonnet sometimes helps show them that this is actually so.

The typical sonnet lover, like Sidney's Astrophil, finds it exceedingly difficult to rise above the level of physical desire. Although professing to celebrate a feminine ideal, Petrarchan poetry is preoccupied with the psychological state of male lovers. These are poems about frustration or, at least, sublimation instead of fulfillment. The ideal woman often plays the role of a personified superego, checking the male libido, which sometimes retires humbly (as in the Wyatt and Surrey translations of Sonnet 140), sometimes breaks into bitter reproach (as in Sidney's Sonnet 31 [1.922]). In contrast, the woman is calm and remote and never seems to experience the emotional turmoil of her lover—except, as in the case of Queen Elizabeth and Lady Mary Wroth, when the woman herself is the speaker.

As we know from both her public life and her private verses, Queen Elizabeth knew her Petrarch well. Lines such as "I am and not, I freeze and yet am burned" from *On Monsieur's Departure* (1.595, line 5) are classically Petrarchan. (Compare that line also with the last line of *Troilus's Song* [1.314], which is the first translation of one of Petrarch's sonnets into English.) In her court, Elizabeth was accustomed to receiving adulation in language similar to that addressed to the Petrarchan mistress. Foreign ambassadors, noble courtiers, and members of Parliament all participated in Elizabeth's cult of love, showering her with extravagant compliments. "We all loved her," her godson Sir John Harrington wrote, "for she said she loved us" (1.594).

Elizabeth was at least as well educated as most of her male courtiers. As we might expect from the one-time pupil of Roger Ascham (1.563), she had mastered classical rhetoric and the complex of linguistic and social values Ascham called "decorum": "a true choice and placing of words, a right ordering of sentences, an easy understanding of the tongue, a readiness to speak, a facility to write, a true judgment both of his own and other men's doings, what tongue soever he doth use" (1.565). The poems

Elizabeth wrote in English, such as *The doubt of future foes* and *On Monsieur's Departure* (1.594–95), are personal in tone, revealing her understanding of her own and other's doings, while testifying to her constant anxiety over appearances and public opinion. Her *Golden Speech* (1.598) and *Speech to the Troops at Tilbury* (1.597), by contrast, are propaganda pieces in which the queen expertly manipulates the emotions of her auditors. The stirring address to the English troops awaiting the Spanish invasion helps us understand the veneration in which she was held by her people. It belongs to a rhetorical tradition that includes Birhtwold's famous lines at the end of *The Battle of Maldon* (1.109) and Winston Churchill's radio speeches during the Battle of Britain.

Naturally there are also anticonventional sonnets rejecting the love of women, such as Wyatt's *Farewell, Love*, where "Senec and Plato call me from thy lore" (1.528); or Sidney's *Leave me, O Love* (1.933). And there are sonnets that satirize hackneyed sonnet images, the most famous of which is Shakespeare's Sonnet 130 (1.1040):

> My mistress' eyes are nothing like the sun;
> Coral is far more red than her lips' red;
> If snow be white, why then her breasts are dun;
> If hairs be wires, black wires grow on her head.

In these lines and in the next two quatrains, Shakespeare ridicules the trite and sometimes silly comparisons used to describe the mistress's beauty in Petrarchan poetry. Hair, for instance, was commonly compared to fine golden wire, as it is in Spenser's Sonnet 37 (1.865), though Spenser too takes issue with the convention:

> What guyle is this, that those her golden tresses,
>   She doth attire under a net of gold:
>   And with sly skill so cunningly them dresses,
>   That which is gold or heare, may scarse be told?

Although Shakespeare's Sonnet 130 can be read on its own as a witty exercise, the so-called Dark Lady of his sonnet sequence is the very antithesis of the Petrarchan mistress. It is important to bear in mind that Sonnets 1–126, which employ many conventional Petrarchan themes, are addressed to a young man. (This is made explicit in, for instance, Sonnets 3, 20, and 126.) Whatever the nature of the poet's love for the young man, this idealized male love is contrasted with sheer lust (powerfully analyzed in Sonnet 129) for the dark mistress. Not only does she consort with the speaker, but she seduces his friend—presumably the young man of the first part of the sequence (Sonnet 144). Unlike the cruelly chaste Petrarchan mistress, the Dark Lady tempts and corrupts. In the context of the Petrarchan tradition these powerful but disturbing poems strike a bitterly discordant note.

In direct contrast to Petrarchan idealism, Elizabethan poets also cultivated a strain of sexual license freely drawn from classical poetry, especially from Ovid. The desire of Faustus for forbidden knowledge is complemented by his desire for supreme sexual pleasure, most memorably expressed in the famous lines addressed to the incubus of Helen of Troy, which Mephastophilis conjures for him:

> Was this the face that launched a thousand ships,
> And burnt the topless towers of Ilium?
> Sweet Helen, make me immortal with a kiss:
> Her lips sucks forth my soul, see where it flies! . . .
> O thou art fairer than the evening air,
> Clad in the beauty of a thousand stars,
> Brighter art thou than flaming Jupiter
> When he appeared to hapless Semele;
> More lovely than the monarch of the sky
> In wanton Arethusa's azured arms;
> And none but thou shalt be my paramour.
> [*Exeunt* (FAUSTUS *and* HELEN).] (1.1020, lines 81–84, 94–100)

This is the kind of imagery that Volpone absurdly imitates as he tries to lure Celia into bed by telling her that they will act out roles in "Ovid's tales, / Thou like Europa now, and I like Jove" (1.1352, lines 220–21).

Marlowe translated Ovid's *Amores,* a series of erotic poems called elegies because they were written in classical elegiac meter. The best example of the type in *NAEL* is Donne's *Elegy 19. To His Mistress Going to Bed* (1.1256), which may well have been written in the 1590s. Carew's *A Rapture* (1.1661) carries on the same tradition.

A genre of erotic narrative called epyllion (little epic) includes Shakespeare's *Venus and Adonis* and Marlowe's *Hero and Leander* (1.970). Marlowe's unfinished poem is packed with playfully prurient imagery and action. Its boy hero, Leander, is completely ignorant about sex:

> Albeit Leander, rude in love and raw,
> Long dallying with Hero, nothing saw
> That might delight him more, yet he suspected
> Some amorous rites or other were neglected. (1.983, lines 545–48)

But when Leander catches on, Hero, who seemingly was willing before, now preserves her maidenhead. Leander still has much to learn. When Neptune tries to seduce him, Leander protests, " 'You are deceived; I am no woman, I.' / Thereat smiled Neptune" (1.986, lines 676–77).

The Elizabethans also revived the Latin *carpe diem* poem of which the most famous is one by Catullus addressed to Lesbia, translated and set to music by Thomas Campion (*My sweetest Lesbia* [1.1196]). This and the other selections by Campion are excellent examples of Elizabethan love songs, which, it should be remembered, not only circulated in manuscripts and books but were constantly being performed. Whether or not lyrics were set to music, sweetness and musicality were among the most prized characteristics of Elizabethan verse: When you get to the early seventeenth century, you might have your students compare these lyrics both for sound and rhythm with some of the love poems by Donne, who obviously breaks with that lyrical style for one less musical and closer to natural speech rhythms.

Perhaps the most famous love poem of the century is Marlowe's *The Passionate Shepherd to His Love* (1.989), which inspired many replies, among them Ralegh's (1.879) and Donne's (1.1247). A comparison of these can make a good topic for discussion or for a paper. You could also invite your students to write a reply to Marlowe's shepherd in the style of some other seventeenth- or eighteenth-century poet.

Spenser and Shakespeare

Edmund Spenser

Even more than most of his contemporaries, Spenser was immersed in the political and religious controversies of his time, and this makes teaching his works in their historical and cultural contexts more than usually urgent—and more than usually rewarding. Spenser's poetry is the response to an exceedingly complex cultural situation by an even more complex mind. His works are examples of how politics can influence literature, but they also suggest the power of literature to shape our responses—for better or for worse—to events, ideas, and people.

In a letter he wrote to his friend Gabriel Harvey in 1580, Spenser demanded, "why a God's name may not we, as else the Greeks, have the kingdom of our own language?" This question sums up the remarkable shift in attitudes toward the English language in the sixteenth century. No longer was English to be viewed as an inferior vernacular, incapable of rising to the literary heights of Latin and Greek. Writers of Spenser's generation were determined to prove that English was second to no other tongue in beauty, dignity, and versatility. Spenser's means to this end was to reject foreign influences and seek a literary and linguistic model in Chaucer, whose work he praised as "the well of English undefiled." *The Shepheardes Calendar* and *The Faerie Queene* abound in archaisms—for example, the *y* prefix in past participles like *yclad*. Elizabethan readers would have still found the language of these poems intelligible, but would have recognized its distinctiveness and occasional difficulty. It is for this reason that Spenser's works, unlike those of his contemporaries, are reproduced in their original spelling.

As discussed in the headnote, Sidney, Jonson, and later Samuel Johnson all objected to Spenser's cultivation of archaic English, Jonson famously remarking that Spenser "in affecting the ancients, writ no language" (1.615). Sidney's *Defense of Poesy* reveals a new consciousness of a national identity expressed through a native language and literature, and praises "English, before any vulgar language I know" (1.953) as fit for both ancient and modern modes of versification; at the same time, however, Sidney is a modernist in matters of language and criticizes Spenser's "old rustic language" (1.949). From Sidney's point of view, English literature stood in need of classical reform, lest its abuses "like an unmannerly daughter showing a bad education, causeth her mother Poesy's honesty to be called in question" (1.952).

Sidney positions himself somewhere between the extremes of the "English purist" position (Spenser), and the stance of the classicizers, who in the sixteenth century were busy transforming the language through the introduction of many thousands of words borrowed from Latin and Greek. (See the discussion of "inkhorn words" in Geoffrey Nunberg's essay "The Persistence of English" [1.1–1i]) One of the most provocative defenders of this practice was Thomas Nashe:

> To the reprehenders that complain of my boisterous compound words, and ending my Italianate coined verbs all in -ize, thus I reply. . . . For the compounding of my words, therein I imitate rich men who, having gathered store of white single money together, convert a number of those small little scutes into great pieces of gold. . . . Our English tongue of all languages most swarmeth with the single money of monosyllables, which are the only scandal of it. Books written in them and no other seem like shop-keepers' boxes, that contain nothing else save half-pence, three-farthings, and two-pences. (preface to *Christ's Tears Over Jerusalem* [2nd ed., 1594])

Spenser himself by writing a pastoral as his first work was following in the footsteps of Virgil whose *Eclogues* set the pattern for future poets aiming to write an epic. Milton's pastoral elegy *Lycidas* heralds the same intention. In Spenser's letter to Ralegh introducing *The Faerie Queene*, the allusions to Homer, Virgil, Ariosto, and Tasso, the explanation of the distinction between a "Poet historical" and a "Historiographer," and the projected number of twelve books all proclaim that Spenser intended his poem to be read as an epic for the English nation to rival the great Greek, Latin, and Italian models.

In the letter, Spenser claims that each of his twelve projected books will treat one of "the twelve private morall vertues, as Aristotle hath devised" (1.625). Aristotle did not in fact devise such a list; and in any case, holiness, the virtue portrayed in the poem's first book, is a concept foreign to classical moral philosophy. The Redcrosse Knight, as Spenser tells the reader, wears the armor of the Christian warrior allegorized by St. Paul in Ephesians 6.13–17. The epic struggle of book 1 turns out to be an allegory of the English Reformation. The book can—and should—be read both as a romance and as a moral allegory; but for an understanding of sixteenth-century English literature, and for much of the literature that follows, it should also be taught for its religious and political allegory.

Except for explaining that the Faerie Queene is Elizabeth, however, Spenser does not unpack the pervasive political allegory, which must have fascinated his Elizabethan audience. He left it to his readers to work out most of the allegorical identifications for themselves, expecting them to be familiar with the religious and political controversies springing from the Reformation. (If it is any comfort to the modern reader, the glosses that Elizabethan readers scrawled in the margins, sometimes identifying characters in the poem with actual people, vary wildly and often seem absurd; but the general outlines of the allegory would have been clear enough to Spenser's contemporaries.) With the help of the notes, which explain the meanings of the characters' names and their associations, the instructor can show how the first book allegorizes the history of the Church of England (Una) in its rivalry with the Roman Catholic Church (Duessa). Spenser sees this history from a militant Protestant perspective, based on an interpretation of the Book of Revelation (chapter 17) in which the Whore of Babylon stands for the Roman Catholic Church. The separation of Redcrosse from Una early in the book and his disastrous partnering with Duessa represent the centuries of separation Protestants saw between the original Christian church and the rule of the Roman Church in England before the English Reformation.

Together with the selections in "The Literature of the Sacred," Spenser's first book can help students grasp the bewildering ideological crosscurrents of the sixteenth century and the religious and political passions they inspired. For Spenser and many of his readers, the triumph of English Protestantism over Spanish Catholicism in the age of Elizabeth I was quite literally the historical fulfillment of biblical prophecies and ushered in a new age in which England would be, as Isaiah (42.6) had prophesied of Israel, a light among nations. The praise of England's Virgin Queen, personified as

> . . . Goddesse heavenly bright,
> Mirrour of grace and Majestie divine,
> Great Lady of the greatest Isle, whose light
> Like Phoebus lampe throughout the world doth shine,
> (1.628–29, lines 28–31)

is not mere flattery. It expresses an almost mystical sense of Elizabeth's historical significance felt by some of her subjects at that historical moment, although the euphoria of the moment (probably inspired by the seemingly divine destruction of the Great Armada) would quickly fade as the century drew to an end. At the same time, the reader often gets the sense that Spenser describes Elizabeth not as she was, but as he wished her to be, as she could be if only she chose to be. The real Elizabeth often seemed reluctant to act as befitted God's instrument, and she was notoriously parsimonious in funding the enterprises of militant Protestantism in the Netherlands and elsewhere.

Spenser's first book also embodies a reinterpretation, again from a Protestant point of view, of holiness. Catholicism celebrated the monastic (contemplative) life above the active and held virginity to be a higher state than marriage (see, for example, *The Wife of Bath's Prologue*). Spenser does not by any means reject the contemplative life, but he suspects monasticism of hypocrisy, and in the figure of the Redcrosse Knight he asserts the active life of Christian warfare as necessary and holy. The evil wizard Archimago, masquerading as a hermit, declares to Redcrosse that holiness has nothing to do with "warre and worldly trouble" (1.636, lines 266–69). Despaire tells Redcrosse that all his "great battels" will only increase his sin and his punishments (1.731, lines 379–87). But the true hermit Contemplation refutes Archimago and Despaire in telling Redcrosse that the knight cannot be admitted to the heavenly city until "thou famous victorie hast wonne" (1.748, 536–40). In the betrothal of Redcrosse and Una, after the victory over the dragon, Spenser celebrates the renewed union between Holiness and the True Church, which for him was the Church of England.

The Middle Ages had a doctrine of two symbolic cities: Babylon, the city representing wickedness, and Jerusalem, the heavenly city, which is not the Jerusalem on earth but the heavenly Jerusalem, which is the goal of every wandering Christian soul. For Spenser, however, there are three symbolic cities: Babylon, the wicked city identified by Protestants with Rome; Jerusalem; and between the two, Cleopolis (famous city, Spenser's name for London), which, Contemplation tells Redcrosse, is "for earthly frame, / The fairest peece, that eye beholden can" (1.747, lines 524–25). Cleopolis thus becomes the symbolic city of earthly wealth, power, and fame, which are no longer to be despised, allied with the One True Church in creating a better world on earth. As the capital city of the English nation, Cleopolis is also the home of the empire just coming into being.

In this connection, one should remember that Spenser was writing the greater part of *The Faerie Queene* in Ireland, where he served an oppressive and often brutal colonial regime. The 1580s and 1590s were troubled years in Ireland, with low-level guerrilla resistance by the native Irish alternating with full-scale rebellion. A succession of English lord deputies in Ireland experimented with various methods of pacifying the country. Spenser himself contributed to the debate over how Ireland could be finally conquered and fully controlled in his unpublished prose tract *A View of the Present State of Ireland* (an excerpt is on the Web site under "Renaissance Exploration"). In the *View,* Spenser endorses both military domination and strategic use of famine as means of pacifying—or eliminating—the troublesome natives.

Book 2, the legend of Temperance, which is represented in *NAEL* by its final canto, does not have the same militant and doctrinaire spirit as book 1. Some critics suggest that Spenser associates the pleasures of the Bower of Bliss, where the witch Acrasia turns men into swine, with the corruption of English settlers by sex with Irish women (see Web site, *A View of the Present State of Ireland*). However, the scene in the Bower—Acrasia, veiled in transparent silk and stretched out beside the sleeping young man on a "bed of roses"—has analogues in many Renaissance paintings of semi-nude Venuses in repose. The Bower is a good example of heavily charged eroticism of other Elizabethan works, which was discussed earlier (pp. 48–49). Spenser had the problem of making sexual fantasy seem at the same time both sensually seductive and morally repelling. How well did he succeed? In stanzas 74 and 75 he has written one of the loveliest *carpe diem* lyrics in the language. Spenser was certainly not puritanically against sex, which he celebrates in the *Epithalamion* written for his own wedding (1.868). He regards sex as divinely ordained for the ends of wedded love and procreation. He does object to voyeurism and sexual exploitation. This is what he condemns in the Bower of Bliss and still more searchingly in the sinister masque of Cupid at the House of Busyrane (book 3, cantos 11–12, 1.840ff.). Canto 6 of book 3, the Garden of Adonis, is a complex allegory of the conflict between love and chastity and the conflict between humanity and time. If you had rather not assign book 1 or prefer to assign only brief selections from it, the Bower of Bliss and the selections from book 3 could make for an absorbing unit on love and time. Such a unit would teach well in relation to Shakespeare's sonnets, which are also preoccupied with the themes of love and time.

William Shakespeare

If your course covers several literary periods, you will probably not have time to teach both *Twelfth Night* and *King Lear*. The choice between them is difficult but will to some extent be dictated by the structure of the course. If you are stopping, temporarily or permanently, at the end of the sixteenth century, then *Twelfth Night* makes a satisfactory and uplifting conclusion to a course. If you are carrying on into the seventeenth century, then the pessimistic Jacobean *Lear* is a good choice. Teaching either play on its own or both together, you will have the opportunity to introduce students to themes and conflicts that were central to Shakespeare's culture and to his art: conflicts between custom and innovation, between men and women, between social classes, and between appearances and inner truth.

In the sixteenth century, power and status were closely bound up with costumes, symbols of authority, and visible signs of rank—with what Stephen Greenblatt in his introduction to *The Norton Shakespeare* terms "the fetishism of dress." In explaining this point, you might begin by referring back to More's *Utopia*. The Utopians put gold and silver to memorably paradoxical uses: children, slaves, and criminals go about adorned with these metals, while their betters dress simply and without ornament (1.513). More's point is that value resides not in the substances themselves but in their social use. If we all agree to regard gold as contemptible or coarse cloth as a mark of honor then that is what it is. It is a point with special relevance to a society in which customs and sumptuary laws dictated what sort of dress and ornaments must—or must not—be worn by people of every office and class. Just as kings and queens wore crowns, so a steward like Malvolio in *Twelfth Night* would inevitably wear a chain, and a Fool, like the one in *King Lear* would wear a fool's cap, or coxcomb. Men and women were of course expected to dress very differently from one another.

Clothing in this culture—as in ours today—was used as a marker of identity. In Shakespeare's plays, however, it often seems as if identity itself resides in clothing. When Viola puts on a young man's clothes and calls herself Cesario in *Twelfth Night* she is taken by everyone for an attractive male youth. The same sort of thing happens in *King Lear* when Kent disguises himself as Caius and Edgar wraps himself in a filthy blanket to become the mad beggar, Poor Tom. These plays challenge us to wonder whether selfhood is really a matter of inner truth, or rather—like the value of gold and silver—a matter of social perception.

At the end of *Twelfth Night*, even though Viola's sex has at last been revealed, Orsino continues to call her Cesario. He will do so, he explains, until she resumes her feminine attire, for only then will she be transformed back into a woman:

> Cesario, come—
> For so you shall be while you are a man;
> But when in other habits you are seen,
> Orsino's mistress and his fancy's queen. (1.1105, lines 380–83)

Is Viola/Cesario at this moment in the play a man or a woman? Is gender a matter of biology or of dress? The question is made still more complex by the fact that, on the Shakespearean stage, the actor playing the part was a boy. Where Orsino sees a woman playing a man, the audience would see a boy playing a woman playing a man. This must have required a large measure of mental agility on the part of the audience, who would simultaneously have to remember that Cesario was Viola, and forget that Viola was an adolescent male actor.

For Puritans in this society, the ambiguities raised by the theatrical convention of cross-dressing were simply unacceptable. They railed against the theater and its adherents, reminding male members of the audience that when they found the "woman" on stage desirable they were really committing the sin of desiring a boy. In a closely related controversy, authors denounced the gender-bending fashions adopted by both men and women in everyday life. Pamphlets such as *Hic Mulier* and *Haec Vir* (excerpted on the Web site) branded masculine women and effeminate men as monstrosities. The authors of such works saw themselves as defending the essential difference between women and men. Yet the very fact that they felt obliged to make such arguments suggests their underlying anxiety about the power of clothing; as the incorrigible fashion for cross-dressing on the stage and on the streets implied, the difference between the sexes might not be so essential after all.

As they begin reading the play, you might ask students to consider in what ways gender in *Twelfth Night* seems to be a matter of biological fact and what aspects of the play suggest, conversely, that gender is no more essential than the clothes one wears. Which point of view, if either, seems to prevail? Is the answer to this question at the end of the play the same as it is at the end of act 3?

The fetishism of dress is also a dominant theme in *King Lear*, though here the determining power of clothing is considered in regard to the fictions of social class rather than those of gender. Lear is first moved to a recognition of common humanity by the sight of Edgar/Poor Tom, and his immediate reaction is to try to strip off his own clothes: "Thou art the thing itself; unaccommodated man is no more but such a poor, bare, forked animal as thou art. Off, off, you lendings! come unbutton here" (1.1154, lines 103–5). Later, in a moment of lucidity-in-madness, the king declares: "Through tattered gowns small vices do appear; / Robes and furred gowns hide all" (1.1174, lines 161–62). *King Lear* properly belongs to the early seventeenth century and to the reign of Elizabeth's successor, James I. In its themes and in its somber mood, the play reveals the precariousness of the Tudor and Stuart establishments and the gloom that seems to have overtaken the country at the turn of the century. *Lear* calls into question all the familial, social, and political bonds that had been invoked to rationalize and justify the Tudor monarchy in the sixteenth century. More fundamentally, the play comes close to shattering the faith in nature on which the whole social order was supposed to rest.

It was not on the stage alone that old certainties were being shattered. The anxious questioning and generalized pessimism of *Lear* reflect wider social processes and ideological tensions. Shakespeare lived and wrote in an era when one very old and well-honored social system was gradually and uneasily giving way to another. According to the traditional values upheld in the play by Lear and Gloucester, one's position in society rested on the relatively intangible bases of rank, lineage, and loyalty; people were supposed to remain in the station to which they were born. But in Shakespeare's lifetime traditional assumptions were increasingly being called into question by new social forces—forces associated in the play with Edmund, Goneril, and Regan—and by historians with the rise of early capitalism. Real authority now seemed to lie not in fuzzy concepts like social rank but in how much power—most fundamental, economic power—one could bring to bear. In one traditional set of terms, then, King Lear's aspiration to remain a king while giving up his power makes perfect sense. But in the coldly pragmatic terms of the emergent society, it is patently absurd.

The ideological debate in *King Lear* does not refer directly to "economics" or "society" but rather to "nature." The word recurs constantly in the play. Both Edmund and Lear refer to nature as a goddess, but with opposing meanings. When Edmund declares "Thou, nature, art my goddess; to thy law / My services are bound" (1.1117, lines 1–2), he means that he is not bound by worn-out old ideas of custom, legitimacy, and loyalty. In "nature," Edmund worships the sort of chaotic social forces unleashed by the market economy (and his prayer foreshadows such modern clichés as "It's a dog eat dog world"). On the other hand, when Lear cries out "Hear, Nature, hear! dear goddess, hear!" (1.1128, line 271), he invokes a traditional conception of nature as upholding the innate authority of fathers and of kings. It is not clear which version of nature is responsible for the storm that batters Lear and his companions in act 3. Perhaps in the storm, nature is revolting against the unnatural cruelty of Goneril and Regan; or perhaps the natural world is simply mocking all human appeals to hierarchy, reason, and morality. As they read the play, students should be encouraged to note all the references to nature. What different meanings are assigned to the word? Does any one sense seem to predominate throughout or at the end?

Sonnets

These translations of Petrarch's sonnets 140, 189, and 190 are reprinted by permission of the publisher from *Petrarch's Lyric Poems*, translated and edited by Robert M. Durling (Cambridge, MA: Harvard UP, 1976).

Sonnet 140

(Cf. Wyatt, *The Long Love*; Surrey, *Love, that doth reign*)

Love, who lives and reigns in my thought and keeps his principal seat in my heart, sometimes comes forth all in armor into my forehead, there camps, and there sets up his banner.

She who teaches us to love and to be patient, and wishes my great desire, my kindled hope, to be reined in by reason, shame, and reverence, at our boldness is angry within herself.

Wherefore Love flees terrified to my heart, abandoning his every enterprise, and weeps and trembles; there he hides and no more appears outside.

What can I do, when my lord is afraid, except stay with him until the last hour? For he makes a good end who dies loving well.

Sonnet 189

(Cf. Wyatt, *My galley*)

My ship laden with forgetfulness passes through a harsh sea, at midnight, in winter, between Scylla and Charybdis, and at the tiller sits my lord, rather my enemy;

each oar is manned by a ready, cruel thought that seems to scorn the tempest and the end; a wet, changeless wind of sighs, hopes, and desires breaks the sail;

a rain of weeping, a mist of disdain wet and loosen the already weary ropes, made of error twisted up with ignorance.

My two usual sweet stars are hidden; dead among the waves are reason and skill; so that I begin to despair of the port.

Sonnet 190

(Cf. Wyatt, *Whoso list to hunt*)

A white doe on the green grass appeared to me, with two golden horns, between two rivers, in the shade of a laurel, when the sun was rising in the unripe season.

Her look was so sweet and proud that to follow her I left every task, like the miser who as he seeks treasure sweetens his trouble with delight.

"Let no one touch me," she bore written with diamonds and topazes around her lovely neck. "It has pleased my Caesar to make me free."

And the sun had already turned at midday; my eyes were tired by looking but not sated, when I fell into the water, and she disappeared.

Contents: Norton Topics Online, The Sixteenth Century
www.wwnorton.com/college/english/nael

Contents: Norton Online Archive, The Sixteenth Century
www.wwnorton.com/college/english/nael/NOA

From Book 1, Chapter 12 [The Need for Revealed Law]
From Book 1, Chapter 16 [Conclusion]
Anonymous Lyrics
Back and Side Go Bare, Go Bare
In Praise of a Contented Mind
Though Amaryllis Dance in Green
Come Away, Come, Sweet Love!
Thule, the Period of Cosmography
Madrigal ("My love in her attire doth show her wit")
The Silver Swan
Constant Penelope Send to Thee

Contents: NAEL Audio Companion, The Sixteenth Century

William Shakespeare
Oh Mistress Mine (*from* Twelfth Night)
setting by Thomas Morley
Thomas Campion
Fain Would I Wed
text and music by Thomas Campion
sung by Dame Janet Baker

CHAPTER 4

The Early Seventeenth Century 1603–1660

Introducing Early-Seventeenth-Century Literature

And new philosophy calls all in doubt;
The element of fire is quite put out;
The sun is lost, and the earth, and no man's wit
Can well direct him where to look for it.
And freely men confess that this world's spent,
When in the planets and the firmament
They seek so many new; they see that this
Is crumbled out again to his atomies.
'Tis all in pieces, all coherence gone;
All just supply, and all relation:
Prince, subject; father, son, are things forgot,
For every man alone thinks he hath got
To be a phoenix, and that there can be
None of that kind of which he is, but he.

These lines from John Donne's *An Anatomy of the World* (1.1267, lines 205–18) introduce several of the themes, moods, and perceptions that characterize the literature of the early seventeenth century and help mark the break between the Elizabethan and Jacobean periods. The sense Donne conveys of a world that has severed its links with the past and fallen under the spell of bewildering innovations is particularly worthy of emphasis, given that both students and instructors may at times be inclined to wonder what exactly is new and different about early-seventeenth-century literature. More than any other division between literary periods, the line dividing literature written under the Tudors from that written under the first Stuarts can seem artificial, a matter of convenience rather than a useful critical tool. The fact that the careers of major authors such as Shakespeare and Donne span the Elizabethan-Jacobean divide makes it easy for the teacher to effect the transition from one era to the next without much fuss.

Nevertheless, there are good reasons to draw attention at the outset to what is new and distinctive in Jacobean literature. Students find periodization a useful aid in grasping long-term historical change—reference to some sort of dividing line, however arbitrary, makes it much easier to grasp the huge gulf that lies between the worlds of More and Milton. Moreover, as the lines from Donne's *Anatomy* indicate, the subjects of James VI and I were themselves acutely aware of the break their society had made with its recent past. Early-seventeenth-century literature is suffused with the sense of a people, or rather a new confederation of peoples, entering into new and uncharted waters.

Indeed, this navigational metaphor applied literally to the successful Jacobean settlement of the New World. While Elizabethan literature abounds in famous celebrations of exploration and discovery, by Ralegh, Hariot, and others, it is important to bear in mind that every attempt at conquest and settlement in that era ended in failure. Without territorial possessions on the European Continent or in the New World, Elizabeth ruled over a realm smaller than any English monarch since before William the Conqueror. Only under James did the realm begin to take on the form of a British state ruling an overseas Empire—political structures still recognizable, if increasingly atrophied, today. James united England and Scotland under one crown if not yet as one kingdom, and his adoption of the title "King of Great Britain" popularized a term that to Elizabethan ears would have had only an odd, antiquarian ring. During James's reign, England established its first successful colonies in the New World, at Jamestown (1611) and Plymouth (1620).

While Donne in another poem gives famous expression to the wonder associated with the New World—"O my America! my new-found-land" (*Elegy 19*, 1.1256, line 27)—in the *Anatomy* he dwells on the discovery of new worlds even farther afield, in outer space. Advances both in scientific instruments (such as the telescope) and in scientific method characterize the early seventeenth century. New scientific approaches afforded new perspectives on society as well as on the stars and played an important role in the other development that Donne identifies as marking his age, the breakdown of traditional hierarchies: " 'Tis all in pieces, all coherence gone; / All just supply, and all relation." The challenges to the old social order leading up to the English Revolution and beyond are recognizable both in the rise of the individual ("every man . . . a phoenix") and in the development of new and subversive forms of class consciousness. Like many members of his society, Donne scanned these new developments with a sense of distinct unease for the future. It is perhaps this peculiar wonder at new worlds balanced against pessimism and nostalgia for a stable past that is the most distinctive of the period and has the capacity to make its literature seem especially relevant to students today.

Emphasizing what is new about early-seventeenth-century literature does not, of course, mean treating the period as if it were itself a phoenix. There are numerous important continuities with the preceding era, and indeed, the larger period 1485 to 1660 (often described as the English Renaissance) has its own intellectual validity. If you are teaching the early seventeenth century as part of an ongoing survey, students will be quick to grasp the ways in which the conflicts of the period represent an extension and a working out of sixteenth-century debates. This is true above all in regard to the consequences of the English Reformation. John Calvin's doctrine of predestination (1.544) was a flashpoint in the theological debates that came to divide England. The Reformation martyrs hallowed by John Foxe, including Anne Askew, served as models and inspiration to later generations of Puritans and freethinkers. In particular, an interesting comparison can be made between the examination of Anne Askew for heresy in 1545 (1.547) and the trial of Anna Trapnell for prophesying in Truro a century later (1.1743). Taking a different tack, you might encourage your students to compare Foxe's accounts of Protestant martyrdom (1.551) with responses to the execution of Charles I by Katherine Philips in *Upon the Double Murder of King Charles* (1.1680) and Andrew Marvell in *An Horatian Ode* (1.1700). The Norton Topics Online sections for the sixteenth and early seventeenth centuries include materials relating to the Reformation and the English Revolution that provide the basis for more comparisons of this kind.

There are many more continuities and points of overlap between the periods on the level of literary forms and styles. While the 1580s and 1590s marked the high point of the English sonnet craze, John Donne and Lady Mary Wroth wrote powerful sequences in the Jacobean era and Milton molded the sonnet into a new form that would influence the Romantics. Wroth's *Pamphilia to Amphilanthus* is particularly interesting for the way it at once carries forward and critiques Elizabethan, Petrarchan, and male assumptions, transforming the traditional relationship between an ardent lover and his cold beloved into a woman's charged dialogue with her own desire.

One point that must be born in mind in any comparison between this period and the century that preceded it is that the early seventeenth century witnessed both a major increase in literacy and the massive growth of the print trade. The number of books being published annually more than doubled between 1600 and 1640; and in the civil war and the Interregnum, with the rise of the newsbook and the temporary collapse of censorhip, the number of titles published exceeded the total printed before that period. These massive cultural shifts allowed for the entry of a chorus of previously excluded voices into the literary sphere. Not only were there many more writers than before, but also there were many more kinds of writers, and more kinds of writing. This era saw the entry of women in significant numbers into the fields of authorship and publication. Ten women writers are represented in the Early Seventeenth Century section of *NAEL*, almost a third of the total. This period saw the emergence, from Ben Jonson onward, of the professional author as a (relatively) respectable member of early capitalist society. And it is also in this era that we begin to hear, if still only faintly and unclearly, the voices of the laboring poor. Faced with such sudden abundance, no anthology and no survey course can hope to represent all the different kinds of writers and writing. Recognizing this inevitable fact, the beginning of this section of your course may be a good time to present your students with the question of canon formation, the drawbacks and advantages of literary canons, and the ways they are continually being transformed and remade.

Casting All in Doubt

Every Man a Phoenix: Jacobean Individualism

In the early Jacobean tragedy *King Lear*, Shakespeare presents his audience with a new and dangerous kind of human being, one who rejects the authority of all social strictures and familial bonds:

> Thou, nature, art my goddess; to thy law
> My services are bound. Wherefore should I
> Stand in the plague of custom, and permit
> The curiosity of nations to deprive me. . .? (1.1117)

The bastard Edmund is a new kind of person brought forth by a new kind of social structure; from our vantage point, his iconoclastic individualism owes less to the circumstances of his birth than to the collapse of feudal structures and the emergence of a market economy. If you have already taught *King Lear*, or are choosing to teach it as a bridge into the Jacobean period, you might ask your students to compare Act 1, Scene 2 of *Lear* with the passage from Donne's *Anatomy* quoted above. They will quickly see that Donne's complaints about the world's decline closely echo Gloucester's astrologically based pessimism: "in countries, discord; in palaces, treason; and the bond cracked 'twixt son and father. . . . We have seen the best of our time" (1.1120). Yet as students read further in Donne's poetry and prose, they will come to see that his perspective on the new phoenixes of the Jacobean era is both more complex and more compromised than is Shakespeare's in *King Lear*.

More than a decade earlier, when writing on the search for the true church, Donne expressed the traditional respect for custom and one's ancestors: "ask thy father which is she, / Let him ask his" (*Satire* 3, 1.1259, lines 71–72). Yet if this pious filial sentiment contrasts sharply with the egotism of an Edmund or Donne's phoenix, it also contrasts with the main bent of *Satire* 3 and with the facts of Donne's own life. The *Satire* was written while Donne was engaged in the painful process of leaving the Roman Catholic Church, the church of his fathers and of his martyred uncle and brother. Like all those who came to the Church of England early or late in the sixteenth century, Donne had to break the bond 'twixt son and father. (The Reformation, among other things, gave official backing to the idea that one thousand years of fathers could be wrong.) While the vast majority of those who joined the Anglican communion did so on the orders of the state, at least preserving thereby the due relation of prince and subject, Donne in *Satire* 3 fiercely attacks those who would let "a Harry, or a Martin" (1.1260, line 97) choose their faith for them. "Fool and wretch, wilt thou let thy soul be tied / To man's laws, by which she shall not then be tried / At the last day?" (1.1259–60, lines 93–95). Painful as is the process the poem describes and reflects, Donne's spiritual seeker must ultimately emulate the individualist stance of Shakespeare's bastard Edmund.

In many of the *Songs and Sonnets*, Donne turns his back with ostentatious indifference on his culture's normative codes and values. In *The Canonization*, for instance, he scornfully tells a friend "Take you a course, get you a place, / Observe His Honor, or His Grace" (1.1240, lines 5–6), but chooses for himself the role of the lover isolated from politics, commerce, and society. Often he declares that he and his lover are capable of replicating, containing, or obliterating the rest of the world: "She is all states, and all princes I, / Nothing else is" (1.1239, lines 21–22). In these defiant verses, Donne makes a show of rejecting the society that had already rejected him. Yet Donne's desire to overmaster or efface the world is frequently matched by his desire, in poems such as *The Good-Morrow* (1.1236), *A Valediction: Forbidding Mourning* (1.1248), and *The Ecstasy* (1.1249), to efface his own individuality in the Neoplatonic union of lovers' souls. In *The Canonization* he declares, "The phoenix riddle hath more wit / By us: we two being one, are it" (1.1241, lines 23–24)—the phoenix, which elsewhere symbolizes the self-made, self-serving individual, here becomes an emblem of the surrender of individuality. (The Audio Companion to NAEL features musical settings of several of Donne's poems.)

Expressions of Donne's desire for self-effacement recur in his religious poetry, notably *Holy Sonnets* 5 and *14* (1.1268, 1271). Similar sentiments are found in such very different later writers as Richard Crashaw, who pleads with Saint Teresa to "Leave nothing of myself in me" (1.1643), and Katherine Philips, who declares her spiritual oneness with various female friends in *Friendship's Mystery, To My Dearest* Lucasia (1.1681) and *To Mrs. M. A. at Parting* (1.1682). Yet in Donne's case, at least, the Neoplatonic or pious desire for union with another spirit inevitably rubs up against his self-concern. In *Meditation 17*, for instance, Donne famously responds to the tolling of the passing bell with the recognition that "No man is an island. . . . Any man's death diminishes me, because I am involved in mankind; and therefore never send to know for whom the bell tolls; it tolls for thee" (1.1278). While Donne stresses his participation in humanity, he does so to deepen and sharpen his introspection, turning another's affliction into his own "gold" (1.1278). Moreover, even this limited form of identification with another, which in an older work such as *Everyman* is simply taken for granted, is achieved by Donne only by means of strenuous mental effort. Donne's self-absorption finds its ultimate expression on his deathbed, where, as Izaak Walton records (1.1583), he had himself painted in his own winding sheet and contemplated that image.

Whatever contempt for court and commerce he may have expressed in his poetry, Donne struggled for years and with little success to follow the advice he gave to a worldly friend in *The Canonization*: "Take you a course, get you a place / Observe His Honor, or His Grace." In this aspect of his career he cut a recognizable and widely distrusted figure in Jacobean society, the would-be courtier casting about for preferment. The malcontent Bosola in Webster's *Duchess of Malfi*, whose motto is "I will thrive some way" (1.1434, lines 36–37), epitomizes the type and the dangers associated with it. *King Lear* also presents a version of this antisocial individual in the Captain who, following Edmund's advice that "men / Are as the time is" (1.1183–84, lines 31–32), slaughters Cordelia. Ben Jonson expresses scorn rather than fear of hangers-on at court in *On Something, That Walks Somewhere* (1.1394) and disgust at those who consented to serve as spies like "Pooly or Parrot" (*Inviting a Friend to Supper*, 1.1398, line 36). In his epigram *Of Spies*, Jonson declares:

> Spies, you are lights in state, but of base stuff,
> Who, when you've burnt yourselves down to the snuff,
> Stink, and are thrown away. End fair enough.

But Jonson's repeated insistence on his own "bluff" honesty and impartiality—"He that departs with his own honesty / For vulgar praise, doth it too dearly buy" (*To My Book*, 1.1394, lines 13–14)—must be read in the context of his own complicated career. The rise from bricklayer's apprentice to unofficial Poet Laureate was not accomplished without compromises, including a change of faith and consenting to serve as a government spy in the aftermath of the Gunpowder Plot. Such compromises were par for the course in the lives of most writers who sought patronage or preferment at court. Hence, much of the reverence that surrounded George Herbert derived from the fact that (willingly or not) he had turned his back on the prospect of court preferment to care for simple souls. The Norton Topics Online cluster on "The New Jacobean Order" (in the Early Seventeenth Century topic "Civil Wars of Ideas") explores some of the changes and controversies that developed during James I's rule.

The notion of the human being as a self-interested, self-seeking individual operating in a society composed of other such individuals is now so familiar that students may find it difficult to understand how in the early seventeenth century this perspective on society could be regarded as both new and profoundly unsettling. Many will be inclined to argue that this is simply a matter of human nature. If you are in the midst of a survey course, you will be able to point out that there is little or no equivalent in the periods you have studied previously to the type of villain delineated in *King Lear* and *The Duchess of Malfi* or to the meticulous personal stock taking of Martha Moulsworth's *Memorandum* (1.1553) or to the sudden intrusion of Milton the private individual into *The Reason of Church Government Urged Against Prelaty* (1.1796). When reading political texts such as Hobbes's *Leviathan* (1.1588) and Milton's *Areopagitica* (1.1801), many of whose assumptions students will be inclined to accept as given, point out that these are foundational texts that did much to shape the ideas about human nature and society they now seem to reflect. To study early-seventeenth-century literature and culture is to some extent to study the developments that culminated both in Hobbes's vision of the state of nature as that of "war of every man against every man" (1.1592) and in Milton's ideal individual questing after truth within the free market of ideas.

All Coherence Gone: Jacobean Pessimism

The supposed "pessimism" of Jacobean drama in particular and early-seventeenth-century English society more generally is a familiar theme. Indeed, reports of the sudden death of hope and gaiety in 1603 have been somewhat exaggerated. The notion of a peculiarly Jacobean form of pessimism arose in part because earlier generations of scholars were often disinclined (for complex ideological reasons) to recognize the increasing gloom and tension of the last third of Elizabeth I's reign. The years after the defeat of the Spanish Armada saw not the outpouring of patriotism and optimism that might have been expected, but rather a breakdown of the Elizabethan consensus, with growing tensions between Puritans and religious conservatives, monarch and Parliament, the queen and her advisers. The last decade of the sixteenth century was an era of severe plague and recurrent dearth, war in Ireland and, bewildering anxiety over the succession whenever the aging and childless queen should finally die. The belief that the Elizabethan era was a Golden Age, which soon gained currency under James, owed less to the reality of the late sixteenth century than to the utility of nostalgia as a covert means of criticizing the new order. It is certainly true that the Spenserian poets who wrote under James idolized Elizabeth in a way that Spenser himself never did.

Nevertheless, it is fair to say that a distinctly gloomy view of human nature, civil society, and the chances of improving either one is characteristic of much early-seventeenth-century writing. The four Jacobean dramas included in whole or in part in *NAEL—King Lear, Volpone, The Duchess of Malfi*, and *The Tragedy of Mariam*—are very different works, but all may be discussed in light of "Jacobean" pessimism. All, that is, depict worlds in which the unjust outnumber and tend to overpower the just, in which those who should uphold morality and order are corrupt or worse, and in which luck itself is almost invariably bad. (The complete text of *The Tragedy of Mariam* is available in the Norton Online Archive.)

Written a year or so after *King Lear*, Jonson's *Volpone* is arguably the more pessimistic play, in spite of its also being a successful comedy. Shakespeare and Jonson both protest in different ways against the rise of a commerce-driven society in which personal interest knows no higher law. Both draw on contemporary fascinations, such as demonic possession and exorcism, for theatrical effect (compare Edgar in *Lear*, act 4, scene 1, with Voltore in *Volpone*, act 5, scene 12). But whereas Shakespeare's play presents us with several heroic models of fidelity and fortitude struggling against the current of a foul society, Jonson offers only Celia and Bonario, whose goodness is more or less proportional to their lack of effectiveness and personality. These characters rarely engage students' sympathies as do Cordelia and Kent, and this is probably because they do not engage Jonson's. Although he scorns and satirizes the society that spews up the likes of Volpone, Jonson seems incapable of imagining a viable alternative; instead, his imagination is drawn, almost against his will, to the ever-expanding frontiers of commodification, in an age when even old corpses had a market value. As Mosca says of Corbaccio in act 4, scene 4, "Sell him for mummia; he's half dust already" (1.1363; line 14). (Jonson is not the only author to latch onto the strange trade in mummy dust as an emblem of the new market economy; Bosola in *The Duchess of Malfi* mentions it [1.1484, lines 113–14], and Sir Thomas Browne is magnificent on the subject: "The Egyptian mummies, which Cambyses or time hath spared, avarice now consumeth. Mummy is become merchandise, Mizraim cures wounds, and Pharaoh is sold for balsams" [*Hydriotaphia*, 1.1580].)

If you are not teaching a course focusing on the drama, you may be able to teach only one or two of the plays in *NAEL*. In that case, Webster's *The Duchess of Malfi* and Cary's *The Tragedy of Mariam*, of which eight scenes are included, make a particularly attractive combination. (Most of your students will probably not be aware that one play is more "canonical" than the other, so it will be up to you whether to make their very different after-histories a topic for discussion.) As pointed out in the headnote for Cary (1.1508), there are a number of parallels in the plots of these two plays, both of which explore issues of marriage, female independence and female choice, jealousy, murder, and madness. Both also have in common an extremely pessimistic vision of society, in which the good can do little or nothing to struggle against the power of the self-willed, sadistic, and corrupt.

But there are also important differences between the two plays, which can form the basis for student exercises and essays. Most obviously, *Mariam* is the first example of a published drama by a female author, and some features of the heroine's situation closely resemble Elizabeth Cary's own difficult marriage to a domineering and "very absolute" (1.1508) husband. (Norton Topics Online includes an interesting excerpt from Cary's biography, written by her daughter; see the "Contesting Cultural Norms" cluster in "The Early Seventeenth Century," "Gender, Family, Household.") In addition, *Mariam* is a closet drama, a form that allowed the author to develop complex ideas and characters and to experiment with perspectives in ways that would not be possible (for political or practical reasons) on the stage. (The gloomy atmosphere of *Mariam* is reminiscent of another closet drama, Fulke Greville's *Mustapha*, represented in *NAEL* by the supremely bleak *Chorus Sacerdotum*, 1.955.) Taken together, Webster's and Cary's plays can provide material for a variety of student exercises or essays. What are the relative advantages and disadvantages of the stage-play and the closet drama as instruments of social analysis and comment? Students will be inclined to imagine actresses playing both title roles: does it make a difference that the Duchess of Malfi was played by a boy and Mariam by no one at all? What similarities can be detected between the two problematic characters of Bosola and Salome? Is it reasonable to associate any of their controversial pronouncements with the views of Webster and Cary? What are the wellsprings of evil and tragedy in Webster's Italy and Cary's Judea?

In the case of Bosola, we are made aware from the first that his dangerous capacity for evil is physical in origin: "This foul melancholy / Will poison all his goodness" (1.1435, lines 69–70). Melancholy, thought to be brought on by an excess of black bile, was unquestionably the master humor of the early seventeenth century. A survey of writings on melancholy in this period offers the advantage of introducing a diverse range of authors and genres relatively quickly, while remaining focused on a defined and historically significant theme. Although standard humor theory (see the brief discussion at 1.1214) taught that it was but one of four possible imbalances in the human constitution, melancholy in many seventeenth-century works seems rather to be the individual's response to an imbalanced society. If Bosola's melancholy poisons his goodness, it also allows him—as it allows Hamlet and Jacques in *As You Like It*—to voice penetrating criticisms of the world he inhabits and the behavior of his betters. Like the Fool in *King Lear*, the melancholic man has a kind of license to speak truth to power. Thus Ferdinand sees Bosola as wearing an advantageous "garb of melancholy" (1.1440, line 185), rather than as suffering from a psychological malady.

If Bosola epitomizes the melancholic as malcontent, Antonio in the same play reveals a different facet of melancholy, the humor of the reclusive philosopher, drawn to ruins and cemeteries: "I do love these ancient ruins. / We never tread upon them but we set / Our foot upon some reverend history" (1.1501, lines 9–11). This is the melancholy of the scholar, hailed by Milton in *Il Penseroso* as "divinest Melancholy" (1.1786, line 12). Both subsequent to and longer than *L'Allegro*, this poem suggests Milton's preference for "staid Wisdom's hue" (line 16)—that is, the dark complexion brought on by black bile. That the poet appears to regard his dominant humor as a matter of choice does not mean that his melancholy is merely figurative; rather, in common with much modern science, Milton believes that the constitution of the body will follow, as well as determine, the constitution of the mind. He or his speaker opts for melancholy because he regards it as a pleasurable state, which in this account it does seem to be. Il Penseroso's melancholy will not prevent him from attending plays, reading Chaucer's *Canterbury Tales*, or dissolving into religious "ecstasies" (line 165).

The extracts in *NAEL* are designed to give students a sense of the style and matter of *The Anatomy of Melancholy*, but they cannot, of course, do more than hint at the extraordinary range and sheer mass of Burton's magnum opus. As Burton acknowledges in his preface, *Democritus Junior to the Reader*, his is a "roving humour" which seeks "to have an oar in every man's boat, to taste of every dish, and sip of every cup" (1.1564). Melancholy offers Burton a means of organizing his boundless interests and erudition around a broad and infinitely capacious subject. Yet if Burton represents himself as a descendant of the "laughing philosopher" Democritus, his treatise draws the reader into a weirdly dark and supremely melancholic world, in which all sources of knowledge and all modes of living seem equal, and equally mad. As he promises in another part of the preface, not included in *NAEL*:

> thou shalt soon perceive that all the world is mad, that it is melancholy, dotes; that it is (which Epicthonius Cosmopolites expressed not many years since in a map) made like a fool's head . . . a crazed head, *cavea stultorum*, a fool's paradise . . . a common prison of gulls, cheaters, flatterers, etc., and needs to be reformed.

(The map referred to here appears on the cover of *The Norton Shakespeare* [1997].) While Burton represents himself as standing amused and apart from it all, the prurient misogyny of the passages of *Love Melancholy* (1.1565) reveals this member of an all-male academic society in a more unsettling light. To round out a survey of melancholic works and writers, you might invite students to compare the treatment of love melancholy in Burton's *Anatomy* and the sonnets of Mary Wroth.

The Science of Self and World

Situated between the age of explorations and the Enlightenment, the early seventeenth century was also an an age of discovery. The range of works gathered in the section "The Science of Self and World" (1.1528) attests to the many modes of self- and social analysis in this era. It is not necessarily an instance of a radical epistemic break with the past, but rather of an intensification of certain preoccupations and the development of a range of styles to accommodate them. There is a growing interest in empiricism in this period, but most of the authors collected here remain primarily interested in the (moral, practical, political) uses of knowledge about self and society, rather than in amassing information of any kind for its own sake.

Useful knowledge is the one goal of the scientists of Solomon's House in Bacon's *New Atlantis*. Rather than seeking to enlarge the bounds of learning per se, they are set on "the enlarging of the bounds of human empire, to the effecting of all things possible" (1.1548). (In this they make for a sharp contrast with the Laputans in Swift's *Gulliver's Travels* [1.2414], theoretical mathematicians whose contempt for practical knowledge prevents them from being able to build proper houses.) Although Bacon made little contribution to the experimental sciences he praised, his approach to social and philosophical questions in the *Essays* was nothing if not utilitarian. Beginning with *Of Studies*, you can use Bacon's works to get your students thinking about ways of reading and the uses of learning in the seventeenth century (and today). Who is the implied reader of Bacon's *Essays*? What can this reader expect to gain from studying them? How is Bacon's style designed to influence the way the information he provides will be absorbed and deployed?

Neither Martha Moulsworth nor Rachel Speght had a place in Bacon's implied readership, but both succeeded in attaining a level of education unusual for women in the early seventeenth century, including a measure of classical learning. Speght gives an allegorical account of her education in *A Dream* (1.1556) and, in the person of Truth, defends the right of women to seek after knowledge, while Moulsworth argues for the establishment of a university for women. Your students will probably warm to Moulsworth in particular, whose personal tone, practicality, and mild earthiness make her seem more modern than many of her contemporaries. Yet the *Memorandum* is far more than an outpouring of bittersweet memories. Moulsworth selects the information she records and uses her chosen form to make points about female education, the married state, and the freedom of widowhood. The form of the poem too encodes a kind of knowledge. With her close attention to patterning and to number, Moulsworth participates in an early modern fascination with numerology. (The *Memorandum*, consisting of fifty-five couplets for the author's fifty-five years, may be compared to Spenser's intricately patterned *Epithalamion* [see the discussion at 1.864].) (For more texts that will help you to examine issues of women in the culture, see Norton Topics Online, the "Contesting Cultural Norms" cluster, in "The Early Seventeenth Century," "Gender, Family, Household.")

Robert Burton, Thomas Browne, and Thomas Hobbes were all, like Francis Bacon, products of the universities. Yet the three scholars not only followed markedly different careers but developed different approaches to knowledge, along with styles that reflect and enable those approaches. Whereas Burton crams his work with dizzying numbers of citations, giving all equal weight and leaving little or any room for reasoning outside the box of his bibliography, Browne wears his learning more lightly, and trusts to it less. Browne's famously well-crafted sentences seem designed to help him run rings around his own reason. "In philosophy, where truth seems double-faced, there is no man more paradoxical than myself" (*Religio Medici*, 1.1573). In matters of religion, Browne's eagerness to subordinate reason to faith leads him to declare "there be not impossibilities enough in religion for an active faith" (1.1574); he is glad not to have lived in the age of miracles, for "then had my faith been thrust upon me" (1.1574). Browne's antipathy to dull proof contrasts sharply with Hobbes's determined pursuit of it. Hobbes's obsession with clarity and distaste for figurative language suggest an attempt to write without style; nevertheless, like Browne and Burton, he can be read for his style today.

Although they can be taught as a group, all of the selections in "The Science of Self and World" can be taught well individually or in combination with other texts. Bacon's *Essays* are particularly attractive as launching pads for the study of various seventeenth-century themes and modes. For instance, *Of Plantations* can be read alongside such colonial texts as Marvell's *Bermudas* (1.1686) as well as those grouped in the sixteenth century section "The Wider World" (1.889). *Of Masques and Triumphs*, with its ambiguous meditation on court entertainments, teaches well alongside Jonson's *Masque of Blackness* (1.1294). The section *Solomon's House* could initiate a survey of early modern versions of Utopia, reaching back to More's seminal text (1.506) and forward to such disparate texts as Gerrard Winstanley's proclamation of Digger communism in *The True Levellers' Standard Advanced* (1.1740), Milton's description of Eden, and Margaret Cavendish's *The Blazing World* (1.1765). (Thomas Traherne's vision of a wondrous world without private property as seen through a child's eyes in *Centuries of Meditation* and *Wonder* [1.1755, 1756] also merits consideration as a version of Utopia.) More ambitiously, the essay *Of Marriage and Single Life* could be the starting point for a wide-ranging survey of the literature of the period organized around the theme of marriage. Such a survey might cover Moulsworth's *Memorandum*, Webster's *Duchess of Malfi*, Cary's *Tragedy of Mariam*, Suckling's *A Ballad upon a Wedding* (1.1666), Philips's *A Married State* (1.1679), Cavendish's *A True Relation* (1.1762), and finally, *Paradise Lost*. (Norton Topics Online offers even more resources that provide historical background and conflicting contemporary views about marriage and the social order.)

The World Turned Upside Down

The Social Order and Its Challengers

The events known to some as the English Revolution, to others as the English Civil War(s), and to the less Anglocentrically minded as the War of the Three Kingdoms continue to challenge and divide historians. For the teacher of literature, the challenges posed by this period can be even more daunting, because the time you have to introduce students to the history of the conflict is extremely limited. On the other hand, opportunities abound to teach important aspects of the great struggle through the texts in *NAEL*. Few if any of the poets and prose writers who lived and wrote in the tumultuous years 1640 to 1660 were successful in avoiding politics, even if they wished to do so. Many were actively involved in contemporary struggles or served as (paid or voluntary) propagandists. Others sought to distance themselves from the disasters of the age; but the events that impinged, often painfully, on their personal and public lives inevitably left traces in their prose and poetry.

Many of the poets who are represented in *NAEL* largely or entirely by their devotional, philosophical, or personal verse were also active commentators on political affairs. There are valid reasons for the bias that tends to exclude works of the latter variety by all but the greatest writers of the age, such as Milton. Poems written in haste in response to current events are often of very mixed quality and generally require copious annotation if they are to be understood today. However, it is good to make your students aware that the minds of early-seventeenth-century poets were not fixed constantly on creative writing. Poets such as Crashaw, Cowley, and Waller, as well as Marvell and Milton, served as hired pens for one side or another (or both) before, during, and after the revolutionary era. Crashaw, for instance, represented in the anthology by *Music's Duel* and his brilliant religious poetry, produced the following effusion on the birth of Prince Henry in 1640, as Charles I made ready for a second campaign against his Scottish subjects:

> Rebellion, stand thou by; Mischief, make room;
> War, blood and death (names all averse from joy),
> Hear this, we have another bright-eyed boy.
> That word's a warrant, by whose virtue I
> Have full authority to bid you die.

Examples of this sort, demonstrating that poetry and politics were not separate spheres, will prepare students to recognize the more oblique politics of many of the poems and prose works in *NAEL*. (For images of, documents about, and literary responses to the execution of Charles I, see Norton Topics Online, "The Early Seventeenth Century," "Civil Wars of Ideas.")

Poems such as Herrick's *The Hock-Cart, or Harvest Home* and Suckling's *A Ballad upon a Wedding* celebrate traditional festivities involving mingling of classes. These are thoroughly ideological works that aim to naturalize the traditional social order. In both works, the poet seeks to enter the minds of agricultural laborers and to assure himself of their fidelity to their aristocratic masters. Herrick, who deliberately courts Puritan disapproval with his praise of superstitious or quasi-Catholic practices such as blessing the cart and kissing the sheaves (1.1650, line 19), represents his rural revelers as the backbone of English society. After drinking their Lord's health, they drink "to the plow (the common-wealth)" (line 39). The phrase closely echoes a remark by Robert Cecil in the House of Commons in 1601, which is in turn indicative of a broad stream of conservative thought: "I do not dwell in the Country, I am not acquainted with the Plough: But I think whosoever doth not maintain the Plough destroys this Kingdom."

Yet particularly in its final lines, *The Hock-Cart* draws attention to the operation of power in the commonwealth maintained by the plow. "And you must know, your Lord's word's true, / Feed him ye must whose food fills you" (lines 51–52). The last part of the poem, with its reiteration of *must* and the emphasis on pain (line 54), draws surprisingly frank attention to the coercion by which the social order is maintained and raises the question of how and by whom wealth and food are produced in this society. Similarly, when Suckling's country yokel recognizes at the end of *A Ballad upon a Wedding* that sex is the same for lords and laborers, the social order seems to wobble very slightly. Both poems, however, allay any doubts they may raise by virtue of their exuberant confidence in the vitality and timelessness of the old order. Read one way, these poems cynically celebrate the power of the aristocracy to pull the wool over the eyes of rural laborers by means of spectacle. Read another, they celebrate the games and festivities that bind the aristocracy and the rural poor together, in opposition to Puritans and the urban middle classes. Part of the point of Suckling's ballad is that his rural speaker has ventured as far as Charing Cross in London, the heart of mercantilism and Puritanism, and, thanks to witnessing the wedding, come away ideologically unscathed. (The Norton Topics Online cluster "Styles of Belief, Devotion, and Culture," in "The Early Seventeenth Century," "Civil Wars of Ideas," offers texts that will allow deeper examination of issues of social order.)

One of the most rewarding ways to study the social order through literature is by focusing on the peculiarly seventeenth-century genre of the country-house poem. Assigning Lanyer's *The Description of Cooke-ham* (1.1287), the first such poem to be published, Jonson's *To Penshurst* (1.1399), and Marvell's *Upon Appleton House* (1.1704) is a remarkably efficient way of shedding light on the complex questions of patronage, class, aristocratic display, the social order, and the rural economy. At the same time, of course, you will be drawing distinctions among them. (Since these distinctions include gender, it is worth reminding students that Lanyer is not the only one of these three poets who "has" gender.) The attractions of this approach are particularly apparent if you are pressed for time in covering the early seventeenth century. One potential drawback is that many students are initially resistant to the "country-house" genre, both because the ostensible subject matter sounds rather dull and because the relationship of poet to patron seems mercenary and antithetical to the spirit of poetry. But such prejudices can be countered, or at least placed in context, by a careful exposition of the poet-patron relationship, and this in itself is an exercise of great value in teaching the literature of the seventeenth century. (Norton Topics Online provides images of country houses, including Penshurst, along with portraits and records of their aristocratic inhabitants; see "The Early Seventeenth Century," "Gender, Family, Household.")

In the years before the outbreak of hostilities, challenges to the traditional social order came from several directions. London was growing exponentially, from a population of 200,000 in 1600 to 375,000 in 1650; and with it grew the power of the urban middle classes. *The Memorandum of Martha Moulsworth* is particularly enlightening in this regard. Although her father was a cleric and landowner "Of gentle birth" (1.1553, line 22), her three husbands were all wealthy men associated with London guilds. Moulsworth lays stress on the fact that her third husband was descended from the Mortimers, an ancient family that at one point could advance a claim to the Crown; she also glances disapprovingly at the practice of purchasing coats of arms, as those who were successful at their trades (including Shakespeare) often did (lines 59–60). Yet in spite of her reverence for gentle birth and noble blood, Moulsworth when she wrote had become a member of a class that, simply by its uncheckable growth and confidence, posed a challenge to the old social order.

Other challengers to that order were far more vocal in their dissent. Puritans vociferously opposed many features of Caroline society, from the rule of bishops to the ancient seasonal festivals celebrated in Herrick's *The Hock-Cart* and *Corinna's Going A-Maying*. As a preface to the latter poem, you might read your students this excerpt from Richard Stubbes's *Anatomie of Abuses*:

> Against May, Whitsunday, or other time all the young men and maids, old men and wives, run gadding over night to the woods, groves, hills, and mountains, where they spend all the night in pleasant pastimes. . . . And no marvel, for there is a great Lord present amongst them, as superintendent and Lord over their pastimes and sports, namely Satan, prince of hell. But their chiefest jewel they bring from thence is their Maypole, which they bring home with great veneration, . . . this Maypole (this stinking idol, rather) which is covered all over with flowers and herbs. . . . And then fall they to dance about it, like as the heathen people did at the dedication of the Idols, whereof this is a perfect pattern, or rather the thing itself. I have heard it credibly reported . . . by men of great gravity and reputation, that of forty, three-score, or a hundred maids going to the wood over night, there have scarcely the third part of them returned home undefiled.

Norton Topics Online offers more examples of Puritan social critique, including selections from the irrepressible William Prynne, who was sentenced to have his books burned and his ears cropped for implicitly comparing the queen to a whore because she took part in masques and pastorals; see "The Early Seventeenth Century," "Civil Wars of Ideas," "Styles of Belief, Devotion, and Culture."

Well before the outbreak of war in 1642, England was clearly divided into two increasingly hostile camps. Although royalists and traditionalists like Herrick and Suckling idealized rural pastimes, their faction was known as "the court"; and while Puritans and Parliamentarians had a powerful base in London, they called themselves "the country." These were charged phrases, as may be seen in Lucy Hutchinson's dramatic recollection of the quarrel between her father and Lord Newark in April 1642, four months before the king unfurled his standard and the Civil War began, over who owns Nottingham's cache of gunpowder (1.1727). When Colonel Hutchinson seeks to preserve the powder for "the country," he means the county, and more specifically the rural districts surrounding the county seat. In this context "country" is not being used in the way we speak of "city and *country*," but he means that it is under the control of Parliament.

The word, constantly repeated with growing vehemence, also means something more general. It stands for a position and a point of view, a way of seeing society for which many thousands were willing to die.

The Experience of Defeat

The old observation that there are no winners in war is particular apt in regard to the internecine conflicts of the middle seventeenth century. Almost every writer who lived through the middle decades of the seventeenth century was deeply affected by the English Revolution and its aftermath. Some took up arms in defense of the old order; others used their pens to justify rebellion and regicide. Almost all had the experience of watching their cause go down to apparently absolute defeat. The consequences of defeat may be traced in terms of shattered careers, crises of faith, and, frequently, brilliant poetry.

Defeat came first to those who served and fought for Charles I and his queen. Thomas Hobbes, Richard Crashaw, Sir John Suckling, Edmund Waller, Abraham Cowley, Margaret Cavendish, and the earl of Clarendon went into exile in Paris; Crashaw and Suckling both died abroad, the latter probably by his own hand. Thomas Carew, Henry Vaughan, Richard Lovelace, and Suckling fought in the king's armies. Lovelace and Waller were imprisoned. Others suffered forms of internal exile. Herrick was ejected from his parish and returned to London, where he published his one volume of verse; Katherine Philips in west Wales found herself in the difficult position of being a royalist married to a regicide. For some, like Richard Crashaw and Henry Vaughan, defeat opened the way to experiences of conversion, the former to Catholicism, the latter to a deeply mystical faith tinged with Hermetic philosophy. The greatest poetry of Crashaw and Vaughan, Hobbes's *Leviathan*, Herrick's *Hesperides*, and the poems Lovelace wrote and prepared for publication in prison—all of these are the fruits of defeat.

Those who took the side of Parliament and Army went down to defeat in stages and to varying degrees, depending on their politics and the compromises they made. Radical opponents of the Cromwellian regime such as John Lilburne, Gerrard Winstanley, and Anna Trapnel were exposed to persecution, interrogation, and often imprisonment in the late 1640s and 1650s. For others, final defeat came with the Restoration in 1660. Lucy Hutchinson's husband died in prison. Milton would most probably have suffered a similar fate if not for the intercession of Marvell, who managed to retain his parliamentary seat after the Restoration without sacrificing his independence. The experience of defeat, as utter as it was unanticipated, lies behind all of Milton's last works, including *Paradise Lost*. (See also "The New Culture Wars: The Restoration" cluster in Norton Topics Online, "The Early Seventeenth Century," "Civil Wars of Ideas.")

Several short poems in *NAEL* bear directly on the conflicts of the time and, taught together, give students a sense of the great and varied impact of the wars on almost every life. Herrick's *The Bad Season Makes the Poet*

Sad, written in the middle to late 1640s, refers to the years before the civil wars and the flight of Henrietta Maria as a "golden age" (1.1653, line 7). Concluding with a line translated from Horace's first ode to his patron Maecenas, Herrick associates this golden age with the reign of the emperor Augustus (and thus anticipates the "Augustan" spirit of the Restoration). Although the poem was written before the execution of the king, the golden age of the prewar years already seems infinitely remote and—except in wishful fantasy—all but irrecoverable.

Lovelace's *Lucasta* was published in 1649, a year after Herrick's *Hesperides* and after Parliament had crossed the bridge of regicide. *The Grasshopper* and *To Althea, from Prison* reveal the response of this quintessential Cavalier to the destruction of his cause, a response that is almost paradoxically optimistic and life affirming. Whereas for Herrick there can be no joy until the wished-for and still conceivable return of the golden age, Lovelace in prison creates a golden world in miniature out of the elements of love, friendship, wine, and unbending royalism. Students tend to respond very warmly to *To Althea; The Grasshopper*, with its comparatively complex rhythms and close-clustered allusions, is more difficult, but involves the finest statement of the Cavalier ideal. For Lovelace, at least, this ideal never boils down to defiant hedonism, but requires self-knowledge and fidelity to the truth found in the heart: "Though lord of all that seas embrace, yet he / That wants himself is poor indeed" (1.1672, lines 39–40).

Two poems in *NAEL* bear directly on the execution of Charles I. (A range of other accounts, illustrations, and perspectives on this event can be accessed on Norton Topics Online.) Katherine Philips's bitterly witty and rhetorically complex *Upon the Double Murder of King Charles* (1.1680) satirizes attempts to justify regicide: "He broke God's laws, and therefore he must die, / And what shall then become of thee and I?" (lines 21–22). By comparison, Marvell's famous account of the execution in the central stanzas of *An Horatian Ode* (1.1702, lines 53–72) is easier to follow but more difficult to grasp. Marvell is concerned to achieve a balanced judgment—or at least the appearance of such a judgment—and these stanzas are particularly finely balanced, breaking in the middle with "While," "But," "But," "So," "And yet" (lines 55, 59, 63, 67, 71). The politics and sympathies of this poem have been and continue to be disputed, and the poem provides an excellent theme for a classroom discussion or debate. It will be important to point out, however, that the implied question "Cromwell or Charles?" already excludes a range of alternative political positions; there is no room in *An Horatian Ode* for the voices of Levellers, Diggers, or Fifth Monarchists (represented in *NAEL* by John Lilburne, Gerrard Winstanley and Anna Trapnel), all active in 1650 and all opposed to Cromwell's rule as well as to kingship.

The compact and highly teachable section "Voices of the War" (1.1725) brings together in less than thirty pages seven men and women who experienced the English Revolution in very different ways. All took risks and suffered losses as a result of the stances they took during and after the war. This section provides an opportunity to introduce representatives of the various political and religious groups important in this period (Puritans, Cavaliers, Levellers, Diggers, Fifth Monarchists, and Ranters) and to observe commonalities as well as the distinctions between them. Students should be prepared to approach each "voice" with certain basic questions in mind. What, for each writer, is the ultimate source of political power? How does God intercede in human affairs, if at all? What is the role of the individual in shaping history? How would each writer respond to Milton's call for freedom of thought and a free press in *Areopagitica*? Answers to these questions could form the basis for essays or a less formal assignment.

"Voices of the War" will also allow you to initiate a discussion of how different voices compete to be heard in the public sphere. Three of the writers included here are women; several espouse positions and spring from backgrounds that in the past would almost certainly have barred them from appearing in print. The breakdown of censorship (1.1801), the challenges to traditional authority, and the blossoming of debate in the 1640s created conditions in which all of these voices could compete for a hearing. They did not, of course, compete on a level playing field—Diggers and Ranters lacked almost all of the cultural and economic resources available to the traditional leaders of opinion. Nevertheless, one of the most remarkable features of Winstanley's and Trapnel's writings is their forthrightness and confidence in laying their controversial cases before the general public.

Milton and Paradise Lost

The first question when it comes to teaching Milton in a survey course must inevitably be "how much?" Along with ample selections of Milton's early verse, the sonnets, and a sampling of the prose writings, *NAEL* includes the full text of *Paradise Lost*. (See also in the Early Seventeenth Century section of Norton Topics Online, the rich selection of materials in "*Paradise Lost* in Context.") Although there can be no substitute for the poem in its entirety, you may well be constrained by other commitments to teaching only a few books, along with some of the shorter works. It is still possible to give students a fulfilling experience of the poem, if not a full one, and you will have the comfort of knowing that they have the whole poem in their possession if they find themselves hooked, as more than a few will be.

It is possible to include a surprising amount of Milton's work in your course, and at the same time do justice to the length and variety of his career, by interspersing his shorter works throughout the weeks or months you spend teaching this period. Thus *On Shakespeare* (1.1782) might be introduced in company with Jonson's *To the Memory of My Beloved . . .* (1.1414), prompting a discussion of how Shakespeare's reputation developed in the seventeenth century (Dryden's comparison of Shakespeare and Jonson [1.2117] could also have a role here). *L'Allegro* (1.1782) and *Il Penseroso* (1.1786) could be used alongside other texts dealing with melancholy and humors (see "All Coherence Gone," p. 68). *On the Morning of Christ's Nativity* (1.1774) makes for an obvious yet interesting pairing with Crashaw's *In the Holy Nativity of Our Lord God* (1.1635). *Lycidas* (1.1790) could be taught alongside Donne's *An Anatomy of the World* (1.1262), another poetic response to a premature death, but it stands perfectly well on its own, and is more useful as a way of introducing the religious conflicts of the middle part of the century. *Areopagitica* (1.1801) can also be brought in at this stage and will work well alongside "Voices of the War." Milton's political sonnets can also be introduced at any point in a discussion of the Revolution, and *To the Lord General Cromwell, May 1652* (1.1813) makes for an obvious comparison with Marvell's *An Horatian Ode* (1.1700). (Alternatively, the sonnets can serve as the culmination of a survey charting the development of the form from the classic Elizabethan sequences, through the works of Donne, Wroth, and Herbert.) Many other linkages between Milton and other and earlier writers are possible. Proceeding in this way, you will find you have been able to cover a great deal of Milton's work before "arriving" at the destination of *Paradise Lost*.

When you reach Milton's epic, there will still be plenty of opportunities to draw connections with texts you have covered earlier on. If you can only cover a few books, say 1, 2, 4, 9, and 12, it will be particularly useful to refer back to other writers for purposes of comparison or to place Milton's themes in context. For instance, the question of Milton's sexism or otherwise in his portrayal of Eve can be explored more fruitfully where representations of Eve by near-contemporary women writers are available for comparison. Lanyer's *Eve's Apology in Defense of Women*, which turns the story of the Fall to feminist account, presents a very different image of Adam and Eve from that found in *Paradise Lost*, and Book 9 in particular. (Another seventeenth-century woman's version of the Fall, Rachel Speght's *A Muzzle for Melastomus*, is included on Norton Topics Online.) Similarly, Milton's first description of Adam and Eve in Book 4 can be situated within a debate about marriage going back to the beginning of the period (see "The Science of Self and World") and including Milton's own notorious *Doctrine and Discipline of Divorce* (extracts of which are on Norton Topics Online).

Paradise Lost can be a great pleasure to teach precisely because students typically expect not to like or even understand it, and are delighted to find themselves doing both. Students generally find as well that they know much more of the story than they think they do. A drawback to this, however, is that some are inclined simply to conflate the plot of *Paradise Lost* with "the Bible story" and Milton's religious views with "Christianity." A good way of countering this is to point out that many of the most memorable events in the poem, including the "great consult" in Hell (1.1836) and Eve's delighted discovery of her reflection in the water (1.1884), have little or no basis in scripture. Moreover, Milton's mature theology, often implied in the epic poem and revealed in his unpublished *Christian Doctrine*, was unorthodox on a number of points; most notably in the poem, Christ is not coequal and coeternal with the Father, as all churches taught, but merely "of all creation first" (1.1866, line 383).

Finally, it is vital that students should bear in mind that *Paradise Lost* is an epic poem. The difficulty with teaching it as one is that you may not have had much occasion to mention the epic genre up until this point in the course (unless you have covered *The Faerie Queene* and emphasized its epic qualities). Providing students with a few examples of epic conventions (in a lecture or on a handout) will prove more effective than simply listing the standard features of an epic poem. Contemporary translations of Homer and Virgil were almost always in rhyme, which Milton abhorred, so you may prefer to use modern unrhymed translations (available on Norton Topics Online) to give students a sampling of epic statements and invocations. Alternatively, let them hear the magnificent opening of Dryden's *Aeneid*:

> Arms, and the man I sing, who, forced by fate,
> And haughty Juno's unrelenting hate,
> Expelled and exiled, left the Trojan shore.
> Long labors, both by sea and land, he bore,
> And in the doubtful war, before he won
> The Latian realm, and built the destined town;
> His banished gods restored to rites divine,
> And settled sure succession in his line,
> From whence the race of Alban fathers come,
> And the long glories of majestic Rome.
> O Muse! the causes and the crimes relate;
> What goddess was provoked, and whence her hate;
> For what offense the Queen of Heaven began
> To persecute so brave, so just a man;
> Involved his anxious life in endless cares,
> Exposed to wants, and hurried into wars!

More examples of epic conventions can be drawn from within *NAEL*. The first twelve lines of Pope's *The Rape of the Lock* can also be compared with the first sixteen lines of *Paradise Lost*. Similarly, the brief passage from Henry Howard's translation of Virgil (1.576) offers a perfect example of an epic simile, and the opening of *The Faerie Queene* (1.628) can be referred to for a largely self-explanatory example of beginning in medias res. Armed with a few such examples, students will be in a better position to appreciate the neatness and audacity with which Milton reinvents such tired epic conventions as the descent into the underworld.

Early-Seventeenth-Century Voices

Style and Authorship

The period that includes the works of Donne, Jonson, Bacon, Browne, Herbert, Vaughan, Marvell, and Milton is ideal for talking about style.

Some eras have a dominant style, and it takes a trained ear to distinguish a sonnet of Sidney's from one by Daniel or Drayton, or Pope's couplets from Dryden's. What is remarkable about the early seventeenth century is the number of excellent writers composing in very distinctive styles. Students can be initially resistant to thinking and talking about style—they think they do not know what it is or take it to be a particularly arcane and difficult branch of knowledge and are afraid of looking foolish. Nevertheless, even students who are convinced they have no "ear for poetry" can learn a great deal about style by comparing and contrasting the poets and prose writers of the seventeenth century.

Certain pairings, such as Jonson and Herrick, Herbert and Donne, work particularly well for making points about poetic style. Herrick is the most prominent of the "Sons of Ben," yet the great difference between him and Jonson can be seen in comparing Jonson's *Still to Be Neat* (1.1414) with Herrick's imitation *Delight in Disorder* (1.1646). The two poems espouse the same aesthetic principles in regard to women's dress and, by implication, poetic art. Yet Jonson's poem is itself nothing if not neat, while Herrick captures something of the "careless shoestring's" playful swish.

Herbert resembles Donne in his use of "metaphysical" conceits (see below); yet the homeliness and simplicity of the language and the quiet tone sound not at all like Donne. The best way to make the difference clear is to read or get students to read a few devotional poems by each poet aloud (say *Death, be not proud* [1.1270] and *Batter my heart, three-personed God* [1.1271] by Donne, *Death* [1.1613] and *The Collar* [1.1609] by Herbert). Nothing is more alien to Donne's style than a poem like *The Collar*, which starts off shouting and finishes, triumphantly, just above a whisper. Donne's poems tend to end with a punch-line; Herbert's end when the poet stops punching.

The prose lends itself to similar comparisons. Bacon's *Essays* may be contrasted both with the works of other prose writers and with each other. Changes in his style—a relaxation of his austere, aphoristic manner, a comparative smoothness and expansiveness—can be traced in comparing the 1597 and 1625 versions of *Of Studies* (1.1541). Essays new in the 1625 edition can be compared with those introduced in 1597 or 1612. Donne, too, can be compared to himself: his prose shares many of the characteristics of his poetry. Burton, Browne, and Hobbes all cultivate distinctive prose styles suited to the purposes of their writings. Hobbes's exceptionally clear style and his hostility to all ambiguity help grant his work the air of pure ratiocination, which we associate with modern philosophy. At times, however, we catch notes of the aphoristic style honed by the young Bacon half a century before. You might, in a quiz or as a competition, ask students to identify the authors of the following phrases:

- "Men in great place are thrice servants: servants of the sovereign or state, servants of fame, and servants of business." (Bacon, *Of Great Place*, 1.1533)

- "So that in the nature of man, we find three principal causes of quarrel. First competition; secondly, diffidence; thirdly, glory." (Hobbes, *Leviathan*, 1.1591)

Differing styles in this period are often connected to differing conceptions of authorship. The two things can and should be discussed together. The introduction to the period includes a brief and clear discussion of the different modes of authorship epitomized by the witty amateur Donne, the polished professional Jonson, and the at once selfless and self-doubting Herbert (1.1217–18). In each case, the poet's self-presentation can be read alongside the responses of their friends, followers, and critics. In Donne's case, Jonson's *To John Donne* (1.1395) praises the poet's wit and (perhaps with subtle criticism) his singularity; yet on another occasion Jonson lambasted Donne for lack of discipline, saying he "deserved hanging" for his metrical irregularities (see 1.1233). In sharp contrast, Carew's *An Elegy upon the Death of the Dean of Paul's, Dr. John Donne* (1.1656) presents Donne as a hyper-masculine poetic legislator whose "strict laws will be / Too hard for libertines in poetry" (lines 61–62). Carew's *To Ben Jonson* (1.1659) offers another version of the poet-as-lawgiver with his "just chastising hand" (line 1), but blames Jonson for taking offense at reasonable criticism. Herrick's *His Prayer to Ben Jonson* (1.1652) is shorter and more playful, lightly twitting Jonson for his former Catholicism by invoking him as "Saint Ben" and, kneeling at his altar, offering him a lyric—this poem—and candles. As for Herbert, while *NAEL* includes no poem addressed to him, Vaughan's *Unprofitableness* (1.1622), opening with a clear echo of Herbert's *The Flower* (1.1610), can be used to illustrate how Vaughan at once emulated and differed from his master.

Authorship is an equally important concept in teaching the works of John Milton and Margaret Cavendish. Milton's discussion of his epic projects in *The Reason of Church Government*, an essential text in preparing the way for *Paradise Lost*, also offers a jumping-off point for a discussion of male and female modes of authorship in the latter part of the period. Compared to the poets who flourished in the earlier decades of the century, Milton and Cavendish both come across as extraordinarily confident, indeed arrogant, in their callings. Milton, whose sense of poetic vocation is already fully developed in *Lycidas* (1.1791), informs the (no doubt perplexed) readers of *The Reason of Church Government* of his determination "to fix all the industry and art I could unite to the adorning of my native tongue . . . to be an interpreter and relater of the best and sagest things among mine own citizens throughout this island in the mother dialect" (1.1798). Cavendish is if anything even more forthright in proclaiming her calling, and her authorial project is even greater in scope: "my ambition is not only to be Empress, but Authoress of a whole world" (1.1770).

Yet if these attitudes strike us as arrogant, we should recognize that they are also compensatory, for both writers were subject to fierce criticism as well as attacks of self-doubt. Cavendish was widely scorned for what were perceived as her pretensions, and her husband was mocked for encouraging and financing her ventures into print. In the slyly witty *The Poetess's Hasty Resolution*, she mocks her own ambition in rushing into print, yet concludes in the confident expectation that readers will "Wipe off my tears with handkerchiefs of praise" (1.1760, line 24). Still more subtle and intriguing is her description of her motives for and manner of writing in *A True Relation of My Birth, Breeding, and Life* (1.1762). Here, her anxiety about the public reception of her work is overmastered by recourse to sheer bravado: "it is true, that 'tis to no purpose to the readers, but it is to the authoress, because I write it for my own sake, not theirs" (1.1765). Yet this triumphant declaration of self-sufficiency is immediately followed by a recurrence of the fear that she will be forgotten or, worse, confused with another wife.

Milton, too, was constantly required to master the self-doubt to which he testifies in works ranging from the early sonnet *How Soon Hath Time* (1.1812) to *Paradise Lost*. The openings of Book 3 (1.1858–59, lines 1–55) and Book 9 (1.1961–62, lines 1–47) in particular reveal the extent to which the mature poet reconceived himself along with the epic genre, in response to political experiences, personal losses, and the devastating experience of defeat in 1660. If Milton at last fulfilled his youthful ambitions in *Paradise Lost*, he had also to come to terms with the inadequacy and failure of youthful dreams. In the opening lines of Book 9, the poet turns his back on "Wars, hitherto, the only argument / Heroic deemed" (1.1962, lines 28–29) in favor of "the better fortitude / Of patience and heroic martyrdom" (lines 31–32). These words testify to the distance Milton had traveled from the epic ambitions expressed in *The Reason of Church Government*. Still more personal is the proem in Book 3, in which Milton confronts and masters his anxieties about his blindness. He was not alone in questioning whether a blind man was fit for such a task. His friend Marvell was frank about his doubts in the verses he wrote for the second edition of *Paradise Lost* (the full text of which is available on Norton Topics Online):

> When I beheld the poet blind, yet bold,
> In slender book his vast design unfold,
> Messiah crowned, God's reconciled decree,
> Rebelling Angels, the Forbidden Tree,
> Heaven, Hell, Earth, Chaos, all; the argument
> Held me a while, misdoubting his intent
> That he would ruin (for I saw him strong)
> The sacred truth to fable and old song,
> (So Sampson groped the temple's posts in spite)
> The world o'erwhelming to revenge his sight.

Yet as Milton mastered his own self-doubt, so he mastered Marvell, who acknowledged, "Just heaven thee, like Tiresias, to requite, / Rewards with prophecy the loss of sight."

Uses and Abuses of the Metaphysical Poets

There never was a school of metaphysical poets, nor would any of the poets generally grouped under that heading—Donne, Herbert, Vaughan, Crashaw, Cowley, and others—have answered to the name. The differences between these poets are so striking and so central to their respective achievements that forcing them into anything resembling a school risks obscuring much more than is revealed. Therefore, we do not recommend that the great poets of the early seventeenth century be introduced under the common heading of metaphysical poets.

On the other hand, it is neither necessary nor advisable to dispense with the term *metaphysical* altogether. If we speak instead of a "metaphysical manner" or "metaphysical wit," we are naming a quality or habit of writing that can be discerned not only in the poets mentioned above but in most of the best writers of the period, including many of those usually classed as "Cavalier," and even Ben Jonson. Central to the metaphysical manner is the metaphysical conceit: a far-fetched, intellectualized, and unusually elaborate comparison. The best poem to use in introducing the concept of the metaphysical conceit is probably Donne's *A Valediction: Forbidding Mourning* (1.1248), with its comparison of the lovers' souls to the legs of a compass:

> If they be two, they are two so
>   As stiff twin compasses are two;
> Thy soul, the fixed foot, makes no show
>   To move, but doth, if th' other do. (lines 25–28)

What makes this conceit metaphysical is not only its unlikeliness at first glance, but also the multileveled quality of the comparison. The lovers are like parts of a compass because, though distinct, they together form a single entity; because the one that is fixed sympathetically leans toward the one that moves; because one part grows "erect" (line 32) when joined to its fellow; because the fixity of one ensures the other's fidelity and eventual return.

Having worked through the last twelve lines of *A Valediction: Forbidding Mourning*, invite your students to discover and describe the elaboration of the conceits in such poems as *A Valediction: Of Weeping* (1.1244), *A Lecture upon the Shadow* (1.1254), and *Hymn to God My God, in My Sickness* (1.1274). You can refer back to such "textbook cases" from Donne when you come to deal with examples of metaphysical conceits in the works of later poets. Donne's *Holy Sonnet 14* ("Batter my heart, three-personed God," 1.1271) and Herbert's *Man* (1.1604) are based on very similar conceits—the human being as a palace or walled town that God is invited to enter—but develop differently and suggest very different relationships between God and the speaker. The complex conceit in Vaughan's *Silence, and Stealth of Days!* (1.1620)—whereby the poet's mental return to the hour of his brother's death is likened to a miner underground rushing back to the lamp that is his "day"—recalls Donne's *The Sun Rising* (1.1239) both in the image of the sun shining in an enclosed space and in the yearning to arrest or turn back time; Vaughan, however, configures the elements of the conceit differently and to different effect than Donne. Finally, Crashaw's epigrammatic conceits, by which Christ's wounds are variously doors (*I Am the Door*, 1.1634), mouths and eyes (*On the Wounds of Our Crucified Lord*, 1.1634), and lactating breasts (*Luke 11.*[27], 1.1635), present a special case. They are neither, in the context of Catholic iconography, strikingly original nor elaborated to any great extent, yet they attain "metaphysical" status when Crashaw steers them to an unanticipated, intense, and typically shocking conclusion: "The Mother then must suck the son." When teaching Crashaw, you can refer back to Donne's praise of "a figurative, a metaphorical God" in *Expostulation 19*:

> How often . . . doth thy son call himself a way and a light and a gate and a vine and bread than the son of God or of man? How much oftener doth he exhibit a metaphorical Christ than a real, a literal? This hath occasioned thine ancient servants, whose delight it was to write after thy copy . . . to make their accesses to thee in such a kind of language as thou wast pleased to speak to them, in a figurative, in a metaphorical language. (1.1279)

The idea of "metaphysical wit," then, has a usefulness and validity even if the category of "metaphysical poets" does not, and the comparison of conceits can be a way of underlining differences as well as commonalities among poets. Also, however misleading or empty it may seem today, the concept of metaphysical poetry was central to later perceptions of seventeenth-century literature and, indeed, to the development of modern literary criticism. The first and second volumes of *NAEL* include important critical appraisals of the metaphysical poets, which testify to a long and fascinating history of reception.

With the rapid shift in intellectual and aesthetic fashions following the Restoration, Donne was one of several major poets suddenly relegated to the status of footnotes in literary history. Those who excelled at metaphysical wit were now seen as clever but difficult, arrogant, and offensive. In *A Discourse Concerning the Original and Progress of Satire*, John Dryden condemned Donne because "he affects the metaphysics . . . and perplexes the minds of the fair sex with nice speculations of philosophy, when he should engage their hearts, and entertain them with the softnesses of love." Samuel Johnson amplified these criticisms, coining the phrase "metaphysical poets" for all those, such as Abraham Cowley, who shared Donne's perceived faults. In his life of Cowley, Johnson complained in particular of the extravagance of metaphysical conceits:

> The most heterogeneous ideas are yoked by violence together; nature and art are ransacked for illustrations, comparisons, and allusions; their learning instructs, and their subtlety surprises; but the reader commonly thinks his

improvement dearly bought, and, though he sometimes admires, is seldom pleased. (1.2737)

In working through Johnson's criticism with students, ask them to consider not only what he can tell us about early-seventeenth-century poetry but what principles of literary taste are stated or implied in his criticisms of the metaphysical poets. What does Johnson consider to be the purpose of poetry? To what extent do we still share his aesthetic criteria?

If you will be using volume 2 of *NAEL* later in the course, you have the opportunity at this point to assign T. S. Eliot's *The Metaphysical Poets* (2.2401), among the most important and influential pieces of twentieth-century criticism. Even if your students do not have volume 2, or if Eliot's essay seems too difficult or time-consuming to assign in its entirety, it is still worthwhile quoting a few passages to give the students a sense of how and why Donne, Crashaw, Herbert, and Vaughan were rescued from literary obscurity. Eliot is much more forgiving than Johnson of the metaphysical conceit: "the elaboration . . . of a figure of speech to the furthest stage to which ingenuity can carry it" (2.2402). More memorable and significant is his assertion that these were the last poets to "feel their thought as immediately as the odour of a rose" (2.2405), before the infamous "dissociation of sensibility" (2.2406), which set in under the influence of Milton and Dryden. It is not, of course, necessary to endorse all of Eliot's sometimes dubious historical claims, nor need you worry that students will swallow his argument hook, line, and sinker. What Johnson and Eliot offer are simply conflicting perspectives that students may enjoy testing against examples of seventeenth-century verse. They also offer radically different (but not mutually exclusive) ways of describing the transition from the literature of the early seventeenth century to that of the Restoration—as triumph of good taste, or as dissociation of sensibility.

Contents: Norton Topics Online, The Early Seventeenth Century
www.wwnorton.com/nael

Contents: Norton Online Archive, The Early Seventeenth Century
www.wwnorton.com/nael/NOA

Though I Am Young
Pleasure Reconciled to Virtue
Robert Herrick
The Lily in a Crystal
To Blossoms
To the Water Nymphs Drinking at the Fountain
Richard Crashaw
On Our Crucified Lord, Naked and Bloody
Elizabeth Cary
The Tragedy of Mariam, The Fair Queen of Jewry
Henry Vaughan
A Rhapsody
I Walked the Other Day (to Spend My Hour)
John Milton
Samson Agonistes
Henry King
The Exequy
Dorothy Osborne
The Letters of Dorothy Osborne
["Servants"]
[Fighting with Brother John]

Contents: NAEL Audio Companion, The Early Seventeenth Century

CHAPTER 5

The Restoration and the Eighteenth Century 1660–1785

Introducing Restoration Literature

The Restoration differs from most other literary periods in that we can say with near precision when and where it began. In March of 1660, General George Monk turned out the rump of the Long Parliament, which had been sitting, on and off, since 1642. This act, which heralded the now-inevitable return of Charles II, was instantly celebrated in a broadsheet ballad titled *The Second Part of St. George for England*:

> Now the Rump is confounded, there's an end to the Roundhead,
> Who hath been such a bane to our nation.
> He hath now played his part, and's gone out like a fart,
> Together with his 'Reformation'.

A more conciliatory note was struck by the playwright and poet Alexander Brome, in his verses for the entertainment of Monk at Clothworker's Hall:

> We'll eat and we'll drink, we'll dance and we'll sing,
> The Roundheads and Cavs, no more shall be named,
> But all join together to make up the ring,
> And rejoice that the many-headed dragon is tamed.
> 'Tis friendship and love that can save us and arm us,
> And while we all agree, there is nothing can harm us.

These two royalist responses to the events of early 1660 serve as a guide to the two main currents of Restoration literature. On the one hand, we find a vindictive and vulgar triumphalism in the face of Puritanism (extending to a tendency to goad and provoke middle-class moralists of all kinds), and, on the other, a longing for harmony and consensus, for a blending of opposites and a healing of old wounds.

It is not, of course, the case that Restoration literary modes sprung fully formed from the brow of General Monk in the spring of 1660. They have roots that go farther back than that, though not very far, and not exclusively in English soil. The crucial year before 1660 was 1645, when Queen Henrietta Maria left war-torn England for Paris. There, the future Charles II and members of the Court were exposed to new currents in French culture and learned to emulate the French emphasis on elegant simplicity, "correctness," and the avoidance of excess and unruliness in manner and matter. As a consequence, the main current of English literature up to 1660—and the contents of *NAEL*—provide relatively little indication of what was to come. Among the English poets writing in the Interregnum, those who influenced their successors most immediately were not the giants Milton and Marvell but the comparatively minor talents of Edmund Waller, himself one of the Parisian exiles, and Sir John Denham. Whether or not you have previously covered the literature of the early seventeenth century, it is worthwhile directing students to Waller's *The Story of Phoebus and Daphne Applied* (1.1675) for a work that exemplifies Restoration and Augustan literary values (though not the values of stylistic dissidents like William Collins, who saw "Waller's myrtle shades" [1.2836, line 69] casting a long shadow over the eighteenth century).

When introducing Restoration literature proper to your students, we advise you to begin at the beginning, with Dryden's *Annus Mirabilis*. Although the technical subject of the extract from this poem in *NAEL* is the destruction of London by fire in 1666 and the rebuilding of the city, Dryden's comparison of the conflagration to a Cromwell-like "dire usurper" sent "To scourge his country with a lawless sway" (1.2073, lines 849–50) makes the wider relevance apparent. The poem conveys a sense of new beginnings, of a nation starting from scratch but with confidence in its unlimited potential. Like Donne at the dawn of the previous literary period, Dryden chooses the legendary phoenix as the emblem of his age:

> More great than human, now, and more August,
> New deified she from her fires does rise
> Her widening streets on new foundations trust,
> And, opening, into larger parts she flies. (1.2073, lines 1177–80)

In this poem, much more than a bigger, better London is rising on new foundations. Dryden's confidence in England's future greatness at the end of this year of disasters may be nine-tenths bluster, but what is most strikingly new is what he is blustering about: naval power and global trade. The resolutely insular and defensive tone that had marked English patriotism since the Reformation has vanished. One has only to compare the defiant bluster of, say, Shakespeare's *King John*—"Come the four corners of the world in arms / And we shall shock them"—with the openness and confidence of Dryden:

> Now like a Maiden Queen, she will behold,
>   From her high turrets, hourly suitors come:
> The East with incense, and the West with gold,
>   Will stand, like suppliants, to receive her doom.
>
> (1.2074, lines 1185–88)

These lines consciously invoke the memory of Elizabeth, the virgin queen. Yet her modern equivalent is not Charles II, but the mercantile city of London. Even for Dryden, a royalist to the bone, the index of English greatness is not the majesty of its monarch, but the balance of its trade.

The quoted quatrain occurs near the end of a poem of more than twelve hundred lines. It is best to prepare your students from the outset for a simple but unavoidable fact: poetry of the Restoration and eighteenth century is almost invariably long. While the lyric retreated steadily into the background in this period, long descriptive and didactic poems, verse epistles, mock epics, and verse essays came to the fore. Unsurprisingly, the first response of many students to page upon page of close-set verse, often lacking even stanzaic divisions, is to recoil. Yet they will soon realize that there are important compensations. Students generally find narrative and didactic poetry (the sort involving plot, character, and/or a "message") much easier to grasp and talk about than lyric. They will also be pleasantly surprised to find that the poetry of this period, dominated by the balanced, end-stopped rhyming couplet and proceeding in a conversational tone, is easy to follow and easy to like.

In the end, then, the challenge may not lie in getting students to appreciate the poetry of this period, but in getting them to appreciate it *as* poetry and to recognize it as belonging to a time and culture far removed from ours. Paradoxically, the main problem with eighteenth-century language is that it looks so close to our own. This makes it easy to read but also easy to skim through without understanding. Many words did not mean quite the same thing that they do now. For instance, dozens of sentences will be misconstrued by a reader who does not know that *doubt* means "fear" or "worry" and that *still* means "always" rather than "yet" or "now as before." (Thus "I doubt he is still there" would mean "I fear he is always there.") Students should also be encouraged to pay careful attention to the unsurpassed artfulness of eighteenth-century verse—unsurpassed, but too often passed over by the hasty reader. Matthew Arnold's remark that the eighteenth century was an "age of prose" (1.2063) may have been unfair, but it is the case that much of the verse of this period reads as smoothly and easily as prose. Thus Matthew Prior was praised by William Cowper for his ability to "make verse speak the language of prose, without being prosaic—to marshal the words of it in such an order as they might naturally take in falling from the lips of an extemporary speaker" (1.2295). This remarkable achievement in versification, by its very nature, runs the risk that it will be overlooked entirely. It is a central task of the instructor to ensure that students are alive to the artfulness of such verse. One way to accomplish this would be to assign and go over lines 289–393 of Pope's *Essay on Criticism* (1.2515–17), pointing out the ways in which Pope's verse illustrates the principles of style, decorum, and versification that he prescribes. A short written assignment might be to ask students to compare the two earlier drafts of the opening lines of Epistle 2 from *An Essay on Man*, printed under Poems in Process (1.2893–94), with the final version (1.2561) and to discuss the likely stylistic and metrical reasons for the revisions that Pope made.

In the past, the Restoration and eighteenth century have been seen as being dominated by a few great (male, Tory) figures. Thus we are used to speaking of the age of Dryden, the age of Pope and Swift, and the age of Johnson. There is some merit in this approach. This was an era in which the dominant modes of literary production made it possible, as rarely before or since, for a few authors to exert a stylistic influence over other writers. What went for Mary Leapor went for most of her contemporaries: "the author she most admired was Mr. Pope, whom she chiefly endeavored to imitate" (1.2603). Yet as the example of Leapor, the daughter of a gardener, indicates, more people than ever were writing in this period, including small but significant numbers of female, working-class, and nonwhite authors. The period thus presents us with an unprecedented diversity of authorship. By adhering to the strict canons of Augustan style, nontraditional authors in this period gained new access to the literary sphere.

"On New Foundations"

Restoration Modes

Annus Mirabilis epitomizes and sets the tone for one current of Restoration literature. Like Alexander Brome in the verses quoted above, Dryden is resolutely (if not quite convincingly) optimistic: the poet paves over recent defeats and lingering divisions within English society by painting a picture of England's imminent exaltation. But another current of Restoration writing has more in common with the vindictive and gleefully indecent royalist ballad *The Second Part of St. George for England*. Royalist writers who had suffered for their cause (and many more who had not) now took pleasure in courting the vanquished Puritans' fury. Some did so by mercilessly satirizing the foes they had feared and hated; others by conducting a more generalized assault on middle-class morality. A good many playwrights and poets of the period delighted in what is now often called "pushing the envelope." It is their work, as sophisticated as it was outrageous, that is most immediately conjured by the term *Restoration*.

Samuel Butler was at work on his comic satire of the roundheads, *Hudibras*, well before the Restoration. When he published the first part in 1662, he was briefly the toast of a king and court eager to laugh at "that stubborn crew / of errant saints" (1.2161, lines 190–91) who had so recently held sway. Parts of *Hudibras* merely cater to popular prejudices, and the burlesque is both broad and shallow. But often Butler's quotable comic couplets convey serious and powerful insights, as when he describes Presbyterians carrying on "As if religion were intended / For nothing else but to be mended" (1.2161, lines 203–4). Butler can be seen as inaugurating the great age of Augustan satire (see "Satire," p. 113), but also as writing within a tradition of satirical social comment in verse stretching back as far as the *General Prologue* to Chaucer's *Canterbury Tales* (1.215).

Chances are that most of us now teaching with *NAEL* did not encounter poems such as the earl of Rochester's *The Imperfect Enjoyment* (1.2163) and Aphra Behn's *The Disappointment* (1.2167) as part of our undergraduate education. Both deal in explicit (and, in Rochester's case, highly obscene) terms with a sexual encounter broken off as a result of male impotence (also the subject of the later *The Reasons That Induced Dr. Swift . . .* by Lady Mary Wortley Montagu [1.2588]). The response of undergraduates to this material is bound to be varied, and some will feel that it is unsuitable for the classroom. Should you encounter such reactions, you can point out that earlier ages tended to be more frank about such matters. Moral objections were of course raised against the licentiousness of much Restoration poetry and drama. These poems by Rochester and Behn were intended to shock, and they belong to a genre dating back to Ovid's *Amores* (and, in English, at least as far back as Thomas Nashe's *The Choice of Valentines*, written in the 1590s). With these points established, it is possible to focus on the important differences between the two poems. Rochester's sexual imagery is harsh and violent, whereas Behn writes an ironic version of pastoral. Behn emphasizes her empathy with the nymph Cloris ("The nymph's resentments none but I / Can well imagine or condole," 1.2170, lines 131–32), while Rochester's poem is male centered ("Corinna" seems to disappear halfway through the poem, leaving the poet alone with his disobedient penis). On the other hand, both works have interestingly ambiguous titles. If you and your students are sufficiently comfortable with the material, there are grounds here for an interesting debate over which lover experiences "Imperfect Enjoyment" and which "Disappointment."

Behn and Rochester both moved, at different levels, in the cosmopolitan world of the court. Both despised and were only too happy to provoke Puritans, and it is part of the political subtext of their works that anyone who is offended must belong to that category. In fact, however, the libertine values espoused by a small but socially influential clique of literary wits offended many who had no sympathy with Puritanism or the "Good Old Cause." Jeremy Collier, whose *A Short View of the Immorality and Profaneness of the English Stage* attacked Dryden, Wycherley, and Congreve among others, was a High Church clergyman, and no more of a Dissenter than Jonathan Swift. Congreve attempts to tar him with the Puritan brush when, in *The Way of the World*, he has Lady Wishfort point out the books over her chimney: "Quarles and Prynne, and the *Short View of the Stage*, with Bunyan's works to entertain you" (1.2241). He also mocks the increasingly vociferous "Societies for the Reformation of Manners" in the Prologue: "Satire, he thinks, you ought not to expect, / For so reformed a town who dares correct?" (1.2218, lines 31–32). But Congreve was thin skinned and easily stung by criticism, and the complaints of Collier and others eventually contributed to his decision to abandon the stage forever.

Congreve's *The Way of the World* has a good claim to be the best as well as the best-known Restoration comedy. To do justice to the play, however, it needs to be seen as a critique as well as an exemplar of Restoration dramatic values. Indeed, compared to some of his predecessors, Congreve is an outright moralist. He might be speaking to the previous generation of playwrights when he has Mrs. Marwood ironically remark, "Besides you forget, marriage is honorable" (1.2253). *The Way of the World* sparkles with wit, yet it is also sharply critical of those for whom wit appears the highest virtue. Congreve and the reader are simultaneously delighted and repelled by the finely observed Fainall, who wittily argues that it would make him miserable to be rid of his wife: "For having only that one hope, the accomplishment of it of consequence must put an end to all my hopes; and what a wretch is he who must survive his hopes!" (1.2231). An equally subtle and scathing portrait is that of the foolish Witwoud, who has covered up his rustic background and one-time apprenticeship (1.2250) to reinvent himself as an endlessly epigrammatic fop. Witwoud might stand for many in Congreve's original audience—perhaps one reason the play was at first not well received.

In contrast to such would-be-wits, Mirabell and Millamant are genuinely witty characters. Their famous "contract" scene (Act 4, scene 5, 1.2257–59) parodies the financial contracts of arranged marriages, like that in Hogarth's *Marriage-à-la-Mode* (2.2654). But unlike Fainall's jokes about marriage, which express real contempt for his wife, Mirabell's "provisos" and Millamant's feigned horror at them actually express their love and their mutual respect for each other's intelligence and individuality. Like other heroes in Restoration comedy, Mirabell needs to repair his squandered fortunes and must secure Millamant's money as well as her love. It is a distinction of Congreve's play, however, that the hero and heroine transcend the way of their brittle and cynical world to establish a fresh and attractive relationship.

Lady Wishfort's reference to "Bunyan's works to entertain you" may be Congreve's little joke, but the fact is that the best-selling *Pilgrim's Progress* entertained as well as instructed many more people in the Restoration era—and for centuries after—than did *The Way of the World*. The book quickly became a children's classic loved by Maggie Tulliver in

George Eliot's *The Mill on the Floss* and the March sisters in Louisa May Alcott's *Little Women*, many chapter titles of which, as all of Alcott's nineteenth-century readers would have recognized, are taken from Bunyan's allegory. But the work was also the imaginative vehicle of Bunyan's radical and political dissent from the accepted ways of Congreve's world. The historian E. P. Thompson says, "*Pilgrim's Progress* is, with *Rights of Man*, one of the two foundation texts of the English working-class movement." Like *Paradise Lost* and Lucy Hutchinson's *Memoirs, Pilgrim's Progress* reveals the response of a boldly eloquent Puritan to the experience of defeat. The Vanity Fair episode (1.2140) offers a devastating allegorical depiction of English society and its treatment of Dissenters after the Restoration. Though Bunyan writes within the age-old tradition of Christian allegory, he is a keen observer of contemporary England, with its emerging consumer society: "at this fair are all such merchandise sold, as houses, lands, trades, places, honors, preferments, titles, countries, kingdoms, lusts, pleasures, and delights of all sorts, as whores, bawds, wives, husbands, children, masters, servants, lives, blood, bodies, souls, silver, gold, pearls, precious stones, and what not" (1.2141). Yet, like the older Milton, Bunyan found himself less concerned with the reformation of the commonwealth than with the transformation of the human soul. In a hostile society, the individual is often required to seek the path to salvation unaided and alone—Christian stops his ears against the cries of his wife and children and runs on, "crying, Life! life! eternal life!" (1.2138). In the long years of defeat, the Puritan mindset still offered experiences of literary and spiritual intensity far surpassing anything available from Restoration rakes and wits.

Party Politics

The Restoration and the eighteenth century saw the rise of party politics, a legacy still too much with us on both sides of the Atlantic. In no other period have poets engaged with the day-to-day stuff of political life—parliamentary intrigue, ever-changing alliances, rising and falling stars—so consistently and on such an intimate level. It is impossible to follow, much less appreciate, a good deal of Dryden, Swift, Pope, and Johnson without at least a rough knowledge of political history. Nor is it possible to appreciate the shape of their checkered careers for, especially in the first part of the period, writers rose and often fell with their parties or factions. Dryden and Pepys were turned out of office with the coming in of William and Mary in 1688. The Tory Aphra Behn suffered arrest in 1682 for her "abusive reflections" on the Whig hero, the duke of Monmouth. The Whigs Steele and Addison enjoyed patronage and public office except for the wilderness years 1710–14, when the Tories were in power. Matthew Prior, on the other hand, was broken in fortune and suffered a year of house arrest after the Tory government fell in 1714. Congreve and Defoe, more conciliatory or less principled, succeeded in making themselves useful to successive parties and governments. Swift broke with the Whigs over the question of the Test Act to become a brilliant Tory propagandist.

The politics of the Restoration and eighteenth century are unavoidably complex. Fortunately, the *NAEL* introduction to the period provides an excellent and easily graspable overview of political history and can be referred to for guidance on such issues as the Test Act, the Popish Plot, the Exclusion Bill, the Act of Settlement, and so on (1.2046–48). It also provides information on such important figures as Robert Harley (Oxford) and Henry St. John (Bolingbroke), whose flamboyant careers provide matter for repeated reference in the works of Pope, Swift, and Montagu, among others. Given the regularity with which these issues and personalities pop up in the literature of the period, you might consider preparing and distributing a handout with basic definitions (Whig, Tory, Jacobite, Bolingbroke, etc.) for students to keep and refer back to.

The bitter factionalism of this period had its origins in the Civil War. Even the names of the two parties originated as terms of abuse. "Tories" were Irish Catholic outlaws; "Whigs" were Scottish Presbyterian rebels or horse thieves. Only in the 1780s were the parties formally established, and not until the early nineteenth century did they assume the titles of Liberal and Conservative. Some Whigs saw all Tories as crypto-Catholics and closet Jacobites, intriguing to overthrow the Church of England and to restore the House of Stuart; some Tories saw all Whigs as Dissenting advocates of mob rule, eager to abolish traditional hierarchies. To a degree, later historians have also taken sides and influenced views of both parties. In what has come to be known as "the Whig version of history," the Whigs are cast as the party of liberty and progress and the Tories as the party of the status quo or reaction. Southey's *Colloquies on the Progress and Prospects of Society* and Macaulay's review (2.1697) are examples of the Tory and Whig versions, respectively. Yet, more recent interpretations of history credit the Tories with their opposition to slavery and to the laissez-faire economics that put a free market economy above all other political and humanitarian considerations. In spite of the deep divisions between the two parties, during the eighteenth century, both parties still served the interests of propertied Anglican Englishmen, whether that property came from the land or from commerce, and they shared certain ethnic and class prejudices. You can remind students of the latter point when teaching Boswell's account of the famous dinner party at which the staunch Tory Johnson and his political enemy Wilkes bond by exchanging mutual pleasantries at the expense of their host Boswell's Scottish compatriots (1.2776).

Just as most of the major writers in the early seventeenth century were Royalists (Marvell and Milton are notable exceptions), so in this period Tories tend to predominate. This is not to say there were not great talents among the Whigs—Defoe, Congreve, Steele, Addison, and Montagu among them—but with Dryden, Behn, Swift, Pope, Gay, and Johnson in their ranks, the Tories could claim an upper hand in literature that was rarely granted them in the political sphere. Literature also provided a forum for political expression for those who were barred from participation in formal politics—which is to say all women and the vast majority of men, including Dissenters like Bunyan and Defoe and Catholics like Dryden and Pope.

There is no better way to introduce the phenomenon of party politics than through Dryden's *Absalom and Achitophel* (1.2075), which allegorizes the events of 1678–81 that resulted in the abiding division between Whigs and Tories. The *NAEL* introduction to the poem provides the essential background on the Popish Plot and the Exclusion Crisis. Students should also be referred to 2 Samuel 13–18 for the biblical events that form the basis of Dryden's allegory. The poem can be made somewhat easier by focusing on the three main characters, David, Absalom, and Achitophel—and their English counterparts, Charles II, his illegitimate son the duke of Monmouth, and the earl of Shaftesbury—letting students skip lines 569–913.

Absalom and Achitophel is at once a piece of party-political propaganda (brought out to influence events in 1681) and a denunciation of party politics. The central issue, from Dryden's point of view, was the danger that renewed Civil War might overthrow the tenuous social order that had been established by the Restoration and leave the nation at the mercy of intolerant and power-hungry political factions. The poem is full of satiric references to the religious and political strife of the early seventeenth century. Dryden's analogy between the English and the people of ancient Israel works on several levels, one of which is to mock parallels the Puritans had observed between the English and the Israelites—see, for example, Gerrard Winstanley's reference to "the poor enslaved English Israelites" (1.1743). In Dryden's poem, the "Jews" are "a headstrong, moody, murmuring race," never satisfied for long with their leaders, "God's pampered [as opposed to "chosen"] people" (1.2078, lines 45–47). Dryden dismisses the widespread fear of a new Catholic persecution under a Catholic monarch as a trumped-up issue, exploited by unscrupulous politicians.

In Achitophel, Dryden has drawn the portrait of a clever politician without principles, interested only in personal power, "Resolved to ruin or to rule the state" (1.2080, line 174). Achitophel's method is to arouse and to manipulate the prejudices of the majority. To accomplish his ends, he seeks to make the handsome, popular, and weak Absalom his puppet. Whereas Milton had seen kings and bishops as oppressors, Dryden feared the oppression of mob rule under the control of radical politicians like Shaftesbury. Dryden admired Milton as a poet (see his *Epigram on Milton*, 1.2108) but opposed his politics. You can capitalize on the allusions to *Paradise Lost* in *Absalom and Achitophel* (especially in the temptation of Absalom, echoing Satan's temptation of Eve) to compare the political as well as stylistic differences between the two poets. A true conservative,

Dryden believed that order and civil rights were better protected by law and the monarch's paternal sway than by democratic processes. David asserts this philosophy in the speech that closes the poem:

> The law shall still direct my peaceful sway,
> And the same law teach rebels to obey:
> Votes shall no more established power control—
> Such votes as make a part exceed the whole:
> No groundless clamors shall my friends remove,
> Nor crowds have power to punish ere they prove.
> (1.2098, lines 991–96)

Several other central works of this period both require some knowledge of political debates and can be used as a means of introducing important political ideas and themes that will be useful later on. Steele's portraits of the members of the fictional Spectator's Club (1.2484) and Addison's sketches of Sir Roger de Coverley at church (1.2488) and at the assizes (1.2490) introduce types of the Tory and the Whig from a Whig perspective (though it should be acknowledged that the Spectator treats most of his fellow club members with gentle satiric humor, regardless of their politics). Note that the one member of the club who may be said to be gainfully employed ("a person of indefatigable industry," 1.2485) is the wealthy London merchant Sir Andrew Freeport, whose politics are thoroughly Whig. He believes that British interests overseas are better advanced by trade than by war, and his little joke is to call the sea "the British Common" (1.2486). In the eccentric Sir Roger de Coverley, on the other hand, Steele and especially Addison have created a condescendingly affectionate portrait of a Tory country baronet "rather beloved than esteemed" (1.2485). Sir Roger is a bumbling but innocuous representative of the old order that must give way to the new. One way of helping students come to grips with the politics of eighteenth-century literature is to refer back regularly to these characters from *The Spectator*, asking them to imagine how Sir Roger or Sir Andrew would respond to a particular proposition.

A very different perspective on British politics emerges in part 1, chapter 4 of *Gulliver's Travels*, with its description of Lilliputian political controversies that unmistakably mirror those of Swift's divided society. In Lilliput, High Church Tories and Low Church Whigs find their equivalents in high-heeled *Tramecksan* and low-heeled *Slamecksan*: "animosities between these parties run so high, that they will neither eat nor drink, nor talk with each other" (1.2353). There exists a further rift between the ruling (Protestant) Little-Endians and the persecuted (Catholic) Big-Endians, who interpret in different ways the sacred text: "*That all true believers shall break their eggs at the convenient end*" (1.2353). Swift's point here is certainly not that the difference between Whigs and Tories, or Protestants and Catholics, is no more meaningful than the height of your heels or how you eat an egg. He was a Tory propagandist and a High

Churchman who wrote in favor of retaining the Test Act in the great satire *Abolishing of Christianity in England* (1.2321). Moreover, the later chapters of part 1 of *Gulliver's Travels* satirize the Walpole (Flimnap) administration and show sympathy for the Tory lords Oxford and Bolingbroke, hounded like Gulliver with accusations of treason. Swift, in other words, was a confirmed high-heeled Little-Endian. His satire is not aimed at political and religious opinions as such, but at the tendency of parties to become more important—as focuses of loyalty and of enmity, as political machines and ladders of advancement—than the causes they were set up to serve.

The speech and behavior of the criminal class in *The Beggar's Opera* satirize the upper classes in general, but certain characters and scenes were aimed directly at Prime Minister Walpole and his government (1.2606). Yet the commercial success of the *Opera* and the universal popularity of *Gulliver's Travels* show that political satire had become a commodity relished by all parties.

Dryden, Steele, Addison, Swift, Gay, and others employ the classic device of satirizing or denouncing party politics as a means of advancing the interests of their party—a tactic that still finds much favor among American politicians today. Throughout most of this period, party membership remained an accusation to be flung at one's opponents (as members of Congress still accuse one another of being "partisan").

New Worlds

> I saw new worlds beneath the water lie,
> New people, and another sky.
> (Thomas Traherne, *On Leaping over the Moon,* 1.1757, lines 1–2)

If the existence of one "New World" had been revealed to Europeans in 1492, many more were discovered, explored, and invented in the course of the Restoration and the eighteenth century. In an era of exploration culminating in Captain Cook's voyage to New Zealand and Australia in 1768, the blank spaces on the map of the earth became filled with well-defined places, all populated by different societies with different customs. The reading public was eager for accounts of these newly discovered places and peoples. This was in part because they promised opportunities for commercial and imperial expansion, but also because they opened windows on other—and potentially superior—ways of living. In the same era, certain sections of the public were no less fascinated by the scientific discoveries made possible by the microscope and the telescope. Suddenly, every star in the heavens and every drop of water could be looked on as a new world. For the devout, the fruits of geographical and scientific exploration offered further reasons to celebrate God's infinite bounty; for the more speculatively inclined, they provided grounds to question the established values and givens of their own society. (For reactions to scientific discoveries, see Norton Topics Online, "The Plurality of Worlds.")

There is a good case—especially if you seek to cover a wide range of texts in a relatively short time—for organizing your syllabus for this period around the theme of "New Worlds." This syllabus would include representative selections from all the major and many secondary writers in a variety of modes and would draw connections between geographical and scientific exploration. Among the texts devoted to travel are Dryden's *Annus Mirabilis* (1.2073), with its celebration of expanding trade routes; the satirical travel narrative *Gulliver's Travels* (1.2329); Johnson's *The History of Rasselas* (1.2678), with its Utopian Abyssinia and cosmopolitan Cairo; Behn's *Oroonoko* (1.2170), with its idyllic images of Africa and Surinam poisoned by the whites' greed and treachery; and, for a sharp contrast, the final part of Goldsmith's *The Deserted Village*, in which the villagers are forced to emigrate from their once-idyllic England to "new-found worlds" of bestial savagery and "poisonous fields with rank luxuriance crowned" (1.2865, lines 372, 351). In the same syllabus, differing attitudes to the new worlds of science could be represented by Newton's letter on optics (1.2151), the selection from Locke (1.2146), Addison's *On the Scale of Being* (1.2502), Pope's *Essay on Man* (1.2554), and (again) *Gulliver's Travels* and *Rasselas*.

In his important essay *On the Scale of Being*, Addison notes that "The author of *The Plurality of Worlds* draws a very good argument upon consideration for the peopling of every planet" (1.2502). Bernard le Bovier de Fontenelle's *Entretiens sur la pluralité des mondes* (1686) was enduringly popular in this period. Its translators included Aphra Behn (1688) and, later, Frances Burney. In the book, a philosopher explains to an intelligent noblewoman his theory of life on other worlds:

> To conclude, every thing lives, and every thing is animated. That is to say, if you comprehend the animals that are generally known, the living creatures lately discovered, and those that will be discovered hereafter, you will find that the Earth is very well peopled, and that Nature has been so liberal in bestowing them, that she has not been at the pains to discover half of 'em. After this, can you believe that Nature, who has been fruitful to excess as to the Earth, is barren to all the rest of the planets? (Behn's translation)

It is noteworthy and deserving of emphasis that two of the translators, as well as a large proportion of the audience for this and similar works, were women. Throughout the period, and perhaps especially as the relative freedom of the Restoration period gave way to the straitjacket of eighteenth-century feminine respectability, women were drawn to discourses that allowed them to imagine worlds and ways of life very different from their own. *The Female Spectator* encouraged women (of a certain class) to make use of the microscope and telescope. The attractions of other worlds, real or imagined, are apparent in Margaret Cavendish's *The Blazing World*, which concludes with the writer's determination to "reject and despise all the worlds without me, and create a world of my own" (1.1770). Cavendish was also the author of a series of poems on the many worlds to be found in this world, including one on a world in an eare-ring:

> An *Eare-ring round* may well a *Zodiacke* bee,
> Wherein a *Sun* goeth round, and we not see. . . .
> But when the *Ring* is broke, the *World* is done,
> Then *Lovers* they into *Elysium* run.

This poem, with other materials, including part of Behn's translation of Fontenelle's *A Discovery of New Worlds*, is available on Norton Topics Online.

Many male writers also gloried in the plenitude of God's creation but were at the same time concerned to insist on its order and to forestall certain kinds of speculation. As Pope writes in *An Essay on Man,* "Through worlds unnumbered though the God be known, / 'Tis ours to trace him only in our own" (1.2555, lines 21–22). Addison, though he writes with wondering admiration of a universe that teems with every form of life, wants to emphasize that all of these forms are organized on a single scale, stretching from the lowest slime to the deity, with humanity nearer the former than the latter. Many worlds, then, but a single hierarchy. It was in the spirit of Addison and Pope, not Cavendish and Fontenelle, that it was said "there could be only one Newton" for "there was only one world to discover" (1.2150). One of the best-remembered heroic couplets of the eighteenth century is that of Pope, cited under "Nature" in Johnson's *Dictionary*:

> *Nature* and *nature's* laws lay hid in night,
> God said, Let Newton be, and all was light. (1.2724)

Readings from Cavendish, Locke, Newton, Addison, Swift, and Pope shed light on the scientific revolution of the late seventeenth and eighteenth centuries from a variety of angles. Good topics for discussions or assignments include the relevance of gender in scientific discourses, the effect of the new discoveries on faith and religion (see 1.2050–51), the tension between delight in multiplicity and delight in universal order, and the place of wonder. This last topic is particularly important in treating the transition from the eighteenth century to the Romantic period. To Romantic and post-Romantic sensibilities, wonder and science often seem utterly opposed. Thus Blake pours scorn on the vain efforts of science and reason to disenchant the world:

> The Atoms of Democritus
> And Newton's Particles of light
> Are sands upon the Red sea shore,
> Where Israel's tents do shine so bright.
> (*Mock on, Mock on, Voltaire, Rousseau,* 2.84, lines 9–12)

For many of our students, this Romantic view of science is second nature. For Addison and Pope, however, the revelation of a regular order beneath the apparent chaos of observed phenomena was not the end but the beginning of wonder. It requires an effort of imagination—but one that is well worthwhile—to recapture the pious wonder with which readers first greeted Newton's revelation that even colors obeyed divine laws. "A naturalist would scarce expect to see the science of those become mathematical, and yet I dare affirm that there is as much certainty in it as in any other part of the optics" (1.2152).

In much eighteenth-century literature, delight in the revelation of Newtonian physics is combined with hostility to most other kinds of science and scientists. For Pope, the role of science (embodied by Newton) was to demonstrate the operation of a universal order. That having been accomplished, any further research—for instance, by the botanist and butterfly collector who appear before the throne of Dulness in *The Dunciad* (1.2576–77)—was at best redundant, at worst an incitement to: "See Nature in some partial narrow shape, / And let the Author of the whole escape" (1.2577, lines 455–56). Even wonder at the divine order was dangerous if it led human beings "To wonder at their Maker, not to serve" (line 458). Other writers of the period show the same mingled suspicion and contempt for scientific enterprises. For Johnson, it is not the business of the poet—or, he implies, anyone with any sense—to "number the streaks of the tulip" (*Rasselas*, 1.2686). The psychological and spiritual dangers of immersion in scientific study are evident in the fate of the astronomer in *Rasselas*, who comes to imagine that he is personally responsible for the weather (chapters 40–44). In *Idler No. 31* (1.2677), Johnson, under the guise of "Mr. Sober," touchingly satirizes his own interest in chemical experiments as an idle amusement. No one was more scathing than Swift in his satire of science. The Laputans in part 3 of *Gulliver's Travels* are so terrified of destruction by comets or the extinction of the sun that they cannot sleep and so preoccupied by abstruse speculations that they must be struck with a bladder to awaken "the organs of speech and hearing" (1.2415).

Whereas part 3 of *Gulliver's Travels* satirizes scientists, the book as a whole is a satire of travel writing, at once reflecting and mocking the public appetite for tales of distant lands and strange peoples. As Gulliver notes in his concluding remarks on travel writing, such books were typically full of "strange improbable tales" and "the grossest falsities" (1.2470), abusing the trust of the reader. The final chapter calls into question not only the veracity of travelers' tales but their purpose. Is it the role of the travel writer, as Gulliver claims, to serve "the PUBLIC GOOD" (1.2470) by providing examples of virtuous societies? How does this tally with Gulliver's other claim that his work has no implications for British politics (1.2331, 2471)? How seriously are we to take his denunciation of conquest and colonialism? *Gulliver's Travels* still challenges its readers to consider their motives—and the sources of their pleasure—in reading tales of new and different worlds.

Eighteenth-Century Civilization and Its Discontents

Slavery and Freedom

Slave labor and the slave trade played crucial roles in Britain's economic and political expansion in the eighteenth century. Both in the sugar colonies of the West Indies and in the port cities of Bristol and Liverpool, the entire economy rested on the ongoing traffic in slaves, and even many who never set eyes on a plantation or a slave ship owed their fortunes to slavery. The problem of slavery, then, is a central one for eighteenth-century society and for eighteenth-century literature—its relevance is by no means limited to the relatively few texts that deal explicitly with the terrible practice. Slavery is never mentioned in Goldsmith's *The Deserted Village* (1.2858), for instance; but according to one contemporary report, the enclosures that the poem laments were conducted by "a great West Indian"—that is, by a landlord who owed his fortune to slave labor on Caribbean plantations. At the end of that poem, the dispossessed villagers embark for a new life in Georgia, another slave economy. Wherever riches are celebrated in the literature of this period, it is pertinent to inquire into their source; wherever rights and liberties are defended, it is necessary to ask to whom they extend and from whom they are withheld. Slavery should be important to the way we teach not only *Oroonoko* and *The Life of Olaudah Equiano* (1.2813), but also Thomson's *Rule Britannia* (which trumpets "*Britons* never will be slaves"; 1.2825), Montagu's *Epistle from Mrs. Yonge to Her Husband*" (which contrasts the lot of a wronged wife unfavorably with that of a wounded slave; 1.2582, line 22), and Mary Leapor's *An Essay on Woman* (which concludes "Unhappy woman's but a slave at large"; 1.2605, line 60). See also "Slavery and the Slave Trade" among the Norton Topics Online for this period.

Just as *Oroonoko* is not the only text to which slavery is relevant, so slavery is not the only question relevant to *Oroonoko*. Although the central narrative deals with the enslavement of an African prince by the English, Behn's is a story of the meeting and clash of three cultures—the English, the Africans, and the natives of Surinam. (If we count the Dutch, who took Surinam in 1665, and who are blamed for treating the natives "not so civilly as the English" (1.2202), there are four cultures.) The unreliable and greedy Europeans contrast unfavorably both with the highly cultured and sophisticated Africans and with the South Americans, who are represented as noble savages living in prelapsarian innocence, strangers to clothing, cowardice, and deceit (see especially 1.2172–73, 2204–6). Behn's narrator is by no means opposed to slavery or to colonialism, though she does imply that both practices have the potential to debase the European character. What makes Oroonoko's tale a tragedy is that he is a *royal* slave, the social superior of those who abuse him as a racial inferior. His tragic end, and the stoicism with which he faces it, are intended to recall the fate of the royal martyr Charles I.

It was in the later eighteenth century, with the rise of the abolitionist movement, that *Oroonoko* began to be read as an antislavery text. Even then, Hannah More's abolitionist verses register a suspicion of *Oroonoko*'s politics and genre, while turning the book's popularity to polemical account:

> For no fictitious ills these numbers flow,
> But living anguish, and substantial woe;
> No individual griefs my bosom melt,
> For millions feel what Oroonoko felt:
> Fired by no single wrongs, the countless host
> I mourn, by rapine dragg'd from Afric's coast.

(The full poem, along with several other abolitionist works, is included on Norton Topics Online.)

When teaching *Oroonoko* and later writings on and against slavery, be prepared to encounter a measure of confusion and disquiet. Some students at least will try to meld proslavery and antislavery positions onto familiar oppositions between liberals and conservatives or progressives and reactionaries, terms that are not very useful for characterizing the politics of slavery in this period. "Progressive"—or Whiggish—thinkers might favor slavery as good not only for the British economy but for Africans, to whom it brought enlightenment and Christianity. This view was endorsed by some former slaves, including the American poet Phyllis Wheatley. On the other hand, Tory "conservatives" might object to the slave trade in part because its profits created a new social order hostile to the values of the gentry. Support for slavery did not overlap with—indeed, it might clash with—support for imperialism. (Referring back to the Spectator's Club, the Politics of Whigs like Sir Andrew Freeport, who disdains foreign conquests, would not be inconsistent with support of slavery.)

The section "Slavery and Freedom" introduces students to two black British writers who have recently begun to receive much critical attention, Ignatius Sancho and Olaudah Equiano. You may wish to teach Equiano's *Interesting Narrative*, or at least his account of the Middle Passage (1.2813), before or alongside *Oroonoko*, as it provides a factual account of conditions aboard a slave ship to which Behn's imagined version (1.2189–91) may be compared. The two examples of Sancho's letters are interesting not only for their content but for their differences in style. While the letter to Jack Wingrave reveals Sancho's ability to write with cold rhetorical force, in his letter to Sterne he emulates the spontaneity, digressiveness, and exuberance typical of Sterne's sermons and *Tristram Shandy*. Although Sterne, like Sancho, is an abolitionist, his response to the letter reveals an element of condescension. The passage from *Tristram Shandy* dealing with the "poor negro girl" (1.2809) in the shop may strike some of your students as an imperfect response to Sancho's request "to give one half-hour's attention to slavery, as it is at this day practised in our West Indies" (1.2808). A short writing assignment based on the "Slavery and Freedom" section might ask students to consider the grounds on which the various writers—Sancho, Sterne, Johnson, and Equiano—base their opposition to slavery, as well as the rhetorical methods they adopt.

A theme running through much writing on slavery from *Oroonoko* onward is that of uneven historical development. Since the late sixteenth century, writers and artists had pondered the relationship between non-European "savages" and the peoples of European and British antiquity. Thus Behn notes that the ornate incisions on the bodies of the noble Africans "resemble our ancient Picts, that are figured in the chronicles" (1.2196). The slave name of Caesar given to Oroonoko also associates him with European antiquity, though in a different way. The parallel between Africans and ancient Romans was later emphasized by Hannah More: "Capricious fate of man! that very pride / In Afric scourged, in Rome was deified." The abolitionist Richard Savage, in another poem featured on Norton Topics Online, took the opposite tack, associating the enslaved Africans with the barbarian tribes who eventually turned the tables on Rome (Britain): "Revolving empire you and yours may doom, / (Rome all subdu'd, yet Vandals vanquish'd Rome)." Many in this period agreed that the difference between Europeans and Africans was more one of historical development than of racial development (though they might not agree on precisely which historical parallels should be drawn). A line can be drawn from Behn's *Oroonoko* as far forward as the famous passage early in Joseph Conrad's *Heart of Darkness* that imagines the feelings of a Roman soldier on duty in ancient Britain:

> I was thinking of very old times, when the Romans first came here, nineteen hundred years ago—the other day. . . . Land in a swamp, march through the woods, and in some inland post feel the savagery, the utter savagery, had closed round him—all that mysterious life of the wilderness that stirs in the forest, in the jungles, in the hearts of wild men. (2.1960)

Debating Women

The condition of women in the Restoration and the eighteenth century presents a complex picture. On the one hand, this was an era in which women's access to certain kinds of power and freedom grew steadily. In the new market economy (including the book market), women's importance as consumers could not be ignored; women were often seen as arbiters of taste and sometimes of morality, and an elite few played important if unofficial roles in politics. More and more women of all classes wrote, some for coteries and others for the public. On the other hand, the intellectual and sexual freedoms that some women had begun to exercise in the Restoration era soon receded, to be replaced by a regime of propriety.

For women not of the upper classes, life remained the same in many respects throughout the period. The "Deb Willet Affair" described by Samuel Pepys (1.2127)—involving the sexual exploitation of a servant and the deception of a wife by a man possessed of unlimited reserves of self-pity—could have occurred in most of its particulars as easily in 1788 as in 1668. An exploration of women's conditions in this period might begin with this passage from the famous diary. Pepys ensures Willet's sexual compliance through violence, initially economic and ultimately physical. After a final sexual encounter achieved through force in a coach, Pepys "did nevertheless give her the best counsel I could, to have a care of her honor and to fear God and suffer no man para haver to do con her—as yo have done—which she promised" (1.2130). As this passage indicates, Pepys takes care to supplement his economic and physical power over Willet with spurious moral authority and superior linguistic mastery. Neither his servant nor his wife would have been able to understand the Spanish Pepys employed for his descriptions of illicit sexual acts.

Unless you are teaching a course on women's writing, there is no need to teach all of the women writers of this period as a group. They are, after all, a highly diverse set, representing different classes and political perspectives, and their writings are no less various. There are, however, several themes that are important to a number of women in this period, as well as some of the men. The arguments over women's moral, social and literary worth gathered in the section "Debating Women: Arguments in Verse" (1.2584) can be seen as an extension of the medieval and early modern *querelle des femmes*. Contributors to this controversy in the previous century include Aemilia Lanyer (1.1281) and Rachel Speght (1.1556). Never before the eighteenth century, however, had so many women, or women from such a range of class backgrounds, written in defense of their sex. The social chasm dividing Leapor, the gardener's daughter, from Anne Finch, countess of Winchelsea, is arguably as great or greater as that separating men and women of the same class, but it manifests itself in different ways. In teaching this section, it is worth laying stress on the clear differences between the women writers, as well as the ways they all seek to defend their sex against male attacks. Leapor could never have risked the playful images of violent retribution in Finch's *The Answer* (1.2591). Montagu's *The Reasons* (1.2588) speaks volumes about class as well as sexual antagonisms, with its transformation of Celia into the vulgar Betty and its glancing blows at those who seek to rise above their proper station (lines 41–44), not to mention the Irish (line 87).

An equally important debate, which also carries over from the previous period and into the next, is that concerning the institution of marriage. Contributions to the debate in this period include Dryden's Song from *Marriage à la Mode* (1.2075); Mary Astell's *Some Reflections upon Marriage* (1.2281); Daniel Defoe's *Roxana* [*The Cons of Marriage*] (1.2285); the discussion of marital conditions and provisos between Mirabell and Millamant in act 4, scene 5 of *The Way of the World* (1.2259); Montagu's *Epistle from Mrs. Yonge to Her Husband* (1.2582); Act I, scene 8 of Gay's *The Beggar's Opera* (1.2614–16); Hogarth's *Marriage A-la-Mode* (1.2654); Frances Burney's rejection of Mr. Barlow and married life (1.2785); and the marriage debate in chapter 29 of *Rasselas* (1.2699).

What is striking is the extent to which almost all of the contributors agree that contemporary marriage is flawed, though for some the flaw lies in those who enter into it, for others in the institution itself. In general, women writers tend to the latter opinion, men to the former. Perhaps the most rhetorically complex text is *Roxana*, in which a male author puts in the mouth of a female character a series of powerful arguments against marriage, which, she admits to the reader, were made from folly and vanity. But Roxana's real objection to marriage, namely the loss of economic independence it entails for women, is as powerful an argument against the institution as any other.

Montagu's *Epistle from Mrs. Yonge* remained unpublished until 1972. There were limits to what even an aristocratic woman could say in print in the eighteenth century. Similarly, Anne Finch suppressed the *Introduction* to her poems, which complains sadly of the double standard imposed on women writers. Women were expected to shine in social diversions, but "To write, or read, or think, or to enquire, / Would cloud our beauty, and exhaust our time" (1.2292, lines 16–17), lines sadly quoted by Virginia Woolf in recalling Finch's example and the hostility she aroused among her contemporaries (*A Room of One's Own*, 2.2184). Whereas the Wife of Bath and Aemilia Lanyer protested against the injustice of antifeminism as a general attitude, upper-class educated women in the eighteenth century were keenly sensitive to a specific prejudice against and fear of learned and intellectual women. Dr. Johnson's words rousing Frances Burney to attack Mrs. Montagu—"*Down* with her, Burney!—*down* with her!—spare her not! Attack her, fight her" (1.2789 and n. 1)—although he intends them humorously, are a good example of what women intellectuals had to put up with even, perhaps especially, from great men who patronized them.

Aphra Behn and Frances Burney stand like brilliant bookends at either end of the period and will likely be among the first and last writers you cover in this part of the course. To reflect on their lives is to reach backward into the early seventeenth century and forward into the Victorian age. Behn was born around 1640, when Charles I's grip on power still seemed secure. Burney died two centuries later, in 1840, the third year of Victoria's reign. There are some marked similarities between their two careers—both moved among wits and in the sphere of the Court, both made money from writing, both lived abroad, and both were caught up in the political tumults of their time—but it is hard to imagine two more different personalities. The difference between Behn and Burney, in terms of voice, self-presentation, attitudes, and social conduct, is one measure of the distance traveled by women—and English society—over the course of the "long eighteenth century." In the milieu of the Restoration, Behn, in spite of her many social, political, and financial troubles, seems relatively more licensed to speak her mind and write as she pleases. Burney would never have produced a bawdy poem about male impotence like Behn's *The Disappointment* (1.2165) or attempted an epic history of a royal slave like *Oroonoko*. Her sphere is the novel of manners, which depicts the social world of the English upper class under the more strait-laced conditions of the latter half of the eighteenth century. She is a keen observer of pretentiousness, presumption, and vulgarity, which her heroines are expert at squelching. She did not write plays as Behn had, but the dialogue in her books, journal, and letters often reads like a play in which she is the heroine, warily playing her part: rejecting an unwanted suitor; keeping up her end of a conversation with a young woman of whom she disapproves; encountering the mad George III in one of his saner moments.

The Country and the City

The theme of the country and (or versus) the city has an exceptionally long history in literature—the ancient Greek Aesop has a fable of the town mouse and the country mouse. The theme is nevertheless especially pertinent to the period of the Restoration and the eighteenth century. This was the era that witnessed the spectacular growth of a host of English and Scottish cities, including Bristol, Liverpool, Manchester, and Glasgow. The most remarkable changes occurred in the capitals—London's population doubled in the century after the Great Fire of 1666, while Edinburgh's New Town is a triumph of Georgian planning. Ever more dominant as the center of cultural and commercial life, London set the tone for business and for pleasure in Britain's emerging consumer society. In the same period, the face of the countryside, where the vast majority of the population still lived and worked the land, altered radically as well. The changes here came from technological advances, the growth and movements of population, and above all, the enclosure of common lands by acts of Parliament. Piecemeal enclosures had been taking place over centuries, but the modern English landscape—dominated by privately owned fields divided by stone walls and hedges—is largely a product of the second half of the eighteenth century.

Although the theme of the country and the city remains prominent throughout the period, it is possible to point to a gradual shift in emphasis from the capital to the countryside over the course of the Restoration and eighteenth century. A survey would begin, naturally, with Dryden's *Annus Mirabilis* and the Fire of London (also described unforgettably by Pepys). In the early eighteenth century, comic contrasts between life in the dull countryside and life in the vibrant capital provide matter for Congreve, Addison, and Pope. Next, early optimism about the new London begins to give way to a pessimistic view of city life, notable in Swift and Gay. In the latter half of the eighteenth century, attention shifts to the country, with Gray's immortal *Elegy Written in a Country Churchyard* and Goldsmith's and Crabbe's angry descriptions of contemporary rural life.

When Dryden wrote *Annus Mirabilis*, the London that would rise in splendor from the ashes was still little more than a blueprint by Christopher Wren. Many were inclined to interpret the fire, along with the horrific plague that preceded it, as a sign of God's unappeasable anger with

England's decadent capital. Yet, at least as far as the city was concerned, Dryden's confidence proved entirely justified. Just two years after the fire that he recorded so vividly, Samuel Pepys was cheerfully doing business at "the Change" (1.2130)—that is, the Royal Exchange, swiftly rebuilt after the fire as a vast shopping mall, which became the hub of city life. The resurrection of London added greatly to the confidence of its citizens that they were indeed living in a new Augustan age. Just as the emperor Augustus had found Rome brick and left it marble, so Wren and others had triumphantly transformed England's capital. Looking back, Samuel Johnson would say that Dryden, the city's panegyrist, had performed the same feat with English poetry (1.2072).

In the Restoration, the habit originated of referring to London, and its fashionable society, as "the town." Thus in the Prologue to *The Way of the World*, Congreve writes "Poets are bubbles, by the town drawn in" (1.2218, line 11), and later in the play Witwoud tells his brother " 'tis not modish to know relations in town" (1.2250). The use of the term involves a complex, self-mocking irony, by which London is at once comically diminished (not a city but a town) and set on a pedestal ("*the* town"). Town is comically contrasted with country in works like *The Way of the World* (the shallow town fop Witwoud opposed to his "great lubberly brothers" from the country; 1.2250) and Pope's *Epistle to Miss Blount*:

> She went, to plain-work, and to purling brooks,
> Old-fashioned halls, dull aunts, and croaking rooks:
> She went from opera, park, assembly, play,
> To morning walks, and prayers three hours a day.
> (1.2544–45, lines 11–14)

Yet these works, and others like them, ultimately criticize the town as much as or more than the country. Congreve's oversophisticated Witwoud is probably a greater fool than his crude but honest brother, and Pope's epistle ends with the poet "Vexed to be still in town" surrounded by "Streets, chairs, and coxcombs" (lines 49, 48).

These and other works explore the idea that the contrast between city and country, while striking on the surface, conceals deeper affinities. In his description of Sir Roger at church, Addison begins by suggesting that country folk are but one remove from "savages and barbarians," but then observes that "a country fellow distinguishes himself as much in the churchyard as a citizen does upon the 'Change" (1.2488). Gray's *Elegy* also plays with such condescending comparisons—"Some village Hampden, that with dauntless breast / The little tyrant of his fields withstood" (1.2831, lines 57–58)—while emphasizing how rural poverty circumscribes human potential. Like Congreve, Pope, and Addison, Gray warns the privileged reader against wearing a too-easy "disdainful smile," for death is the equal lot of peasant and potentate, and "The paths of glory lead but to the grave" (lines 31, 36).

As you teach these works, encourage students to examine and express their own feelings and preconceptions about urban and rural life. As with so much else, our modern notions of the countryside are heavily tinged with Romanticism. Yet Pope's antipathy to stultifying country life still resonates for some, and when it comes to the city, both positive and negative ideas about urban environments have strong roots in the Augustan period. While some writers celebrated the splendor and variety of eighteenth-century London (as Johnson declared, "When a man is tired of London, he is tired of life"), others came to regard the city as a sink of moral and physical corruption. For Goldsmith, the city was the place "To see ten thousand baneful arts combined / To pamper luxury, and thin mankind" (*The Deserted Village*, 1.2864, lines 311–12). Gay, who had honed his satirical skills in the mock georgic *Trivia, or the Art of Walking the Streets of London*, put London's seedy underworld on stage in *The Beggar's Opera* (described by Swift as a "Newgate pastoral"). Finally, Swift's deservedly famous *Description of a City Shower* shows us all the filth the city breeds, following the course of "dung, guts, and blood, / Drowned puppies, stinking sprats, all drenched in mud, / Dead cats, and turnip tops" through London's foul open sewers (1.2301, lines 61–63). The reader is not encouraged to suppose that the city is in any way purified by the rain. (Like Travis Bickle in the movie *Taxi Driver*, Swift can at best hope that "Some day a real rain will come and wash all the scum off the streets.") For texts and images portraying the city, view "A Day in Eighteenth-Century London," Norton Topics Online.

In the latter half of the eighteenth century (the period that saw more than two thousand separate acts of parliamentary enclosure), the focus of many writers shifted to the British countryside. Few works can be paired so effectively in a course as Goldsmith's *The Deserted Village* (1.2858) and Crabbe's *The Village* (1.2867). These works can challenge students to think more deeply about the politics of poetry and the ways in which a poem can make a statement. The two poems are sharply opposed to one another, yet they do not take opposite "sides"—both are written in anger at the dispossession and impoverishment of country people, chiefly by enclosure.

Goldsmith's method is to present an ideal image of rural life and then to lament its destruction by greedy landowners. Although Goldsmith sentimentalizes the "rural mirth and manners" of ancient village life—a literary view with political implications that goes all the way back to Chaucer's Yeoman, Plowman, and Parson—the elimination of the small family farm, resulting in emigration to the cities and to the New World, was part of the prelude to the industrial revolution. Like many of his contemporaries, Goldsmith blamed these changing conditions on the corruption of wealth:

> But times are altered; Trade's unfeeling train
> Usurp the land and disposses the swain;
> Along the lawn, where scattered hamlets rose,
> Unwieldy wealth, and cumbrous pomp repose. (lines 63–66)

Crabbe's poem is a reply to Goldsmith's and in some places a direct rebuke, as when he quotes and mocks the description of the village preacher as "passing rich with forty pounds a year" (line 303 in Crabbe, line 142 in Goldsmith). With its picture of a rural life that has always been and grows ever more ugly and painful, *The Village* denies its readers the pleasurable solace of nostalgia. It concludes with a funeral ceremony, that is itself inconclusive (the "busy priest" never arrives), and this absence of closure leaves the reader unsettled, and potentially angry. Crabbe, then, is more effective than Goldsmith in stirring a desire for action and redress in the reader's breast. But what sort of action is desirable, or even possible? A heavy air of fatalism hangs over *The Village*, and while Crabbe complains that "The wealth around them makes them doubly poor" (line 139), he avoids naming the direct connection between the gentry's wealth and the laborers' poverty. In the end, the reader is able to wish for nothing more radical than the provision of better doctors and better ministers than those who so absymally fail Crabbe's aged pauper.

Both *The Deserted Village* and *The Village* are written for readers of the classes that profited, directly or indirectly, from enclosure. Goldsmith addresses himself to "Ye friends to truth, ye statesmen" (line 265), whereas Crabbe mockingly interrogates the pampered, self-indulgent city folk who would make up the bulk of his audience (lines 250–61). Neither poet draws the radical implication that the dispossessed villagers might rise against their oppressors any more than Gray conceives that one of the villagers buried in the country churchyard might actually have become a Hampden or a Cromwell. Nevertheless, the working-class movement was already under way during the latter part of the eighteenth century and would find voices in Blake, Burns, Paine, Wollstonecraft, and Shelley. Shelley's *Song: "Men of England,"* which may be heard on the Audio Companion, became the hymn of the British Labor Movement:

> Men of England, wherefore plough
> For the lords who lay ye low?
> Wherefore weave with toil and care
> The rich robes your tyrants wear? (2.727)

Augustan Modes

Satire

Literary satire is hardly exclusive to the early eighteenth century, but it reached some of its greatest heights in this period and is the age's dominant mode. Although the term designates a distinctive genre derived from the satires and epistles of the Roman poets Horace and Juvenal, it can be defined rather more broadly. The object of satire is to expose; to ridicule; and, by attacking, to correct ignorance, folly, vices, and abuses. Satire could be blunt and vicious, but Restoration and eighteenth-century satirists tended to prefer a subtler and stealthier mode. As Dryden says in his *Discourse Concerning the Original and Progress of Satire*, "there is . . . a vast difference betwixt the slovenly butchering of a man, and the fineness of a stroke that separates the head from the body, and leaves it standing in its place" (1.2121).

Satire often speaks tongue in cheek, professing to admire and advocate the very things toward which the audience is meant to react critically. And just as Swift's *A Modest Proposal* was misconstrued by some of its original readers as seriously endorsing infanticide and cannibalism, so eighteenth-century satire can prove confusing and frustrating to our students today. The natural tendency of students is to read literally, and many have never been trained to respond to wit or irony. Moreover, contemporary American culture provides few obvious examples of the mode (except for the ever-popular "spoof"). Although you must expect to meet with a measure of incomprehension, it is probably best not to "explain" too much at the beginning. (To explain a joke is usually to spoil it.) As they read works like *A Modest Proposal,* students will begin to get it on their own. Those who do so first will probably be better equipped than you are to enlighten their peers by reference to contemporary popular culture.

Roman satire was revived in the Renaissance along with other classical forms (for background, see Donne's *Satire* 3, 1.1257). Poems written in imitation of Horace or Juvenal employ direct discourse instead of fiction: the poet or a persona closely resembling the poet comments, either directly to the reader or in a letter to a friend, on whatever is found absurd or corrupt. The stance of the Horatian satirist is that of a sophisticated and worldly spectator who ironically surveys the vanities and follies of the time. The Juvenalian satirist, by contrast, is an angry moralist. Johnson's *Vanity of Human Wishes* is loosely based on Juvenal's *Satire 10* and holds up as examples famous men and women whose lives and ambitions ended in disgrace, imprisonment, madness, and violent death. Yet these careers are not so much satirical prototypes of human vice and folly as they are typical instances of the tragic outcomes of all human desire and striving. Even the virtuous and innocent are victimized by "Misfortune" (lines 291–310). Only religion offers sure basis for hope or true comfort against fear. Johnson was not by temperament an angry satirist like Juvenal, Swift, or Pope. He was far too critical of his own ambitions and weaknesses so as not to feel a kinship with the faults of others. Pope, on the other hand, always looked back to Horace, though the satirical mode of which he was the indisputed master is better termed "Augustan." The *Epistle to Dr. Arbuthnot* is both a satire and a vindication of the author and his mercilessly personal method of satire. Pope thought himself engaged in a moral warfare in which no quarter could be given, no retreat into bland generalities admitted.

Pope was also one of the masters of the mock-heroic, another form of Augustan satire. Early examples of this mode are Butler's *Hudibras*, a caustic burlesque of the Puritan revolutionaries, and Dryden's *MacFleck-*

noe, a mock-epic sendup of a literary and political antagonist. The characters are drawn more delicately in Pope's *The Rape of the Lock*, the textbook example of the mock-heroic genre and style. The ingenious adaptations of epic motifs include Belinda's dressing-table ritual (the traditional "arming" scene), the card game (the battle), the Cave of Spleen (the descent to the underworld), and the metamorphosis of the lock into a constellation. Yet while all these devices satirize the heroine and her social milieu, Belinda and her world are made astonishingly concrete, alive, and for all their petty vanities, highly attractive.

Swift was a major prose stylist, and he turned prose into a powerful medium of satire. In satires such as *A Modest Proposal*, he adopts the persona of a "projector," a man who presents himself as enlightened, reasonable, progressive, and civic-minded, and who argues rationally and ingeniously for projects that are obviously insane. The narrator of *A Tale of a Tub*, who has discovered that madness is caused by frustrated sexuality rising as vapors to the brain, demonstrates that delusions and madness are essential to our survival; that the lunatics in Bedlam are unfortunate victims of having been in the wrong place at the wrong time and, if set free, would make excellent soldiers, businessmen, lawyers, and scientists (1.2319). Only gradually does it dawn on the reader that Swift's point is that the enlightened, reasonable, and progressive leaders of society are really as crazy as these narrators.

The satire of *Gulliver's Travels* is somewhat more complex. The descriptions of Lilliput, Brobdingnag, and Laputa satirize different aspects of eighteenth-century English society—its politics, its wars, its new science. But increasingly the satire also focuses on the human animal. Physically, the Lilliputians appear charming and delicate—like toys—to Gulliver, and he seems repulsive to them. Only gradually does he come to see their pride, pettiness, and meanness. In Brobdingnag these conditions are exactly reversed, and Gulliver's own pride and nastiness emerge in his offer to make gunpowder for the king. Harder questions are raised by the great and controversial fourth book. Here, for once, Swift's point of view is not entirely clear. Are the purely rational Houyhnhnms really ideal beings, or are we right to be horrified by the proposal that the Yahoos be exterminated by means of sterilization (1.2458–59)? Did Swift, to some degree, share Gulliver's misanthropy, or is Gulliver's rejection of his Yahoo identity and his wish to pass for a Houyhnhnm the ultimate insanity of pride?

Criticism

Many instructors will be teaching the Restoration and eighteenth century at the end of the semester or term, when final papers are coming due. If yours is an introductory survey course, many of your students may be largely or wholly unfamiliar with what is expected of them in a college-level critical paper. It's fortunate, then, that the Augustan age was an era of great critics, witnessing the birth of literary criticism in a recognizably modern form. There is a good case for throwing chronology to the winds and teaching the critical writings of Dryden, Addison, Pope, and Johnson together as a unit, around the time final paper assignments are handed out. Though none of these writers can or should be taken as exemplars for slavish imitation, each excels at one or more of the critical skills that we strive to pass on to our students. Thus Dryden, in *An Essay of Dramatic Poesy* and *The Author's Apology for Heroic Poetry*, provides a model of a close attention to imagery and word choice. Addison in his essay on true, false, and mixed wit applies his considerable acumen to an aspect of language that students find it notoriously difficult to analyze. And Johnson is not only among the most eloquent and searching of critics but, in his even-handed judgments of Shakespeare and Milton, one of the fairest.

Of course, even as you demonstrate what can still be learned from these critics, you will want to place them in their historical context, for they provide powerful insights into Restoration and eighteenth-century social values. Dryden's criticism cannot be appreciated without recognizing the patriotic prejudices that drive him on. His purpose in *An Essay of Dramatic Poesy* is "chiefly to vindicate the honor of our English writers from the censure of those who unjustly prefer the French before them" (1.2114, n. 1). Thus, for Dryden, Ben Jonson's crowning achievement is to have "laid down . . . as many and profitable rules for perfecting the stage, as any wherewith the French can furnish us" (1.2118).

It is a commonplace of eighteenth-century criticism that art should be mimetic, that is, in the parlance of the age, it should "follow nature." "Chaucer followed Nature everywhere, but was never so bold to go beyond her," Dryden wrote in his *Preface to Fables Ancient and Modern* (1.2121). Addison, following his French models, declared himself convinced that "it is impossible for any thought to be beautiful which is not just, and has not its foundation in the nature of things" (1.2497). Pope's *Essay on Criticism* is in large part an essay on truth to nature: "Those rules of old discovered, not devised, / Are Nature still, but Nature methodized" (1.2511, lines 88–89). "Nature and Homer," he declares a little farther on, are "the same" (line 135).

Johnson expresses the same principle with the qualification (implicit in most of the others) that art should imitate not the unique elements of a particular specimen of nature but the universal qualities of its kind. As Imlac famously puts it in *Rasselas*: "The business of a poet . . . is to examine, not the individual, but the species; to remark general properties and large appearances; he does not number the streaks of the tulip" (1.2686); or Johnson himself in *The Preface to Shakespeare*: "Nothing can please many, and please long, but just representations of general nature" (1.2727). The same principle accounts for Johnson's objections to the school he dubbed "the metaphysical poets": "If the father of criticism [Aristotle] has rightly denominated poetry *tekhne mimetike, an imitative art*, these writers will without great wrong lose their right to the name of poets, for they cannot be said to have imitated anything: they neither copied nature nor life" (1.2736). That is also the theoretical ground for

Johnson's famous attack on *Lycidas*: "In this poem there is no nature, for there is no truth; there is no art, for there is nothing new. Its form is that of a pastoral, easy, vulgar, and therefore disgusting" (1.2738). Johnson's judgment may also have been influenced by Milton's attack in *Lycidas* on the Anglican clergy and by a plethora of trite pastoral poetry produced in the eighteenth century. Many of your students will probably agree with Johnson that "Passion plucks no berries from the myrtle and ivy, nor calls upon Arethuse and Mincius, nor tells of 'rough satyrs and fauns with cloven heel.'"

Johnson's own career illustrates the rise in the eighteenth century of the author/journalist/critic/scholar as a man of letters who could support himself by his writings. The *Dictionary*, his edition of Shakespeare, and his *Lives of the Poets* stand as landmarks in an age in which literary criticism and theory became instruments for creating and educating the literary appetite and taste of an ever-expanding public.

Contents: Norton Topics Online, The Restoration and the Eighteenth Century www.wwnorton.com/nael

The Telescope
Galileo, drawings of the phases of the Moon
James Thomson, *from* Autumn
Scales of Values
Blaise Pascal, *from* Pensees
Margaret Cavendish, A World in an Eare-Ring
Popularizing Science
Bernard le Bovier de Fontanelle, *from* Coversations on the Plurality of Worlds
Letter to the Female Spectator
Reactions to the New Philosophy
Joseph Addison, The Plurality of Worlds and The Spacious Firmament
Christiaan Huygens, *from* Cosmotheoros
Stephen Duck, On Mites
The Expanding Universe
The Solar System: Pictures of the Orrery
The Milky Way: Thomas Wright, *from* An Original Theory . . . of the Universe
Laurence Sterne, A Dream
J. J. Granville, The Juggler of Worlds
Explorations
Web Resources

SLAVERY AND THE SLAVE TRADE IN BRITAIN
South Sea Company
The Middle Passage
John Newton, *from* Thoughts Upon the African Slave Trade
Captain William Snelgrave, *from* a New Account . . . of the Slave Trade
British Views of Liberty
John Locke, *from* The First and Second Treatises of Government
William Blackstone, *from* Commentaries on the Laws of England
Phillis Wheatley, On Being Brought from Africa to America
Abolitionist Poets
Richard Savage, *from* Of Public Spirit in Regard to Public Works
Hannah More, *from* Slavery, a Poem
William Cowper, The Negro's Complaint
Hester Piozzi, extract of a letter
William Blake, *from* The Little Black Boy
Explorations
Web Resources

Contents: Norton Online Archive, The Restoration and the Eighteenth Century www.wwnorton.com/nael/NOA

Contents: NAEL Audio Companion, The Restoration and the Eighteenth Century

CHAPTER 6

The Romantic Period 1785–1830

Introducing the Romantics

It is always tempting to begin the Romantics section with the *Lyrical Ballads* and then work forward and backward from William Wordsworth's 1802 Preface. When Wordsworth breaks so decisively with the neoclassical poetic theory that dominated the eighteenth century, it gives the students the reassuring sense that the last section of the survey has been left behind and that the new section can be organized around certain concrete precepts: for instance, poetry should depict "incidents and situations from common life"; it should do so in "ordinary" rather than figurative language; a poem should give the impression of "the spontaneous overflow of powerful feelings" (2.241–42).

It is also tempting to begin with *Lyrical Ballads* because so many of us now teaching from *NAEL* learned as students that the Romantic era was dominated by five great (male) poets: Wordsworth, Samuel Taylor Coleridge, Lord Byron, Percy Bysshe Shelley, and John Keats. (William Blake might be included as an eccentric sixth figure.) However, recent scholarship has challenged this limiting view of Romanticism by emphasizing the extraordinary diversity of Romantic prose and poetry. The Seventh Edition of *NAEL*, in turn, contains an extraordinary range of Romantic voices, including a number of woman authors whose nineteenth-century fame equaled or eclipsed that of their male peers. Thus we recommend that you begin teaching the Romantics by emphasizing the heterogeneous nature of Romantic literature written in the 1780s and 1790s.

Blending canonical and noncanonical figures may be more of a challenge for the instructor than the students, because the instructor may be encountering women poets like Charlotte Smith and Mary Robinson for the first time. But some of your students may begin the course unable to name a single Romantic text or even author. The disadvantages of this are obvious, but the unexpected bonus is that your students will not be surprised when you ask them to contrast Smith's sonnets with Wordsworth's or Robinson's *Haunted Beach* with Coleridge's *Rime of the Ancient Mariner*: they will approach the material without preconceived notions of which authors are worth studying and which texts are prototypically Romantic.

Romanticism's break with the eighteenth century, of course, was not so decisive as a reading of Wordsworth's Preface alone would lead us to believe, and if you are teaching the Romantics as part of an ongoing survey, it will be useful to emphasize continuities as well as differences. If not, you will still need to contextualize these writers who are so self-consciously engaging and resisting literary, philosophical, and political traditions of earlier decades. In *January, 1795*, for example, Robinson uses the iambic tetrameter couplets favored by Jonathan Swift and the iterative mode of caustic observation found in such Juvenalian satires as Samuel Johnson's *Vanity of Human Wishes*. When Anna Letitia Barbauld invokes a "domestic Muse" who will "sing the dreaded Washing-Day" (*Washing-Day*, 2.29, lines 3, 8), her mock-heroic style is clearly indebted to Alexander Pope and John Dryden. (Later works, like Byron's satire *Don Juan* and Keats's *Lamia*, were influenced by neoclassical models as well.) Joanna Baillie's *Winter's Day* seems to strike a balance between Oliver Goldsmith's idealized picture of village life and George Crabbe's more realistic one. Smith's melancholic sonnets, particularly *Written in the Church-Yard at Middleton in Sussex*, can be read against such productions of the "graveyard poets" as Thomas Gray's *Elegy Written in a Country Churchyard*. William Cowper's *The Castaway* and Robert Burns's *To a Mouse*, however dissimilar in tone, can be compared as poems of sensibility, both exploring the dynamics of sympathetic identification—as Cowper puts it, "misery still delights to trace / Its semblance in another's case" (1.2881, lines 59–60). (And because Cowper's poem appears in the first volume of *NAEL* but postdates Burns's in the second, the pairing can inspire an interesting discussion about periodization.) Norton Topics Online provides a rich archive of material to help you contextualize Dorothy Wordsworth's journal entries, William Wordsworth's *Lines Composed a Few Miles above Tintern Abbey*, Coleridge's *Frost at Midnight*, and Percy Shelley's *Mont Blanc* within a number of late-eighteenth-century discourses on nature, including writings on tourism, theories of the sublime, and landscape painting.

These last-mentioned poems are instances of what is often considered the "typical" Romantic lyric: where the speaking "I" is indistinguishable from the poet, where the occasion of the poem is the poet's intensive interaction with the natural world, where the poem nonetheless may focus less on the natural world itself than on the poet's own mental processes as these are inspired by nature. (See the "Introduction" to the Romantic Period, 2.7–8, for further discussion.) And while this "typical" lyric certainly is prevalent across the Romantic period, and one can interestingly trace its development in the earlier Romantic texts (particularly if one begins with Barbauld's 1773 *A Summer Evening's Meditation*), these selections experiment quite variously with voice, subject matter, and style. For instance, many texts are far more interested in the observation and description of the external referent than in the detailing of poetic subjectivity. In Robinson's *London's Summer Morning* (2.92), no speaking "I" is in evidence: the poem begins by asking "Who has not wak'd" (line 1) to the pleasing cacophony of London street life on a hot summer's morning and goes on to describe in rich detail the noise and splendid chaos of the busy city. The "poor poet" appears only briefly and in the third person, as if her own voice had been overpowered by the "din of hackney-coaches, . . . Knife-grinders, coopers, squeaking cork-cutters, . . . and the hunger-giving cries / Of vegetable venders" (lines 10–14). Other texts—Blake's dramatic monologues and persona poems in *Songs of Innocence* and *Songs of Experience*, several of Wordsworth's contributions to *Lyrical Ballads*—explore the workings of subjectivities quite distinct from the poet's. Indeed, Blake continually plays with voice and reminds the reader that he is doing so, writing as various prophet-personae (demonic and otherwise) like "the voice of the Bard" (*Introduction*, 2.49, line 1), "The Voice of the Devil" (*The Marriage of Heaven and Hell*, 2.74), and "The Voice of one crying in the Wilderness" (*All Religions Are One*, 2.41). Smith's sonnets, wherein the speaking and poetic "I" do merge, are often intensely self-regarding, but what they describe is a longing for the dissolution of subjectivity—Smith's speaker looks upon the bones of the "village dead," torn from their graves and commingled with "shells and sea-weed" (*Written in the Church-Yard*, 2.34, lines 7, 9), or upon the lunatic stalking the headland, "uncursed with reason" and self-consciousness (*On Being Cautioned against Walking on an Headland*, 2.35, line 13), and feels only envy. And adaptations of multiply-authored songs and ballads (Burns's *Green grow the rashes*, Baillie's *Song: Woo'd and married and a'*), or new works undertaken in these traditional forms, allow the author to experiment with effacing or perhaps masking an individual poetic voice and striving for the effect of an anonymous or collective one. (The *NAEL* Audio Companion features a reading of Burns's *Green grow the rashes* and Baillie's *Woo'd and married and a'*.)

Romantic Radicalism

The French Revolution and the "Spirit of the Age"

Literary history has not always credited the extent to which Romantic writers were engaged in the political movements of their day, and those critics who have charted the symbiotic relations between Romantic authorship and the contemporary political sphere have not always approved. For the Victorian Matthew Arnold, Romantic literature was not great literature because its practitioners produced "poetical works conceived in the spirit of the passing time, and which partake of its transitoriness" (*Preface to Poems*, 2.1512). While the French Revolution was perhaps "the most animating event in history" admitted Arnold a bit grudgingly in *The Function of Criticism at the Present Time* (2.1519), it inspired intellectual and literary movements that were "political" and "practical" rather than "disinterestedly intellectual and spiritual" (2.1518).

From the perspective of most Romantic writers, however, the French Revolution promised both practical and political changes and the transformation of "intellectual and spiritual" and imaginative life as well. "Bliss was it in that dawn to be alive, / But to be young was very Heaven!" wrote William Wordsworth in *The Prelude* (2.360, lines 108–9), remembering the first flush of enthusiasm that followed the early days of the Revolution and his belief that "Reason," turned "Enchantress," would soon transfigure "the whole earth" (2.360, lines 113–17). In his *Defence of Poetry*, Percy Shelley argued that "the literature of England . . . has arisen as it were from a new birth" (2.802), and that this renaissance was the result of literature's engagement in the thrilling affairs of the world, not Arnoldian disinterestedness:

> It is impossible to read the compositions of the most celebrated writers of the present day without being startled with the electric life which burns within their words. They measure the circumference and sound the depths of human nature with a comprehensive and all-penetrating spirit, and they are themselves perhaps the most sincerely astonished at its manifestations, for it is less their spirit than the spirit of the age. (2.802)

And these writers who burned with "electric life" were in turn to impress their visions on the world and effect further transformation. "The most unfailing herald, companion, and follower of the awakening of a great people to work a beneficial change in opinion or institution, is Poetry. . . . Poets are the unacknowledged legislators of the World" (2.802).

The special section "The French Revolution and the 'Spirit of the Age' " demonstrates how enthusiastically Romantic thinkers were involved in political debate, struggling to realize such abstractions as liberty, justice, and equality in concrete social terms. It can be difficult for students to grasp the import of cataclysmic events for a historically distant people, so you may wish to underscore what's already emphasized in the introduction to the section (2.117), the extent to which the French Revolution transfixed the Romantic imagination. Beginning with the group of prose selections concerned with the English controversy about the Revolution, ask your students to speculate about why the French Revolution appeared so disastrous to some and so thrilling to others—how it could be seen to presage both the downfall of Western civilization and the dawning of an era of justice and equality. What traditional ideas, institutions, and social orders seemed likely to be overthrown as a result of the French Revolution, and what new ones threatened or promised to take their places? Ask your students to attend carefully to the rhetoric and argumentative strategies of each author. (If your students have read the slavery selections in volume 1 of *NAEL*, ask them to compare the rhetoric and argumentative strategies of those pieces.) When do the authors appeal to readerly sensibility (and what emotions are being played upon), and when do they deploy the language of rationality? How can the modern reader differentiate between a conservative argument, a moderate argument, and a radical argument?

At the end of his selection, Richard Price writes enthusiastically of the "glorious" revolutions in France and America and the "ardour for liberty catching and spreading" across Europe (2.121), but he begins by celebrating England's "bloodless" revolution of 1688 (2.119). Revolution, he seems to reassure his readers, is quintessentially English, and thus the support of revolution is almost a patriotic duty, particularly because that earlier English revolution did not ensure religious freedom or equality of representation. Edmund Burke also alludes to 1688, but not as a revolution: he instead emphasizes the stability and continuity of English law and English "privileges, franchises, and liberties" (*Reflections on the Revolution in France*, 2.122), and argues that necessary change can and should be effected gradually, not through social upheaval. Burke undermines such concepts, beloved of revolutionary sympathizers, as the "spirit of innovation" and "the spirit of freedom"—one is "generally the result of a selfish temper and confined views," and the other is prone "to misrule and excess" (2.122–23)—and offers in their stead "the spirit of a gentleman" and "the spirit of religion" (2.127). Burke rivets his reader's attention with his sensational account of the tribulations of the king and queen of France, and at the same time appeals to his reader's sentimentality and a sense of "chivalry." He works openly on the fears of his upper-class readers by warning that European civilization is soon to be "trodden down under the hoofs of a swinish multitude" (2.127).

Mary Wollstonecraft and Thomas Paine both object to Burke's appeal to tradition and inherited rights, and both ground their responses in rationalist principles. Because men are "rational creatures," Wollstonecraft argues, they inherit their "natural rights" at birth from God, not from their forefathers (*A Vindication of the Rights of Men*, 2.131). She demonstrates just how pernicious long-standing tradition can be: if one takes Burke's argument to its logical conclusion, one must argue that slavery should not be abolished because it is a social custom sanctified by long usage. For Paine the corruption of the French government was so ingrained and so widespread that its overthrow through violent revolution can be seen only as a "rational" action (*Rights of Men*, 2.136). Each attacks the style of Burke's argumentation—Wollstonecraft accuses him of inconsistency, illogic, and a love of "slavish paradoxes" (2.130); Paine denounces Burke's theatricality, sentimentality, and "spouting rant" (2.137)—as well as his content. Yet each is capable of rhetorical excesses of her or his own, as when Wollstonecraft terms the European gentleman "an artificial monster" (2.131) and when Paine describes the French government as an "augean stable of parasites and plunderers" (2.135).

The second set of readings on the French Revolution (2.137) shows how, among other things, Romantic writers might appropriate biblical discourse on apocalypse for secular ends: the millennium would be brought about by human rather than divine agency and would fulfill the twin promises of the seemingly incompatible eighteenth-century doctrines of rationalism and sensibility by achieving both universal justice and universal amity. When teaching these readings, you may wish to consult the Explorations questions and other materials found on Norton Topics Online under the heading "The French Revolution: Apocalyptic Expectations." If you are pressed for time, you may decide to substitute *The Marriage of Heaven and Hell* for the Blake selections in "Apocalyptic Expectations" so that your students can read in its entirety one of Blake's longer works. *Marriage* responds directly to the French and American Revolutions, particularly in *A Song of Liberty* ("France, rend down thy dungeon," 2.83), but is perhaps more important in this context for its celebration of revolutionary energy, its thorough rejection of religious and other ideological orthodoxies that constrict human potential, and Blake's willingness to accept contradiction and ambiguity in the place of intellectual certainty. *The Marriage of Heaven and Hell* is probably the most teachable of Blake's longer works, wherein newcomers to Blake will find his cryptic pronouncements accessible enough to reward close reading.

The Rights of Women

Wollstonecraft would deploy similar arguments to those she used in *Rights of Men*—that all humans are *by nature* rational beings, that society should not constrain any individual's pursuit of reason and virtue, that the most long-standing social traditions may be the most tyrannical ones—a year later in *A Vindication of the Rights of Woman*. The social orthodoxy Wollstonecraft challenged was the belief that women were less rational and more emotional than men, possessing a weaker ethical sense but greater sensibility. Thus women were designed (by Nature, by God) not for work in the public sphere but for domestic duties: raising children, managing a household, providing emotional support to their menfolk. The selections from *Vindication* included in *NAEL* especially demonstrate Wollstonecraft's claim that women's subjugation results not from their native inferiority, but from social convention and faulty education. And whereas sentiment and sensibility could be important tools for eighteenth- and nineteenth-century radicals (men as well as women), who would argue that sympathetic identification of the empowered with the disempowered proved the basic humanity of women, slaves, the laboring classes, and other marginals, Wollstonecraft rejects them wholesale here. Women appear to be irrational creatures because they are trained *only* in sensibility, she argues. "Novels, music, poetry, and gallantry, all tend to make women the creatures of sensation, and their character is thus formed in the mould of folly" (2.186).

Even if you don't assign the selections from *Rights of Woman*, you should ask your students to read the headnote to Wollstonecraft's writings (2.163) to get a sense of British women's legal and social standing at the turn of the century and to understand the extent to which women lacked basic political rights and opportunities for meaningful or well-paid employment. The English jurist Sir William Blackstone wrote in 1756 that

> the husband and wife are one person in law: that is, the very being or legal existence of the woman is suspended during the marriage, or at least is incorporated and consolidated into that of the husband: under whose wing, protection, and *cover*, she performs every thing; . . . and her condition during her marriage is called her *coverture*.

Coverture meant that women's bodies, earned and inherited monies and possessions, and children belonged by law to their husbands; nor was a married woman allowed to carry on legal or business matters as her own person. (Coverture also meant that the identity of an unmarried female minor was submerged into that of her father; a single woman of age, however, enjoyed relative autonomy.) When radicals attacked the institution of marriage, then, it was more than a matter of abstract principle: defined as the ownership of another person's body, children, and labor power, marriage looked uncomfortably similar to the institution of slavery. An understanding of the legal ramifications of marriage and the near-impossibility of divorce during the Romantic period should encourage your students to darken their readings of even a sparkling novel of courtship and marriage like Jane Austen's *Pride and Prejudice* (1813).

Blake's *Visions of the Daughters of Albion* (1793) can be usefully taught with *Vindication*, and not only because Blake, who knew and admired Wollstonecraft, also saw democracy, the abolition of slavery, and the rights of women as interconnected causes. Blake's championing of sexual freedom for women, and indictment of the "hypocrite modesty" (2.70, line 16) in which women were trained, is all the more striking given the furor that ensued when William Godwin, proud of his dead wife's political, religious, and sexual radicalism, published what proved to be a scandalous memoir of Wollstonecraft in 1798. For Blake, religion's "Thou shalt not" (*The Garden of Love*, 2.56, line 6) had turned the Garden of Love into a graveyard. Woman's sexuality was like a tremendous force of energy waiting to be released in order to generate joy and creativity, but that force had been locked up and abused by conventional morality, thus bringing the whole world under the curse of repression, jealousy, prostitution, and, what amounted to the same thing as prostitution, marriage without love. Prophetic works like *Daughters* and *The Book of Thel* project this fallen world in language imitating the Old Testament prophets and in terms of Blake's personal mythology. In that world, women are in bondage, like the slaves in America; not only the slaves but the slave owners, too, wear mental chains, of which the prime example is the forbidding sexual code. Oothoon, the heroine of *Daughters*, expresses a redemptive vision: "Love! Love! Love! happy happy Love! free as the mountain wind! . . . every thing that lives is holy!" she cries out to her lover; but he denies her and her vision because she has been raped and thus, in his eyes, defiled (2.71, plate 7, line 16, plate 8, line 10). Oothoon's martyrdom is compared to Prometheus's suffering for humankind (2.67, line 13); she thus anticipates not only Prometheus in Percy Shelley's *Prometheus Unbound*, but also Asia, the daughter of Ocean, whose reunion with Prometheus overthrows Jupiter's tyranny and redeems the fallen world (2.754, n. 7). In these mythical and symbolic works, the redemptive role of woman resembles that of the Virgin Mary in medieval literature, with the important difference that it is woman's sexuality, not her virginity, that saves humankind, and the promised heaven is a heaven on earth.

You might also wish to follow *Vindication* with Barbauld's *The Rights of Women* (2.27). Barbauld's satire of Wollstonecraft was probably inspired by Wollstonecraft's attack (in a selection of *Vindication* not included in *NAEL*) on Barbauld's 1773 *To a Lady, with Some Painted Flowers*, a poem that begins by offering "Flowers to the fair," and concludes by telling the Lady that "Your best, your sweetest empire is—to please." As if deliberately misreading Wollstonecraft's argument (Wollstonecraft despised female coquetry and hoped that male-female relations would be governed more by friendship than by passion), Barbauld sardonically urges "injured Woman" to use the tools of "wit and art" to "bend / Of thy imperial foe the stubborn knee," and "Make treacherous Man thy subject, not thy friend" (2.27, lines 17–19). Barbauld concludes by suggesting that the feminist position is an unnatural one: the militant female will soon find her "coldness" and "pride" melted when "Nature's school" instructs her womanly heart that "separate rights are lost in mutual love" (2.28, lines 28, 31–32).

We do recommend that, if you are teaching a general historical survey (as opposed to a survey of woman writers), you not teach the Romantic woman writers en masse, as a homogeneous group of authors. Romantic-era women, who wrote fiction, essays, reviews, plays, and verse of all kinds, can hardly be said to share a common aesthetic practice. While Romantic woman writers read one another's work, they also read and were influenced by male authors and, in turn, were read by and influenced male authors. And as the Wollstonecraft-Barbauld disagreement makes abundantly clear, the Romantic women writers included in *NAEL* held a range of divergent opinions on questions of women's rights, women's proper place, women's duties, and women's nature—and on other political and social issues, for that matter. Wollstonecraft's female contemporaries might not challenge gender ideologies to the extent that she did, but they nonetheless take a stance radical for its time: for example, arguing that a woman's education should include philosophy, politics, and the sciences so that she might prove a better wife and mother; upholding the doctrine of separate spheres and yet speaking out on public issues; agreeing that woman's nature differed from men's, but claiming that woman's "natural" characteristics—her greater emotionality and sensibility—made hers an important voice against slavery and other forms of social injustice. (Barbauld, for instance, published the antislavery *Epistle to William Wilberforce* in 1791, and the anti-imperialist *Eighteen Hundred and Eleven, a Poem* in 1812.) Romantic-era feminism, if we want to call it that, came in many varieties; and perhaps the best way to illustrate this is to teach several of the Barbauld selections with Wollstonecraft. Though Barbauld rejected the idea of women's rights in her satire of Wollstonecraft, she does not reject women's experiences as inappropriate for poetry. *To a Little Invisible Being Who Is Expected Soon to Become Visible* (2.28), for instance, frankly describes the emotions of a pregnant woman while drawing subtle parallels between childbirth and literary production; and in the witty *Washing-Day* (2.29) Barbauld insists that women's work and the domestic sphere are worthy topics of poetry even as she uses the mock-heroic form to undermine her own claim: "Then I would sit me down and ponder much / Why washings were" (lines 78–79).

Representing the Laboring Classes

Indebted to works like *The Dunciad* and *The Rape of the Lock*, *Washing-Day* nonetheless breaks with the neoclassical tradition in its choice of subject matter, depicting ordinary people engaged in ordinary activities. While there were certainly eighteenth-century precedents for the widespread Romantic interest in what Wordsworth called "incidents and situations from common life" (Preface, 2.241), such an interest was heightened by the American and French Revolutions and the ensuing hope that "the people" were poised to seize power across Europe. Though political democracy would be slow to catch on in England—at the turn of the century, only 5 percent of adult men held the vote—democratic principles were much in evidence in literary theory and literary practice. In the "Introductory Discourse" to her 1798 *Plays on the Passions*, an essay that influenced Wordsworth and Coleridge, Baillie suggested that ordinary people were in fact more interesting than their aristocratic betters: "those works which most strongly characterize human nature in the middling and lower classes of society, where it is to be discovered by stronger and more unequivocal marks, will ever be the most popular." Wordsworth similarly argued that "the essential passions of the heart" were best displayed in "low and rustic life" (Preface, 2.241).

But Baillie and Wordsworth both disapproved of the pastoral tradition that depicted rustic people as quaint or charmingly primitive. (Baillie's countryman Robert Burns was hailed as such a primitive and was often willing to don the persona of the charming and canny peasant-poet. However, his dramatic monologue *Holy Willie's Prayer*, a satire of a particularly intolerant version of Scottish Calvinism, shows that rustic ignorance and narrow-mindedness are anything but quaint.) Baillie's narrative poem *A Winter's Day* (2.210) depicts a day in the life of laboring people in rural Scotland with sympathy and attentiveness, but Baillie glamorizes neither her laborers nor their relationship with the natural world. Wordsworth reclaims the pastoral by portraying the tragedy of a shepherd and his family in *Michael*, subtitled *A Pastoral Poem* (2.270); there and in poems like *Simon Lee* (2.222) and *The Ruined Cottage* (2.259) he attempts to depict the suffering and poverty of common people in unsentimental terms. Charlotte Smith makes the unusual move of incorporating the pastoral into the sonnet *The Sea View* (2.35), wherein the "serene" idyll of an "upland shepherd" reclining on the mountain is disrupted by a violent battle between two "war-freighted ships" in the seas below (lines 8, 1, 11). In *Michael* the narrating "I" is quite distinct from the events detailed in the poem, and *A Winter's Day* works to efface the presence of the narrator altogether. But in *The Sea View*—which according to Smith's note is based on her own experience of witnessing a conflict at sea—the perspective of the sonnet writer is split between the third-person narrator and the "rustic" himself. Here the rustic both occupies the moral high ground (literally and figuratively) of the poet pronouncing on the horrors of war and serves as a persona for the poet.

As the *NAEL* introduction to the period notes, Romantic texts did not portray just "humble people" sympathetically, but also "the ignominious, the outcast, the delinquent" (2.11). Thomas De Quincey, for instance, defends the "noble-minded Ann" and other prostitutes who befriended him when he was a destitute teenager alone in London (*Confessions of an English Opium-Eater*, 2.530); and if you are not discussing them in another context, you might wish to contrast some of Blake's deceptively simple, eminently teachable *Songs of Innocence* and *Songs of Experience* with Wordsworth's *The Thorn* (2.229) or one or two of the poems of rural poverty mentioned above. In the dramatic monologues *The Little Black Boy* (2.45) and the first *Chimney Sweeper* (2.46), Blake speaks in the voice of the utterly marginalized subject, inviting the reader to inhabit the innocent consciousness of the child who is literally enslaved and the child who is practically enslaved, and yet to share with the poet the terrible knowledge that each child has internalized the ideology that oppresses him. The child in the second *Chimney Sweeper* in *Songs of Experience* (2.52) has rejected the pieties that consoled his counterpart but is still enslaved, and arguably more miserable than the boy who takes comfort in dreams of the afterlife. "Innocence" is an ambiguous state, and "experience" offers no easy solutions to the social injustice Blake decries here and elsewhere. Analyzing other matched pairs (the two *Holy Thursday* poems (2.47, 2.51), *The Lamb* (2.45) and *The Tyger* (2.54), the two versions of *Nurse's Song* (2.48, 2.52) and *The Divine Image* (2.47, 2.59) confuses matters further: experience might be wisdom, an awareness that brings disillusionment and pain, or cynicism; innocence might be pureheartedness, naiveté, or blind orthodoxy.

Blake invites his readers to draw a moral (perhaps multiple, conflicting morals) from the *Songs*, but doesn't make it easy for them; the reader must first struggle with Blake's allusiveness and layers of irony. Wordsworth's *Simon Lee* (2.222) also forces its readers to uncover its political or ethical or emotional meaning with minimal help from the poet: the narrator interrupts the story to inform the "gentle Reader" that he or she is almost certainly misinterpreting the poem (lines 61–72), but doesn't specify a correct reading. (Wordsworth compounds his unhelpfulness in the Preface [2.242–43], noting cryptically that in *Simon Lee* he placed his readers "in the way of receiving from ordinary moral sensations another and more salutary impression than we are accustomed to receive from them.") If you are teaching these poems in the context of Romantic radicalism, your students may wish to discuss their political efficacy: do they contribute more or less to social causes than such overtly political works as Percy Shelley's *A Song: "Men of England"* (2.727), eventually adopted as a hymn of the British labor movement? (The Audio Companion features a performance of *Men of England.*) It is also interesting to contrast *England in 1819* (2.72) and *To Sidmouth and Castlereagh* (2.728), wherein Shelley explicitly criticizes the British government after the Peterloo massacre, to Wordsworth's indirect treatment of social issues in *The Ruined Cottage* (2.259). Agricultural depression, industrialism's displacement of handloom weavers, and the revolutionary wars cause the destruction of Margaret's family, yet these events are alluded to only briefly, kept very much in the background, while Wordsworth—or rather the internal narrator Armytage—concentrates on Margaret's misery when her unemployed husband enlists in the army and does not return. One can criticize Wordsworth for refusing openly to engage with the events that so devastated the laboring-class people he claimed to champion. Alternatively, one can argue that Wordsworth's attentiveness to the emotional effects of poverty and war (Margaret's grief is infectious, spreading to Armytage, then the narrator, then presumably the reader) makes *Ruined Cottage* a more effective social critique, while his focus on Margaret rather than on Robert, on the breakup of the domestic sphere rather than on the experience of warfare, makes the poem a more inclusive social critique.

Revolution in Style

"There will . . . be found in these volumes little of what is usually called poetic diction," wrote Wordsworth in the Preface to *Lyrical Ballads*. "I have taken as much pains to avoid it as others ordinarily take to produce it" (2.244). In their deliberate break with neoclassical precepts, Baillie and Wordsworth each called for a revolution in literary style as well as subject matter. Wordsworth deplored "the gaudiness and inane phraseology of many modern writers" (2.241), the kind of florid writing Baillie mocks in her send-up of bad eighteenth-century pastoral: "A shepherd whose sheep, with fleeces of the purest snow, browze the flowery herbage of the most beautiful vallies; whose flute is ever melodious; and whose shepherdess is crowned with roses" ("Introductory Discourse"). Both suggested that poetry should abjure figurative language, or what Baillie called "the enchanted regions of simile, metaphor, allegory and description" (2.210), and substitute (in Wordsworth's phrase) "language really used by men" (2.241). Humble people, Wordsworth argued, spoke in "simple and unelaborated expressions," using a more beautiful and even "far more philosophical language" than that of the poets who indulge in "arbitrary and capricious habits of expression" (2.241–42).

The Preface is important to teach as a text that displays "the spirit of the age" by advocating the incorporation of democratic principles into poetic practice. And it's very useful to teach in tandem with the *Lyrical Ballads* themselves, especially because students beginning or continuing a survey may expect their poetry to be more "poetic" and find the *Ballads* bafflingly like prose. After discussing the arguments of the Preface, you might ask your students to look carefully at Gray's *Sonnet on the Death of Richard West* and Wordsworth's analysis of it (2.245–46): go line by line to try to determine why Wordsworth argues that the italicized passages "in no respect differ from good prose" and are moreover the only passages in the sonnet "of any value." Then ask them to make a similar analysis of some of the *Lyrical Ballads* to see if Wordsworth himself has succeeded in eradicating the "difference between the language of prose and metrical composition" (2.245) by using plain diction and conversational syntax, incorporating dialogue, and so on. Ask your students to speculate about why Wordsworth does indulge in a limited amount of figurative language despite his own injunctions against it: for instance, the homely simile in *Simon Lee* ("the centre of his cheek / Is red as a ripe cherry," 2.222, lines 7–8), the adjoined metaphor and simile that make up the second stanza of *She dwelt among the untrodden ways* (2.252) in its entirety, the personification of Nature in *Three years she grew* (2.252). If you are not teaching Coleridge in another context, you could at this point introduce *Rime of the Ancient Mariner* (2.422), included in the *Lyrical Ballads*, or *Christabel* (2.441), intended for it but unfinished, and consider the extent to which the precepts set out in the Preface can be usefully applied to poems other than Wordsworth's.

You may also wish to compare Wordsworth's poetry about laboring-class people to poetry written by the farm laborer John Clare, the self-educated son of an illiterate mother and near-illiterate father (see the headnote, 2.802). Clare's 1820 *Poems Descriptive of Rural Life and Scenery* brought him briefly into vogue as the "Northamptonshire Peasant," and he seemed to inhabit this poetic persona quite comfortably in poems like *The Peasant Poet* (2.810) and *Pastoral Poesy* (2.805). That Clare shared the Preface's antipathy to elaborate poetic diction is clear from such descriptive, even naturalistic verse as *Mouse's Nest* ("When out an old mouse bolted in the wheats / With all her young ones hanging at her teats," 2.807, lines 5–6) and *The Nightingale's Nest* (2.803). The latter is particularly interesting to teach with *Ode to a Nightingale* (2.849) in light of Clare's disparaging comments about Keats (whom he in many ways admired) as a nature poet. Keats's writing, according to Clare, was overwrought and overstuffed with literary allusion, and "the frequency of such classical accompaniment makes it wearisome to the reader where behind every rose bush he looks for a Venus & under every laurel a thrumming Appollo." Keats was the son of an London stableman, though his class origins would probably not be visible to a modern reader impressed by the intense and passionate erudition of such sonnets as *On First Looking into Chapman's Homer* and *On Seeing the Elgin Marbles.* Clare, perhaps, saw Keats's ecstatic displays of classicism as a betrayal of his lower-class origins, but many critics ridiculed them as the pretensions of a vulgar *arriviste* attempting to rise above his station. In an 1818 essay, the critic John Gibson Lockhart called *Endymion* a work of "drivelling idiocy" and Keats an "uneducated and flimsy stripling" who lacked the learning "to distinguish between the written language of Englishmen and the spoken jargon of Cockneys." A vital peasant-poet who composed verse in the fields was a pleasing novelty, but a "Cockney" apothecary-turned-professional-poet who wrote about mortals in love with goddesses was apparently not to be borne. In any case, a comparison of Clare and Keats shows the danger of generalizing about the language and literary ambitions of lower-class writers.

Several selections from Coleridge's *Biographia Literaria* teach well with the Preface, including Coleridge's critique of the intellectual and formal properties of Augustan poetry (2.468), his praise of Wordsworth's earlier work (2.474), his discussion of the inception of the *Lyrical Ballads* and the place of his own contributions or intended contributions within them (2.478), and the adumbration of his differences from his erstwhile collaborator (2.483). In later years, Coleridge saw Wordsworth's idealization of the rustic subject as a form of anti-intellectualism, arguing that the "best part of human language . . . is derived from reflection on acts of the mind itself," not the simple ruminations of "uneducated man" (2.484); and that because language usage varies according to education and situation, the writings of philosophers counted as "the REAL language of men" (2.484) no less than the speech of "a common peasant." Wordsworth, he said, meant "ordinary" rather than "real" language—and furthermore, who could say what this ordinary language was, because the dialect of humble people varied from county to county and village to village (2.485)?

"Ha! whare ye gaun, ye crowlan ferlie!" This colloquial opening interjection from Robert Burns's *To a Louse* (2.106) is clearly an instance of "ordinary" language use, but it might seem incomprehensible to a Grasmere shepherd (or an urbane Londoner, for that matter). Coleridge could have been thinking of Burns's 1786 *Poems, Chiefly in the Scottish Dialect* when he argued that so-called real or ordinary language was fractured into regional variants. Born into poverty, Burns became known as the

"Heaven-taught ploughman" and was lionized as an untutored rustic genius (despite being quite well read). Burns's career is thus usefully contextualized within the Romantic-era interest in "the common people" (see the headnote, 2.99), and his own democratic sympathies are in evidence in his depictions of rural subjects and sensibilities and his archival work (also practiced by his countryman Sir Walter Scott) with Scottish ballads and other folk material. Burns was skilled at reworking genteel eighteenth-century English forms in Scots dialect (see, for instance, the mock-heroic *Tam o' Shanter*, 2.109; also included on the Audio Companion), and his conviction that rural Scotland was a worthy subject and rural Scots dialect a worthy language of poetry perhaps owes as much to his nationalist as his democratic sympathies. Both are in evidence in *Robert Bruce's March to Bannockburn* (2.114). Although its subject is the Battle of Bannockburn, which had secured the liberty of Scotland in the fourteenth century, the poem is certainly inspired by recent events in France:

> Lay the proud Usurpers low!
> Tyrants fall in every foe!
> Liberty's in every blow!
> Let us Do—or Die!!! (lines 21–24)

And Burns looks forward to revolution and the coming of the millennium in *Song: For a' that and a' that*: "It's coming yet, for a' that, / That Man to Man the warld o'er / Shall brothers be for a' that" (2.116, lines 38–40).

After the Revolution

The Fate of Late-Romantic Radicalism

Of all the Romantic-era readings included in *NAEL*, the selections from *The Prelude* (2.305) best demonstrate the disillusionment—the sense of intellectual and even personal betrayal—many revolutionary sympathizers experienced as a result of the Reign of Terror and its aftermath, Napoleon's dictatorship and imperial ambitions, and Britain's war with France. The youthful Wordsworth, enamored of the Revolution, had looked forward to the secular millennium, to a paradise found "in the very world, which is the world / Of all of us,—the place where in the end / We find our happiness, or not at all!" (361, lines 142–44). But although Wordsworth, in his own words, "Became a Patriot" (2.356, line 123), and embraced the revolutionary cause fervently, what is striking in the selections from books 9 and 10 of *The Prelude* is Wordsworth's ambivalence about the Revolution. When he first visits the Paris landmarks of the Revolution in 1791, he listens to "Hawkers and Haranguers" and "hissing Factionists" with "a Stranger's ears" and a sense of unreality (2.355, lines

57–59). He pockets a sacred "Relic," a stone from the ruins of the Bastille,

> in the guise
> Of an Enthusiast; yet, in honest truth,
> I looked for Something that I could not find,
> Affecting more emotion than I felt. (2.355, lines 70–73)

Later Wordsworth compares the Revolution and its aftermath to an important book written in a foreign language, and he is the man who "questions the mute leaves with pain, / And half-upbraids their silence" (2.357, lines 62–63). Whether Wordsworth actually felt such estrangement from the events in France during his stay there, or colors his emotions retrospectively, is impossible to know. (On 2.336–37, lines 256–76, he acknowledges by means of an extended simile how difficult it is for him to distinguish a real from an imagined past.) But in any case, for Wordsworth as well as for many of his contemporaries, the idea of revolution would prove much better than its actuality. Betrayed by world history (by "the times / And their disastrous issues," 2.365, lines 51–52), Wordsworth would turn to mythic history—as when, in *The Prelude*'s mystical "Vision" of prehistoric England, he feels his own kinship with the Druids at Stonehenge, those "barbaric" poet-seers from "Our dim Ancestral Past" (2.375–76, lines 319, 325)—and, of course, turn more famously to personal history through the very act of adapting the epic to describe the development of his poetic consciousness.

One can also track Wordsworth's gradual turn from political radicalism in the sonnet *London, 1802* (2.297), which begins, "Milton! thou should'st be living at this hour: / England hath need of thee" (lines 1–2). Though he longs for a modern-day Milton to clean up the "fen / Of stagnant waters" that England has become (lines 2–3), Wordsworth seems less interested in Milton as the great poet of the Puritan Revolution (and thus a heroic figure to most Romantics) than in a more domesticated Milton who points the way to the "inward happiness" the English have lost through selfish pursuits (line 6). Milton's voice was powerful like the sea, pure as the sky, but he traveled "life's common way, / In cheerful godliness" and subjected his heart to "lowliest duties" (lines 12–13, 14). Thus Wordsworth's image of Milton in the sonnet is not of a stormy reformer but of a man who dutifully and cheerfully submits to the will of God and accepts the miseries of the human condition. However, the ideal poet described in the sestet sounds less like Milton than like Wordsworth himself after he had turned away from his youthful enthusiasm for the French Revolution.

Wordsworth grew increasingly conservative in his later years, to the dismay of younger authors like Byron, Hazlitt, Keats, Percy Shelley, and later Robert Browning, who saw his electioneering for Tory candidates and his acceptance of government patronage and eventually the poet laureateship in 1843 as a betrayal of his youthful principles (see Browning's

The Lost Leader, 2.1355). Shelley's 1816 sonnet *To Wordsworth* (2.701; an interesting match with *London, 1802*) is a sort of elegy for the optimistic young Wordsworth who sang of "truth and liberty" in "honoured poverty" (lines 12, 11). The sonnet suggests that Wordsworth's preoccupation with the past—his nostalgia for "Childhood and youth" (line 3)—has replaced his more idealistic pursuits.

The second generation of Romantic authors grew up during a period of harsh political repression, governmental paranoia, and widespread social distress in England. The spirit of the revolution was still alive in radical and intellectual circles, but those with radical tendencies had to maintain their optimism within a conservative, often reactionary cultural milieu. Percy Shelley's sonnet *England in 1819* (2.728) deplores the excesses of the times—a corrupt monarchy, a brutal military, "leechlike" rulers bleeding their people dry, the Peterloo massacre (line 5)—but prophesies nonetheless that the "glorious Phantom" of revolution would rise from the dead "to illumine our tempestuous day" (lines 13–14). Shelley was not always the most practical revolutionary, for instance launching his broadsheet *A Declaration of Rights* (1812) off to Ireland in bottles across the St. George's Channel and in air balloons above it, but he was arguably the most radical of the later Romantic authors included in *NAEL*, with a seemingly inextinguishable faith in the ultimate victory of revolution and the betterment of the human condition. As late as 1821 this faith was still visible in *Hellas* (2.769; a chorus from *Hellas* is featured on the NAEL Audio Companion), written to raise money for the Greek struggle for independence from the Turkish empire:

> The world's great age begins anew,
>   The golden years return,
> The earth doth like a snake renew
>   Her winter weeds outworn;
> Heaven smiles, and faiths and empires gleam
> Like wrecks of a dissolving dream. (2.771, lines 1–6)

Shelley wrote more political verse, pamphlets, and essays than could possibly be included or excerpted in *NAEL*, including *The Necessity of Atheism*, 1811 (for which he and Thomas Jefferson Hogg were expelled from Oxford), *An Address to the Irish People* (1812), *An Address to the People on the Death of Princess Charlotte* (1817), *The Revolt of Islam* (1818), *The Mask of Anarchy* (1819), *Ode to Naples* and *Ode to Liberty* (1820), and *A Philosophical View of Reform* (1820). Within *NAEL*, the revolutionary Shelley is in evidence at his most grandiose in the allegory *Prometheus Unbound* (2.736), which looks forward to the overthrow of tyrannical leaders and despotic states, and a new golden age in which humans will live "Sceptreless, free, uncircumscribed . . . / Equal, unclassed, tribeless, and nationless, / Exempt from awe, worship, degree" (2.753, lines 194–96). But since teaching even the abridged version of *Prometheus* requires such a commitment of time, you might instead emphasize breadth of genre (song, sonnet, satire) with the three poems written after Peterloo, *Men of England* (2.727), *England in 1819* (2.728), and *To Sidmouth and Castlereagh* (2.728); excerpt the Preface to *Prometheus* (2.733) and teach it with *A Defence of Poetry* to illustrate Shelley's belief that imaginative practice and political activism were inextricably intertwined; or pair either text with *Ode to the West Wind* (2.730). When the speaker-poet of the *Ode* invokes the "fierce" spirit of the wind to bring him poetic inspiration and creative energy (line 61), the images of death and rebirth are linked as well to the fall of despotism and the rise of democracy (cf. *Prometheus* and *England in 1819*); and the poet, as suggested in the *Defence*, will not only record but inspire the "new birth" of human liberty when his "words among mankind" shall arouse "unawakened Earth" with the "trumpet of a prophecy" (lines 64, 67–69).

The fact that Shelley wrote so many of these works in exile—and that even the radical editor Leigh Hunt, imprisoned in 1811 for criticizing the prince regent, did not dare publish poems like *England in 1819* and *The Mask of Anarchy* during Shelley's lifetime lest he be sued for libel and imprisoned again—illustrates the difficulty of actually maintaining a radical stance within England during the later Romantic period. When the Shelleys returned to England in 1816, Percy found himself vilified for sexual immorality and atheism as well as for his politics, and the two left for Italy in 1818, Percy for good. It was left to Mary Shelley to resuscitate his reputation after his death.

Marginal Subjects in Frankenstein

According to her biographers, Mary Shelley, having seen her mother's and husband's reputations destroyed, became mistrustful of political radicalism—or, to take it from a slightly different angle, became all too aware of the personal costs of political and philosophical idealism. In later years, she would distance herself from the revolutionary fervor of her parents and husband, as is clear from the 1838 journal entry excerpted in the headnote to Mary Shelley (2.903), wherein she professes "respect" for those who "have a passion for reforming the world," but rejects "violent extremes." Yet it is hard to credit her claim that "I am not a person of opinions." While her most famous novel, *Frankenstein*, does not take an unambiguously radical stance, it is in many ways a radical and provocative text.

"I was benevolent and good; misery made me a fiend," Victor Frankenstein's monster reproaches his creator. "Make me happy, and I shall again be virtuous" (2.960). Are monsters born or made? That is, are irrational and even violent behaviors by certain groups (working-class mobs, slaves, women) the result of their imperfect nature or a product of social injustice? While the novel does not answer it definitively, *Frankenstein* thoroughly engages this question. Shelley's journals indicate that she was rereading radical texts by her famous parents while composing *Frankenstein*: William Godwin's 1793 *Enquiry concerning Political Justice*, which maintained that a corrupt society debased and perverted its subjects, while only just and benevolent social institutions could ensure a virtuous, enlightened, and contented populace; and Wollstonecraft's *Vindication of the Rights of Woman* and *An Historical and Moral View of the Origin and Progress of the French Revolution* (1795). *Vindication* argues that faulty education and social indoctrination, not defective feminine nature, spawned the narrow-mindedness and petty venalities of the middle-class woman (see "The Rights of Women," above). *Origin and Progress* acknowledges the excesses of the French Revolution, but focuses on the ways in which the tyranny of the French state drove its people to retaliatory violence: "People are rendered ferocious by misery; and misanthropy is ever the offspring of discontent," wrote Wollstonecraft. Burke and other conservatives had figured the revolutionaries as inhuman, characterizing them variously as monsters, demons, cannibals, ghouls, and fiends; debates over the abolition of the slave trade similarly hinged on the question of the basic humanity (or lack thereof) of non-Europeans. (See also the Norton Topics Online discussion "Slavery and the Slave Trade in Britain.") Violent uprisings in Haiti and other European colonies seemed to confirm a basic kinship between these two breeds of "monster": the dangerous spirit of Jacobinism was spreading and infecting the empire; slaves and colonized peoples proved their unworthiness by revolting against their "betters."

The nineteenth-century reader would likely have been familiar with these debates about the basic humanity of marginals in a way that your students will not, and because the novel clearly hints that the monster is *some* kind of marginal subject, but does not directly identify it as a slave, disenfranchised woman, or *sans culotte,* you will need to remind your students to attend carefully to the subtler details of the text as they pursue this problem. (Such an admonition is especially worth making here because students often assume that "popular" fiction does not require close reading.) For instance, when the monster is first introduced to the reader it is coded in racial terms: Walton notes its peculiar physiognomy and takes it for "a savage inhabitant of some undiscovered island," as opposed to the obviously "European" Victor, who is introduced shortly thereafter (2.918). Like nineteenth-century women ("the sex"), the monster—"the filthy mass that moved and talked"—is associated with the register of reproduction and childbirth and the abject materiality of the body. The monster and Victor's two best-beloved women are phantasmatically interchangeable at the level of his unconscious fears and desires: after he flees his newborn creation in "breathless horror and disgust," Victor dreams that his beautiful Elizabeth becomes "livid with the hue of death" within his embrace and melts into the shrouded "corpse of [his] dead mother" crawling with "graveworms," and then awakens to find the "demoniacal corpse" grinning at his bedside (2.935). Like the most destitute vagrant or pauper, the creature is starved and left to the mercy of the elements; and in volume 3, chapters 2 and 3, when the "daemon" appears at the remote Orkney workshop where Victor is engaged in the "detestable occupation" of constructing its mate, monstrosity is metonymically associated with the "miserable" poverty of the island's inhabitants ("the squalidness of the most miserable penury").

The creature, in other words, can be read as a composite type of the oppressed subject. And in many ways *Frankenstein* insists on the basic humanity of this oppressed subject, even when it appears monstrous to unsympathetic eyes. The creature gives ample evidence of its educability when it observes the De Laceys and learns "to admire their virtues, and to deprecate the vices of mankind" (2.976) and of its benevolence when it labors in secret for the De Laceys or saves a young peasant girl from drowning. The savage rejection of the creature's friendly overtures—Felix De Lacey beats the creature, and the peasant girl's father shoots it—lends credence to the creature's claim that its intrinsic good nature has been perverted by cruel treatment. Moreover, the creature, with its "fine sensations" (2.988), displays the sensibility and rationality that are hallmarks of human identity; indeed, it is in many ways the most philosophical character in the novel, struggling to understand its own origins, the meaning of existence, and the place of the individual in society.

And yet the creature is also prone to violent rages, and commits one murder after another. It torches the De Laceys' cottage and dances around the flames like a lower-class incendiary or a rebellious slave. In other words, if one wishes to read the creature as a composite oppressed subject, the novel seems to invite as much horror as sympathy for this subject who veers between reason and unreason, benignity and malice—who at one moment demands justice and compassion from Victor, the master/aristocrat/patriarch, and at another threatens to usurp his authority entirely: "Slave, I before reasoned with you, but you have proved yourself unworthy of my condescension. Remember that I have power. . . . You are my creator, but I am your master;—obey!" (2.1001). One is tempted to say that Mary Shelley's own ambivalence is on display throughout *Frankenstein*, but it is difficult to locate the author and specify her political views because she has hidden behind—or rather scattered herself among—so many narrators. The novel carefully maintains an ambiguous stance throughout, refusing to pronounce definitively on the causes and effects of oppression, or to imagine utopian solutions to social injustice, and in this sense it constitutes a break from Romantic radicalism, or perhaps a tempering and critique of Romantic radicalism. (See also the Norton Topics Online discussion "Literary Gothicism.")

Late-Romantic Irony and the Byronic Hero

The Shelleys' friend Lord Byron had no sympathy for Wordsworth's attempts to wed democratic principles and poetic practice. Wordsworth, he thought, was a "vulgar" and tedious "blockhead," and he skewered him mercilessly in *Don Juan* (2.622), begging Wordsworth to indulge in a little classicism rather than writing "trash" about "Pedlars" and "boats" and "waggons." "Oh! Ye shades / Of Pope and Dryden, are we come to this?" (2.679, lines 889–891). Nonetheless, the aristocrat Byron did espouse liberal causes throughout his lifetime, supporting democratic principles and the common people so long as they were not portrayed in Wordsworth's poetry. From his seat in the House of Lords he spoke up for Irish Catholic rights and against the Frame Work Bill (1812), which demanded the death penalty for the unemployed textile workers who destroyed the machinery that was putting them out of work. "The perseverance of these miserable men in their proceedings, tends to prove that nothing but absolute want could have driven a large, and once honest and industrious, body of the people, into the commission of excesses so hazardous to themselves, their families, and the community," argued Byron in his maiden speech. Later in life Byron supported the Carbonari, a secret society of revolutionaries dedicated to the cause of Italian nationalism, then the Greek war of independence against the Ottoman Empire. In Greece—"The land of honourable Death" (*January 22nd. Missolonghi*, 2.563, line 34)—Byron died of fever while working to outfit an expedition against the Turks.

Nonetheless, Byron's poetry could almost serve as an antidote to the revolutionary idealism and utopian exuberance of earlier Romantic authors:

> When a man hath no freedom to fight for at home,
>   Let him combat for that of his neighbors;
> Let him think of the glories of Greece and of Rome,
>   And get knock'd on the head for his labours. (2.561, lines 1–4)

Characterized by its skepticism and irony, and often a late-Romantic malaise, Byron's work neither idealizes an imaginary past nor manifests an Enlightenment belief in human perfectibility and progress nor hopes for a new golden age in the present. In *Written after Swimming from Sestos to Abydos* (2.555), the speaker-poet mocks his own attempt to perform a noble feat and swim across the Hellespont like Leander; a "degenerate modern wretch" like himself, exhausted by making the crossing in "the genial month of May," is no match for the heroes of antiquity (lines 9–10). But the ironic, even facetious tone of the poem makes light of everything: Leander's grand and tragic passion as well as the uninspired inadequacy of modern times, and the poet's own half-wistful longing to emulate the heroics of Leander most of all. Byron did not take himself too seriously as a revolutionary; after all, his periods of radicalism were interspersed with bouts of almost frenzied hedonism, like the sexual excesses described in an 1819 letter (2.695). But however far removed from that flush of idealism that marked the 1790s, Byron was still irresistibly drawn to noble, impossible causes, as he acknowledges with ironic resignation in *When a man hath no freedom to fight for at home*.

"And thus, untaught in youth my heart to tame, / My springs of life were poison'd" (*Childe Harold's Pilgrimage,* 2.567, lines 59–60). Elsewhere Byron would adopt the pose of the world-weary roue, oppressed by the "fulness of satiety" like his character/persona Childe Harold, who has run through "Sin's long labyrinth" for too many long years (2.565, lines 34, 37). The "Byronic hero" or antihero, as described in the headnote to Byron, is "an alien, mysterious, and gloomy spirit, superior in his passions and powers to the common run of humanity, whom he regards with disdain" (2.552; see also the Norton Topics Online discussion "The Satanic and Byronic Hero"). The Byronic hero is too grimly antisocial to pursue political causes: Childe Harold, "the most unfit / Of men to herd with Man" (2.568, lines 100–1), shuns "the hot throng" and the "contentious world" (2.575, lines 657, 661). But however apolitical, this iconoclastic figure is nonetheless a child of the Revolution in his intellectual rebelliousness and contempt for conventional morality. And his studied gloom spoke to the discouragement of postrevolutionary Europe. Childe Harold's fierce melancholy darkens further as he tours the continent where the hope of freedom has turned to dust and red clay mingled with the blood of the slain at Waterloo. Napoleon, presented as something of a Byronic figure himself, serves as yet another reminder that no unsullied heroes are to be found in the modern world. "Extreme in all things," Napoleon inspires contempt as well as admiration: "An empire thou couldst crush, command, rebuild, / But govern not thy pettiest passion . . . nor curb the lust of war" (2.320, lines 320, 338–41).

Characterized by its playful irony, urbanity, and satiric wit, *Don Juan* (2.622) breaks from the lugubriousness and self-indulgence that sometimes characterize *Childe Harold* and *Manfred.* "I want a hero," *Don Juan*'s narrator asserts, seemingly in earnest, in the opening line of the opening canto. But because he "can't find any in the present age" worth writing about (2.623, line 38), he looks to the past for his hero—and then chooses not an "Agamemnon," or some other "valorous and sage" warrior, but the notorious rake, Don Juan (lines 33–34)—and even then depicts his subject as no profligate libertine, but as an amiable innocent, naive rather than worldly, seducing women with his charming good looks rather than his sexual potency. This same narrator has already explained in a parenthetical aside of the prefatory *Fragment* that "I write this reeling / Having got drunk exceedingly to day / So that I seem to stand upon the ceiling" (2.622, lines 4–6). *Don Juan* proceeds in similarly giddy fashion, extemporized by the author over a number of years, and as much picaresque as epic, its plot driven by chance, accident, and the narrator's whim. In *Don Juan* Byron decisively turns his back on the idea of heroism and all that goes with it—belief in the meaningfulness of human experience and in the coherence and stability of meaning, knowledge systems, narrative, history, and so on. Here teleological uncertainty—the loss of faith in such master narratives as Enlightenment progressivism or the coming of the new millennium—allows for comedy, play, excess, exuberance, rather than inspiring despair.

Romantic Imagination and Subjectivity

"The Modifying Colors of Imagination"

In the Preface to *Lyrical Ballads,* Wordsworth writes that the poet who depicts "incidents and situations from common life" should "throw over them a certain colouring of the imagination, whereby ordinary things should be presented to the mind in an unusual way" (2.241). Coleridge makes a similar argument in *Biographia Literaria*: poetry should have "the power of exciting the sympathy of the reader by a faithful adherence to the truth of nature, and the power of giving the interest of novelty by the modifying colors of imagination" (2.478). Both emphasize that poets must carefully attend to and accurately portray the natural world and human emotions and situations—and yet fidelity, accuracy, and truthfulness do not mean that the poet has apperceived, analyzed, and transmitted an objectively discernable external world. Poetry should startle the reader into an intense and very personal engagement with the world: it works to defamiliarize what's familiar, so that readers are able to regard those scenes and activities to which they are accustomed with a "freshness of sensation" (*Biographia Literaria,* 2.476). (Compare Percy Shelley's dictum that "Poetry lifts the veil from the hidden beauty of the world, and makes familiar objects be as if they were not familiar," *Defence of Poetry,* 2.796.) Poetry trains the reader not in objective observation but in vision, sensitivity, responsiveness, and interpretation, "awakening the mind's attention from the lethargy of custom and directing it to the loveliness and wonders of the world before us" (*Biographia Literaria,* 2.476).

Such an "awakening" is made possible by the transfiguring power of the poetic imagination: the world is made anew within the mind of the poet. Percy Shelley argues that, while reason "may be considered as mind contemplating the relations borne by one thought to another," the imaginative process is "mind acting upon those thoughts so as to colour them with its own light, and composing from them, as from elements, other thoughts, each containing within itself the principle of its own integrity" (*Defence*, 2.790). The creative process described here is twofold. To "colour" the object of apprehension is to infuse it with one's own subjectivity and thus transform it. And moreover, whereas reason analyzes but does not alter its objects, imagination's power is synthetic: it recombines the constituent elements that reason provides and creates something new. Poetry "marries exultation and horror, grief and pleasure, eternity and change; it subdues to union under its light yoke all irreconcilable things" (*Defence*, 2.799–800).

Biographia Literaria also emphasizes what Coleridge calls the "esemplastic" qualities of the imagination, its ability to shape disparate elements into a new unity (see 2.478, n. 6). The imagination's "synthetic and magical power . . . reveals itself in the balance or reconciliation of opposite or discordant qualities" (2.482). Such a "reconciliation" occurs in *Kubla Khan* (2.439), wherein Coleridge describes "a miracle of rare device, / A sunny pleasure-dome with caves of ice!" (lines 35–36). Throughout Romantic literature one finds such startling conceits, whereby binary oppositions are impossibly reconciled, contradictions fused into a striking image or phantasmic landscape. Mary Shelley also proposes a marriage of fire and ice in the conclusion of *Frankenstein,* as the monster travels to "the most northern extremity of the globe" to build its own "funeral pile" on the frozen wastes and "exult in the agony of the torturing flames" (2.1034). Byron describes Jean-Jacques Rousseau as a man both irradiated and destroyed by passion: "as a tree / On fire by lightning; with ethereal flame / Kindled he was, and blasted" (*Childe Harold,* 2.577, lines 734–36). In book 5 of *The Prelude,* Wordsworth tells of a fabulous dreamscape that combines desert and deluge: the "sandy wilderness, all blank and void" (2.342, line 72) is covered over with "the fleet waters of a drowning World" (2.343, line 138). Oppositions are insistently collapsed in Keat's works, as when Lamia, herself a figure of the exuberant imagination, is described as an amalgam of innocence and experience, "A virgin purest lipp'd, yet in the lore / Of love deep learned to the red heart's core" (*Lamia,* 2.861, lines 189–90). In a more pensive register, Keats's *Ode on Melancholy* concludes that melancholy

> dwells with Beauty—Beauty that must die;
> And Joy, whose hand is ever at his lips
> Bidding adieu; and aching Pleasure nigh,
> Turning to poison while the bee-mouth sips:
> Ay, in the very temple of Delight
> Veil'd Melancholy has her sovran shrine." (2.854, lines 21–26)

For Keats, to be "a dreaming thing"—a poet—is to be unable to experience "The pain alone; the joy alone; distinct" (*The Fall of Hyperion,* 2.878, lines 168, 174). As De Quincey writes in *Confessions of an English Opium-Eater,* "the exuberant and riotous prodigality of life naturally forces the mind more powerfully upon the antagonistic thought of death. . . . Wherever two thoughts stand related to each other by a law of antagonism, and exist, as it were, by mutual repulsion, they are apt to suggest each other" (2.541).

Coleridge argues that the poet's power of synthesis demonstrates the godlike potential of human beings. His "primary IMAGINATION," or creative apperception, is "as a repetition in the finite [human] mind of the eternal act of creation in the infinite I AM," and unfolds through the workings of the "secondary imagination," which "dissolves, diffuses, dissipates, in order to recreate" (*Biographia Literaria,* 2.477). This difficult passage is worth teaching with an equally difficult passage from *The Prelude,* Wordsworth's vision on Mount Snowdon in book 14. Here the poet is able to behold in the spectacular beauties of nature "the type / Of a majestic Intellect," the "emblem of a Mind / That feeds upon infinity," but the "transcendent power" of such a mind also infuses the mortal minds of visionary poets (2.378–79, lines 66–67, 70–71, 75):

Them the enduring and the transient both
Serve to exalt; they build up greatest things
From least suggestions. . . .
Such minds are truly from the Deity,
For they are powers; and hence the highest bliss
That flesh can know is theirs,—the consciousness
Of whom they are, habitually infused
Through every image, and through every thought,
And all affections by communion raised
From earth to heaven, from human to divine.
(2.379, lines 100–2, 112–18)

In passages like these, which some of your students will find grandiose and others inspirational, the visionary poet, by virtue of the divine imagination, is exalted to the status of bard or seer. The speaker-poet of *Kubla Khan* figures himself as a sort of magician whose "flashing eyes" and "floating hair" should thrill the onlooker with "holy dread"—"For he on honey-dew hath fed, / And drunk the milk of Paradise" (2.441, lines 50, 52–54). Keats promises to be the "oracle," "prophet," and "priest" of Psyche and build for her "a fane / In some untrodden region of my mind" (*Ode to Psyche*, 2.848, lines 48–51). In *To a Sky-Lark* (2.765) Percy Shelley hopes to be like the bird that soars higher and higher while pouring out its "profuse strains of unpremeditated art" (line 5) and never returns to earth; for then "Such harmonious madness / From my lips would flow / The world should listen then—as I am listening now" (lines 103–5). Barbauld sends her mind to roam among "the trackless deeps of space" in *A Summer Evening's Meditation* (2.26, line 82), though unlike Shelley she is "Content and grateful" to alight again amongst the ordinary realities of the familiar world (line 118). Other texts figure the poetic imagination in relatively modest terms, as when Barbauld compares her "verse" to soap bubbles "sent aloft" to "Ride buoyant through the clouds" (*Washing-Day*, 2.26, lines 86, 80, 83). The poet is represented by the ladybug, hidden like Ariel in the cowslip's blossoms, in Clare's *Clock a Clay* (2.809, lines 1–2); and by the "ever patient and ever contented" old woman, singing in her "poor little hovel," in Robinson's *The Poor Singing Dame* (2.95, lines 33, 14).

The "Egotistical Sublime"

In each case, the text is concerned with the process of imaginative apperception, as the Romantic lyric depicts the complex interplay between the poetic imagination and the natural objects that it observes, engages, and responds to. But it would be misleading to focus on imaginative apperception alone, because the Romantic lyric is concerned in general with all of the intricacies of subjectivity, detailing the most subtle workings of emotional and mental life. As Wordsworth argues, poetry should show "the fluxes and refluxes of mind when agitated by the great and simple affections of our nature" (Preface, 2.242). In *This Lime-Tree Bower My Prison* (2.420), for example, Coleridge initially frets because his friends have left him behind on their walk. But the speaker-poet looses his imagination from his disabled body and by recalling each detail of the walk to a point overlooking the sea, enters into sympathetic identification with the friends who view heath and "blue ocean" (line 37); he is thus able to reawaken his faculties of poetic observation and appreciate the many beauties of the "little lime-tree bower" that no longer imprisons, but inspires him (line 46). Like Wordsworth's *Lines Composed a Few Miles above Tintern Abbey* (2.235), *Lime-Tree Bower* describes an act of mind, "the fluxes and refluxes" of subjectivity as memory, imagination, speculation, and attentiveness to the natural world feed off of one another. Similarly, *Ode to a Nightingale* (2.849) charts the speaker-poet's fluctuations of mood as Keats both responds to the hypnotic song of the nightingale and intensifies his own trancelike state by pursuing the chain of associations the bird's singing inspires; nature is narcotic, poetic imagery and language perhaps more so. Such intensive focus on the intricate workings of subjectivity may seem so familiar as to be unremarkable to your students, so it is worth reminding them that the conception of the self as a complex and layered interiority demanding careful study is—like such quintessentially "modern" formations as industrialism, democracy, secularism, and urban culture—relatively new to the nineteenth century.

Tintern Abbey is in many ways more concerned with the observing self than the landscape the self observes, as Wordsworth tracks the changes that have overtaken him since he last visited the banks of the Wye, laments that "I cannot paint / What then I was" (2.236, lines 75–76), and is consoled by finding in his sister, Dorothy, a type of his younger, more spontaneous, and impassioned self. The description of the landscape proper only occupies about an eighth of this 159-line poem, and even within this description the speaker-poet constantly intrudes himself: "again I hear" (line 2), "Once again / Do I behold" (lines 4–5), "I again repose" (line 9), "Once again I see" (line 14). As this example begins to make clear, close attentiveness to the complexities of subjectivity also has its dangers. In the Preface Wordsworth writes that poetry "takes its origin from emotion recollected in tranquillity: the emotion is contemplated till by a species of reaction the tranquility gradually disappears, and an emotion, kindred to that which was before the subject of contemplation, is gradually produced, and does itself actually exist in the mind" (2.250). Poetic sensibility, by this definition, requires a hypersensitivity to one's own internal state, and an artificial enhancement of the emotions. (See also the Norton Topics Online discussion "*Tintern Abbey,* Tourism, and Romantic Landscape.")

Too-acute self-awareness can serve as a form of entrapment, as is the case in Letitia Elizabeth Landon's *Love's Last Lesson* (2.1037), a poem that describes a woman's experience of passionate love and then the anguish of rejection in such a way as to yield the most minute and nuanced details of her pain and sorrow. As Byron the narrator writes in *Childe Harold's Pilgrimage,*

> Yet must I think less wildly:—I *have* thought
> Too long and darkly, till my brain became,
> In its own eddy boiling and o'erwrought,
> A whirling gulf of phantasy and flame. (2.567, lines 55–58)

Such disabling self-consciousness is also visible in Byron's *Manfred* (2.588), whose gloomy tragic hero is perhaps rather too preoccupied with contemplating the magnificence of his own ruin. That this state is akin to egoism the text makes clear when we learn that Manfred's misery stems from the loss of a narcissistic double who "had the same lone thoughts and wanderings," a sister/love object "like me in lineaments—her eyes, / Her hair, her features, all, to the very tone / Even of her voice, they said were like to mine" (2.602, lines 109, 105–7). (Compare the tragic youth of Shelley's *Alastor*, doomed by his love for an imagined "veiled maid" whose "voice was like the voice of his own soul / Heard in the calm of thought," 2.707, lines 151, 153–54.)

In an 1818 letter, Keats writes that "A Poet . . . has no Identity—he is continually in for—and filling some other Body" (2.895). When Keats criticizes the self-aggrandizing tendencies of the Romantic lyricist, he singles out Wordsworth as the most offensive "Egotist" (2.890), although a few months later he expresses his admiration for Wordsworth in another letter, praising him as a compassionate and insightful thinker (2.892). In still another letter, he coins the memorable phrase "the wordsworthian or egotistical sublime" (2.894) to describe a poetic sensibility overly enamored of itself. William Hazlitt satirizes the tendency of mere mortals to worship at the shrine of the egotistical sublime as much as poets' willingness to accept such worship when he writes that "ever after" hearing Wordsworth praise a sunset, "when I saw the sunset stream upon the objects facing it, [I] conceived I had made a discovery, or thanked Mr. Wordsworth for having made one for me!" (*My First Acquaintance with Poets,* 2.523). The Romantic era was an era of celebrity poets—Robinson, Byron, and Landon among the most notorious—and Wordsworth found himself the object of some adulation as his fame grew. Keats, however, is less concerned with Wordsworth's public persona than with his poetic persona when he writes sardonically, "How beautiful are the retired flowers! how would they lose their beauty were they to throng into the highway crying out, 'admire me I am a violet! dote upon me I am a primrose!' " (2.890).

The Prelude itself—so many thousands of lines devoted to what Wordsworth called "the growth of my own mind" (2.303)—is certainly the most visible artifact of the "wordsworthian sublime," thought it would be a mistake to reduce such a massive achievement to a mere exemplum of Keats's criticism. Certain key moments of *The Prelude* nonetheless would seem to illustrate Wordsworth's tendency to let a too-finely honed poetic sensibility intervene between the self and the world. In book 6, for example, the young Wordsworth is "grieved" to discover that the actual Mont Blanc isn't nearly as sublime as the Mont Blanc of his imagination (2.346, lines 524–29), and again "grieved" to find that the experience of crossing the Alps hasn't lived up to his expectations (2.347, lines 587–92). Here the poetic imagination—which serves Wordsworth so beautifully elsewhere in *The Prelude*—appears delimiting and even disabling, leaving him unable to really *see* the natural world, or relish his sensations as he moves through it. However, one need not assume that the older Wordsworth, expanding *The Prelude* a decade or more after these experiences took place, always identified completely with the persona of his younger self in the poem. Instead of failure of imagination, it is also possible to credit him with a modicum of humor at his own expense as in the case of the "Relic" stone he pocketed from the rubble of the Bastille.

A more obvious example of the "egotistical sublime" is *Resolution and Independence* (2.280). Wordsworth begins *Resolution* as the intently observing poet of nature, able to translate what he sees into striking images like this description of a hare running playfully in the morning sunshine: "And with her feet she from the plashy earth / Raises a mist; that, glittering in the sun, / Runs with her all the way" (lines 12–14). As the speaker-poet turns his focus inward, however, he is less and less able to observe, and instead frets that he won't always be a "happy Child of earth" like that "playful hare" (lines 31, 30). By the time he meets the old leech gatherer—described, rather problematically, as a natural artifact himself (a "huge stone," a "sea-beast crawled forth," lines 57, 62)—the speaker-poet has become self-absorbed to the point of solipsism:

> The old Man still stood talking by my side;
> But now his voice to me was like a stream
> Scarce heard; nor word from word could I divide;
> And the whole body of the Man did seem
> Like one whom I had met with in a dream;
> Or like a man from some far region sent,
> To give me human strength, by apt admonishment. (lines 106–12)

You can pair *Resolution and Independence* with Lewis Carroll's wicked parody, *The White Knight's Song* (2.1668), which satirizes Wordsworth's self-absorption, his elevation of humble folk and their humble professions, and the solemn portentousness of his conclusion (Carroll, by contrast, lapses into pure nonsense at the end of his poem, line piled on rhyming line sheerly for pleasure's sake).

The Dissolution of Subjectivity

It is also interesting to compare *Resolution and Independence* with the entry in Dorothy Wordsworth's *Grasmere Journals* that partly inspired it (2.387). Dorothy describes the old leech gatherer's utter destitution—all but one of his ten children are dead; badly injured in a cart accident, he cannot ply his trade and is reduced to begging—but she points no moral and draws no conclusion. Or compare Dorothy's journal entry about a walk during which she and William came unexpectedly upon a sea of daffodils (2.391) with William's *I wandered lonely as a cloud* (2.284; William, interestingly, rewrites the encounter as a solitary one). Each text has its own strengths: the latter is primarily concerned with the process by which the poet-speaker responds to the natural world and renders it meaningful to himself; the former abjures interpretation of the scene but is much richer and more finely nuanced in detail. In general, Dorothy Wordsworth's descriptive language is both precise and subtle, as in this depiction of the heath near Alfoxden: "Its surface restless and glittering with the motion of the scattered piles of withered grass, and the waving of the spiders' threads" (2.386). But except for the occasional "I saw" (which strikes one more as a refusal to pretend to render an omniscient point of view than as an interposition of self), Dorothy Wordsworth's passages detailing stormy nights, seascapes, trees, and flowers are almost entirely unflavored by her own subjective impressions. She focuses inward in certain entries, like the one describing her hysteria during the wedding of her brother (2.395), but otherwise seems content to remain an attentive observer of the natural world.

Clare's *The Nightingale's Nest* (2.803) not only practices but also emphasizes the importance of careful and respectful observation of nature. Of all the Romantic lyrics describing nightingales and other rhapsodic birds, this is the only one that describes what a nightingale looks like when she sings, what materials she uses to make her nest, the number and color of her eggs. Clare's nightingale is no figure for the poet or poetic imagination: she is a wild creature that humans must approach humbly and "softly . . . for fear / The noise may drive her from her home" (lines 3–4). Many a time, Clare tells his companion, he has crept "on hands and knees through matted thorns" just to get a glimpse of her (line 13), and "if I touched a bush or scarcely stirred, / All in a moment stopt. I watched in vain: / The timid bird had left the hazel bush" (lines 28–30). *Nightingale's Nest* teaches well with not only Keats's *Ode to a Nightingale* (2.849) but also William Wordsworth's *Nutting* (2.258), about the poet's plundering and even ravishment of the natural world. Clare, by contrast, looks and listens intently, but is careful not to disrupt; he does not rob the nightingale's nest when he finds it unexpectedly ("So even now / We'll leave it as we found it," lines 61–62), only pausing to learn how the nightingale weaves her nest and to note the precise color of her "curious eggs . . . / Of deadened green, or rather olive brown" (lines 89–90).

In *Nightingale's Nest* the subject only observes and does not interpose itself upon the natural world; Clare's *I Am* (2.808) describes, in a very different tone, the dissolution of subjectivity. "I am," the speaker-poet begins in what seems a simple and forceful assertion—but he qualifies that assertion steadily throughout the long sentence that takes up two-thirds of the poem. "None cares or knows" what he is; he has been "forsake[n] . . . like a memory lost" (lines 1–2); his unhappy thoughts are "like vapours tossed / Into the nothingness of scorn and noise" (lines 6–7). In the final stanza, he fantasizes about death, the final dissolution of self, much as Charlotte Smith longs for oblivion in *Written in the Church-Yard at Middleton in Sussex* (2.34).

It is easy to understand *I Am* within the context of Clare's long struggle with mental illness, but it's also possible to read it as one of many Romantic texts exploring the impermanence and instability of the self, whether in a melancholic or an ecstatic or a gothic register. Coleridge's *Pains of Sleep* (2.462), for instance, describes the dissipation of self-identity within the dream-state, where one finds "Desire with loathing strangely mixed / On wild and hateful objects fixed. / Fantastic passions! maddening brawl! / And shame and terror over all!" (lines 23–26). De Quincey's opium-induced visions are more phantasmic still, dissolving not only self but also all logic and narrative sense: space and time are amplified or collapsed or distorted surreally in his dreams of the court of Charles I being overrun by Roman legions; of Piranesi's labyrinthine interiors; of oceans swelled with human faces; of landscapes that

> brought together all creatures, birds, beast, reptiles, all trees and plants, usages and appearances, that are found in all tropical regions, and assembled them together in China or Indostan . . . I was stared at, hooted at, grinned at, chattered at, by monkeys, by paroquets, by cockatoos. I ran into pagodas: and was fixed, for centuries, at the summit, or in secret rooms; I was the idol; I was the priest; I was worshiped; I was sacrificed." (*Confessions of an English Opium-Eater,* 2.540)

Percy Shelley's *Mutability* (2.701), by contrast, rejoices in the fluctuability of subjectivity; humans are like clouds that cross the moon and "speed, and gleam, and quiver, / Streaking the darkness radiantly!" (lines 2–3). Though in his more bardic moments Shelley might seem like a good candidate for the egotistical sublime, he is not invested in the fantasy of an utterly self-possessed, all-powerful, and all-knowing subject, as satirized in his sonnet *Ozymandias* (2.725). He emphasizes the susceptibility and permeability of subjectivity ("Man is an instrument over which a series of external and internal impressions are driven") as much as the poet's ability to shape and control in his metaphor of the eolian lyre in *Defence of Poetry* (2.790), or when he compares himself to the "Ravine of Arve," receptacle of the thunderous "Power" of the icy river, and not the Arve itself, in *Mont Blanc* (2.720, lines 12, 16):

> I seem as in a trance sublime and strange
> To muse on my own separate phantasy,
> My own, my human mind, which passively
> Now renders and receives fast influencings,
> Holding an unremitting interchange
> With the clear universe of things around. (lines 35–40)

Such passages resonate with Keat's discussion of "negative capability," when he praises the poet who can remain "in uncertainties, Mysteries, doubts, without any irritable reaching after fact & reason. . . . With a great poet the sense of Beauty overcomes every other consideration, or rather obliterates all consideration" (2.889–90). Receptivity, rather than the struggle for mastery, brings wisdom. Elsewhere, as in the very beautiful letter that describes the world as a "vale of Soul-making" (2.896) or *The Fall of Hyperion* (2.873), Keats celebrates the poet's powers of sympathetic identification. None may approach the shrine guarded by Moneta "But those to whom the miseries of the world / Are misery, and will not let them rest" (*The Fall of Hyperion,* 2.878, lines 148–49). Acute awareness of this "World of Pains and troubles" (2.899) brings sorrow, but is preferable to an egoistic self-consciousness that blocks out one's view of the world. Best of all is to dissolve one's identity entirely by losing oneself in "richer entanglements, enthralments far / More self-destroying," like love (*Endymion*, 2.831, lines 798–99): "Melting into its radiance, we blend, / Mingle, and so become a part of it" (2.832, lines 810–11).

Contents: Norton Topics Online, The Romantic Period
www.wwnorton.com/nael

Contents: Norton Online Archive, The Romantic Period
www.wwnorton.com/nael/NOA

William Hazlitt
  From Mr. Wordsworth
Thomas Love Peacock
  The Four Ages of Poetry
  The War Song of Dinas Vawr
George Gordon, Lord Byron
  The Vision of Judgment
Percy Bysshe Shelley
  Song of Apollo
  To Jane. The Invitation
  The Triumph of Life
William Lisle Bowles
  To the River Itchin, near Winton
  Languid, and sad, and slow
Walter Savage Landor
  The Three Roses
  Dirce
  Well I remember how you smiled
George Darley
  The Phoenix
  It is not Beauty I demand
  The Mermaidens' Vesper Hymn
Thomas Lovell Beddoes
  Song ("How many times do I love thee, dear?")
  Song ("Old Adam, the carrion crow")
  The Phantom Wooer

Contents: NAEL Audio Companion, The Romantic Period

Robert Burns
  Green grow the rashes
    Performed by Jean Redpath
  Tam o' Shanter
    Read by David Daiches
George Gordon, Lord Byron
  She walks in beauty
    Music by Isaac Nathan. Performed by Malcolm Bilson and Judith Kellock
Percy Bysshe Shelley
  A Song: "Men of England"
    Performed by Susan Bender, Neil Gladd, and Myrna Sislen
  Choruses from *Hellas*: "Worlds on worlds"
    Music by William Christian Selle. Performed by Susan Bender and Carol Feather Martin
Joanna Baillie
  Song: "Woo'd and married and a' "
    Read by Gowan Calder

CHAPTER 7

The Victorian Age 1830–1901

Introducing the Victorians

The Victorian era is a messy, crowded, miscellaneous era: a confusing array of contradictory ideologies, intellectual, political, and religious controversies, and social and technological changes are grouped together almost arbitrarily, by virtue of the longevity of Queen Victoria. It is difficult to teach the Victorians in a survey course for this reason, and also because it is arguably the period of British literature about which first-time students (American students, at least) have formed the most stereotypes. Ask your students to begin the class or this section of the survey by listing what they think are typical Victorian characteristics, and they will likely say that the Victorians were complacent, stodgy, class-bound, formal, prudish, sexually and emotionally repressed, hypocritical, earnest, materialistic, and so on.

It is hardly a uniform period, however, as the *NAEL* period introduction makes clear: the country changed drastically between 1830 and the turn of the century; "The Victorian Age" (2.1043) subdivides its topic into three historical periods, and in the section "The Late Period (1870–1901): Decay of Victorian Values" it identifies more than a third of the era as being atypically Victorian, or anti-Victorian. And within any given decade Victorian lives differed drastically, depending on one's class status, whether one was a man or a woman, where one lived. The daughter of a prosperous merchant would receive an upbringing and education quite unlike her brother's, yet she would have more in common with him than with a pieceworker and part-time prostitute living in a London slum, who would in turn know nothing about the lives of rural laborers in the country village where her great-grandparents had lived. Those who love the Victorian period love it precisely because it *is* a messy, crowded, miscellaneous era; and for every literary instance that confirms a stereotype of "the Victorian," one can find another that explodes it.

In the nineteenth century one can see the invention, or new prominence and consolidation, of certain ideologies, practices, and structures characteristic of later modernity. The Industrial Revolution had begun in the late eighteenth century with James Watt's steam engine and the improvement of machines for processing textiles, and by the 1850s Britain's transformation from an agrarian-based to an industrial economy was complete. National prosperity was fueled by large-scale manufacturing and commerce—coal mining and processing, steelworks, and textile mills; railways and steamships—rather than agriculture. Power shifted from the land-holding and -inheriting aristocracy to those in manufacturing and trade, the middle classes, whose values, beliefs, and social customs were increasingly identified as those of the Victorian mainstream. Landless laborers and small peasant farmers migrated to the newly important industrial centers, and thus was created a new class, the urban proletariat, earning a wage within a capitalist and laissez-faire economic system rather than subsisting on the products of his or her own labor. With industrial capitalism there came an increasing separation of public and private spheres and an increasing identification of each sex with one of them. The Victorian period also witnessed the continued spread of democracy, including the progressive institution of universal manhood suffrage and the gradual extension of other basic rights to the lower classes and to women; increased literacy rates and new educational opportunities for all groups; and, with imperialism, the rise of global culture. New modes of producing and distributing commodities and new technologies like electric telegraphy and the steam press (both of which allowed for immediate coverage of news events), photography, railway and steamship travel, phonographic recording, and the typewriter transformed the texture of daily life. A concomitant to the consolidation of secular culture was the rise of not only evolutionary biology and other materialist sciences but also the human sciences: ethnography, psychology (especially alienism, the study of mental aberrations), sexology, criminology, and sociology.

"What is all this but a mad Fermentation; wherefrom, the fiercer it is, the clearer product will one day evolve itself? Such transitions are ever full of pain." As the introduction, "The Victorian Age," makes clear (see especially 2.1043–45), such rapid, unprecedented changes evoked wildly differing responses—enthusiasm, despair, optimism, anxiety, exhaustion, or some combination thereof, as in the above passage from Thomas Carlyle's *Sartor Resartus* (2.1078). Many Victorians lamented the loss of an older, more stable social order (whether real or imagined) and regarded the new age, unfolding beneath their feet, with both anticipation and terror. In *Characteristics* (1831) Carlyle complains that "the doom of the Old has long been pronounced, and irrevocable; the Old has passed away: but, alas, the New appears not in its stead; the Time is still in pangs of travail with the New." "The old order changeth, yielding place to new," the dying King Arthur says to Sir Bedivere in Alfred, Lord Tennyson's *Idylls of the King*. "Comfort thyself: what comfort is in me?" (2.1302, lines 408, 411). In *Stanzas from the Grand Chartreuse,* Matthew Arnold writes of being caught "between two worlds, one dead, / The other powerless to be born, / With nowhere yet to rest my head" (2.1495, lines 85–87).

Arnold's description of a journey through the Alps contrasts strikingly with book 6 of William Wordsworth's *Prelude* or Percy Shelley's *Mont Blanc*. The only insight that Arnold's speaker gleans is into his own inconsequentiality and displacement ("what am I, that I am here?" [2.1494, line 66]); the only certainty he finds is that his "faith is now / But a dead time's exploded dream" (2.1495, lines 97–98). Here and in many similar Victorian works, loss of religious faith stands in for, or is simultaneous with, a general cultural malaise, resulting from the relentless confusion of the times, as well as personal despair. "In our age of Down-pulling and Disbelief, the very Devil has been pulled down, you cannot so much as believe in a Devil. To me the Universe was all void of Life, of Purpose, of Volition, even of Hostility: it was one huge, dead, immeasurable Steam-engine, rolling on, in its dead indifference, to grind me limb from limb" (*Sartor Resartus,* 2.1081). Yet *Sartor*'s Professor Teufelsdröckh, at least tentatively, manages to reconcile himself to the seeming meaninglessness of the times, and the loss of his religious faith, by quenching his thirst at "little secular wells" rather than at "Saints' Wells" (2.1083). The barge bearing the dead King Arthur passes on "Down that long water opening on the deep / Somewhere far off" and vanishes, but it vanishes "into light," not darkness, while "the new sun rose, bringing the new year" (2.1303, lines 466–69): Tennyson sounds a cautious note of hope for a new social order, a new regime of meaningfulness, whose outlines are as yet unknown. Elizabeth Barrett Browning was a fierce critic of the social injustices of her era, but she also defended it against those who deemed it "unheroic," an "age of scum," an "age of mere transition." In *Aurora Leigh* she celebrates "this live, throbbing age, / That brawls, cheats, maddens, calculates, aspires. . . . The full-veined, heaving, double-breasted Age" (2.1193, lines 157, 161, 163; 2.1194, lines 203–4, 216).

From Revolution to Reform

Students who have just finished studying Romantic writings on the French Revolution will find it hard to believe that the three Reform Bills systematically enfranchising all adult men caused such furor among the Victorians. Yet, while the spread of democracy took place more or less peacefully in Victorian England, it was not accomplished without great social uproar. The First Reform Bill (1832) largely served more equitably to distribute power between Tories and Whigs, country and city. It extended the franchise to only about half the population of middle-class men; five out of six adult males still could not vote. Yet opponents of the First Reform Bill raged as if its passing would mean the end of England: church, monarchy, and government were about to be pulled down by ravening mobs of working-class hooligans, and private property would be abolished. When the Second Reform Bill (1867) was passed, giving voting rights to the remainder of middle-class men and to town workers, Arnold foresaw "anarchy," and deplored the distribution of power among England's "raw and uncultivated" masses. The working classes, he said satirically, are "beginning to assert and put in practice an Englishman's right to do what he likes; his right to march where he likes, meet where he likes, enter where he likes, hoot as he likes, threaten as he likes, smash as he likes" (*Culture and Anarchy,* 2.1531). In *Shooting Niagara: and After?* (1867), an older, increasingly conservative Carlyle described the progress toward democracy as England's headlong rush down the rapids, perhaps to shatter on the rocks below.

For Britain's poorest classes, of course, the spread of democracy and the pace of reform must have seemed bitterly, painfully slow. As the period introduction makes clear, reform was desperately needed, particularly in the early decades of Queen Victoria's reign, when the laboring classes suffered from intolerable working and living conditions and were hardest hit by the food shortages, economic depression, and typhus and cholera epidemics that ravaged the country (see especially 2.1046–68; see also the 1832 parliamentary report to the Sadler Committee on the Web site). This was the "condition of England" problem, and it included the "problem" of labor discontent and unrest, particularly after the working classes found that the passage of the First Reform Bill had failed to make any real difference in their situation. Feeling betrayed by the bourgeoisie with whom they had allied to champion the bill, they turned to working-class movements like Chartism, which unsuccessfully petitioned Parliament to pass the People's Charter, an electoral bill of rights, in 1839, 1842, and 1848.

Working-class demonstrations were largely peaceful, despite press to the contrary. Yet they often elicited hysterical anxiety. "Slowly comes a hungry people, as a lion, creeping nigher, / Glares at one that nods and winks behind a slowly-dying fire," Tennyson wrote in *Locksley Hall* (2.1223, lines 135–36). Perhaps the working classes were unjustly treated and deserving of compassion, or perhaps they were monsters—animalistic predators prepared to savage their "betters," like the *sans culottes* of the French Revolution. The specter of the French Revolution haunted the Victorians, especially during the earlier decades. Every trade unionist was a Jacobin, every Chartist an incendiary; every working-class demonstration was in danger of turning into a fearsome spectacle of mob violence like Burke had described, and Carlyle after him. Carlyle's *The French Revolution* describes condemned prisoners being tossed into a "howling sea" of revolutionaries, into a chaos "of wild sabres, axes and pikes," and "hewn asunder. And another sinks, and another; and there forms itself a piled heap of corpses, and the kennels begin to run red" (2.1104).

Reformists and antireformists alike told and retold the cautionary tale of the French Revolution: the Reform Bill would mean anarchy, an "unwonted wild tumult howling all round" (2.1104); conversely, only the Reform Bill could save England from France's gruesome fate. But Carlyle himself looked back with a certain admiration, and even nostalgia, at the "miracle" of the revolution. "A whole People, awakening as it were to consciousness in deep misery, believes that it is within reach of a Fraternal Heaven-on-Earth. With longing arms, it struggles to embrace the Unspeakable." At the end of the last century idealism and "Faith" had briefly inflamed "the heart of a People," and these were sadly needed to set right the sorry "condition of England" in this one (2.1109). Carlyle compares the French Revolution to a "Fireship," whose crew of radical incendiaries has torched the "gunpowder" and other combustibles of the "old French Form of Life." The corrupt *ancien regime* and Jacobinism burn alike in the resulting firestorm. "Wild are their cries, and their ragings there, like spirits tormented in that flame. But, on the whole, are they not *gone,* O Reader?" The flames have not spread to England, as so many Romantic authors had either hoped or feared: after "frightening the world," the Fireship has sailed away "into the Deep of Time." Two generations later the historian can only look back with wonder and terror and try to draw what lessons he can from this traumatic event. "Standing wistfully on the safe shore, we will look, and see, what is of interest to us, what is adapted to us" (2.1110). Two generations later England's leadership was sorely troubled as to how to solve the problem of an increasingly intolerable class disparity.

The "Condition of England"

In *A Review of Southey's* Colloquies, Thomas Babington Macaulay attacks Robert Southey's contention that "the manufacturing system" has brought nothing but misery to the people of England. It is not the case that industrialism "destroys the bodies and degrades the minds of those who are engaged in it" (2.1698), Macaulay asserts: drawing on statistics about the longevity and prosperity of the urban laborer, he concludes that "the people live longer because they are better fed, better lodged, better clothed, and better attended in sickness, and that these improvements are owing to that increase of national wealth which the manufacturing system has produced" (2.1699).

The aesthetic critique of industrialism would become a powerful tool in the hands of political reformers like Charles Dickens and John Ruskin. In the excerpt from *Hard Times,* for instance, Dickens emphasizes the monotonous ugliness of Coketown, whose red-brick houses, built around "a river that ran purple with ill-smelling dye," are disfigured by smoke, ashes, and soot. The starkly hideous houses and streets are "all very like one another," and the lives of the unhappy people who work in Coketown are "equally like one another . . . every day was the same as yesterday and tomorrow, and every year the counterpart of the last and the next" (2.1712). Southey also saw the uniform and drab living quarters of the urban working classes ("as offensive to the eyes as to the mind") as symptomatic of the misery of working-class lives and contrasted them unfavorably to the picturesque, homey cottages of poor rural laborers. Macaulay, however, jeers at a social critique that rests on the fact that "the dwellings of cotton-spinners are naked and rectangular" (2.1700). "Here is wisdom," he writes contemptuously. "Here are the principles on which nations are to be governed. Rosebushes and poor rates, rather than steam engines and independence. Mortality and cottages with weather stains, rather than health and long life with edifices which time cannot mellow" (2.1699).

Macaulay was famous for articulating a view of Victorian progress that would prevail throughout much of the nineteenth century: that economic improvement was natural and inevitable, and that the march toward greater and greater national wealth would be steady and triumphant. British prosperity, in fact, was divinely sanctified, a gift of "the supreme being" and of "those general laws"—such as the laws governing a laissez-faire economic system—"which it has pleased him to establish in the physical and in the moral world" (2.1700). While acknowledging that the "present moment is one of great distress" for certain classes of people, he predicts an England that will grow "richer and richer," so long as its government is careful not to overregulate its industries (2.1701). "Our rulers will best promote the improvement of the nation by strictly confining themselves to their own legitimate duties, by leaving capital to find its most lucrative course, commodities their fair prices, industry and intelligence their natural reward" (2.1702).

The laissez-faire economy Macaulay champions, Carlyle takes as a sign of widespread social indifference to the terrible plight of the working poor. In *Past and Present* Carlyle, himself born into poverty, in many ways sympathizes with and champions the working classes. "It is not to die, or even to die of hunger, that makes a man wretched. . . . But it is to live miserable we know not why; to work sore and yet gain nothing; to be heartworn, weary, yet isolated, unrelated, girt-in with a cold universal Laissez-faire: it is to die slowly all our life long, imprisoned in a deaf, dead, Infinite Injustice" (2.1111). In passages like this the laboring classes are not a "they" but a "we," as if Carlyle were one of them: like other reformers, he proposes to speak for those who have no voice. Yet epithets like the "Dumb Class" or the "dumb millions" (2.1111) seem condescending in light of Carlyle's argument that the working classes do not require reform bills, or suffrage, or the other liberties prized by Romantic revolutionaries but rather secretly crave the sort of kindly, beneficent leadership that prevailed in feudal times. "Liberty? The true liberty of a man," in the days of feudalism, "consisted in his finding out, or being forced to find out, the right path, and to walk thereon." The lower-class individual who tries to forge out "the right path" toward freedom on his own is like a "madman" who must be restrained for his own good, lest he do himself some irreparable harm (2.1112).

Thus the type of the ideal laborer in *Past and Present* is a swineherd from Scott's *Ivanhoe*, Gurth, "born thrall of Cedric the Saxon. . . . Gurth to me seems happy, in comparison with many a Lancashire and Buckinghamshire man, of these days, not born thrall of anybody! Gurth's brass collar did not gall him: Cedric *deserved* to be his Master" (2.1112). However, in the debased days of modernity, the traditional hereditary aristocracy has given up its prerogative of noble leadership and is characterized by "withered flimsiness" and "godless baseness and barrenness." The "mild" and highborn "Benefactress" no longer dispenses her charity and "blessings" (2.1111–12); there is no gallant and generous Cedric who *deserves* to be Gurth's master.

For the Gurths of the industrial age, then, the "grand problem [that] yet remains to be solved" is "how to find government by your Real-Superiors!" Because the landed aristocracy can no longer provide the leadership cadre, "this immense Problem of Organizing Labour, and . . . of Managing the Working Classes, will . . . have to be solved by those who stand practically in the middle of it; by those who themselves work and preside over work" (2.1115). Carlyle pins his hopes on a new kind of "aristocracy," the "Captains of Industry," who must be turned from their pursuit of wealth and awakened to their duty. "The leaders of Industry, if Industry is ever to be led, are virtually the Captains of the World; if there be no nobleness in them, there will never be an Aristocracy more" (2.1116). A version of this scenario—where the factory owner learns to be not so much a feudal lord as a father figure to his working-class operatives, who are revealed as dependents sorely in need of his benevolent guidance—occurs again and again in "condition of England" novels like Elizabeth Gaskell's *Mary Barton* (1848) and *North and South* (1855), Benjamin Disraeli's *Sybil* (1845), and *Hard Times* (1854). In a Victorian-only survey you may wish to supplement *NAEL* with one of these; *Mary Barton* in particular (see the *Preface* on the Web site) works well with the readings both on industrialism and on "the woman question."

Into "Darkest England"

Friedrich Engels, of course, would propose a more radical solution than paternalistic benevolence to the conflict between manufacturer and worker, which he identifies outright as "class warfare" in the selection from *The Condition of the Working Class* (2.1703). Your students, who likely have encountered Marxist philosophy only in the most ahistorical of circumstances, may be interested to know that both Marx and Engels studied in Victorian England (Engels was sent to Manchester by his father, a German cotton-mill owner, to complete his training in the family business), and their critique of capitalism resulted from firsthand observation of what had gone wrong in the country that was the first fully to industrialize. Like Annie Besant, who describes manufacturers as parasites who "suck wealth out of the starvation of helpless girls" working in their factories (2.1717), Engels argues that the prosperity that Macaulay celebrates enriches only a few, who maintain their wealth, and achieve full self-realization, through continued exploitation of the poor. "The vast majority" of the working classes "have had to let so many of their potential creative faculties lie dormant, stunted and unused in order that a small closely-knit group of their fellow citizens could develop to the full the qualities with which nature has endowed them." Like Carlyle, Engels attacks laissez-faire political economy as a system based on "barbarous indifference and selfish egotism" (2.1704).

"In one of these courts, just at the entrance where the covered passage ends, there is a privy without a door. This privy is so dirty that the inhabitants of the court can only enter or leave the court if they are prepared to wade through puddles of stale urine and excrement" (2.1707). As they read the horrifying descriptions of the slums of Manchester and London in the excerpts from *Condition of the Working Class* and Charles Kingsley's *Alton Locke,* it is important that your students know that Engels and Kingsley are not exaggerating. The rural poor had poured into London and the industrial centers in search of employment and found no decent housing ready to receive them. There was no public planning, and no regulation of slum development: just a "chaotic conglomeration of houses, most of which are more or less uninhabitable" (2.1709). Neighborhoods of cheap, shoddy houses were thrown up in haphazard fashion—"unplanned wildernesses," Engels calls them—on streets "unpaved and full of holes," and with "neither gutters nor drains" (2.1704–5). Whole families, or a "group of families," might be crowded into a single room, as we see in *Alton Locke* (2.1711). Landlords had no financial incentive to improve their ramshackle properties or hook up the tenements to the sewage and water systems, if these even existed. One filthy, overflowing privy might serve two hundred families; thus Engels's recurrent emphasis on the "heaps of dirt and filth" spread about the Manchester slum neighborhoods he explores (2.1707). "How can these people wash when all that is available is the dirty water of the Irk?" Engels asks—the Irk, a "narrow, coal-black, stinking river full of filth and rubbish," whose banks are covered with "revolting blackish-green puddles of slime" (2.1709, 1708).

And yet it was possible for such misery to remain invisible to those who did not choose, or did not know where, to look for it. "Owing to the curious lay-out of the town it is quite possible for someone to live for years in Manchester and to travel daily to and from his work without ever seeing a working-class quarter" (2.1705–6). Manchester's business district was a "central or inner core that is packed by day and deserted at night." Laborers needed to walk to their workplaces, so the slums were built up in belts around this inner core; the middle classes who conducted their business in the city core, and had once lived there, had moved to the "suburban heights" connected by direct thoroughfares to the factories and shops at the city center. Thus "plutocrats" and their families could travel in and out of town, by omnibus or carriage, on streets that run "entirely through working-class districts, without even realizing how close they are to the misery and filth which lie on both sides of the road" (2.1706).

In London, too, the poor were hidden from sight in slum neighborhoods so tortuous and inaccessible, so dangerous, even, that investigative parties would not venture in without a policeman for a guide. "As there is a darkest Africa is there not also a darkest England?" asked William Booth, founder of the Salvation Army (*In Darkest England and the Way Out,* 1890): only the most intrepid and dedicated "social explorers" could, or dared, make their way through the wilds of "darkest England." "Deep are the mysteries of London," George Godwin wrote in *London Shadows: A Glance at the "Homes" of the Thousands* (1854), "and so environed by difficulties, that few can penetrate them. The condition of large sections of its inhabitants is wholly unknown to the majority of those above them in the social pyramid, the wide base of which is made up of poverty, ignorance, degradation, crime, and misery." Reformers hoped to bring that misery to light. Carlyle, Engels, and Besant are particularly concerned with the plight of the working poor, as is Elizabeth Barrett Browning, whose *The Cry of the Children* describes underage factory workers ground under by the "mailed heel" of industry (2.1178, line 155). Dickens's *A Visit to Newgate* focuses on "the guilt and misery" of the criminal classes (2.1336), and Henry Mayhew's *London Labour and the London Poor,* the residuum: the vagrants, beggars, and street-finders who exist on the margins of the wage economy, like the "boy inmate of the causal wards," a former child factory hand who has "begged [his] way from Manchester to London" (2.1714; see also *Statement of a Vagrant* from the Web site). Philanthropists, journalists, missionaries, sociologists, and novelists believed that the worst miseries would be alleviated once public sympathy was aroused: their main goal, besides providing facts and statistics urgently required by Royal Commissions, was to dramatize the evils and tragedies of poverty for middle-class readers in hope of stimulating reform. Early sociology was for this reason often more sensational than any Victorian potboiler, as evidenced by such evocative, melodramatic titles as *Horrible London, The Great Unwashed, The Seven Curses of London, Town Swamps and Social Bridges, The People of the Abyss,* and *The Bitter Cry of Outcast London.*

The Aesthetics of Reform

In Dickens's *The Old Curiosity Shop* (1841), Nell and her grandfather lose their way among the damp and soot-covered streets of industrial Birmingham, rest overnight in a factory like an Inferno, whose workers move "like demons among the flame and smoke, dimly and fitfully seen, flushed and tormented by the burning fires," then travel for two long days through the slag heaps and blasted landscape outside the city. The surreal ugliness of the industrial landscape corresponds to the misery and abject poverty of the "savage" people who live in the "unroofed, windowless, blackened, desolate" company houses and work in the endless factories "crowding on each other, and presenting that endless repetition of the same dull, ugly form, which is the horror of oppressive dreams." In *How I Became a Socialist,* William Morris explains that it was not just a consciousness of "the wrongs of society" and "the oppression of poor people" that led him into radicalism (2.1619). He also reacted, as an artist and designer, against the "sordid, aimless, ugly confusion," the "dull squalor," of the industrial age. "Apart from the desire to produce beautiful things, the leading passion of my life has been and is hatred of modern civilization" (2.1620).

Arnold's *Culture and Anarchy* also combines an aesthetic critique of modernity with social analysis, though of course to very different political ends than Morris. On the one hand indicting the Puritanism, pragmatism, crass aesthetic sensibilities, and materialism of the middle classes, and on the other, the coarse hooliganism of the working classes, Arnold condemns his era for its "vulgarity, hideousness, ignorance, violence" (2.1534). The Second Reform Bill, as far as Arnold is concerned, was the last straw, placing political power in the hands of the brutes as well as the philistines, so that England now is "in danger of drifting towards anarchy" as well as ugliness (2.1530). Arnold's solution to the "vulgarity" of modern life is to return to what he defines as "Hellenic" values: to pursue the timeless ideals of beauty and truth, to "see things as they really are," to cultivate "spontaneity of consciousness," better to integrate morality and intellect—to reverence "sweetness and light," in his perhaps most famous phrase (2.1532, 1534).

Arnold's was one of the most eloquent Victorian voices to speak against middle-class cultural insularity and anti-intellectualism. Above all else, he writes in *The Function of Criticism at the Present Time,* the English value "material progress" ("our railways, our business, and our fortune-making") and being "perfectly comfortable"; they care nothing for the "free play of the mind," for the cultivation of the intellect for its own sake. "The Englishman has been called a political animal, and he values what is political and practical so much that ideas easily become objects of dislike in his eyes" (2.1521–22). By insisting on a rigid separation between intellectual speculation and political practice, however, Arnold ends up dismissing political idealism (whether associated with Romantic-era revolutionary sympathies or Victorian reform) as crass and short-sighted pragmatism, even another form of anti-intellectualism. The French Revolution was admirable because of "the force, truth, and universality of the ideas which it took for its law, and . . . the passion with which it could inspire a multitude for these ideas," but "the mania for giving an immediate political and practical application to all these fine ideas of the reason was fatal" (2.1519). Thus, in *Culture and Anarchy,* the Second Reform Bill's extension of democracy is merely another symptom of the Victorian "idolatry of machinery"; the extension of democracy to working-class men is conflated with the middle-class worship of material well-being; and, in a *reductio ad absurdum*, "liberty" is redefined as selfishly "doing as one likes" (2.1530).

Similarly, while in *Function of Criticism* Arnold wittily excoriates middle-class Victorian complacency—"Such a race of people as we stand, so superior to all the world! The old Anglo-Saxon race, the best breed in the whole world! I pray that our unrivaled happiness may last!" (2.1524)—he criticizes English philistinism with blunt-edged instruments. Describing an article about a young working-class woman named Wragg, arrested for strangling her illegitimate child, Arnold lets loose with a stream of sardonic invective:

> how eloquent, how suggestive are those few lines! . . . If we are to talk of ideal perfection, of "the best in the whole world," has anyone reflected what a touch of grossness in our race, what an original shortcoming in the more delicate spiritual perceptions, is shown by the natural growth amongst us of such hideous names—Higginbottom, Stiggins, Bugg! In Ionia and Attica they were luckier in this respect than "the best race in the world"; by the Ilissus there was no Wragg, poor thing! . . . And the final touch—short, bleak and inhuman: *Wragg is in custody.* The sex lost in the confusion of our unrivaled happiness; . . . the superfluous Christian name lopped off by the straightforward vigor of our old-Anglo-Saxon breed! There is profit for the spirit in such contrasts as this; criticism serves the cause of perfection by establishing them. (2.1524–25)

The woman Wragg is an object lesson in what is "harsh and ill-favored" (2.1524) in her social class and in modern life; she has an aesthetically displeasing name and has committed an aesthetically displeasing crime. Arnold's contrasting of Wragg's miserable situation and the graciousness of Greek culture is almost shockingly inappropriate. Here we see the limitations, and the dangers, of the aesthetic critique of modernity.

In Ruskin's work, by contrast, we see Victorian socioaesthetic critique at its most powerful. Ruskin's *The Storm-Cloud of the Nineteenth Century* charts the atmospheric changes wrought by decades of industrialism—the clouds of pollution that block the sun, the "plague-wind," fitful and "feverish," that "looks partly as if it were made of poisonous smoke. . . . But mere smoke would not blow to and fro in that wild way. It looks to me as if it were made of dead man's souls" (2.1444, 1446). "Blanched Sun,—blighted grass,—blinded man." The plague-wind denotes not just industrial contamination, but also the "moral gloom" of an era in which "every man [is] doing as much injustice to his brother as it is in his power to do" (2.1450). The "animation" of England's "multitudes is sent like fuel to feed the factory smoke," Ruskin argues in *The Stones of Venice* (2.1437). In the opening pages of this essay Ruskin seems simply to be training his readers in aesthetic valuation, inviting them to consider art and architecture from an organicist perspective, as he shows how forms of architecture should be in harmony with and suitable to their environment. Thus Greek and Italian standards of beauty are not timeless and universal standards, as Arnold would have it: one must learn to value seemingly ruder, more primitive forms of art, to "reverence" the "rough strength" of the Gothic builder of the north, who "smites an uncouth animation out of the rocks which he has torn from among the moss of the moorland" (2.1434).

Gradually, Ruskin shifts into an explicitly ethical critique of art. Gothic architecture is "noble" not just because it so well suits the northern landscape and temperament: "it possesses a higher nobility still, when considered as an index, not of climate, but of religious principle." The classical architectures (Greek, Ninevite, and Egyptian) usually so much admired, Ruskin considers immoral, for they relied on "Servile ornament," whereby "the execution or power of the inferior workman is entirely subjected to the intellect of the higher." The Greeks could not "endure the appearance of imperfection in anything," and thus chose to work with "geometrical forms . . . which could be executed with absolute precision by line and rule" (2.1434). The workman who executed the forms was literally a slave—but more important, was rendered servile by his engagement with work that required no invention, no creativity, no imagination. Gothic architecture, by contrast, deployed the system of "Revolutionary ornament" (also called medieval or Christian ornament), whereby "no executive inferiority is admitted at all." This system recognizes the "individual value of every soul" of every workman, and thus encourages creativity in each workman, with the understanding that the finished product will then, of necessity, be flawed—but paradoxically, more beautiful for its imperfection (2.1434–45).

"And therefore, while in all things that we see, or do, we are to desire perfection, and strive for it, we are nevertheless not to set the meaner thing, in its narrow accomplishment, above the nobler thing, it its mighty progress; not to esteem smooth minuteness above shattered majesty" (2.1435). Making an argument rather like Robert Browning's in *Andrea del Sarto*—"a man's reach should exceed his grasp, / Or what's a heaven for?" (2.1387, lines 98–99)—Ruskin sweeps the reader up in his eloquent aesthetic valuation, but then suddenly turns midparagraph to consider the more controversial topic of present-day labor relations. Modern English consumers demand "smooth minuteness" and technical perfection in their jewelry, housewares, and other commodities; and thus the modern factory owner is not willing to accept errors and imperfections from his workers, but requires, like the Greek slave drivers, that they "work with the accuracy of tools" and "be precise and perfect in all their actions." To demand such accuracy, such precision, is to "unhumanize" the workers (2.1436), says Ruskin the social conservative, in an argument that resonates startlingly with that of his contemporary Marx on dehumanized and alienated industrial labor:

> All their attention and strength must go to the accomplishment of the mean act. The eye of the soul must be bent upon the finger point, and the soul's force must fill all the invisible nerves that guide it, ten hours a day, that it may not err from its steely precision, and so soul and sight be worn away, and the whole human being be lost at last—a heap of sawdust, so far as its intellectual work in this world is concerned. (2.1436)

Ruskin also looks back to feudalism for a solution to the "condition of England" problem. Ruskin's workers, engaged in "vain, incoherent, destructive struggling for a freedom of which they cannot explain the nature to themselves," require wise guidance more than liberty, like Carlyle's Gurth the swineherd. "I know not if a day is ever to come when the nature of right freedom will be understood, and when men will see that to obey another man, to labor for him, yield reverence to him or to his place, is not slavery. It is often the best kind of liberty—liberty from care" (2.1437). Ruskin, however, proposes a certain leveling of class distinctions, a sort of meritocracy in the workplace, whereby one distinguishes operatives "only in experience and skill." Intellectual and manual labor should not be separate activities: "always in these days . . . we want one man to be always thinking, and another to be always working, and we call one a gentleman, and the other an operative; whereas the workman ought often to be thinking, and the thinker often to be working; and both should be gentlemen, in the best sense" (2.1441). Morris, who successfully implemented Ruskin's ideas in his workshops, also pushed his philosophy to a more radical conclusion. In *How I Became a Socialist* he hopes for "a condition of society in which there should be neither rich nor poor, neither master nor master's man, neither idle nor overworked, neither brain-sick brain workers, nor heart-sick hand workers" (2.1618).

The "Woman Question"

> A queen in opal or in ruby dress,
> A nameless girl in freshest summer-greens,
> A saint, an angel;—every canvass means
> The same one meaning, neither more nor less.
> (Christina Rossetti, *In an Artist's Studio* [2.1586, lines 5–8])

Even the most radical authors on "the woman question" seldom argued that men and women were essentially similar. They debated instead about the extent of their dissimilarity, what proper relations between the sexes ought to be, which "womanly" qualities were fixed and inherent and which culturally determined, and what sorts of activities women were best suited to or disabled from attempting. In *The Subjection of Women,* John Stuart Mill points out the fallacy of claiming that certain characteristics are "natural" to women. Whatever is customary always seems natural, he argues, and those in power "hold it to be Nature's own dictate that the conquered should obey the conquerors" (2.1156). "All women are brought up from the very earliest years in the belief that their ideal of character is the very opposite to that of men; not self-will, and government by self-control, but submission, and yielding to the control of others" (2.1158).

Thus women cannot know themselves, Mill argues; art, history, science, medicine, all traditions paint a portrait of femininity that "is wretchedly imperfect and superficial, and always will be so, until women themselves have told all that they have to tell" (2.1163). Lizzie Siddal, the model in *In an Artist's Studio*, remains "hidden just behind those screens" (line 3)—that is, behind the canvases, which "mirror" the desire of the painter, Christina's brother Dante Gabriel Rossetti, and conceal the real woman's complex desires, disappointments, and aspirations from the onlooker and even, perhaps, from herself. Clothing his model in all the conventional forms of femininity ("A saint, an angel"), the painter shows her "Not as she is, but as she fills his dream" (line 14). (Christina herself was painted as the Virgin Mary by her brother; see *Ecce Ancilla Domini* [The Annunciation] on the Web site.) In Mary Elizabeth Coleridge's *The Other Side of a Mirror* (2.1861), the speaker tries to understand what lies behind the facade of complacent and cheerful womanhood (the "aspects glad and gay") she has been taught to maintain (line 3). Looking beyond and behind the mirror of traditional representation she finds a "wild" vision of herself (line 5) that's terrifying, yet oddly compelling:

> And in her lurid eyes there shone
>   The dying flame of life's desire,
> Made mad because its hope was gone,
>   And kindled at the leaping fire
> Of jealousy, and fierce revenge,
>   And strength that could not change nor tire. (lines 19–24)

"I am she!" the speaker concludes, preferring this "speechless," "distracted," "hideous," and enraged specter of femininity to "fairer visions" of angels and saints (lines 30, 17, 29, 15, 27).

The "Woman Question" readings on 2.1719–39—supplemented by those on the Web site and easily matched with Charles Darwin on sexual selection, George Eliot's *Margaret Fuller and Mary Wollstonecraft*, Mill's *Subjection of Women*, and the Besant and Ada Nield Chew selections in the special section "Industrialism: Progress or Decline?"—can be taught as a self-contained unit, or in tandem with literary works such as Barrett Browning's *Aurora Leigh*, Gaskell's *The Old Nurse's Story*, Christina Rossetti's *Goblin Market*, or Bernard Shaw's *Mrs. Warren's Profession*. If you are teaching a Victorian-only survey and have time to include a novel that deals explicitly with the situation of women (Charlotte Brontë's *Jane Eyre* or Eliot's *Middlemarch*, for example), you may find it useful to break up your discussion midway through and use some or all of the woman question readings to historically contextualize and deepen your readings of the novel. There are a number of helpful resources you can place on reserve or otherwise use to supplement your discussion of the woman question, such as *Victorian Women: A Documentary Account of Women's Lives in Nineteenth-Century England, France, and the United States* (1981), the two-volume *Women, the Family, and Freedom: The Debate in Documents* (1983), and the three-volume *The Woman Question: Society and Litera-*

ture in Britain and America, 1837–1883 (1983). All of these excerpt or liberally quote from nineteenth-century sources.

Separate Spheres

The selection from Tennyson's *The Princess* (2.1229), however much it upholds the ideal of the complementarity of the sexes, insists that men and women, "Distinct in individualities," are at the core radically unlike. *The Princess* advocates woman's rights in a very guarded way, arguing against a woman-centered or separatist version of feminism. Instead, man must make woman's battles his own, for their fates are intertwined. "The woman's cause is man's: they rise or sink / Together, dwarfed or godlike, bond or free." A limited version of the "woman's cause" in fact serves male interests, for, as the speaker points out, uneducated, narrow-minded women make poor wives: "If she be small, slight-natured, miserable, / How shall men grow?" Man should foster woman's growth and self-improvement, and help "clear away the parasitic forms / That seem to keep her up but drag her down." However, she should not be encouraged to grow *outside* her basic nature: let her "live and learn and be / All that not harms distinctive womanhood" (lines 243–58).

Women's education should not make them more like men, but should develop their "distinctive womanhood." *The Princess* emphasizes the separate and discrete essence of femininity. "For woman is not undevelopt man, / But diverse: could we make her as the man, / Sweet Love were slain" (lines 259–61). The difference between the sexes is mandated by nature, here represented by romantic desire. In the ideal future, perhaps, men and women will grow to be more alike—but not too much; necessary distinctions between the sexes must remain intact.

> Yet in the long years liker must they grow;
> The man be more of woman, she of man;
> He gain in sweetness and in moral height,
> Nor lose the wrestling thews that throw the world;
> She mental breadth, nor fail in childward care,
> Nor lose the childlike in the larger mind. (lines 263–66).

While morally enlightened by the woman, the man will retain the strength (the "wrestling thews") that enables him to contend with the duties of the world; while intellectually enlightened by the man, the woman will retain the "childlike" innocence that suits her for domestic duties.

Similar arguments—that the sexes complement one another in their differences; that each sex's essential characteristics befit men and women for certain duties and activities and disqualify them for others; that each sex is best suited for a particular social space—underpin the Victorian ideology of separate spheres: men's work lies in the marketplace, women's in the home. One of the most thorough mid-Victorian explications of this ideology can be found in Ruskin's *Of Queen's Gardens* (1865), one of two lectures collected under the title *Sesame and Lilies* (excerpted at length on the Web site and more briefly on 2.1057):

> Now their separate characters are briefly these. The man's power is active, progressive, defensive. He is eminently the door, the creator, the discoverer, the defender. His intellect is for speculation and invention; his energy for adventure, for war, and for conquest, wherever war is just, wherever conquest necessary. But the woman's power is for rule, not for battle,—and her intellect is not for invention or creation, but for sweet ordering, arrangement, and decision. She sees the qualities of things, their claims, and their places. Her great function is Praise: she enters into no contest, but infallibly adjudges the crown of contest.

"By her office, and place," the woman, safe at home, is "protected from all danger and temptation." The man, meanwhile, is busy with "his rough work in the open world," and he is battered and bruised by his efforts in the public sphere: "often he must be wounded, or subdued, often misled, and *always* hardened." But then he returns at night to his household, which is a "sacred place, a vestal temple" watched over by the domestic angel. Here he is soothed and softened by the feminine influence (just as he guards his wife from the dangers of the marketplace), and can return to his "rough work" the next day with fresh vigor and a renewed moral sense.

The excerpt from Sarah Stickney Ellis's *The Women of England* (2.1721) presents an argument quite similar to Ruskin's. Men pursue "worldly aggrandizement" and "clos[e] their ears against the voice of conscience" when they labor within "the mart, the exchange, or the public assembly." Thus they return home with "a mind confused," with their "inborn selfishness" reinforced, with their "integrity . . . shaken"—only to stand "corrected before the clear eye of woman." The "influence of women" is necessary to "counteract . . . the growing evils of society"; in fact, woman goes into the workplace herself in a certain sense, as man's "second conscience," a "secret influence" borne inwardly (2.1722).

A troublesome contradiction underlies arguments like these, and Victorian gender ideology in general: woman is said to be intrinsically nobler than man, yet is at the same time an inferior who must learn (in Ruskin's words) "true wifely subjection." Though Ellis argues adamantly for the constriction of women's roles, she aggrandizes women nonetheless and argues that they "have obtained a degree of importance in society far beyond what their unobtrusive virtues would appear to claim" because theirs is "the high and holy duty of cherishing and protecting the minor morals of life, from whence springs all that is elevated in purpose, and glorious in action" (2.1722). In Coventry Patmore's best-selling poem *The Angel in the House* (2.1725), which celebrates woman's "worth as Maid and Wife" (line 38), the angel-woman is eulogized as "The best half of creation's best" (line 29), nature's "aim and its epitome" (line 32), almost as if in compensation for her delimitation within the domestic sphere. "I'll teach how noble man should be / To match with such a lovely mate" (lines 43–44).

The ideal woman in *Of Queen's Gardens* is "enduringly, incorruptibly good; instinctively, infallibly wise—wise not for self-development, but for self-renunciation" (2.1057). Ellis also values self-renunciation, or what she calls "disinterested kindness," in women. They should not aspire to philosophical knowledge or learnedness in general, but rather to "the majesty of moral greatness," and train themselves to begin and end each day "on the watch for every opportunity of doing good to others" (2.1722–23). Dinah Maria Mulock, though she laments the lack of "something to do" in the average middle-class woman's life, proposes as a solution something very like Ellis's disinterested kindness in *A Woman's Thoughts about Women* (2.1732). Rather than wasting her time with embroidery, piano playing, dancing, and idle chatter, each woman should find meaningful work (teaching, care taking) "lying very near to hand" within the household, or "extend her service out of the home into the world," because "hardly one of [life's] charities and duties can be done so thoroughly as by a wise and tender woman's hand." (Ruskin also argues that charity work is a logical extension of domestic duties.) Her ideal woman is nobly, unfailingly selfless and beloved of all who know her. "You will rarely find she thinks much about herself; she has never had time for it" (2.1733). Dickens is often criticized for his representations of self-sacrificing, humble, and tirelessly helpful little women like little Nell, Florence Dombey, and Esther Summerson, but he also shows how such qualities may be ruthlessly exploited or abused, as in *The Old Curiosity Shop* and *Dombey and Son* (1848), or pushes them to the point of parody, as in *Bleak House* (1853).

Mulock claims that middle-class women, unless they actively seek it, have no meaningful work to perform and waste their time in idle pursuits. Nightingale, on the other hand, argues that middle-class women have too much to do. They are in fact encouraged and even obligated to while away their hours with trivial activities ("sitting around a table in the drawing-room, looking at prints, doing worsted work, and reading little books"); they "find it impossible to follow up . . . systematically" any worthier occupation, because they must "allow themselves *willingly* to be interrupted at all hours" by the exigencies of social engagements. The self-abnegation that Ellis and Mulock praise, Nightingale criticizes: women "have accustomed themselves to consider intellectual occupation as a merely selfish amusement, which it is their 'duty' to give up for every trifler more selfish than themselves" (2.1735–36). As Harriet Martineau points out in the selection from her *Autobiography*, even Jane Austen, "the Queen of novelists," could not work without interruption, but "was compelled by the feelings of her family to cover up her manuscripts with a large piece of muslin work . . . whenever any genteel people came in." Before her family had the good luck, as she saw it, to fall on straitened means, Martineau herself had to pursue her "first studies in philosophy . . . with great care and reserve. . . . If ever I shut myself into my own room for an hour of solitude, I knew it was at the risk of being sent for to join the sewing-circle, or to read aloud" (2.1725).

Education, Work, and Marriage

In the Ruskin quote above, woman is "enduringly" good, "instinctively" wise, yet a great deal of training must be expended in making her realize her enduring goodness and instinctive wisdom. Ellis speaks rather ominously of "the kind of education [that] is most effective in making woman what she ought to be" (2.1722), as if nature could not be trusted to do its work of developing the intrinsically feminine trait of self-renunciation. And many authors, of course, argue that unselfishness (however laudable in men and women both) is not intrinsically feminine at all. In Mill's *Subjection of Women*, the overvaluation of female self-sacrifice is the result of cultural convention and even coercion, used to hold "women in subjection, by representing to them meekness, submissiveness, and resignation of all individual will into the hands of man, as an essential part of sexual attractiveness" (2.1159).

It might be useful here to ask your students to review the selections from *A Vindication of the Rights of Woman*, wherein Wollstonecraft argues that systems of female education "degrade one half of the human species, and render women pleasing at the expense of every solid virtue" (2.173). In her essay *Margaret Fuller and Mary Wollstonecraft*, Eliot deplores "the folly of absolute definitions of woman's nature and absolute demarcations of woman's mission," and urges "the removal of unjust laws and artificial restrictions, so that the possibilities of [woman's] nature may have room for full development" (2.1459, 1456). Like Wollstonecraft, like Mill (who claims that "What is now called the nature of women is an eminently artificial thing—the result of forced repression in some directions, unnatural stimulation in others" [2.1161]), Eliot regards woman's "nature" as something as yet unknown—something that has till now been stunted by an upbringing and education that work consistently to delimit and diminish women.

Eliot satirizes such an education through her character Rosamond Vincy in her novel *Middlemarch*. Rosamond is the "flower of Mrs. Lemon's school" for young ladies, "where the teaching included all that was demanded in the accomplished female—even to extras, such as the getting in and out of the carriage." We can find a more detailed account of such a regimen in Barrett Browning's *Aurora Leigh* (2.1180). Aurora's education is superintended by her aunt, who likes "a woman to be womanly," and believes that genteel Englishwomen are "models to the universe." Aurora is trained in religious orthodoxy, modern languages (the "tongues," not the literatures), "a little algebra," a little science, useless "useful facts" about geography and royal genealogies, and accomplishments like music, drawing, dancing, sewing, and modeling wax flowers.

She reads "a score of books on womanhood" that tell young ladies how to demur to husbands and fulfill their "angelic reach / Of virtue, chiefly used to sit and darn." "By the way," says Aurora with ironic fury, "The works of women are symbolical." Women ruin their eyesight and prick their fingers and waste the hours to produce useless things—a stool to trip over, a pair of slippers, a cushion the man might lean on "And sleep, and dream of something we are not / But would be for your sake" (lines 402–61). Aurora grows ill and depressed under this regimen, struggling to keep her "will and intellect" alive (line 479).

The product of such an educational plan, Eliot warns, quoting Wollstonecraft, will likely be a woman characterized by "ignorance and childish vanity," by "selfish coquetry and love of petty power" (2.1457). Ellis writes approvingly of the domestic woman's pervasive and invisible power: "female influence" guides the husbands, fathers, sons, and brothers who inhabit the public realm, and spreads even to the far reaches of the Empire—"as far as the noble daring of Britain has sent forth her adventurous sons, and that is to every point of danger on the habitable globe" (2.1722). Eliot, however (citing Tennyson's *The Princess* in support of her argument), warns about the pernicious nature of this power behind the throne, wielded by one "debased" by "slavery and ignorance" (2.1460): the poorly educated woman will infect her husband with her own small-mindedness, encourage him to forward her own petty intrigues and designs, and inhibit any higher ambitions toward which he might have aspired. In a passage that seems to describe the eventual fate of *Middlemarch*'s Dr. Lydgate, married to the elegant and accomplished Rosamond Vincy, Eliot warns that the "meridian years of many a man of genius have to be spent in the toil of routine, that an 'establishment' may be kept up for a woman who can understand none of his secret yearnings, who is fit for nothing but to sit in her drawing-room like a doll-Madonna in her shrine" (2.1460). Compare Nightingale's description of the typical middle-class marriage, whose partners chatter about dinner guests, social engagements, and other trivialities, and "never seem to have anything to say to one another . . . about any great religious, social, political questions or feelings" (2.1737).

Ruskin and Ellis, of course, would be in agreement with Eliot in wishing women to have greater educational opportunities than can be found at Mrs. Lemon's school for genteel young ladies. Yet they warn that such opportunities should not promote women's seeking knowledge for its own sake or to forward ambitions any greater than marital, domestic, and charitable duties. Martineau confesses (innocently enough) to a "strange passion for translating" Tacitus and other Latin authors (2.1725), but Ellis asks disapprovingly, "what man is there in existence who would not rather his wife should be free from selfishness, than be able to read Virgil without the use of dictionary?" (2.1723). Ruskin argues that a woman should be educated "only so far as may enable her to sympathise in her husband's pleasures." His "command" of language and science "should be foundational and progressive; hers, general and accomplished for daily and helpful use." Thus St. John Rivers trains Jane Eyre in the rudiments of "Hindostanee" that she might become his wife and assist him in his work as a missionary, and *Middlemarch*'s Dorothea is eager to "learn to read Latin and Greek aloud" to Casaubon, "as Milton's daughters did to their father, without understanding what they read," so that she may help her husband complete his *Key to all Mythologies*. When Romney Leigh proposes to his cousin Aurora, he asks her to give up poetry and be his "helpmate" in liberal causes. "If your sex is weak for art . . . it is strong / For life and duty" (lines 372–75).

Jane finally refuses St. John's demand that she submerge her identity in his, just as she had earlier refused Rochester's demand that she sacrifice herself to be his "better self," his "good angel." Aurora Leigh rejects Romney's offer of marriage indignantly: "You misconceive the question like a man, / Who sees a woman as the complement / Of his sex merely . . . . / I too have my vocation,—work to do" (lines 434–36, 455). Victorian literature is full of women who seek a "vocation," or at least a discrete identity, outside of marriage. Few succeed so triumphantly as Barrett Browning's heroine or as Harriet Martineau, whose supportive brother urged her to "leave it to other women to make shirts and darn stockings" and "devote yourself" to writing (2.1727). In *Middlemarch*'s conclusion we learn that Dorothea has renounced her own ambitions as a reformer and is "absorbed into the life of another," her second husband, Will Ladislaw; she expends her energies giving "wifely help" to Will, a rising politician, and is even relieved to find her life filled with "beneficent activity which she had not the doubtful pains of discovering and marking out for herself."

"The nuptial contrasts are the poles / On which the heavenly spheres revolve" (2.1724, lines 63–64). Your students may find Patmore's sentimental depictions of marriage inane, or feel that Jane Eyre and Dorothea sell themselves short when they settle into domestic contentment at the end of their respective novels, but it's worth reminding students that for women, the prospect of marital unhappiness was far more dire than it is today. "How fortunate it is they're friends / And he will ne'er be wroth with her!" Patmore says brightly, describing an indulgent and loving husband; within the domestic circle, or so the official story goes, the wife is reverenced and pampered, and the husband is solicitous and appreciative. However, not all husbands were benign, and marriage could be a dangerous trap for a woman. See 2.1055 for a brief summary of the laws surrounding marriage until 1870: before the Married Women's Property Acts, unless a woman's male relatives had taken care to procure certain rights for her in her marriage settlement, she effectively lost her legal and even bodily identity when she entered into matrimony. Marriage was said to be woman's mission, but it was a perilous mission, as we see from the following excerpt from Barbara Leigh-Smith Bodichon's *A Brief Summary in Plain Language of the Most Important Laws Concerning Women* (1854):

> A man and wife are one person in law; the wife loses all her rights as a single woman, and her existence is entirely absorbed in that of her husband. . . .
>
> A woman's body belongs to her husband; she is in his custody, and he can enforce his right by a writ of *habeas corpus*.
>
> What was her personal property before marriage, such as money in hand, money at the bank, jewels, household goods, clothes, etc., becomes absolutely her husband's, and he may assign or dispose of them at his pleasure whether he and his wife live together or not. . . .
>
> Money earned by a married woman belongs absolutely to her husband. . . .
>
> The legal custody of children belongs to the father. During the life-time of a sane father, the mother has no rights over her children, except a limited power over infants.

Thus Mill, like Romantic-era philosophers before him, compares marriage to slavery. Women are "compelled" into marriage, their "alleged natural vocation": compelled by the force of tradition, compelled because they have internalized cultural proscriptions about woman's duty, compelled because "all other doors" are closed against them. The "clue to the feelings of those men, who have a real antipathy to the equal freedom of women," says Mill, is their fear that if given the opportunity to support themselves, "all women of spirit and capacity should prefer doing almost anything else" than "degrading" themselves through marriage, "when marrying is giving themselves a master, and a master too of all their earthly possessions" (2.1164–65). Novels like Anne Brontë's *The Tenant of Wildfell Hall* (1848), Wilkie Collin's *The Woman in White* (1860), and Anthony Trollope's *He Knew He Was Right* (1869) depict the terrible circumstances of women trapped within unhappy marriages. In Gaskell's *The Old Nurse's Story*, after proud Miss Maude disgraces her class standing and allies herself to a "dark foreigner" (2.1329), she and her child are deserted by her husband, renounced by her cruel father, and driven out into the freezing night to die. Maude's ghost haunts the pages of the text, rather as the figure of the abused and miserable wife haunts Victorian society as the spectral double of Patmore's Angel in the House.

"Odd Women," Working Women, Fallen Women, Monster Women, "New Women"

"I am not an angel," Jane Eyre tells Rochester with characteristic bluntness, "and I will not be one till I die. . . . I had rather be a *thing* than an angel." Middle-class women who did not fulfill the role of domestic angel—women who rebelled against their proscribed fates, like Aurora Leigh, or who wished for but could not achieve marriage—were considered to be strange, unfeminine, anomalous "things." (St. John tells Jane that her "words are such as ought not to be used: violent, unfeminine, and untrue.") Journalists referred to them as "surplus" or "redundant" women (2.1056), the eponymous women of George Gissing's 1893 *The Odd Women* (excerpted on the Web site); the feminists among them were a national scandal, the unwilling spinsters, a national embarrassment.

Trained only in dependency, in impractical ladylike accomplishments, and in the arts of catching a husband, "odd women" like the Madden sisters of Gissing's novel, left without money or male relatives to support them, languish in genteel destitution. Gainful employment for such women was difficult to come by. Middle-class and lower-middle-class women might obtain work, without compromising their class status too badly, as teachers or governesses, paid companions, nurses, shop girls, and later in the century, typists; but a middle-class working women was always something of an unwelcome oxymoron, giving the lie to a domestic ideology that celebrated women's vulnerability and helplessness within the public sphere. As well, women turned increasingly to writing, especially fiction writing, to earn money, as Eliot notes grudgingly in *Silly Novels by Lady Novelists.* The popular novelist Mary Elizabeth Braddon wrote to support her partner's five children (John Maxwell could not divorce his insane wife to marry Braddon), her own five children, and Maxwell himself as he moved in and out of bankruptcy. Eliot is perhaps overhasty in asserting that nineteenth-century women write more "from vanity" than "from necessity," because "society shuts them out from other spheres of occupation" (2.1468).

It is important to remember that the doctrine of separate spheres for men and women was largely a middle-class doctrine; lower-class women, married and otherwise, could not afford to stay within the domestic sphere. By midcentury, one-quarter of England's female population worked, the majority as domestic servants, seamstresses, factory operatives, and rural laborers. Like men of their class, they frequently worked under atrocious conditions, with the added indignity of receiving less pay (because it was assumed that their wages supplemented those of their menfolk). In *The "White Slavery" of London Match Workers* (2.1715)—a reading that resonates with Ruskin's indictment of glass-cutting factory work, also likened to "the slave trade," in *The Stones of Venice* (2.1439)—Besant describes the inhumane, grueling working conditions of women in the match factory who perform tedious and repetitive tasks for hours on end and receive a pittance in return. In *A Living Wage for Factory Girls at Crewe* (2.1717), Chew laments that "To take what may be considered a good week's wage the work has to be so close and unremitting that we cannot be said to 'live'—we merely exist. We eat, we sleep, we work, endlessly, ceaselessly work, from Monday morning till Saturday night, without remission." Chew longs for some of the leisure hours that Nightingale finds so oppressive. "Cultivation of the mind? How is it possible?" (2.1718). The factory girls have no time to read, to enjoy nature, to take recreation.

" 'A living wage!' " says Chew reproachfully. "Ours is a lingering, dying wage" (2.1718). Lower-class women in particular were likely to turn to prostitution to supplement their "dying wage," or as an alternative to the life of privation and toil Besant and Chew describe. The anonymous author of *The Great Social Evil* defends the "poor women" who labor to obtain "starvation wages, while penury, misery, and famine clutch them by the throat and say, 'Render up your body or die' " (2.1731). When she was a young girl, she recalls, finely dressed, well-fed young women would show up in her poverty-stricken neighborhood "with a profusion of ribands, fine clothes, and lots of cash," treat their families and former friends with food and drink, and then "disappear and leave us in our dirt, penury, and obscurity. You cannot conceive, Sir, how our young ambition was stirred by these visitations" (2.1729). "Anonymous" was not the only writer to attack middle-class society for the hypocrisy of exploiting working-class labor, then condemning those women who sought to escape a life of poverty and overwork through prostitution. In his preface to *Mrs. Warren's Profession*, Shaw argues that "prostitution is caused, not by female depravity and male licentiousness, but simply by underpaying, undervaluing, and overworking women so shamefully that the poorest of them are forced to resort to prostitution to keep body and soul together" (2.1810). But it is instructive to contrast Bracebridge Hemyng's definition of prostitution in Mayhew's *London Labour and the London Poor*: "the using of her charms by a woman for immoral purposes." This definition is more typically Victorian in its failure to recognize prostitution as an economic transaction and in its combination of moral outrage with a sort of prurient interest in the outrageous topic. Even the most sympathetic reformers were made uneasy by "the great social evil," and were likely to overwrite Anonymous's narrative of economic want with melodramatic or monitory stories of women who "fell from virtue" through vanity or greed, though the perversion of their best and most "feminine" qualities (sacrificing themselves, generously, to a beloved but unscrupulous man), or through their own lasciviousness.

Prostitutes were especially troubling within middle-class gender ideology because they were considered sexual agents or sexual objects, and "angels" were supposed to be ethereal and desexualized. "I should say that the majority of women (happily for them) are not very much troubled with sexual feeling of any kind," declared William Acton in *The Functions and Disorders of the Reproductive Organs* (1857). Victorian "wives, mothers, and managers of households" knew no passions except "love of home, of children, and of domestic duties," according to Acton. His views were by no means shared by all medical experts, but he did speak to a fairly commonplace Victorian belief that female sexual desire was problematical, indelicate, even shocking, in a way that male sexual desire was not. Both Maude and her sister Grace are destroyed by "their jealousy and their passions" in Gaskell's story (2.1330). When the eponymous heroine of Tennyson's *The Lady of Shalott* first learns sexual desire, she cries, "The curse is come upon me," and sickens and dies of longing for Sir Lancelot (2.1206, line 116). In Christina Rossetti's *Goblin Market* (2.1589), "sweet-tooth" Laura (line 115) pays a heavy price for her lascivious indulgence in the fruits of the goblin men:

> She never tasted such before,
> How should it cloy with length of use?

She sucked and sucked and sucked the more
Fruits which that unknown orchard bore;
She sucked until her lips were sore. (lines 132–36)

Laura pines away for tasting too early "joys brides hope to have" (line 314), but unlike the Lady of Shalott, she has a sister to save her from a wasting death. Lizzie rescues Laura through a Christlike self-sacrifice, or by offering the alternative of lesbian sexuality ("Hug me, kiss me, suck my juices. . . . / Eat me, drink me, love me"), however one chooses to read it. "For there is no friend like a sister," Rossetti concludes blandly (lines 468, 471, 562).

Medical doctors and psychologists did agree that women were by nature prone to nervous and other disorders—and likely as not unable to pursue sustained intellectual and imaginative work—because the female body was ceaselessly wracked by the upheavals of puberty, menstruation, childbirth, lactation, and menopause. The nineteenth-century perception of women as "the sex" (fully constrained within a sexualized identity, and so both corporeal and animalistic) stands in sharp contradistinction to Victorian celebration of woman as a domestic angel, an essentially disembodied creature. Thus, as critics like Nina Auerbach (*Woman and the Demon*, 1982) have pointed out, Victorian representations of women tend to polar extremes: women are saintly or demonic, spiritual or bodily, asexual or ravenously sexed, guardians of domestic happiness or unnatural monsters. For every Lizzie there is a Laura, for every innocent Esther Summerson a sinner like Lady Deadlock, for every proper Jane Eyre a Bertha Mason, a "clothed hyena" who "snatched and growled like some strange wild animal." The same woman may even embody both extremes, like Catherine Earnshaw in Emily Brontë's *Wuthering Heights* (1847) or Lucy Westenra in Bram Stoker's *Dracula* (1897).

Sexually predatory monster-women like Lucy are especially prevalent in Gothic literature from the end of the century: for instance, H. Rider Haggard's *She* (1887), Arthur Machen's *The Great God Pan* (1890), and Richard Marsh's *The Beetle* (1897). Ask your students to look through Bram Dijkstra's archive of gothic femininity from late-Victorian Europe, *Idols of Perversity: Fantasies of Feminine Evil in Fin-de-Siècle Culture* (1986), with its wealth of images of sphinxes, Circes, sirens, snake women, medusas, and maenads. The Mona Lisa appears in Pater's *The Renaissance* as just such a strange and compelling monster. "She is older than the rocks among which she sits; like the vampire, she has been dead many times, and learned the secrets of the grave; and has been a diver in deep seas, and keeps their fallen day about her." For Pater, the demonic woman epitomizes decadent modernity: her beauty, "into which the soul with all its maladies has passed," is "the symbol of the modern idea" (2.1642). In Wilde's *The Harlot's House* (2.1750) the "strange mechanical grotesques," the "Slim silhouetted skeletons" glimpsed through the blind are figures of horror, but are nonetheless invested with a fantastic and uncanny beauty (lines 7, 14).

Women appear as both sexual decadents and sexual agents in Morris's *The Defense of Guenevere* (2.1606), whose adulterous heroine admits frankly that "in Summer I grew white with flame," as the blood "beat right through / My eager body" (lines 70, 76–77), in the erotic lesbian poetry of Michael Field (2.1742), and in the paintings of Dante Gabriel Rossetti and other pre-Raphaelite artists (see the Web site). The later decades of the century were in general marked by a more open discussion of sexuality, in which the "New Woman," or *fin-de-siècle* feminist, played an important part. The New Woman was considered something of an unnatural monster herself. Like earlier Victorian feminists, New Women were concerned with such issues as education and jobs for women, reform of marriage and divorce laws, and female suffrage. More alarmingly, New Women proposed new codes of sexual behavior and sexual ethics, urging that women be given access to information about contraception and venereal disease, calling for an end to sexual double standards, and championing women's rights to sexual freedom within and outside of marriage. In *The Girl of the Period* (excerpted on the Web site), Eliza Lynn Linton ridicules the New Woman as a "loud and rampant modernization, with her false red hair and painted skin, talking slang as glibly as a man, and by preference leading to conversation to doubtful subjects." Walter Besant provides a more laudatory account of the independent young woman of the 1890s in the selection from *The Queen's Reign* (2.1738). *Mrs. Warren's Profession* may be considered a New Woman play with its depiction of Vivie, a progressive young woman who distinguishes herself "in the mathematical tripos" at Cambridge (2.1813) and proposes to work as an actuary, and its forthright discussion of sexual mores. Mrs. Warren and her sister Liz, raised in poverty, turn to prostitution as a reasonable alternative to the "respectable" options their half-sisters chose: one married a laborer who turned to drink, and the other "worked in a whitelead factory twelve hours a day for nine shillings a week until she died of lead poisoning" (2.1831). The play openly compares marriage to prostitution. The aging roue Crofts essentially offers to buy Vivie from her mother, promising to "die before her and leave her a bouncing widow with plenty of money" (2.1827). As Mrs. Warren asks, "What is any respectable girl brought up to do but to catch some rich man's fancy and get the benefit of his money by marrying him?" (2.1833). Shaw, however, splits the New Woman into two characters: the sexually knowing, rakish, but quite vulgar Mrs. Warren, and the self-reliant but sexually repressed Vivie, who talks baby-talk to her admirer Frank. Mrs. Warren accuses her daughter of being a "pious, canting, hard, selfish woman"; Vivie reproaches her mother with being "a conventional woman at heart" (2.1855). Neither is able to break free of traditional roles, but they are perhaps the predecessors of future generations of truly "new" women.

Victorian Poetry

One has many options when presenting Victorian poetry in a Victorian-only survey. Besides organizing the syllabus in terms of poetic genre (dramatic monologue, sonnet, and so on), one can proceed thematically: poems that describe Victorian crises of faith, like Tennyson's *In Memoriam*, can be taught with prose works detailing spiritual and emotional turmoil and its resolutions, for instance, Mill's *Autobiography*, John Henry Cardinal Newman's *Apologia Pro Vita Sua*, and Carlyle's *Sartor Resartus*. Robert Browning's *Caliban upon Setebos: Or Natural Theology in the Island* (2.1403) and verses 54, 55, 56, 118, and 120 of *In Memoriam*, which deal with nineteenth-century evolutionary science ironically in the one case and despairingly in the other, can be folded into the "Victorian Issues" special section "Evolution" (2.1679). Browning's *Porphyria's Lover* (2.1349) and *My Last Duchess* (2.1352), which describe women who are "killed into art" as a result of the tyranny or insane possessiveness of their men, are well-matched with Christina Rossetti's *In an Artist's Studio*, discussed above (pp. 164–65). The Web site topic "The Painterly Image in Poetry" gives a number of suggestions for teaching works by Browning, Tennyson, and the Rossettis, among others.

If you are teaching a year-long survey, perhaps the easiest way to make the transition from Romantic to Victorian poetry is to start with Victorian prose works like the excerpt from Mill's *Autobiography* and Arnold's *Preface to* Poems. Writing in 1873, Mill remembers the crisis of his youth, when he lost all pleasure in his usual occupations, all confidence in the Utilitarian social philosophy promoted by his father, and all belief in his life's ambition, "to be a reformer of the world" (*Autobiography*, 2.1166). Mill was able to overcome his intense depression with the help of Romantic poetry, which taught him to balance his too-ingrained "habit of analysis" with the "cultivation of the feelings" (2.1168, 1170). William Wordsworth's poems in particular, he thought, "expressed, not mere outward beauty, but states of feeling, and of thought colored by feeling, under the excitement of beauty. . . . In them I seemed to draw from a source of inward joy, of sympathetic and imaginative pleasure, which could be shared in by all human beings" (2.1172).

Arnold, too, admired the "healing power" of Wordsworth, whose "soothing voice" roused both "tears" and "smiles" from the spiritually deadened nineteenth-century person entrapped with "this iron time / Of doubts, disputes, distractions, fears" (*Memorial Verses*, 2.1482, lines 63, 35, 47, 50, 43–44). Poetry, Arnold wrote in the *Preface*, should not only gratify the reader's "natural interest in knowledge of all kinds" but also "inspirit and rejoice the reader; . . . convey a charm, and infuse delight" (2.1505). But whereas Mill believed that such delight stemmed from "the delineation of the deeper and more secret workings of human emotion" by poets like the Romantic poets, "highly delicate and sensitive specimen[s] of human nature" who were carefully attentive to the nuances of their own inner lives (*What Is Poetry?* 2.1141), Arnold argued that the poet should strive for self-effacement, rejecting the Romantic aesthetic that "a true allegory of the state of one's own mind" is "the highest thing that one can attempt in the way of poetry." Modern poetry, he believed, suffered from too much emphasis on the poet's own subjective states, too much "interruption from the intrusion of his personal peculiarities" (2.1509). As Ruskin put it in his essay *Of the Pathetic Fallacy*, an "excited state of the feelings" makes one "irrational"; a mind "affected strongly by emotion" is a mind "unhinged," whose perception and representation of objects is tinged by its own lurid colors, like Coleridge's "morbid" representation of nature in *Christabel*. "All violent feelings . . . produce in us a falseness in all our impressions of external things" (2.1430–31).

"For the Victorians, the egotistical sublime no longer revealed the universal mind underlying all individual imaginations but came to pose the threat of solipsism" (Carol Christ, *The Finer Optic: The Aesthetic of Particularity in Victorian Poetry,* 1975). Arnold, who idealized what he saw as "the calm, the cheerfulness, the disinterested objectivity" of classical Greek literature, also worried about the "morbid" nature of modern poetry (2.1505). Romantic poetry's preoccupation with imaginative apperception, Arnold feared, might lead to disabling self-consciousness and self-absorption. "I sometimes hold it half a sin / To put in words the grief I feel" (lines 5.1–2): Tennyson himself wondered if his immensely popular *In Memoriam* (2.1231)—the long, episodic lyric poem in which he described the most minute fluctuations of his grief over the death of his friend Hallam—was self-indulgent. Perhaps he prolonged his despair by atomizing it, and made "parade of pain" by publically luxuriating in it (line 21.10). Such overattentiveness to one's own subjectivity, Arnold believed, was an especial danger in the present, an "age wanting in moral grandeur" that offered no "sufficiently grand, detached, and self-subsistent object[s]" for poetic contemplation (2.1513, 1508). Entrapped within his own highly wrought sensibility, entrapped within debased modernity, the poet suffered from "sick fatigue" and "languid doubt," the symptoms of "this strange disease of modern life" (*The Scholar Gypsy,* lines 164, 203).

Thus poets were drawn to "situations" from which "no poetical enjoyment can be derived": "those in which the suffering finds no vent in action; in which a continuous state of mental distress is prolonged, unrelieved by incident, hope, or resistance; in which there is everything to be endured, nothing to be done" (2.1505). For instance, the speaker of Tennyson's intensely melancholic dramatic monologue *Tithonus* (2.1215), condemned to eternal life without eternal youth, broods within an autumnal landscape seemingly attuned to his own melancholy ("The woods decay, the woods decay and fall" [line 1]). "Marred and wasted" by the millennia, a "white-haired shadow" of a man, Tithonus is doomed to "wither slowly in [the] arms" of his beloved, the goddess Aurora (lines 8, 19, 6). Embittered by the constant reminder that a human, though he be immortal, is nothing like the gods, Tithonus years only for death.

Tennyson's *Mariana* (2.1202) is another poem in which the protagonist languishes "without hope of change" (line 29). Nature affords no relief to

Mariana: pent up within her own misery, she cannot "look on the sweet heaven" with pleasure, and birdsong and wind and sunshine irritate and "confound" rather than soothe her senses (lines 15, 76). Moreover, in large part the natural world seems to reflect Mariana's own gloom. The moat that surrounds the grange is a "sluice with blackened waters"; the flower beds are "thickly crusted" with "blackest moss"; from her window she sees only the "level waste" of a dead, "gray" country (lines 38, 2, 1, 44, 31). The reader suffers from the same sense of claustrophobia as Mariana, as each verse describes Mariana's surroundings in almost oppressive detail, only to conclude again and again with a nearly identical quatrain:

> She only said, "My life is dreary,
> He cometh not," she said;
> She said, "I am aweary, aweary,
> I would that I were dead!"

"It is a land with neither night nor day, / Nor heat nor cold, nor any wind, nor rain, / Nor hills nor valleys." In her sonnet *Cobwebs* (2.1585), Christina Rossetti describes a "twilight grey" and featureless landscape even more bleak than the one Mariana sees from her window (line 5). This place of utter negation is perhaps the terrain of the mind, an inner wasteland of spiritual and emotional deadness ("No future hope no fear for evermore" [line 14]). Despite joyous and lushly sensuous poems like *A Birthday* (2.1587), Rossetti's works often detail the plight of one who is *Dead before Death:* "Grown hard and stubborn" from a lifetime of disappointments, "Grown rigid" with the effort of self-repression (2.1585, lines 5–6). This theme of claustrophobic entrapment within one's own subjectivity is even more startling in *After Death* (2.1585), a sonnet spoken from the perspective of a dead woman, spurned by the man she loved when living, who closely observes him as he visits her corpse. Her disappointed love embitters her even after death, for the man expresses no emotion more tender than pity, and the sonnet ends with sardonic fury: "very sweet it is / To know he still is warm tho' I am cold."

"Give us long rest or death, dark death, or dreamful ease" (*The Lotos-Eaters,* 2.1211, line 98). When Arnold urged that contemporary poets draw their subjects from classical models, because the literature of Homer and Virgil offers far worthier scenarios than the trivial "domestic epic dealing with the details of modern life which pass daily under our eyes" (2.1507), he must have had something other in mind than poems like Tennyson's *Lotos-Eaters*. Tennyson chooses a relatively obscure episode from the *Odyssey* that illustrates neither the valor of Greek heroes nor the wiliness of Odysseus: the lotos-eaters wish only to withdraw from the world and lose themselves in "drowsy numbness," like the speaker of John Keats's *Ode to a Nightingale* (2.849) who has "been half in love with easeful Death" (lines 1, 52). "We have had enough of action, and of motion we": the mariners refuse to voyage any longer, rejecting all thought of duty, "Fatherland," family, "toil" (lines 150, 39, 60). They prefer the stasis of "a land / In which it seemèd always afternoon"—"A land where all things always seemed the same!"—where they might "dream and dream" with "half-shut eyes. . . . Eating the Lotos day by day" (lines 3–4, 24, 102, 100, 105). In Keats's ode, and in the Romantic tradition generally, one might deliberately seek out a narcotized state to enable flights of imaginative fancy, but in Tennyson the narcotized mind that turns inward on itself is lethargic, torpid, even paralyzed. The poem in many ways condemns such escapism: the *Choric Song* sung by the mariners is full of self-serving rationalization for inactivity, and celebrates an unpleasantly decadent version of nature ("The full-juiced apple, waxing over-mellow, / Drops in a silent autumn night. . . . The flower ripens in its place, / Ripens and fades, and falls, and hath no toil" [lines 78–79, 81–82]).

And yet the language of *The Lotos-Eaters* is on the side of languor and dreamy indolence. Odysseus calls for "Courage!" at the very beginning of the poem, but this opening spondee, immediately disrupting the meter, is awkward to read, so that the reader spurns the idea of courage and turns with relief to the "charmèd" landscape (line 19), described in lushly alliterative language and the luxurious rhythms of spenserian stanza ("And, like a downward smoke, the slender stream / Along the cliff to fall and pause and fall did seem" [lines 8–9]). By contrast, the language of the metrically choppy final stanza, describing the harsh everyday world the lotos-eaters are renouncing, is turbulent, plosive, and ungainly:

We have had enough of action, and of motion we,
Rolled to starboard, rolled to larboard, when the surge was seething free,
Where the wallowing monster spouted his foam-fountains in the sea. . . .
Blight and famine, plague and earthquake, roaring deeps and fiery sands,
Clanging fights, and flaming towns, and sinking ships, and praying
hands. (lines 150–52, 160–61)

"Produce! Produce! Were it but the pitifullest infinitesimal fraction of a Product, produce it, in God's name! . . . Work while it is called Today; for the Night cometh, wherein no man can work," Carlyle's Professor Teufelsdröckh exhorts the Victorian reader (*Sartor Resartus*, 2.1095–96). But poems like *Lotos-Eaters* reveal a certain ambivalence about those supposed Victorian desiderata, activity, labor, and struggle and thus, by extension, a discontent with the frenetic pace and clamor of modern times. Such discontent could take a hedonistic turn: Edward FitzGerald's translation of *The Rubáiyát of Omar Khayyám* (2.1305) urges the reader to "Waste not your Hour, nor in the vain pursuit / Of This and That endeavor and dispute" (lines 213–14). Time is a "Bird . . . on the Wing," the "Wine of Life keeps oozing away drop by drop," the "Leaves of Life" are "falling one by one." *Carpe diem:* far better to relax and enjoy "the fruitful Grape" (lines 28–32, 215) than to labor "with thy whole might," as Carlyle urges (2.1096). Such sentiments are echoed in later Victorian decadent verse like Ernest Dowson's *Cynara* and *They Are Not Long* (2.1894–95).

Or such discontent might give rise to the melancholy and pessimism that deformed (in his own opinion, not most critics') Arnold's poetry. In the *Preface to* Poems Arnold explains why he has excluded his long work *Empedocles on Etna* from the collection. In wishing to "delineate the feelings of one of the last of the Greek religious philosophers, . . . having survived his fellows, living on into a time when the habits of Greek thought and feeling had begun fast to change," Arnold had taken on a "poetically faulty" scenario—the situation of a man of an older era entrapped within a new and inimical one, and convulsed with longing for what he has lost—and found himself unable to describe timeless emotions, only "doubt" and "discouragement," those "exclusively modern" sentiments (2.1504–6). In Arnold's *Dover Beach* (2.1492) as well, the speaker suffers from a sense of displacement. Nostalgic for a more meaningful age ("The Sea of Faith / Was once, too, at the full" [lines 21–22]), he rejects modernity entirely:

> the world, which seems
> To lie before us like a land of dreams,
> So various, so beautiful, so new,
> Hath really neither joy, nor love, nor light,
> Nor certitude, nor peace, nor help for pain;
> And we are here as on a darkling plain
> Swept with confused alarms of struggle and flight,
> Where ignorant armies clash by night. (lines 30–37)

"Time and the gods are at strife. . . . The old faiths loosen and fall, the new years ruin and rend" (lines 19, 40). The speaker of Algernon Charles Swinburne's *Hymn to Proserpine* (2.1625), a Roman patrician and poet who witnesses what is for him a devastating cultural transformation, the transition from paganism to Christianity, is in the same position as Arnold's Empedocles. "I have lived long enough," he says with bitter resignation: the new religious and philosophical beliefs that supercede his own are "barren" to him (lines 1, 17). More decadent than Arnold's speaker in *Dover Beach*, Swinburne's speaker does not regret the certainties of a lost religion so much as the sweet graciousness ("delicate days and pleasant" [line 47]) of his past life. In a tumultuous stanza (lines 47–74) that seems modeled on the final stanza of *Lotos-Eaters*, he rejects the "travail" and "trouble" of the world, described as a roiling ocean beneath which lurk "unspeakable things." Even pleasure has become "grievous" to him (line 10); he longs for oblivion, like Tennyson's mariners, and prays that Proserpine will grant him the gift of death.

The protagonist of Robert Browning's *"Childe Roland to the Dark Tower Came"* (2.1367) is another man who has outlived his time: not only have Roland's fellow knights died, but they been humiliated and disgraced, and the age of chivalry has died out with them. Beaten down by failure and despair, the last of "all the lost adventurers my peers" (line 195), Roland no longer has any faith in his own capacity for heroism. As he comes to the end of his quest for the Dark Tower, he feels "neither pride / Nor hope . . . So much as gladness that some end might be" (lines 16–18):

> For, what with my whole world-wide wandering,
> What with my search drawn out through years, my hope
> Dwindled into a ghost not fit to cope
> With that obstreperous joy success would bring,
> I hardly tried now to rebuke the spring
> My heart made, finding failure in its scope. (lines 19–24)

Roland travels through a surreal landscape—reminiscent of the wasteland of the Fisher King of Arthurian legend (see 2.2368–69), or a blighted modern industrial landscape—as bleak as the one Rossetti describes in *Cobwebs*, but far more grotesque. Nature offers no consolation here, only nightmarish spectacles, like that of a "stupefied" and "stiff blind horse" with "every bone a-stare," or the "dank" plashed soil of a battlefield where long-forgotten men struggled savagely and died (lines 76–77, 130). "What penned them there, with all the plain to choose? / No footprint leading to that horrid mews, / None out of it" (lines 134–36). The natural world is described as a mutilated or deformed human body: thistles are beheaded, leaves are "bruised," grass grows "scant as hair / In leprosy" on muddy ground which "underneath looked kneaded up with blood" (lines 70–75).

Despite all this, *Childe Roland* ends on a note of very cautious optimism. As the hideous mountains crowd around him "like giants at a hunting" (line 190) and the ghosts of his dead friends assemble to watch, all signs point to the likelihood that Roland will die when he fights whatever is to come out of the Dark Tower. He is nonetheless "dauntless" as he sounds his challenge and the poem ends, abruptly and ambiguously. One does not know whether Roland successfully completes the quest and avenges his friends or dies alone, in pain and terror. But perhaps it does not matter: despite so many years of self-doubt and discouragement, at the end Roland displays both courage and a sense of duty, qualities necessary in the difficult nineteenth century no less than in the age of chivalry. *Childe Roland* is well-matched with Tennyson's *Ulysses* (2.1213), another dramatic monologue whose speaker expects to find failure and death at the end of his quest but still is determined to journey on even in his extreme old age:

> It may be that the gulfs will wash us down;
> It may be we shall touch the Happy Isles,
> And see the great Achilles, whom we knew.
> Though much is taken, much abides; and though

We are not now that strength which in old days
Moved earth and heaven, that which we are, we are—
One equal temper of heroic hearts,
Made weak by time and fate, but strong in will
To strive, to seek, to find, and not to yield. (lines 62–70)

Contents: Norton Topics Online, The Victorian Age
www.wwnorton.com/nael

Prose Descriptions of Paintings
Explorations
Web Resources

Contents: Norton Online Archive, The Victorian Age
www.wwnorton.com/nael/NOA

Thomas Carlyle
Carlyle's Portraits of His Contemporaries
[Charles Lamb at 56]
[William Makepeace Thackeray at 42]
from Characteristics
John Henry Cardinal Newman
Apologia Pro Vita Sua
From Chapter 3. History of My Religious Opinions from 1839 to 1841
From Chapter 5. Position of My Mind Since 1845
Elizabeth Barrett Browning
A Year's Spinning
A Musical Instrument
Alfred, Lord Tennyson
Sonnet ("She took the dappled partridge flecked with blood")
Maud
Part 1
6.5 ("Ah, what shall I be at fifty")
6.8 ("Perhaps the smile and tender tone")
6.10 ("I have played with her when a child")
8 ("She came to the village church")
11 ("O let the solid ground")
12 ("Birds in the high Hall-garden")
16.3 ("Catch not my breath, O clamorous heart")
18 ("I have led her home, my love, my only friend")
Part 2
4 ("O that 'twere possible")
In the Valley of the Cauteretz
Pelleas and Ettare
Northern Farmer: New Style
To Virgil
"Frater Ave atque Vale"
The Dawn
Robert Browning
Women and Roses
A Woman's Last Word
Youth and Art
Dis Aliter Visum; or, Le Byron de Nos Jours
Apparent Failure

Walter Pater
From The Child in the House
William Ernest Henley
Madam Life's a Piece in Bloom

Contents: NAEL Audio Companion, The Victorian Age

Elizabeth Barrett Browning
Sonnets from the Portuguese, Sonnet 43
Music by Elizabeth Everest Freer. Performed by Susan Bender and Carol Feather Martin
Alfred, Lord Tennyson
The Charge of the Light Brigade
Read by Alfred, Lord Tennyson
Christina Rossetti
Song: "When I am dead, my dearest"
Music by Ralph Vaughan Williams. Performed by Susan Bender and Carol Feather Martin
Gerard Manley Hopkins
The Windhover
Spring and Fall
—both read by M. H. Abrams
W. S. Gilbert
If You're Anxious for to Shine in the High Aesthetic Line
Recorded by Walter Passmore

CHAPTER 8

The Twentieth Century

Introducing the Twentieth Century

The "philosophy" of *The Importance of Being Earnest*, said Oscar Wilde in an interview, is "that we should treat all the trivial things of life seriously, and all the serious things of life with sincere and studied triviality" (2.1761). This 1895 play provides an excellent means to make the transition from the nineteenth century, whether one is continuing a year-long survey or beginning a course on modernism or the twentieth century. *Earnest* turns its back decisively on the high moral seriousness associated with Victorianism, satirizing Victorian middle-class love of possessions and property, concern with social proprieties, investment in social position, and hypocritical championing of respectability (qualities that would, of course, continue to dominate in the Edwardian era). Its characters are concerned only with appearances, not substance. Lady Bracknell sternly rejects Jack's pretensions to her daughter's hand when she discovers he is an adopted foundling abandoned at Victoria Station cloakroom. "To be born, or at any rate, bred in a handbag . . . seems to me to display a contempt for the ordinary decencies of family life that reminds one of the worst excesses of the French Revolution. . . . I would strongly advise you, Mr. Worthing, to try and acquire some relations as soon as possible" (2.1773). Believing he is named Ernest, Gwendolyn claims to love Jack only because the name "inspires absolute confidence" ("my ideal has always been to love someone of the name of Ernest" [2.1769–70]); Cecily falls in love with Jack's appealingly dissolute but imaginary younger brother Ernest because it's "always been a girlish dream of mine to love someone whose name was Ernest" (2.1787). As Jack and Algernon scramble to please the women by becoming earnest/Ernest in name only, such seeming verities as identity, character, personality begin to appear tenuous and ephemeral, even nonsensical.

Similarly, "matters of grave importance" like education, marriage, family, politics, and work are treated with methodical irreverence, for in such matters, "style, not sincerity is the vital thing" (2.1796). The play has no patience with Victorian propriety, complacency, and self-congratulatory earnestness and delights in role-playing and wordplay, wit and paradox. Social identities and social conventions are revealed as artificial constructs rather than essences, but this is hardly cause for alarm. The world is instead opened up to play and improvisation. For instance, Algernon advocates "Bunburyism"—the philosophy of the trickster, who systematically pursues pleasure by manipulating appearances and spinning elaborate lies (2.1766–67)—and Cecily delights in her own extravagant exaggeration of narrative conventions when she invents an entire courtship between herself and the nonexistent Ernest, complete with diary entries, a ring, and letters. "The three you wrote me after I had broken off the engagement are so beautiful, and so badly spelled, that even now I can hardly read them without crying a little" (2.1787).

Compare the far darker, bitterly ironic perspective of another transitional text, Thomas Hardy's *On the Western Circuit* (2.1918), which describes a world in which neither religion nor any other traditional belief system lends shape or meaningfulness to human existence. The first paragraph of the story, in which the male protagonist strains and fails to catch a glimpse of the Cathedral at Melchester in the falling darkness, alerts us to the bleakly secular nature of Hardy's vision, emphasized in his poetry as well. (In *The Impercipient* the speaker laments that the "faiths by which my comrades stand / seem fantasies to me" [2.1935, lines 3–4].) Rather like *The Importance of Being Earnest*, but in a very different tone, *Western Circuit* rejects earlier fictions of heroic identity. As the narrator tells us bluntly, interrupting himself in the middle of the very first sentence to do so, Charles Bradford Raye is "no great man, in any sense, by the way." Insignificant human beings are jerked and tossed by the machinations of fate: the people at the street fair look like "gnats against a sunset" as they are flung about by the steam circus rides (2.1918). Rigid social conventions deform and delimit human lives no less than the cruelty of blind chance. Edith Harnham, for instance, was pressured into an unhappy marriage because of "the belief of the British parent that a bad marriage with its aversions is better than free womanhood with its interests, dignity, and leisure" (2.1927). All human aspirations are doomed; all emotions are futile. While Wilde undermines the "revolting sentimentality" (2.1802) of Victorian literature ("The good ended happily, and the bad unhappily. That is what Fiction means" [2.1778]) with wit and formal parody, Hardy attacks it with almost savage cynicism. In the first flush of their attraction, Anna and Charles smile at one another "with that unmistakable expression which means so little at the moment, yet so often leads up to passion, heart-ache, union, disunion, devotion, overpopulation, drudgery, content, resignation, despair" (2.1920).

On the Western Circuit moves remorselessly toward its apotheosis of disillusionment (much as James Joyce's *Araby* concludes with the narrator's climactic realization of his own misery and humiliation: "Gazing up into the darkness I saw myself as a creature driven and derided by vanity; and my eyes burned with anguish and anger" [2.2240]), as Charles and Edith confront the certainty of life-long unhappiness with "dreary resignation" (2.1934). For Hardy, Nature is "grotesque, slimed, dumb, indifferent" to the human affairs that Fate manipulates with random and unmotivated cruelty (*The Convergence of the Twain*, 2.1945, line 9). If some "vengeful god" were oppressing him with demonic glee, says the speaker of *Hap*, then he could bear the "suffering," knowing at least that one "Powerfuller than I" shaped his life to some purpose, however malevolent (2.1934, lines 1–2, 7). But life unfolds according to chance, guided by those two "purblind Doomsters," "crass Casualty" and "dicing Time" (lines 11–13). Thus in *The Darkling Thrush* (2.1937), written on December 31, 1900, Hardy hears the "death-lament" of Victorianism (the "Century's corpse"), and looks out across the landscape of the dawning twentieth century, "hard and dry" and "fervourless" and "bleak," with only the ghost of a hope that it will bring something better (lines 10–18). Poetry is dead, or dying: the "tangled bine-stems" are like the "strings of broken lyres," and the one bird who sings, though he sings ecstatically, is an "aged thrush, frail, gaunt, and small," whose joy contrasts starkly with "the growing gloom" that envelops him (lines 5–6, 21, 24).

In Wilde and Hardy we see two exemplary responses to the promise, or threat, of a new century: one that welcomes the flux and indeterminacy of a new and "modern" world in which identities, social relations, and meaning structures can be made and unmade according to need, opportunity, and desire; another that regards the prospect of this modern world, wherein human beings can expect to find neither truth nor certainty, with dark pessimism, stoicism, or outright despair. The works of most twentieth-century writers incorporate both kinds of responses. "Things fall apart; the center cannot hold; / Mere anarchy is loosed upon the world" (lines 3–4). In William Butler Yeats's *The Second Coming* (2.2106), the old order disintegrates into a whirling chaos, and the new human subject that emerges from the wreckage is an admixed monstrosity—a "rough beast" with "lion body and the head of a man, / A gaze blank and pitiless as the sun"—abominable and yet compelling (lines 21, 14–15). In *A Sketch of the Past* Virginia Woolf describes the overwhelming vibrancy and confusion of a world unanchored by any transcendental meaning ("certainly and emphatically there is no God" [2.2224]). She nonetheless discerns a "pattern" hidden "behind the cotton wool" of everyday life: "that we—I mean all human beings—are connected with this; that the whole world is a work of art; that we are parts of the work of art." Such a secular revelation can only be achieved by allowing the boundaries of the self to crumble, by leaving oneself open to "exceptional moments," or "sudden shocks" of insight—a process that can bring with it "a peculiar horror and a physical collapse" as the self dissolves, but also "ecstasy" and "rapture" (2.2224, 2220).

Modernism and Postmodernism

Modernity and Postmodernity

The inception of modernity proper is much debated by historians, but whether we understand a modern society as a postfeudal (or in contemporary times, a posttraditional) society, or situate modernity as a post-Enlightenment phenomenon, "modern" societies are said to be characterized by innovation, novelty, and dynamism. They are secular societies, governed by science and reason rather than superstition and tradition. Modernity is associated with urbanization, industrialism, capitalism, and commodity culture; the rise of individualism, democracy, class mobility, and universal education; rapid and continuous technological change; and the globalization of culture, resulting from faster and more efficient communication and transportation systems as well as imperialism.

"Modernity is the transient, the fleeting, the contingent," Charles Baudelaire wrote in 1863 (*The Painter of Modern Life*). Clearly modernity is nothing new to the twentieth century, but in the twentieth century, even more so than in the fast-paced nineteenth, the rate and intensity of sociocultural and technological change came to seem almost unbearable. In an extended moment that the philosopher Jacques Derrida refers to as a "rupture" in intellectual history (*Structure, Sign, and Play in the Discourse of the Human Sciences*, 1966), Nietzsche and other antimetaphysical thinkers argued that there was no such thing as absolute truth, only knowledge obtained perspectivally; the rising science of ethnology showed that human cultural practices and beliefs were variant and situational rather than universal; Freud and other theorists of the unconscious challenged the Cartesian view of human beings as rational, integral, self-aware, and self-present; Darwin's theory of natural selection described an imperfect, half-animal human species, whose continued mutability was governed by chance rather than providential design. Twentieth-century authors like Joyce, Woolf, Joseph Conrad, and D. H. Lawrence "wrote in the wake of the shattering of confidence in the great old certainties about the deity and the Christian faith, about the person, knowledge, materialism, history, the old Grand Narratives" (2.1905). As David Harvey argues, the twentieth century also struggled to come to terms with the failure of the Enlightenment project, which had proposed the scientific domination of nature to protect humans from calamity and need, and promoted rational, just forms of social organization rather than a state founded on superstition, oppression, and the arbitrary practice of power (*The Condition of Postmodernity: An Enquiry into the Origins of Cultural Change*, 1990).

The Enlightenment promise of universal democracy, justice, and liberty, however, seemed shattered by the events of twentieth-century history. Science had provided human beings with the means to warfare and genocide; the domination of nature meant widespread environmental destruction; and democracy threatened to yield to fascism and other forms of totalitarian government, or seemed inseparable from the brutal exploitation of workers under capitalism.

Postmodernity, variously situated as beginning sometime after World War II, first of all involves a continuation and intensification of the dynamism that characterizes modernity. Thus technological innovation continues apace (the postmodern era is the era of space travel, television, the computer, photocopying, the fax machine, nuclear weaponry, genetic engineering, and so on); market capitalism evolves into multinational and consumer capitalism; and the continued rise of a global (and increasingly homogenous) culture is ensured through advertising and entertainment media. One may speculate that the extended moment of postmodernity also constitutes a "rupture," in Derrida's term: the immediacy of communications by fax and e-mail, the ready availability of information on the Internet, the casual knowledge that global extinction is a daily possibility, the penetration of technology into everyday life, the confusion of domestic and work space, the ubiquity of visual media, has meant that postmodern humans enjoy (or suffer) new and unprecedented modes of experience and subjectivity. Donna Haraway, for instance, argues that the thoroughly intimate relation between postmodern humans and their technologies means that human beings have become "cyborgs": that is, human identity can no longer be conceived fully within the realm of the organic (*A Manifesto for Cyborgs: Science, Technology, and Socialist Feminism in the 1980s*, 1985). Jean Baudrillard describes postmodernity as an "age of simulation" and "hyperreality" in which actuality and representation are impossible to distinguish and representations refer to one another rather than to some underlying reality (*Simulacra and Simulations,* 1981). (Thus the premise of the 1997 film comedy *Wag the Dog*, that an entire imaginary war could be convincingly simulated on television.) Indeed, given the pervasiveness of images from film, television, the internet, and advertising, mediated images may seem more "real"—more vital, compelling, desirable, and true—than lived experiences for postmodern subjects.

Although neither literary modernism nor literary postmodernism can be neatly defined as a uniform body of aesthetic practices (for both concepts are highly contested), it is true nonetheless that specific literary forms and techniques have grown out of the historical situations of modernity and postmodernity. In his 1921 essay *The Metaphysical Poets* (2.2401), T. S. Eliot argues that modern poetry "must be *difficult*" to match the recalcitrance of modern times. "Our civilization comprehends great variety and complexity, and this variety and complexity, playing upon a refined sensibility, must produce various and complex results. The poet must become more and more comprehensive, more allusive, more indirect, in order to force, to dislocate if necessary, language into his meaning" (2.2406–7). In general, modernist (as well as postmodernist) literary practice is characterized by its difficulty (Eliot's erudite allusiveness, Yeats's esoteric symbolism, Conrad's impressionism, Woolf's narrative innovation, Joyce's intricate wordplay), its antitraditionalism, and its high degree of formal experimentation. As Astradur Eysteinsson argues, the many movements that make up literary modernism comprise "a paradigmatic shift, a major revolt, beginning in the mid- and late nineteenth century, against the prevalent literary and aesthetic traditions of the Western world," especially realist traditions (*The Concept of Modernism*, 1990). Postmodernist texts continue this revolt against tradition—including the "traditions," newly defined, of literary modernism.

Clearly modernism and postmodernism are diffuse concepts that can perhaps too easily be made to encompass all nonrealistic (especially all self-reflexive) literature after 1880 or so. And not all twentieth-century texts deploy radically experimental techniques, including certain texts by paradigmatically "modernist" or "postmodernist" authors. Joyce's *Araby*, for instance, is more naturalist than modernist, concerned with realistically describing the young narrator's entrapment within Roman Catholicism (he lives in a house whose former tenant, "a priest, had died in the back drawing-room"), the family, and "decent" lower middle-class values of an Ireland "hostile to romance" (2.2236–37). It is certainly possible to arrange your syllabus to focus more fully on those authors who found traditional forms like fictional realism more suitable to the handling of the bewildering complexity of the twentieth century, or to refuse to foreground the question of which twentieth-century texts are "experimental" and which are not, perhaps by grouping the readings thematically. For instance, the final two sections of this chapter give suggestions about how to organize a set of readings around the issues of colonialism and postcolonialism. The Web site offers study questions and supplementary readings on the topic of twentieth-century technology and warfare.

Woolf's *A Room of One's Own* (2.2153) could be used to begin a unit on the position of the woman writer in the twentieth century, or on the difficulties of authorship for socially marginal groups in general. Alternatively, Woolf's *Professions for Women* (2.2214) provides a useful transition from the previous chapter's discussion of the Victorian "Woman Question." In this essay Woolf confesses (only half-humorously) to murdering Coventry Patmore's "Angel in the House" because the "shadow of her wings" fell over Woolf's page and inhibited her from writing. "It was she who bothered and wasted my time and so tormented me that at last I killed her" (2.2215). Doris Lessing's *To Room Nineteen* (2.2542) and Katherine Mansfield's *The Daughters of the Late Colonel* (2.2409) both describe women who have internalized the role of domestic angel with disastrous results. Susan Rawlings has sacrificed all to assume the part of devoted wife and mother, until she fears that "nothing existed of me except the roles that went with being Mrs Matthew Rawlings" (2.2558).

Constantia and Josephine have squandered their youth tending to their father, the tyrannical colonel. Their lives, spent "looking after father and at the same time keeping out of father's way," seem unreal, seem "to have happened in a kind of tunnel," but they have so muted their own desires that even after their father's death neither can sustain a vision of walking out of the tunnel and into freedom (2.2422, 2423).

"Have you any notion how many books are written about women in the course of one year?" Woolf writes in *A Room of One's Own*. "Have you any notion how many are written by men?" (2.2166). After a frustrating afternoon at the British Library in which she attempted to research the topic "Women and Poverty," Woolf, distracted by the proliferation of volumes propounding the nature of femininity (and written by "men who have no apparent qualification save that they are not women"), stares at a notebook scribbled over with her randomly generated subheadings about woman:

> *Condition in Middle Ages of,*
> *Habits in the Fiji Islands of,*
> *Worshipped as goddesses by,*
> *Weaker in moral sense than,* . . .
> *Offered as sacrifice to,*
> *Small size of brain of,*
> *Profounder sub-consciousness of,*
> *Less hair on the body of,*
> *Mental, moral and physical inferiority of,* . . .
> *Shakespeare's opinion of,*
> *Lord Birkenhead's opinion of,*
> *Dean Inge's opinion of,* (2.2167–68)

Very likely "*Small size of brain of*" can account for "*Weaker in moral sense than*," though "*Less hair on the body of*" may not adequately explain "*Worshipped as goddesses by*," or "*Dean Inge's opinion of.*" In any case, this list reads like a hodgepodge of miscellaneous opinion, presented as scientific fact, historical and anthropological verity, and authoritative pronouncement by Literature, Church, and State. Compare Jean Rhys's *Mannequin* (2.2438), with its satirical depiction of the various stereotypes of the sexual woman. The "mannequins" in the Paris salon are asked to assume exaggerated feminine roles while modeling the dresses for customers and to maintain those roles even outside of the display room: the child-woman, the gamine, the femme fatale, the tomboy, the cat-woman, the mysterious devil-woman, and so on. "Each of the twelve was of a distinct and separate type: each of the twelve knew her type and kept to it, practising rigidly in clothing, manner, voice and conversation" (2.2440). The danger, Woolf argues, lies in internalizing the "truths" generated by scientific fallacy, or embracing popular stereotypes too enthusiastically: in mistaking social constructions of femininity as one's own essential identity.

"Art for Art's Sake": The Beginnings of Modernism

As noted in the period introduction, it is impossible to talk about modernism without beginning in the later nineteenth century and discussing such interrelated movements as Aestheticism, Decadence, and Symbolism (2.1897; see also 2.1054–55 and 1740–41). Aestheticism advocates "the love of art for its own sake," to quote Walter Pater's highly influential *The Renaissance* (2.1644). Aesthetes maintain that art is self-sufficient, need serve no ulterior purpose, and should not be judged by moral, political, or other nonaesthetic standards. "There is no such thing as a moral or immoral book. Books are well written, or badly written. That is all . . . All art is quite useless," Wilde proclaims in the "Preface" to *The Picture of Dorian Gray* (2.1760–61): Aestheticism emphatically rejects the Victorian bourgeois assumption that the work of art should edify and improve its consumer.

Such a stance owes much to Matthew Arnold, who in *The Function of Criticism at the Present Time* argues that "real criticism . . . obeys an instinct prompting it to try to know the best that is known and thought in the world, irrespectively of practice, politics, and everything of the kind; and to value knowledge and thought as they approach this best, without the intrusion of any other considerations whatever" (2.1521). The average Englishman—the crass "philistine" of *Culture and Anarchy*—is too concerned with "the practical consequences and applications" of ideas to appreciate the "disinterested love of a free play of the mind on all subjects, for its own sake" (2.1522, 1521). Aesthetic disinterestedness, by contrast, allows one to "see the object as in itself it really is" (2.1514): that is, accurately to assess the extent to which the work of art conforms to a timeless ideal of Truth or Beauty (an ideal that Arnold believed was most fully manifested in Hellenic art, and poorly represented in the present day).

Pater accepts Arnold's precept that the critic should "see the object as in itself it really is," but only to the extent that all aesthetic objects are "powers or forces producing pleasurable sensations, each of a more or less peculiar or unique kind," and the critic must train himself to heighten his "susceptibility" to these sensations. He rejects the idea of abstract, universal, and objective standards of artistic value. "Beauty, like all other qualities presented to human experience, is relative; and the definition of it becomes unmeaning and useless in proportion to its abstractness." The critic should not attempt to fashion a universal law that would explain beauty (to seek such is to ask profitless "metaphysical questions"), but instead discover the best means of expressing each "special manifestation of it." And rather than seek an objective measure, the critic should ask, what is the work of art "to *me*? . . . One must realize such primary data for one's self, or not at all" (2.1638). Wilde puts this argument even more strongly in *The Critic as Artist* when he claims that in its "most perfect form," criticism is "purely subjective," and the critic's "sole aim is to chronicle his own impressions." Paradoxically, then, the "primary aim of the critic is to see the object as in itself it really is not" (2.1756, 1758). In his famous interpretation of *La Giaconda*, for instance, Pater may have "put into the portrait of Mona Lisa something that Leonardo never dreamed of," but it doesn't matter to Wilde (2.1756). "The meaning of any beautiful created thing is . . . as much in the soul of him who looks at it, as it was in his soul who wrought it. Nay, it is rather the beholder who lends to the beautiful thing its myriad meanings, and makes it marvelous for us, and sets it in some new relation to the age" (2.1757).

Compensating for the erosion of traditional values, Arnold substitutes literary and intellectual activity for religious belief and attempts to create timeless and stable value systems within the realm of art. The late-nineteenth-century movement called Decadence, by contrast, embraces the chaos and flux of a world that has become unmoored from tradition and meaningfulness. Experience, thought, subjectivity, even seemingly solid bodies and objects are "flamelike" and ephemeral, Pater writes; they are merely "the concurrence, renewed from moment to moment, of forces parting sooner or later on their ways." Each of us is a "solitary prisoner" isolated within a "thick wall of personality"; our "impressions" are "unstable, flickering, inconsistent"; "all that is actual" within the world is "a single moment, gone while we try to apprehend it" (2.1642–43). The goal of criticism, then, is to learn to analyze, fully inhabit, and intensify the moment:

> The service of philosophy, of speculative culture, towards the human spirit is to rouse, to startle it to a life of constant and eager observation. . . . Not the fruit of experience, but experience itself, is the end. A counted number of pulses only is given to us of a variegated, dramatic life. How may we see in them all that is to be seen in them by the finest senses. . . . To burn always with this hard, gemlike flame, to maintain this ecstasy, is success in life. . . . While all melts under our feet, we may well grasp at any exquisite passion, or any contribution to knowledge that seems by a lifted horizon to set the spirit free for a moment, or any stirring of the senses. (2.1643–44)

The Decadent movement, then, is associated with this proto-existentialist belief that in a world without transcendent value, life must be lived intensely and carefully. But with his emphasis on sensation and pleasure, Pater also seemed to authorize hedonistic self-indulgence (perhaps justifying his fear that the "Conclusion" to *The Renaissance* "might possibly mislead some of those young men into whose hands it might fall" [2.1642, n. 6]) and the search for ever more novel, arcane, and exquisite sensations. Thus Decadence came to be associated with the love of artificiality, the pursuit of the "unnatural" or the "perverse," and with ennui, neurosis, eroticism, morbidity, and decay. The Decadent's world-weary sensualism is epitomized by the speakers of Algernon Charles Swinburne's *Hymn to Proserpine* (2.1625) and Ernest Dowson's *Cynara* (2.1894):

> Surely the kisses of her bought red mouth were sweet;
> But I was desolate and sick of an old passion,
> When I awoke and found the dawn was gray:
> I have been faithful to thee, Cynara! in my fashion. (lines 9–12)

To quote the passage on the Mona Lisa that Wilde admired, the Decadent seeks out "strange thoughts and fantastic reveries and exquisite passions," and admires the beauty "into which the soul with all its maladies has passed" (2.1641–42). Decadence is a lifestyle and a pose, indulged in by the protagonists of *Dorian Gray* and Joris-Karl Huysmans's *Against Nature* and satirized in W. S. Gilbert's *If You're Anxious for to Shine in the High Aesthetic Line* (2.1676). As an aesthetic practice, Decadence emphasizes form rather than content, deploying elaborate stylistic ornamentation and syntactical and tropic experiment.

Like Aestheticism and Decadence, the Symbolist movement (especially associated with the French poets Baudelaire, Mallarmé, Rimbaud, and Verlaine) reacted against bourgeois and utilitarian standards of aesthetic value, taking issue in particular with realism and naturalism and their goals of objective and accurate representation of physical reality. The symbolist work strives instead to evoke a mood, a sense of dreamy suggestiveness, like Wilde's *Impression du Matin* (2.1749). While this poem paints a cityscape (a "Thames nocturne in blue and gold" [line 1]), it's not interested in the physical world so much as the atmosphere—the lights, colors, shadows, and sound—that envelops it. *Impression du Matin* ends with the striking image of "one pale woman all alone, / The daylight kissing her wan hair," who lingers "beneath the gas lamps' flare, / With lips of flame and heart of stone" (lines 13–16). This image signifies richly, but in indeterminate fashion: the woman is sensuous, wistful, melancholy, faintly sinister, pensive, poignant. Compare T. S. Eliot's haunting images of the catlike, strangely insidious fog (the "yellow fog that rubs its back upon the window-panes, . . . the yellow smoke that slides along the street") in *The Love Song of J. Alfred Prufrock* (2.2364, lines 15, 24). Eliot "saw in the French symbolists how an image could be both absolutely precise in what it referred to physically and at the same time endless suggestive in the meanings it set up because of its relationship to other images" (2.2361)—in this case images of the desolation of the "half-deserted" streets and the lost souls who inhabit them. "I have gone at dusk through narrow streets / And watched the smoke that rises from the pipes / Of lonely men in shirt-sleeves, leaning out of windows" (2.365, lines 70–73).

As the *NAEL* introduction to Yeats explains, the poet "sought all his life for traditions of esoteric thought that would compensate for a lost religion," exploring various kinds of mysticism, "folklore, theosophy, spiritualism, and neoplatonism" (2.2085). In an early essay titled *Magic* Yeats describes a kind of universal consciousness, formed by the flowing together of human minds and wills and "the memory of Nature herself," and suggests that "this great mind and great memory can be evoked by symbols." While the Aesthete, Decadent, and Symbolist have much in common, the Decadent's insistent materialism contrasts sharply with the strain of idealism found in much of Symbolism. The Symbolist work might be marked by a certain distaste for physical reality simultaneous with the distaste for realist representation. Or rather, physical reality is valued as it serves to provide symbols: signs that are indeterminately but portentously charged with meaningfulness. The symbol, an almost incandescent force, serves as a link between the visible and the invisible, between the world of appearances and the world of essences (however defined) that lies above, or perhaps beneath, the physical realm. Thus Symbolism seeks a kind of secular transcendence through a precise but inspired manipulation of language. Yeats acknowledges his own tendency toward mysticism in *The Trembling of the Veil*: "I am very religious, and [was] deprived by Huxley and Tyndall, whom I detested, of the simple-minded religion of my childhood." Cheated of meaningfulness by materialist science, Yeats searched for universal images and narratives "created out of the deepest instinct of man" (2.2128).

"Trivial, Fantastic, Evanescent": Modernist Form

Twentieth-century modernism shares with its *fin-de-siècle* predecessors like Aestheticism a continuing preoccupation with literary form. David Lodge summarizes characteristic modernist techniques as follows: "formal experiment, dislocation of conventional syntax, radical breaches of decorum, disturbance of chronology and spatial order, ambiguity, polysemy, obscurity, mythopoeic allusion, primitivism, irrationalism, structuring by symbol and motif rather than by narrative or argumentative logic, and so on" (*Modernism, Antimodernism, and Postmodernism,* 1981). Traditional poetic and fictional forms are no longer adequate to encompass, or even adequately represent, chaotic modernity and the inchoate human subject newly theorized by evolutionism and psychoanalysis.

However, much more is at stake, self-avowedly, in the formal experimentation of the modernist. In *Tradition and the Individual Talent*, Eliot rejects literary practices associated with Decadence such as "eccentricity" and frivolity in "seek[ing] for new human emotions to express"; in its "search for novelty in the wrong place," the decadent text merely "discovers the perverse" (2.2400). While the Aesthete delights in the autonomy and magnificent uselessness of art, the modernist is disturbed by "high" art's perceived irrelevance to a public increasingly enthralled by popular (and conventional) literary forms. Ambivalent about this mass public, the modernist both seeks and fears artistic disengagement from the public sphere, deploying literary forms that are too difficult to please a general audience, but nonetheless concerned that the artist has become detached from a world ever more in need of the guidance and consolation that the work of art provides.

As he sits in a "pitch dark" so absolute "that we listeners could hardly see one another," alienated from his interlocutors, Conrad's Marlow concludes that "it is impossible to convey the life-sensation of any given epoch of one's existence—that which makes its truth, its meaning—its subtle and penetrating essence. It is impossible. We live, as we dream—alone" (*Heart of Darkness*, 2.1977). Here Conrad seems to echo Pater's thoughts about human isolation within "the narrow chamber of the individual mind" (2.1643). "We think of the key, each in his prison / Thinking of the key, each confirms a prison" (Eliot, *The Waste Land*, 2.2382, lines 414–15).

But Marlow also speaks to the incommensurability of modern experience. The brutality and outrages committed in the Congo in the "cause of progress" (2.1963) defy Marlow's powers of description. "Do you see him? Do you see the story? Do you see anything? It seems to me I am trying to tell you a dream—making a vain attempt" (2.1977). Forced to confront the lies that Western civilization tells itself about its high state of evolution and enlightenment, forced himself into a stupendous lie to Kurtz's fiancée, Marlow questions the possibility of any meaningful human communication whatsoever. Similarly, confronted by the unprecedented horror of trench warfare in World War I, Wilfred Owen bitterly rejects the "old Lie" that it is glorious and honorable to die for one's country. Platitudes about patriotism and national pride are grotesquely inappropriate for a comrade dying in agony of gas poisoning, "guttering, choking, drowning," his blood "gargling from the froth-corrupted lungs, / Obscene as cancer" (*Dulce et Decorum Est*, 2.2069, lines 27, 16, 22–23). In a letter to his mother. Owen writes of the "strange" expression on the faces of the soldiers who lie in a "vast, dreadful encampment" during a lull in the fighting. "It was not despair, or terror, it was more terrible than terror, for it was a blindfold look, and without expression, like a dead rabbit's." This expression—a "look . . . which a man will never see in England"—is "incomprehensible" to all but those who also await the uniquely gruesome deaths meted out during the Great War: "It will never be painted, and no actor will ever seize it. And to describe it, I think I must go back and be with them" (2.2073–74).

"These fragments I have shored against my ruins" (2.2383, line 431). In Eliot's *The Waste Land*, only the scattered remnants of culture, shattered like shell fragments, can be used to describe a Europe left spiritually empty and sterile by World War I. Eliot borrows from the myth of the Fisher King, which describes the eventual regeneration of a desolate land after long drought and hopelessness (see the headnote 2.2368–69). But in *The Waste Land*, the thought that a fertile and joyous new world might spring from the site of mass slaughter ("so many, / I had not thought death had undone so many" [lines 62–63]) is grotesque and unreal. "That corpse you planted last year in your garden, / Has it begun to sprout? Will it bloom this year?" (lines 71–72). No new life springs from the dead soil of the waste land ("what branches grow / Out of this stony rubbish?" [lines 19–20]), and arid human relations provide no more consolation than nature. Sex is not life-affirming but sordid, and brings no pleasure—the "bored and tired" typist yields with indifference to her unskilled lover the clerk, a "young man carbuncular" (lines 256, 231)—and thirty-one-year-old Lil's many pregnancies have only gotten her the wreck of her youthful good looks ("Well, if Albert won't leave you alone, there it is, I said" [line 163]) and the indifference of her husband. In place of vision or enlightenment, the poem offers a "heap of broken images," shards of narrative, and the tag-ends of inconsequential conversations, uncontrolled by any singular or omniscient narrative perspective. As is the case in *Prufrock*, the abundant and arcane literary allusions scattered throughout the poem don't lend dignity or grandeur to its characters and settings, but only emphasize, by means of ironic contrast, the vacuity and inanity of modern times. The poetry of Andrew Marvell and John Day, for instance, finds its debased echo in a present-day pastoral moment: "But at my back from time to time I hear / The sound of horns and motors, which shall bring / Sweeney to Mrs. Porter in the spring" (lines 196–98).

In general modernist form works to disperse rather than collect, to break apart rather than to construct meaning. Some authors like Eliot deploy modernist form while deploring its necessity for an incoherent and bewildering age, and seek to counteract the disorderliness of modernity as best they can. In *Tradition and the Individual Talent*, Eliot (rather like Matthew Arnold) finds coherence and fullness in literary history, which is an "ideal order" that fuses "the timeless" and "the temporal" (2.2396). Those writers who can absorb "the consciousness of the past" contained in this ideal order while simultaneously experiencing and yet disengaging themselves from the present—"the progress of an artist is a continual self-sacrifice, a continual extinction of personality"—will win for themselves a place in the great tradition (2.2398). For while "the ordinary man's experience is chaotic, irregular, fragmentary" (*The Metaphysical Poets*, 2.2406), the poet is able to synthesize the fragments: "The poet's mind is in fact a receptacle for seizing and storing up numberless feelings, phrases, images, which remain there until all the particles which can unite to form a new compound are present together" (*Tradition*, 2.2399).

Others modernists like Woolf regard the break-up of traditional meaning structures and formal unity with something close to exhilaration. "Why, if one wants to compare life to anything, one must liken it to being blown through the Tube at fifty miles an hour—landing at the other end without a single hairpin in one's hair! . . . Yes, that seems to express the rapidity of life, the perpetual waste and repair, all so casual, all so haphazard," Woolf writes in *The Mark on the Wall* (2.2144). Traditional narrative form cannot do justice to the tumultuous randomness of life so understood. The novel that commences cleanly, unfolds a sequence of events logically and evenly, and concludes unambiguously is too much like "Whitaker's Almanack" with its "Table of Precedency" that explains how the various ranks of society must comport themselves in public life. "The Archbishop of Canterbury is followed by the Lord High Chancellor; the Lord High Chancellor is followed by the Archbishop of York. Everybody follows somebody, such is the philosophy of Whitaker; and the great thing is to know who follows whom." Fiction should instead convey the brevity and disjunction of relations and experiences: life is much like looking out the window of a fast-moving train and being "torn asunder . . . from the old lady about to pour out tea and the young man about to hit the tennis ball in the back garden of a suburban villa" (2.2145, 2143). One glimpses a series of brief impressions, unfinished vignettes, unfolding in random order, unrelated to one another, and of no particular consequence. As she writes in *Modern Fiction*, "Let us not take it for granted that life exists more fully in what is commonly thought big than in what is commonly thought small" (2.2151).

In this essay Woolf criticizes realist novelists John Galsworthy, Arnold Bennett, and H. G. Wells because they are too intent on representing the details of the physical world. If their characters "were to come to life they would find themselves dressed down to the last button of their coats in the fashion of the hour." But while attending too closely to inconsequential matters, they fail to capture "life or spirit, truth or reality, . . . the essential thing." By contrast, novelists like Conrad and Joyce are "spiritual"—by which Woolf does not mean they are transcendentalists, but rather analyze "the quick of the mind." Joyce "is concerned at all costs to reveal the flickerings of that innermost flame which flashes its messages through the brain," and when necessary to disregard "probability" and "coherence" in his plotting in order better to represent the erratic motion of subjectivity (2.2150, 2151). (For the editors' discussion of Joyce's stream-of-consciousness narrative, see the headnote, 2.2234.)

> Examine for a moment an ordinary mind on an ordinary day. The mind receives a myriad impressions—trivial, fantastic, evanescent, or engraved with the sharpness of steel. From all sides they come, an incessant shower of innumerable atoms; and as they fall, as they shape themselves into the life of Monday or Tuesday, the accent falls differently from of old. . . . [Fiction should have] no plot, no comedy, no tragedy, no love interest or catastrophe in the accepted style, and perhaps not a single button sewn on as the Bond Street tailors would have it. . . . Let us record the atoms as they fall upon the mind in the order in which they fall, let us trace the pattern, however disconnected and incoherent in appearance, which each sight or incident scores upon the consciousness (2.2150–51).

Like Pater, Woolf regards the changefulness and ephemerality of human subjectivity and experience without nostalgia or regret. And like Pater, Woolf advocates living intensely and perceptively in order best to negotiate a world without inherent meaningfulness. To quote Pater, "Not to discriminate every moment some passionate attitude in those about us, and in the very brilliancy of their gifts some tragic dividing of forces on their ways, is, on this short day of frost and sun, to sleep before evening" (*The Renaissance*, 2.1644). "Every day includes much more non-being than being," Woolf writes in *A Sketch of the Past* (2.2222)—too many hours in which life is experienced passively and listlessly. Thus one must learn to sharpen one's powers of observation and train oneself to an almost painful susceptibility to nature, to other people, to the work of art.

The "moments of being" that result from such susceptibility are the religious visions of the secular materialist, wherein ordinary experience is suddenly irradiated and charged with significance. In *A Portrait of the Artist as a Young Man* Joyce adapts the religious term *epiphany* to describe these heightened experiences, like "a sudden spiritual manifestation," that briefly rend "the vestment of [the] appearance" of the everyday world. "The soul of the commonest object . . . seems to us radiant." Gabriel achieves such an epiphany as he watches the snow fall at the conclusion of *The Dead*. Startled out of his complacency by his wife's story of her youthful romance, exhausted by rapid play of emotions that have shifted from amorous tenderness to humiliation to "dull anger" to "vague terror" (2.2265–66), Gabriel, at least briefly, is released from the burden of self. "His own identity was fading out into a grey impalpable world: the solid world itself which these dead had one time reared and lived in was dissolving and dwindling. . . . His soul swooned slowly as he heard the snow falling faintly through the universe and faintly falling, like the descent of their last end, upon all the living and the dead" (2.2268). In his *Preface to The Nigger of the "Narcissus,"* Conrad hopes that literature itself might provide this sort of epiphany—a "moment of vision"—and not just for individuals in their isolation. The writer must try to convey the "vibration" and "form" and "colour" of a "rescued fragment" of experience: if he succeeds, his "presented vision of regret or pity, of terror or mirth, shall awaken in the hearts of the beholders that feeling of unavoidable solidarity; of the solidarity in mysterious origin, in toil, in joy, in hope, in uncertain fate, which binds men to each other and all mankind to the visible world" (2.1955–56).

Postmodernism and the Implosion of Form

"Finished, it's finished, nearly finished, it must be nearly finished," says Clov "tonelessly" in *Endgame*'s very first line of dialogue (2.2473). Throughout the play Samuel Beckett's characters hope for some resolution, some event that will bestow meaningfulness on their empty lives, some emotional apotheosis that will bring release—or perhaps they just wait for death. But no closure is achieved, or ever can be achieved. As the headnote to Beckett explains, "Not much happens in a Beckett play; there is very little plot, very little incident, and very little characterization. Characters engage in dialogue or dialectical monologues that go nowhere. There is no progression, no development, no resolution" (2.2471–72). Hamm and Clov are locked into some kind of interminable relationship displeasing to both of them: Hamm keeps Clov on as his servant because "There's no one else," and Clov stays on because "There's nowhere else" (2.2474). Nagg and Nell can't get out of their bins, and Hamm can't get up from his chair. Even if they could escape the tiny, claustrophobic house, there's no place of happiness or safety: "Outside of here it's death." Some disaster—perhaps nuclear war, perhaps an environmental catastrophe—has overtaken the world, and "there's no more nature" left (2.2475, 2476). There are only four people closed up together in a shabby room, performing the same repetitive activities, indulging in the same petty bickering, thinking the same fruitless thoughts, again and again and again.

Is Beckett a modernist or postmodernist author? He shares with a number of other modernists, beginning with Hardy, the themes of the random meaninglessness of existence, the hollowness of human relations, and the blank hostility of fate. But something is different—these themes are worked out to the point of absurdity, and played for dark humor. Rather than high modernist anguish and despair, we have the flat affect, the blankness and apathy, of characters with little psychological depth. Symbolism is present in such excess that it is ridiculous: we know that we are witnessing the breakdown of human identity because Nagg and Nell and Hamm are going blind, Nell is going deaf, Clov is half-crippled, Nagg has only "stumps" for limbs, Clov can't sit, and Hamm can't stand. Hamm clearly has oedipal problems—he keeps his parents in bins, and treats his adopted son as a servant, or his servant as an adopted son—yet an interpretation of this play as a critique of the nuclear family seems inadequate and futile. In fact, any interpretation of the play seems inadequate and futile. In what we may identify as one typically postmodern move, Beckett, working within an exhausted literary form, makes no attempt to resuscitate it: he rather exhausts it still further.

In *The Postmodern Turn* (1997), Steven Best and Douglas Kellner argue that postmodern artistic forms "renounce, implode, deconstruct, subvert, and parody conventionally defined boundaries such as those between high and low art, reality and unreality, artist and spectator, and among the various artistic media themselves." Like *Endgame*, they subvert the very idea of artistic legibility. Postmodern artists reject "structure, order, continuity, and cause-effect relations in favor of disorder, chaos, chance, discontinuity, indeterminacy, and forces of random or aleatory play." They manipulate "language, forms, images, and structures, appropriating material and forms from the past, finding aesthetic pleasure in appropriation, quotation, and the play of language, reveling in linguistic and formal invention, puns, parody, and pastiche."

Modernists, of course, also challenge traditional generic and formal boundaries. But postmodernists do so at a more extreme level, and in a different tone. Postmodernists might argue that the modernists were more like the Victorians than they would have cared to admit: both felt entrapped within the tumult and incoherency of modernity, and yearned for that lost, perhaps imaginary time when the "Sea of Faith" was "at the full, and round earth's shore / Lay like the folds of a bright girdle furled" (Arnold, *Dover Beach*, 2.1492, lines 21–23). Think of Yeats's lament for a "Romantic Ireland" that's "dead and gone" (*September 1913*, 2.2099, line 15), his desire to create "a national literature that made Ireland beautiful in the memory" (*Reveries over Childhood and Youth*, 2.2127). The modernist is like the speaker in Eliot's *Journey of the Magi*, "no longer at ease here": he has witnessed the birth of something new and unprecedented, but finds the change to be a "hard and bitter agony, . . . like Death, our death" (2.2387, lines 41, 39). The postmodernist, by contrast, is unlikely to indulge in nostalgia for a past whose integrity and meaningfulness seems increasingly distant, and most likely imaginary.

Such nostalgia is in fact dangerous, Salman Rushdie suggests in *The Prophet's Hair* (2.2843). The "wealthy money-lender" Hashim is a self-satisfied hypocrite with two spoiled, Westernized children; the "glassy contentment of that household, of that life of porcelain delicacy and alabaster sensibilities," seems to mark it out as the likely object of satire. But when Hashim accidentally comes into "possession of the famous relic of the Prophet Muhammad," tradition is reinstated with a vengeance, and disastrously so (2.2845, 2846). Hashim starts to look "swollen, distended," as if "he had filled up with some spectral fluid which might at any moment ooze uncontrollably from his every bodily opening." He gushes forth "long streams of awful truths": he never loved his wife and is miserable in the marriage; he has a mistress; he visits prostitutes; he will disinherit his wife; his son is stupid; his daughter is shameless for going "barefaced." He becomes a religious fanatic, forcing his family to pray five times a day, and burns all household books but the Qur'an. He goes into violent rages with his delinquent debtors, attacking them with bullwhips and knives, and begins beating his family as well: "From now on . . . there's going to be some discipline around here!" (2.2847–48).

Hashim and his children are dead by the end of the story, and his wife has been driven mad: religious fundamentalism and the "old ways" have utterly destroyed this family. And yet *The Prophet's Hair* is as much comedy as tragedy. The grand denouement, with its mayhem and disaster, is unexpectedly hilarious. The story is excessive, parodic, flippant, horrifying, and exhilarating. All characters, all possible positions, all beliefs, are objects of satire; nothing is sacred. Set in the disputed state of Kashmir, the story takes on such thorny issues as religious intolerance, sexual stereotyping, domestic violence, crime, poverty, class disparity, and the erosion of "traditional" culture, yet combines its genuine social engagement with a principled refusal to identify a moral high ground. With its irreverent tone, and its casual mixing of realistic and nonrealistic narrative modes (for the relic is a truly magical artifact, effecting miraculous cures), *The Prophet's Hair* is typically postmodern fiction.

Modernist writers were fully committed to the modernist experiment, and struggled to fashion genuinely innovative literary forms. Postmodernists, in general less concerned with originality, borrow from existing literary forms indiscriminately—*The Prophet's Hair* combines elements of traditional realism, magical realism, satire, moral fable, and cinematic screwball comedy—admixing seemingly incompatible narrative styles, diction, and tone. Nor do postmodernists scorn popular and mass culture forms, as the modernists were inclined to do. Tom Stoppard's *The Real Inspector Hound* (2.2786), for instance, even as it satirizes the popular country house murder-mystery play like Agatha Christie's *Mousetrap*, borrows liberally, and quite affectionately, from that genre. As befits a play whose entire plot derives from the parody of genre conventions, *Inspector*

Hound is always calling attention to the conventions of the drama in general. "The first thing is that the audience appear to be confronted by their own reflection in a huge mirror," we learn at the beginning of the stage directions (2.2786). Spectatorship and literary interpretation are rendered visible: the stage set includes another stage set and a theater's front row, where critic-characters sit and discuss the play. But lest Stoppard's audience be tempted to take the play's experimentalism and self-reflexivity too seriously, a high-minded interpretation of the drama is parodied by the pontificating critic Moon: "the play . . . aligns itself uncompromisingly on the side of life. . . . But is that enough? . . . It is my belief that here we are concerned with what I have referred to elsewhere as the nature of identity. I think we are entitled to ask—and here one is irresistibly reminded of Voltaire's cry, "*Voila!*"—I think we are entitled to ask—*Where is God?*" (2.2800). Here even Beckett is satirized—or perhaps it is only the critics who did not know that they were allowed to laugh at *Waiting for Godot* who are satirized.

The Literature of Empire

Imperialism and Colonialism

As the *NAEL* introduction to "The Rise and Fall of Empire" (2.2017–18) makes clear, British imperial activities date back some centuries, but reached their height in the later nineteenth century. Between 1876 and 1915, British overseas territories comprised some four million square miles, or one-fourth of the globe. If we understand imperialism as not just the "ownership" or control of territories outside of one's strict national boundaries, Eric Hobsbawn argues, but also "include the so-called 'informal empire' of independent states which were in effect satellite economies of Britain," then nearly "one-third of the globe was British in an economic, and indeed cultural, sense" (*The Age of Empire 1875–1914*, 1987). Whether they thought about it or not—and the religious, economic, political, and military ramifications of empire were topics of often heated discussion in Britain in the second half of the nineteenth century—imperialism touched the lives of all Victorians. Thus, though the bulk of the *NAEL*'s readings in the literature of empire are found in the last third of the volume in the section "The Twentieth Century," instructors of the year-long survey will probably wish to begin discussing British imperialism as a Victorian issue, starting with the John Ruskin and John Atkinson Hobson excerpts (dated 1870 and 1902, respectively, but found in "The Twentieth Century" in the special section "The Rise and Fall of Empire") and moving on to Rudyard Kipling's *The Man Who Would Be King* (2.1865). Conrad's *Heart of Darkness* (2.1958)—more often classed as a modernist rather than late-Victorian text, though it was first published in 1899—can be taught in either the Victorian or twentieth-century segment of a year-long survey or used to conclude a Victorian-only survey.

Although the British Empire was far-reaching and powerful, it was hardly a coherent or consistent entity. In other words, though the Empire was a great source of power for the British, that power was wielded in a uneven and often confused fashion, and the readings in the literature of empire will reflect this unevenness. As Bernard Porter writes in *The Lion's Share: A Short History of British Imperialism, 1850–1970* (1975):

> There was no single language covering the whole empire, no one religion, no one code of laws. In their forms of government the disparities between colonies were immense: between the Gold Coast of Africa, for example, ruled despotically by British officials, and Canada, with self-government in everything except her foreign policy. . . . In between, Nigeria was ruled by a commercial company, the states of Australia by their own prime ministers, Sierra Leone by a governor, Sarawak by a heredity English rajah, Somaliland by a commissioner responsible to India, Egypt by a consul-general who in theory only "advised" a native Egyptian cabinet, Ascension Island by a Captain as if it were a ship.

In addition to consulting the map "The British Empire ca. 1913" at the front of volume 2 of *NAEL*, your students may find it useful to look at something like Martin Gilbert's *Atlas of British History* (1993) to get a sense of the range of the British Empire, its expansion and retraction over the centuries, and the varieties and complexities of the relations between Great Britain and its overseas territories.

Imperialism is a difficult word to define, referring as it does to both a set of practices and a set of ideological justifications for those practices. Raymond Williams (*Keywords: A Vocabulary of Culture and Society*, 1983) complicates matters further by noting that imperialism can be understood on the one hand as "a political system in which colonies are governed from an imperial centre, for economic but also for other reasons held to be important," and on the other as "an economic system of external investment and the penetration and control of markets and sources of raw materials." (Economic imperialism does not end with the granting of independence to a colony, nor does cultural imperialism, as will be addressed below in the discussion of postcolonialism.) At the turn of the twentieth century economic and noneconomic motives for imperialism were simultaneous and nearly indistinguishable, as the example of Kurtz in *Heart of Darkness* makes clear. Kurtz is a member of what a jealous competitor calls the "gang of virtue": he's an idealist who proposes to bring enlightenment, civilization, and progress—European education, democracy, and religion—to the continent of Africa. In a report written for "the International Society for the Suppression of Savage Customs" he asserts triumphantly that the European in Africa "can exert a power for good practically unbounded" (2.1975, 1995). But at the same time, Kurtz is driven by the "imbecile rapacity" that motivates his more pragmatic or cynical colleagues, hungry for the wealth and power that he can wring out of the Congo and its people. "I saw him open his mouth wide—it gave him a weirdly voracious aspect, as though he had wanted to swallow all the air, all the earth, all the men before him" (2.1974, 2002).

The distinction between imperialism and colonialism is also difficult to pin down, because the two activities can seem indistinguishable at times. Roughly speaking, imperialism involves the claiming and exploiting of territories outside of one's own national boundaries for a variety of motives: for instance, an imperialist nation might wish to seize a territory to increase its own holdings and enhance its own prestige, to extract labor and raw materials (sugar, spices, tea, tin, rubber, and so on) from the territory, or to procure a market for its own goods (Britain exported everything from textiles to insurance and banking services). Colonialism involves the settling of those territories and the transformation (the colonialist would say "reformation") of the social structure, culture, government, and economy of the people found there. Kipling's *The Man Who Would Be King* illustrates the distinction. Peachey Carnehan and Daniel Dravot would be simple imperialists if they were content to travel to Kafiristan, trick the locals into giving them gold and turquoise and garnets and amber (2.1879), and return with the loot. Daniel, however, wants to settle among the villagers and make them more like Englishmen: "I won't make a Nation. . . . I'll make an Empire!" (2.1881). The men introduce modern weaponry to the villagers, teach them to fight and drill like Englishmen, consolidate the local government, and start a Freemasons' lodge. In *Heart of Darkness*, Kurtz can only accomplish his more idealistic goals—"Each station should be like a beacon on the road towards better things, a centre for trade of course, but also for humanising, improving, instructing" (2.1981)—by settling among the people of the Congo as a sort of missionary and (at least so he plans) re-educating them. His more mercenary goals are thus forwarded as well, for he amasses great stores of ivory with his tribe's help: Kurtz the colonialist can exploit the Congo in a far more thoroughgoing and efficacious manner than the "pilgrims" who pass through the Central Station and have no intention of settling.

Parts II and III of *Things Fall Apart* give a systematic account of the process of colonization. The white men take over not just because of their superior firepower but because they gradually convert the Igbo to their ways. The missionaries win over the outcast (the *efulefu*, or "worthless empty men") and the disaffected, like Okonkwo's oldest son Nwoye, alienated from his father and "haunted" by the memory of Ikemefuna's death (2.2679, 2681). The English preach Western-style capitalism as well as Christianity: "The white man had indeed brought a lunatic religion, but he had also built a trading store and for the first time palm-oil and kernel became things of great price, and much money flowed into Umuofia" (2.2692). Igbo resisters are found guilty under British law, and their punishment administered by collaborators from Umuru. As Obierika says, "Our own men and our sons have joined the ranks of the stranger. They have joined his religion and they help to uphold his government. . . . How do you think we can fight when our own brothers have turned against us?" (2.2692).

E. M. Forster's *A Passage to India* explores the fraught relations between Englishman and Indian after the British conquest and colonization of India has become a long-established fact. Dr. Aziz has been dispossessed of his own homeland: "The roads, named after victorious generals and intersecting at right angles, were symbolic of the net Great Britain had thrown over India. He felt caught in their meshes" (2.2137). The English treat the Indians as if they were invisible, or inconsequential, or faintly disgusting, as when the city magistrate (the "red-nosed boy" Ronnie Heaslop) insults Mahmoud Ali in the courtroom, or the two ladies commandeer Aziz's tonga without asking his permission and turn "instinctively away" from his polite greeting (2.2133, 2137). It is not their fault, Hamidullah says magnanimously: the Englishmen "come out intending to be gentlemen, and are told it will not do" (2.2134). Aziz and Mrs. Moore are able to connect cordially and meaningfully only because she does not behave like the typical English colonist; Aziz knows by her courteous treatment of him that she is "newly arrived in India" (2.2140). Your students should know that despite the rapport that Aziz and Mrs. Moore achieve at the end of the *NAEL* selection, much of the rest of the novel will go on to show that friendly relations between colonizer and colonized are inevitably, terribly, tragically impossible. Aziz and his friends discuss "whether or no it is possible to be friends with an Englishman" (2.2133), and in the final sentence the novel answers, "No, not yet . . . No, not there."

Justifications for Empire

"I ventured to hint that the Company was run for profit," Marlow notes drily after his aunt, expressing sentiments similar to those found in Kurtz's pamphlet, has gotten "carried off her feet" with her effusions about the civilizing mission of the European imperialist (2.1965). Marlow has said earlier that imperialism is "just robbery with violence . . . The conquest of the earth, which mostly means the taking it away from those who have a different complexion or slightly flatter noses than ourselves, is not a pretty thing when you look into it too much. What redeems it is the idea only" (2.1961). Most pro-imperialist thinkers chose to underplay or discount the economic motives that fueled imperialism, focusing on "the idea" that exalted it instead. The great English "knights-errant" like Sir Francis Drake might have returned home with ships "full of treasure," says the frame narrator of *Heart of Darkness*, but what matters most is their devotion to the "dreams of men, the seed of commonwealths, the germs of empires." Whether "hunters for gold or pursuers of fame," British imperialists are "bearers of a spark from the sacred fire" (2.1959). In *Imperial Duty*, Ruskin deplores "the obscene empires of Mammon and Belial," and argues that England must develop colonies not for hope of gaining "terrestrial gold," but because the "sceptred isle" of England should become "for all the world a source of light, a centre of peace" (2.2019).

For Ruskin, the establishment of an empire is thus England's "destiny," the "highest ever set before a nation." Englishmen are descended from "a race mingled of the best northern blood," have the "firmness to govern," are guided by "a religion of pure mercy," are "rich in an inheritance of honour," can boast "a thousand years of noble history," and have made great advances in industry and science (2.2019). Thus England has not only a right but also a *duty* to found colonies and bring its advanced values to inferior peoples. Kipling would make this same argument in more jingoistic terms in poems like *A Song of the White Men* and *The White Man's Burden* (both 1899), the former extolling the valor and selflessness of the European imperialist ("Now, this is the road that the white men tread / When they go to clean a land . . . Oh, well for the world when the white men join / To prove their faith again!"), the latter lamenting the ingratitude of the subject races ("Your new-caught, sullen peoples, / Half devil and half child") who scorn the white man's sacrifices.

Such thinking had its strong opponents, as we see in the excerpt from Hobson's *Imperialism: A Study*. Those who believe that British imperialism is motivated by benevolent aims—that Britain's "colonial and imperial policy is animated by a resolve to spread throughout the world the arts of free self-government which we enjoy at home"—are self-deluded, says Hobson. The Empire has not the slightest interest in helping its subjects achieve self-government: vast numbers of British subjects who live outside of the British isles have no political or civil freedom; the franchise "is virtually a white monopoly in so-called self-governing colonies"; most possessions are in any case Crown colonies or protectorates, where "there is no tincture of British representative government; the British factor consists in arbitrary acts of irregular interference with native government." Less than 5 percent of the "population of the Empire are possessed of any appreciable portion of the political and civil liberties which are the basis of British civilisation" (2.2021–23). England has not "civilized" its colonies, but only brought terror and disarray.

A "white man in an unbuttoned uniform" was "looking after the upkeep of the road, he declared. Can't say I saw any road or any upkeep, unless the body of a middle-aged negro, with a bullet-hole in the forehead, upon which I absolutely stumbled three miles farther on, may be considered as a permanent improvement" (*Heart of Darkness*, 2.1971). Traveling through the Congo, Marlow witnesses the miserable effects of European imperialism: acts of inexplicable violence (in the "empty immensity of earth, sky, and water," a French man-of-war anchored off the coast fires its guns aimlessly "into a continent"); "abandoned villages"; a chain-gang of starving "criminals" who have run afoul of the white man's laws; slave laborers reduced to "black shadows of disease and starvation," dying in slow agony like doomed souls within "the gloomy circle of some Inferno" from Dante (2.1966, 1971, 1968–69).

Imperialism corrupts the conquering as well as subject peoples, as Dr.

Aziz's friends note in *Passage to India* (2.2133–34), fostering cruelty and egotism. In *Shooting an Elephant* George Orwell remembers the hatred, callousness, and despair that he came to feel working as a "sub-divisional police office" in Lower Burma; such terrible emotions, he argues, "are the normal by-products of imperialism" (2.2457). He shoots the elephant "solely to avoid looking like a fool," having lost the ability or will carefully to make rational and ethical decisions, having indeed lost all sense of individuality: "when the white man turns tyrant it is his own freedom that he destroys. He becomes a sort of hollow, posing dummy, the conventionalised figure of a sahib. . . . He wears a mask, and his face grows to fit it" (2.2462, 2460).

Throughout *Heart of Darkness* we find that Europeans are more brutal than the "savages" they purport to enlighten. At the end of his journey down the river Marlow finds a mud hut surrounded by shrunken human heads on wooden stakes. These heads have not been placed there at the behest of some Congolese ruler, but to gratify Kurtz—the idealist, the missionary, erudite, charismatic, and eloquent. Marlow's African cannibal companions on board the steamer prove themselves to be men of principle, unexpectedly capable of "restraint" despite their month-long fast, whereas Kurtz, the exemplary European ("All Europe contributed to the making of Kurtz") utterly lacks "restraint in the gratification of his various lusts" (2.1988, 1995, 2001).

Kurtz has become the metaphorical cannibal, a murderous despot hungry for power and adulation. In *The Man Who Would Be King*, Dravot, too, sounds rather like a cannibal when he advises Carnehan to choose a wife—"a nice, strappin', plump girl"—from among the fair-skinned villager women. "Boil 'em once or twice in hot water, and they'll come as fair as chicken and ham" (2.1883). (This culminating instance of rapaciousness will finally prove to be the two men's undoing.) Kurtz concludes his pamphlet, "that moving appeal to every altruistic sentiment," with a crazed sentence scrawled across the bottom of the page: "Exterminate all the brutes!" (2.1995). The heads on the stakes outside Kurtz's hut, alarmingly, are facing inward: "turned to the house" as if in worship of its megalomaniacal inmate (2.2001). Such behaviors only seem to contradict the sentiments used to justify imperialism, Conrad reveals; and they are in fact sanctioned by the ideologies that support imperialism. The "altruistic" passages of Kurtz's pamphlet are shot through with the arrogance and insolent self-importance of the colonizer: "He began with the argument that we whites, from the point of development we had arrived at, 'must necessarily appear to them [savages] in the nature of supernatural beings—we approach them with the might as of a deity' " (2.1995).

Dravot and Carnehan are tricksters, not failed idealists like Kurtz, but Dravot in particular also proves to be a megalomaniac with delusions of grandeur. Kipling's protagonists travel to an obscure corner of Afghanistan because it's the "only one place in the world that two strong men" with no particular aptitude or skill ("Soldier, sailor, compositor, photographer, proof-reader, street-preacher. . . . We have been boiler-fitters, engine-drivers, petty contractors, and all that") can set themselves up as kings and semidivinities. "They have two and thirty heathen idols there, and we'll be the thirty-third" (2.1870–71). The colonies were thought to be places to which a young, upwardly mobile European like Kurtz could travel to make his fortune or implement his visions, but they also presented opportunities for the "Loafer" and the "vagabond" (Kipling, 2.1865), for stolid and unimaginative Englishmen like Forster's colonial bureaucrats, and for mediocrities like the manager of the Central Station in *Heart of Darkness*, who has nothing to recommend him but stubborn good health. "He had no genius for organising, for initiative, or for order even. . . . He had no learning, and no intelligence. His position had come to him—why? Perhaps because he was never ill" (2.1972). Nineteenth-century ethnology, physical anthropology, psychology, and social evolutionism insisted on the inherent superiority of the European, so that the most untalented individual, who might be a social marginal or a failure at home, could lord it over even high-caste non-Europeans in the colonies.

"Orientalism" and the Psychology of Empire

Edward Said's ground-breaking study *Orientalism* (1978) provides a useful model for framing your discussion of the literature of imperialism. "Orientalism," as Said describes it, is first of all a scholarly discourse, or set of interconnecting scholarly discourses, produced in the West in the eighteenth, nineteenth, and twentieth centuries, and includes writings in such fields as anthropology, philology, linguistics, history, sociology, literature, and literary criticism that take as their object the people, societies, cultures, and histories of the Middle East, East Asia, Southeast Asia, the Indian subcontinent, and Eastern Europe. Though one might expect that Orientalism as defined here is about the pure and disinterested pursuit of scientific and cultural knowledge, Said argues that Orientalism is anything but politically disengaged. The exchange of information is one-sided, for one thing: the Western scholar sets the terms of the study, asking the questions, interpreting the data, and writing up the results—while "the Orient" and "the Oriental" are the objects of study, scrutinized and dissected by the Orientalist scholar. Orientalism is furthermore a reductive and homogenizing discourse, which analyzes people and cultures in the mass rather than individually. Phrases like "the Oriental temperament"—which might be used to describe Mongolian nomads, ancient Egyptians, Japanese feudal lords, Tibetan monks, high-caste urban sophisticates in India, farmers in Guangdong Province, and so on—serve utterly to level the distinctions between diverse populations, cultures, and histories.

In *A Passage to India* (in a chapter much later than the one excerpted in *NAEL*), Superintendent of Police McBryde, opening the prosecution's case against Aziz, cannot forbear interrupting himself to make a few remarks on "Oriental Pathology, his favourite theme." As if "enunciating a general truth," he notes that "the darker races are physically attracted by the fairer, but not vice versa—not a matter for bitterness this, . . . but just a fact which any scientific observer will confirm." McBryde is a strictly amateur Orientalist, more of a bureaucrat than a pathologist, but as a white man he is privileged to make sweeping statements about the psychological makeup and intrinsic inferiority of "the darker races." (You might ask your students if they would make a distinction between McBryde's generalization and the narrator's when he says on 2.2135 that Aziz and his friends "generalized from [their] disappointments—it is difficult for members of a subject race to do otherwise.") McBryde's "scientific" observation reduces Aziz to a type rather than an individual, and "general truths" applied to all dark-skinned peoples confirm Aziz's guilt before the trial is even under way. Here we see the noninnocence of a purportedly objective scholarly discourse: Orientalism justifies and reinforces the colonial power structure, and the Orientalist's conclusions are shaped, consciously or otherwise, by the racist assumptions that enabled colonialism in the first place. Orientalism is what Said (working from the social philosopher Michel Foucault) would call a "knowledge-power formation": as McBryde's double status as policeman and scholar of "Oriental Pathology" makes clear, knowledge serves the workings of power, and power functions by wielding knowledge (representations, "general truth," scientific facts) as well as through brute force.

McBryde might remind one of another colonial bureaucrat and amateur scholar, the "District Commissioner" who appears in the final chapter of *Things Fall Apart.* Achebe's District Commissioner is both a "resolute administrator" and an avid "student of primitive customs." Okonkwo's story, he thinks, will make "interesting reading. One could almost write a whole chapter on him. Perhaps not a whole chapter but a reasonable paragraph, at any rate" (2.2705–6). The complex and tragic history of Okonkwo, intertwined as it is with the complex and tragic history of British conquest of the lands that would become present-day Nigeria, will be reduced to a "reasonable paragraph" of a work titled, ominously, *The Pacification of the Primitive Tribes of the Lower Niger.* Though we are considering British representations of Africa and not the Orient, clearly Said's work is very relevant here as well—Achebe shows the interrelation of scholarship and brute power (knowledge will be put to the service of "pacification"), and criticizes Western scholarship's tendency to reduce non-Western individuals, families, villages, whole cultures to homogeneous types, or perhaps anthropological curiosities.

And in fact, many postcolonial critics have modified *Orientalism*'s argument to discuss Western attitudes toward other colonized regions ("Africanist" representations of Africa, for instance), or discourses on and around imperialism in general. Particularly useful is Said's assertion that Orientalism is not only made up of material texts: it is also "a style of thought based upon an ontological and epistemological distinction made between 'the Orient' and 'the Occident.' " In other words, Orientalist thinking—or we may now say, imperialistic thinking—works in terms of oppositions: the Occident is civilized, but the Orient is barbaric; the

Westerner is rational, democratic, cerebral, Christian, and self-restrained, while the colonized subject is superstitious, despotic, sensual, heathen, and perverse. These opposed terms are in fact mutually self-defining, as J. M. Coetzee's *Waiting for the Barbarians* makes clear. Constantine Cavafy's poem by the same name, excerpted in the *NAEL* headnote to Coetzee, asks, "And now what shall become of us without any barbarians? / Those people were a kind of solution" (2.2828). Coetzee's novel shows how the dominant culture can only maintain its exalted self-image by identifying another group as its "Other," its dark mirror image: a group of aboriginals (innocuous "river people"), identified as enemies of the "Empire" and taken captive, are regarded as "strange animals" and "savages" with "frank and filthy habits" (2.2830–31). The agents of the Empire may then understand themselves as fully human and properly civilized by contrast. One cannot recognize oneself as an "emissary of light" (to borrow a phrase from Marlow's aunt) unless one stands out in relief against a heart of darkness (2.1965).

Among other things Said performs a sort of psychoanalysis of culture: imperialist discourses like Orientalism involve denial (of one's own animalism, physicality, potential for brutality, and so on) and displacement and projection (of those disavowed attributes onto a demonized Other). Such discourses, then, teach us more about the culture producing them than their purported objects. They construct an imaginary Other who bears little or no resemblance to the actual colonial subject, with his or her own complex history, customs, beliefs, and desires; for instance, Dr. Aziz cannot be recognized in the portrait of the sexually predatory "darker races" McBryde paints in his remarks on "Oriental Pathology." Steaming down the river in *Heart of Darkness*, Marlow hears the beating of drums and sees "a whirl of black limbs, a mass of hands clapping, of feet stamping, of bodies swaying, of eyes rolling." He does not see individuals, only a "black and incomprehensible frenzy," a spectacle of undifferentiated African-ness that speaks to him of his own ongoing concerns—the terrifying affinity of "prehistoric man" and himself, the tenuousness of the European's civilized identity, the ephemerality of Western culture (2.1983–84). We learn a great deal about Marlow, and about turn-of-the-century European anxieties, from this incident, but nothing about the people he describes with such apprehension. It is interesting to compare this scene (one of the scenes Achebe singles out for criticism in *An Image of Africa*, 2.2037) with chapters 5 and 6 of *Things Fall Apart*, wherein another village celebration accompanied by pounding drumbeats is used to explore social relations among the people of Umuofia and further to develop the troubling, intricate character of Okonkwo. In Achebe an African festival is presented as not irrationally frenzied but exuberant, not "incomprehensible" but deeply meaningful, carefully planned by the community rather than the result of some obscure savage impulse.

The literature of empire sometimes practices and sometimes critiques the strategies whereby an imperialist culture interprets and represents the disempowered colonized subject, or the unresisting colonial landscape, in ways that suit its own needs and reflect its own hopes, fears, and desires. You might ask your students to identify and track some of these rhetorical and/or psychological strategies—to analyze Ruskin's rhetoric, for instance, when he argues that English "must found colonies as fast and as far as she is able, . . . seizing every piece of *fruitful waste ground* she can set her foot on" (2.2019, emphasis added). In this shrewd oxymoron Ruskin suggests that the colonial lands are "fruitful" because rich in natural resources, but "waste" because inhabited by savages who don't know how to use those resources. Indeed, Ruskin's "waste" lands seem not to be populated by indigenous peoples at all, as is true also of the fantasized Congo of Marlow's childhood, appearing on the map and in the young Marlow's imagination as "a blank space of delightful mystery—a white patch for a boy to dream gloriously over" (2.1962).

The colonial landscape and subject often become confused and blend into one another, the former anthropomorphized and the latter evacuated of its human identity, as when a "wild and gorgeous apparition of a woman" appears toward the end of *Heart of Darkness*. "And in the hush that had fallen suddenly upon the whole sorrowful land, the immense wilderness, the colossal body of the fecund and mysterious life seemed to look at her, pensive, as though it had been looking at the image of its own tenebrous and passionate soul" (2.2003). Non-Europeans are dehumanized by a number of other rhetorical moves as well: described as animals, associated with filth and abjection, exoticized, eroticized. Marlow describes the "savage" who works as his fireman as "an improved specimen . . . to look at him was as edifying as seeing a dog in a parody of breeches and a feather hat, walking on his hind legs" (2.1984). The American Pat in Anita Desai's *Scholar and Gypsy* is disgusted by the smell and hot physicality of "the wild jungles of the city of Bombay," filled with "the greasy Indian masses, whining and cajoling and sneering—oh, *horrible*" (2.2770, 2780), just as the narrator of Coetzee's *Waiting for the Barbarians* complains of the captives' "filth" and "smell" and "the noise of their quarrelling and coughing" (2.2831). Those same "greasy" city dwellers are exotic objects of fascination to Pat's sociologist husband David, while Pat views the mountain people of Manali—whose "squalid" streets filled with beggars and "snot-gobbed urchins" sicken David (2.2783)—as delightful exotics in turn. Coetzee's soldiers are titillated by the "animal shamelessness" of the captives they claim to find so disgusting: the narrator spies on them furtively ("from my window I stare down, invisible behind the glass"), while his men "lounge in the doorways watching them" and sexually assault one of the women (2.2831). In *The Moment before the Gun Went Off* (2.2573), the same Afrikaners who speak angrily of the moral turpitude, improvidence, and indolence of the South African blacks they employ claim them as sexual possessions nonetheless, as we discover at the end of the story when Nadine Gordimer's narrator reveals that the favorite servant Van der Vyver shot accidentally was his own son, born to another servant.

Postcolonial Voices

"The Empire Writes Back"

Postcolonialism—postcolonial literature and theory—is concerned with the situation of former subject nations and cultures whose histories have been irremediably altered by the experience of colonialism. Postcolonialism looks critically at imperialism and its legacy and seeks to undo the ideologies that underpin and justify imperialist practices. Postcolonial writers also work to reclaim the past, because their own histories were often erased or discredited under imperialism, and to understand their own cultural and personal identities, and chart their own futures, on their own terms rather than the terms superimposed on them by imperialist ideology and practice.

The first of these activities should already be quite familiar from the preceding discussion. Postcolonial writers document the strategies—economic, military, ideological, rhetorical—whereby one nation gains control over, subjugates, and maintains power over another, and analyzes the stories the dominant culture tells itself about why imperialism is justified and necessary. *NAEL*'s selections from the literature of empire are by and large highly critical of, or at least ambivalent about, imperialism, so that thinking we might characterize, anachronistically, as "postcolonial" was taking place during the period when the British Empire was at its most powerful. Thus it makes a good deal of sense for an instructor to pair the 1899 *Heart of Darkness* with the 1960 *Waiting for the Barbarians*, because both works show the arbitrariness and hollowness of such concepts as "barbarian" and "civilized," satirize the rationalizations that the imperialist employs, and portray empire building as a nightmarish and brutal activity founded on self-delusion.

But it also makes good sense to pair *Heart of Darkness* with Achebe's critique of it in *An Image of Africa*. Achebe does not consider the novel a great anti-imperialist document by any means; in fact, he calls Conrad "a thoroughgoing racist" (a "bloody racist" in the original version), and argues that even through the novel criticizes nineteenth-century European beliefs, it uses the African continent merely as a "backdrop" against which to do so. Africa is thus evacuated of its actual history, and becomes a "metaphysical battleground" wherein Europeans confront the possibility of their own barbarism (2.2040). In a novel renowned for psychological complexity, Achebe argues, Africans are given neither motivation nor subjective depth, presented as fearsome enigmas or nonentities, scarcely allowed articulate speech (2.2038). "This also . . . has been one of the dark places of the earth," says Marlow, noting that England, the center of the Empire, was once a site of "utter savagery" populated by "wild men" (2.1959, 1960), and the novel will go on to show how European identity is fluctuable and unstable, because reversion to that "wild" state is always a possibility. Africa, however, remains inert, a mute symbol of the savagery of which humans are capable, or even of the essential meaninglessness of human existence.

In Achebe's piece the Empire writes back, to borrow a phrase from a 1989 study by Bill Ashcroft, Gareth Griffiths, and Helen Tiffin (*The Empire Writes Back: Theory and Practice in Post-Colonial Literatures*). Students are often unnerved by this article. Achebe challenges the aesthetic value of a novel that may have given them pleasure or challenged them intellectually, arguing that *Heart of Darkness* should not "be called a great work of art" (2.2040). They may feel that Achebe's deliberately and consistently indignant, sometimes anguished, tone is inappropriate to academic discourse. Students of European descent often assume that Achebe's anger is somehow directed at them personally (an assumption a close reading of the piece will not bear out, of course) rather than at the long history of colonialist representations of Africa. One might say that the article is useful precisely because it provokes such distress. Achebe reminds us of how much is at stake in the game of literary representation: texts and images have the power to shape the attitude of whole generations, and present a certain version of "reality" so convincingly that it becomes impossible to imagine alternatives.

Heart of Darkness does indeed, most students will conclude, develop a quite scathing critique of imperialism, far more so than Achebe gives Conrad credit for. But it is also important to note that while the novel works consistently to break down the oppositions that underlie imperialist ideology—white/dark, civilized/barbaric, modern/prehistoric, human/animal, England/Africa—it displays no interest in African subjects and cultures in their own right, offers us no "alternative frame of reference" to the White Man's (*An Image of Africa*, 2.2039). *A Passage to India*, by contrast, struggles to realize the complex subjectivities of colonizer and colonized alike. Its narrator, as if in compensation for the discourtesy of the English characters, is closely attentive to the nuances of Indian life, explaining the subtleties of the interactions at Hamidullah's home—Hamidullah Begum's oblique and unspoken courtesy, for instance—that might otherwise go unnoticed by the non-Indian reader. "It was difficult to get away, because until they had had their dinner she would not begin hers, and consequently prolonged her remarks in case they should suppose she was impatient" (2.2135). Whether *Heart of Darkness should* have done the same is another question; perhaps it is enough that it so scathingly denounces the hypocritical cruelty and deceit that underlay imperialist practice at the turn of the century. But *Heart of Darkness* only describes the disillusionment and tragic self-deception of the European confronting modernity. Its African subjects, also crushed by the weight of European modernity, are mostly silent. Postcolonial fiction allows those subjects to speak.

Things Fall Apart, then, provides a more indirect but also more thorough critique of *Heart of Darkness* than *An Image of Africa*. As the headnote to Achebe makes clear (2.2616), *Things Fall Apart* responds to and revises British representations of Africa, thus intervening in a tradition represented in *NAEL*, and works as well to establish a countertradition. The novel shows that before colonialism Africa was not a "blank space" on the map (a place without history or culture, an undifferentiated site of primitivism): the Igbo had their own social traditions, civil order, and religious beliefs before the English came to "civilize" them. Like other postcolonial literature, *Things Fall Apart* attempts to describe and explain a reality that has as yet (at least in the Western tradition) escaped representation. While this reality may seem alien to many of your students, the example of the District Commissioner should alert them to the temptation of regarding *Things Fall Apart* as no more than a source of ethnographic data about a preindustrial, noncapitalist culture. (Similarly, they would not confine themselves to an ethnographic reading of the unfamiliar and exotic culture of preindustrial England.)

By choosing a title and epigraph from Yeats, Achebe places himself squarely within the European modernist tradition, and yet the simplicity (most critics would say, the deceptive simplicity) of *Things Fall Apart*'s prose contrasts markedly with the insistent complexity of *Heart of Darkness* (whose extravagant diction—"It was the stillness of an implacable force brooding over an inscrutable intention"—Achebe discusses sardonically in *An Image of Africa*, 2.2036). Your students will want to consider how their understanding of historical and aesthetic modernism alters when imperialism is identified as an integral part of modernism; why Achebe chose the realist novel rather than one of the more experimental narrative forms associated with aesthetic modernism as his medium; and the relationship between novelistic story-telling and the traditional oral forms of story-telling represented within the text. (As Geoffrey Nunberg points out in "The Persistence of English," Achebe's writing "reflects the influence not just of Shakespeare and Wordsworth but of proverbs and other forms of discourse drawn from West African oral traditions.")

Things Fall Apart was published in 1958, just after Ghana had become the first African nation to achieve independence, and just before Nigeria itself became an independent state (in 1960). The novel negotiates this cultural watershed not by looking forward to independence but by revisiting another cultural upheaval, the breakup of Igbo society under British imperialism. Postcolonialism is never fully "post," at least in the twentieth century: one must struggle to imagine the shape and import of what was lost (traditional ways of life, for instance) and the trauma of the imperial encounter must be retold and reinterpreted from one's own perspective, and somehow come to terms with.

And of course, the long-term effects of imperialism still linger long after independence, as shown in Gordimer's account of life under apartheid in *The Moment before the Gun Went Off*. Here we see the terrible interconnectedness of black and white during postcolonial times ("the young black man's blood was all over the farmer's clothes, soaking against his flesh as he drove"; 2.2576), yet power is still divided starkly along racial lines, and racial identity is understood in no less agonistic terms than at the end of the nineteenth century. "Certain things here are quietly American," writes Derek Walcott in *Midsummer* (2.2584, line 1), deploring the effects of cultural and economic imperialism in Trinidad. The poem uses the language of militaristic imperialism and warfare ("Occupation," "fealty") to describe the Americanization of Trinidad, a process that brings relative prosperity but will transform Trinidad's landscape ("Bulldozers jerk / and gouge out a hill") and subjects ("My own corpuscles / are changing as fast") into something as yet unknown (lines 17–18, 23–24). Long after independence, Desai's *Scholar and Gypsy* (2.2768) examines the persistence of imperialistic thinking with a satirical eye. The American farm girl Pat and her more urbane husband, David, each misread and try to appropriate the Indian culture they observe, both "going native" in their very different ways. David "had bought himself crisp bush-shirts of madras cotton and open Kolhapur sandals. . . . He looked so right, so fitting on the Bombay streets" (2.2768–69). He eagerly enters into the night life of Bombay's sophisticated set, joking that he's "disappointed at finding them so westernised. I would have liked them a bit more primitive—at least for the sake of my thesis" (2.2770). Pat joins up with a group of Western hippies who have resolved to "live the simple life, wash themselves and their dishes in a stream, cook brown rice and lentils, pray and meditate in the forest, and, at the end, perhaps, become Buddhists" (2.2785). In an ironic reversal, these European and American indigents, begging in rags, are objects of horrified fascination to the Indian tourists who visit Manali. They give these "fair and tattered hippies" food and alms, and watch them with "condescension" and "pity" and incredulity, "exactly as if they were watching some disquieting although amusing play" (2.2782). Santosh, the narrator of V. S. Naipaul's *One Out of Many*, feels the same combination of attraction and revulsion when he sees some American hippies dressed in Indian clothes, "chanting Sanskrit words in praise of Lord Krishna" and dancing by a fountain. "I felt for the dancers the sort of distaste we feel when we are faced with something that should be kin but turns out not to be, turns out to be degraded, like a deformed man, or like a leper, who from a distance looks whole" (2.2728).

Hybrid Identities, Hybrid Cultures

In *A Far Cry from Africa* (2.2580), Walcott confronts his own ambivalent, anguished responses to the Kikuyu insurrection in 1950s Kenya. The poet hears the "far cry from Africa" (a cry from Kikuyu or white settler or both) and cannot fix its meaning. Moreover, the Caribbean-born Walcott—the descendant of slaves, brought up on the former British colony of Saint Lucia—is himself "a far cry from Africa" and cannot gauge his own responses to its turmoil. The poem cannot locate a place of ethical certainty from which to respond to the convulsive violence that often accompanies the break from colonial rule, which it condemns while also wishing to condemn the history of British imperialism in Africa. The first stanza invites sympathy for the settlers, members of the oppressing class who may yet be innocent (like "the white child hacked in bed") while noting bitterly that black "savages," too, as "expendable as Jews," have also been subject to genocide (lines 9–10). The poet, "poisoned with the blood of both," asks, "Where shall I turn, divided to the vein?" He has despised "British rule," yet he loves the "English tongue," and does not want to choose between his beloved English language and Africa—especially "this Africa," "scattered" with corpses (lines 26–30, 4). To reject either is to betray himself. "How can I face such slaughter and be cool? / How can I turn from Africa and live? (lines 32–33).

A Far Cry from Africa illustrates the dilemma of the hybrid subject, often considered to be the typical subject of postcoloniality. (Students from the United States, a diverse culture that values assimilation, may have difficulty understanding the urgency of this dilemma.) Postcolonial subjects find themselves asked to choose between incompatible cultures or dispersed among multiple cultures: they cannot lay claim to a singular, an unambiguous, a racially or culturally unmixed identity. As we have discussed, one project of postcolonial writing is to retrieve and re-examine precolonial indigenous experience, lost under imperialism—but given that colonialism changes things irremediably, is it possible or even desirable to recreate this experience again? And if one were somehow able to return to that indigenous experience (or perhaps the imaginary postcolonial version thereof), would it yield a more "authentic" identity? Conversely, does adopting the values or practices of the colonizer (embracing Western-style capitalism, converting to Christianity, reading Western literature and philosophy) constitute a betrayal of one's own people?

Roberto Fernández Retamar approaches these questions through the figures of Caliban and Ariel from Shakespeare's *The Tempest* (*Caliban: Notes towards a Discussion of Culture in Our America*, 1974). From the perspective of European imperialism, Caliban is the "bad native" (animalistic, rebellious, unregenerate), Ariel the "good" one (assimilated to the condition and mentality of the colonizers). Both are slaves, but Ariel is rewarded for his docility. The postcolonial subject may wish to reappropriate the discredited persona of Caliban, and step forth as the legitimate and resistant native, uncompromised by European imperialism. And yet thusly to claim the status of authentic and proper subject is to mark some other as illegitimate, no less so after than during imperialism. For instance, the one who was educated in the English language and chooses to write literature in that language may be deemed a collaborator (Ariel) or a traitor. Nunberg writes in "The Persistence of English" that "it has been hard to slough off the sense of English as a colonial language" (2.1vi). Postcolonial Anglophone writers may themselves be haunted by a sense of dispossession when they use the "native tongue" that is not "native."

It may not be possible to locate and identify "Caliban" in any case. What is authentic indigenous culture in the Caribbean, settled by the Spanish, Dutch, French, and English, largely populated by the descendants of Africans imported as slaves, and often Indians imported as servants? The speaker of Walcott's *The Schooner* Flight (2.2583) has red hair, dark skin, and "sea-green eyes": "I have Dutch, nigger, and English in me, / and either I'm nobody, or I'm a nation" (lines 36, 42–43). In *Omeros*, wherein a Caribbean Achille dreams of Africa (2.2585), the classically trained Walcott deploys a hybrid (or one might say, postmodern) literary form, infusing the Homeric epic with the dialect and syntax of the islands.

Nor does Achebe claim to represent *the* authentic indigenous culture of Nigeria, a geographically diverse area whose nearly 250 different ethnic groups were yoked together arbitrarily through the accident of British rule. Achebe is himself a hybrid subject, a Western-educated Nigerian who has done much of his teaching in the United States, born into a family with roots in both traditional Igbo society and the new Christian elite that supplanted it. While *Things Fall Apart* describes precolonial Umuofia in careful and rich detail, and with a certain nostalgia for its lost culture, the novel does not romanticize or idealize it, presenting such traditional practices as the exposure of twins in the Evil Forest, or the ritual sacrifice of Ikemefuna, as ethically troubling. Okonkwo is in some ways a Caliban figure, an authentic "man of the people"—a physically powerful man who is a hard worker and prosperous farmer—but he is in other ways atypical within his community. "Among the Ibo the art of conversation is regarded very highly," but Okonkwo speaks with "a slight stammer and whenever he was angry and could not get his words out quickly enough, he would use his fists" (2.2619, 2618). While Okonkwo is "a man of action and a man of war," his strength results from "the fear of failure and weakness . . . the fear of himself, lest he should be found to resemble his father," Unoka, a "lazy and improvident" man who was only happy "when he was drinking or playing on his flute." Okonkwo has overinvested in physical strength and violence to avoid seeming "*agbala*" (womanish, unsuccessful) like Unoka (2.2621, 2622, 2618). A man of fiery temper and inflexible masculinity, Okonkwo bullies his wives and children, particularly his *agbala* son Nwoye, and makes trouble within the community with his imprudent and violent actions. He dies a victim of a new colonial order that has no room for the traditional warrior-hero, but it's important to note that he could not live comfortably in traditional society either—Okonkwo is sent into temporary exile by his own people at the conclusion of part 1.

Naipaul's *One Out of Many* is about exile and dispossession of a different sort. Its narrator, Santosh, is twice dislocated: first, he leaves his village and his wife and children to work in Bombay and grows into a new identity as a "city man." He cannot bear to return to rural poverty and be "barefoot in the hills" (2.2723), so he follows his employer to the United States, where he then loses himself utterly. He suffers radical culture shock and comes to feel shame in his own ethnic and class identity. Corrupted by television and American consumer culture, he becomes "obsessed" with his own looks and his clothes. "It was like an illness" (2.2731). He is swept up within the confusing race relations of the United States: in India he considered the "*hubshi*," or black Africans, to be degraded, but in the United States the African-Americans claim him as a "Soul Brother," and the *hubshi* women, "attracted by [his] smallness and strangeness," find him sexually exotic (2.2745, 2730). He learns about the interchangeability of people of color in the United States from the Mexicans who work in the Indian restaurant—"when we put turbans on them they could pass" (2.2738)—and learns firsthand about the exploitation of illegal immigrants as well. Finally he gains American citizenship and a measure of stability through marriage to the "*hubshi* woman," but feels himself a "stranger" in his own house, in his black neighborhood, in the American city (2.2744). Here hybrid identity brings only despair: Santosh has lost his old culture, but is ill at ease in his new one. There is no place where he might feel at home.

The hybrid or "transnational" subject shares allegiance to multiple geographical sites and multiple cultures. This quintessentially postcolonial and postmodern subject may experience transnationality as a state of dispossession, melancholy, and exile, like Santosh. But it is also possible deliberately to embrace the hybridized identity that is perhaps the inevitable product of postcolonialism. As Rushdie writes of the novel that made him, arguably, the most famous exile of postcolonial times:

> If *The Satanic Verses* is anything, it is a migrant's-eye view of the world. It is written from the very experience of uprooting, disjuncture and metamorphosis . . . that is the migrant condition, and from which, I believe, can be derived a metaphor for all humanity. . . . *The Satanic Verses* celebrates hybridity, impurity, intermingling, the transformation that comes of new and unexpected combinations of human beings, cultures, ideas, politics, movies, songs. It rejoices in mongrelization and fears the Pure. . . . It is a love-song to our mongrel selves. (2.2842)

Contents: Norton Topics Online, The Twentieth Century
www.wwnorton.com/nael

Keith Douglas, *from* Alamein to Zem Zem
Richard Hillary, *from* The Last Enemy
Adrian Weale, *from* Eye-Witness Hiroshima
Explorations
Web Resources

THE MEANING OF THE MILLENNIUM: APOCALYPTIC VISIONS AND REVISIONS
St. John of Patmos, *from* Revelation
The Reverend Alfred Jones, *from* Armageddon
William Butler Yeats
The Valley of the Black Pig
From A Vision
Hal Lindsey, *from* The Late Great Planet Earth
Explorations
Web Resources

Contents: NAEL Audio Companion, The Twentieth Century

W. B. Yeats
Down by the Salley Gardens
Benjamin Britten's arrangement of a traditional Irish tune
The Lake Isle of Innisfree
Read by W. B. Yeats
Edith Sitwell
Still Falls the Rain
Read by Edith Sitwell
Robert Graves
To Juan at the Winter Solstice
Read by Robert Graves
W. H. Auden
Musee des Beaux Arts
The Shield of Achilles
—both read by W. H. Auden
Dylan Thomas
Poem in October
Read by Dylan Thomas
Philip Larkin
MCMXIV
Aubade
—both read by Philip Larkin
Thom Gunn
Considering the Snail
My Sad Captains
—both read by Thom Gunn
Derek Walcott
The Glory Trumpeter

Read by Derek Walcott

Ted Hughes

Wind

Pike

Theology

—all read by Ted Hughes

Seamus Heaney

The Skunk

Read by Seamus Heaney

Eavan Boland

That the Science of Cartography Is Limited

Read by Eavan Boland

CHAPTER 9

Making Up Courses

Chapters 2–8 suggest ways of grouping texts within each period under several topics. This chapter takes the topical approach to the next step, that is, offering examples of how one might construct a syllabus around a broad unifying topic. The discussions of particular texts that follow are not intended to be comprehensive, but only to indicate how these selections relate to the broad topic in question; they are often cross-referenced to discussions in earlier chapters. Our hope is that these sample courses may give you ideas for writing your own syllabus. There is, of course, no limit to the number of ways in which general survey or individual period courses can be structured to reflect a teacher's historical, critical, and theoretical interests. The topics we present here can easily be revised, narrowed, or expanded. We intend only to indicate how the anthology and the materials on the Norton Web site can help you to devise many different kinds of courses to meet your needs and those of your students and the requirements of your department for its majors. (For sample syllabi developed to be used with *NAEL*, see www.wwnorton.com/college/english/nael7/historical_intro.htm and www.wwnorton.com/college/english/nael7/gender_list.htm.)

ENGLISH 1: English/England/Englishness

> For last year's words belong to last year's language
> And next year's words await another voice.
>
> (2.2392, lines 118–19)

"Who cares,"
he jeered, "any more? The English language
belongs to us. You are raking at dead fires."
(2.2827, lines 40–43)

Poets have always been concerned about language. The first of the two passages above, both of which are written in slant-rhymed terza rima, is spoken by the "compound ghost" Eliot encounters in the air-raid sequence of *Little Gidding*. The meeting is modeled on Dante's with his old master Brunetto Latini (*Inferno* 15). Eliot's ghost is compounded of many old masters; he chiefly echoes Yeats but also, in a line translated from the French symbolist poet Stéphane Mallarmé, declares that the poet's mission is "To purify the dialect of the tribe" (line 127). Perhaps it is ironic that an expatriate American poet should have an Irish poet remind him in the words of a French poet that the purpose of poetry is to purify the speech of the "tribe." One may ask, whose tribe? In the second passage, which surely recalls the first, Seamus Heaney encounters the ghost of James Joyce in *Station Island*. Heaney alludes to a passage in *Portrait of the Artist* that has been a "sort of password," sanctioning the use of the English language by an Irish poet. Joyce replies that this is a dead issue: "The English language / belongs to us." But to whom does the English language belong?

To begin answering that question, the new essay in *NAEL*, "The Persistence of English" (1 & 2.xlvii) is a good place to start. The basic plan here will be to trace the history of the English language, its diffusion through the British Isles and all over the world, and the historical development of a national English identity through literature. Finally, we want to ask to whom the language and literature belong at the beginning of the third millennium. This is not intended in any way to be a "language" course, but it does trace the interaction of the language and the culture in all periods and emphasizes attitudes toward language and literature on the part of English-speaking peoples, especially, of course, the authors who created that literature. The selections take into account "the detachment of English from Englishness," which begins in the late nineteenth century, in colonial and postcolonial literature in English. But they begin with the gradual "attachment" of English to Englishness from the time a few Germanic tribes began their conquest of the island, displacing its Celtic-speaking inhabitants.

The fact that the language and literature that today we call Old English were both until late in the nineteenth century usually referred to as Anglo-Saxon shows that the ancestor of Modern English could just as well be thought of as a branch of early Germanic literature. For his learned European audience, Bede translated Cædmon's *Hymn*, the earliest English poem to survive, into Latin. *Beowulf* contains only a short digression with even a remote connection to England (see 1.73–74, lines 1931–61 and n. 7). In the *Battle of Maldon* the poet refers to Birhtnoth's men as East-Saxons; one identifies himself as coming from Mercia, another is a Northumbrian (1.106, 108); but there is no reference to them as English.

The section entitled "Anglo-Norman England" contains selections translated from Latin, Old French, Early Middle English, Old Irish, and Middle Welsh, all of them preserved in manuscripts written in the British Isles in the twelfth century or a little later, although the Old Irish work dates from around the eighth century. Several deal with King Arthur, the legendary king of the Britons, who became a European culture hero. How Arthur became a national hero for English writers is a story you can explore when teaching *Sir Gawain and the Green Knight*, Malory, Spenser, and Tennyson, and by asking students to view "King Arthur," a Norton Topic Online for the Middle Ages.

Students can sample two specimens of Old English (Caedmon's *Hymn* and a famous passage from *Maldon* [1.24–25, 104]) and the opening stanza of *Sir Gawain and the Green Knight* (1.157–58) in the original with interlinear translation. You can perform these for your class or play the recording on the Audio Companion. When you come to Chaucer, the students can see for themselves how relatively "modern" his language is compared to Anglo-Saxon. The introduction to the Middle Ages contains a section on "Medieval English" and "Old and Middle English Prosody." For a few practical suggestions on teaching Chaucer's language, see pp. 31–33 of this Guide. Obviously there won't be time to teach all the Chaucer selections. If you assign *The Nun's Priest's Tale*, you will probably also want to assign Henryson's retelling of it, *The Cock and the Fox*, where your students will learn something about English dialects.

Chaucer's decision to write in English rather than in French or Latin marks a new stage in what we can now properly speak of as *English* literature. There is a deliberate attempt here not just to translate works from Latin or French for English readers not familiar with those languages but to create poems of high culture, comparable to those Chaucer read in Latin, French, and Italian. You might want to tell your students about the awareness Chaucer expresses in *Troilus and Criseyde* of the change in speech (Book 2, lines 22–25) and of the "diversitee / in English, and in writing of oure tonge" (Book 5, lines 1795–96). Chaucer also has a sense of the Englishness of the company of "sondry folk" traveling to Canterbury "from every shires ende / of Engelond" (1.216, line 25; 215, lines 15–16).

You will want to focus mainly on content in other texts in Middle English—the drama, the lyrics, Julian of Norwich's *Showings*, the *Book of Margery Kempe*, and Malory's *Morte Darthur*—but these texts also present an opportunity to talk about different levels of style in Middle English poetry and prose. For example, you could contrast the formal and often poetic analytic style of Julian with Kempe's colloquial narrative style.

On the Norton Topics Online "King Arthur," you can see how, as William Caxton says in his *Preface* to *Morte Darthur*, Malory "reduced [his French Book] into English." More than any other author, it was Malory who bestowed Englishness upon Arthur and his knights. In his final book, which Caxton entitled "The Dolorous Death and Departing out of this World of Sir Launcelot and Queen Guinevere," Malory seems to be holding up the destruction of the Round Table as a tragic example to the English knights who were destroying one another in the Wars of the Roses. Five hundred years later, Tennyson's King Arthur in the *Idylls* tells Sir Bedivere, "The old order changeth, yielding place to new, / And God fulfills himself in many ways" (2.1302, lines 408–9). Tennyson is thinking of his friend Arthur Hallam and of the changing Victorian order.

In English literature, the old feudal Plantagenet order changed to the new Tudor order, and Middle English slowly turned into Early Modern English. You can trace these developments through many texts in *NAEL*. Sir Thomas More wrote his *Utopia* in Latin for "an international audience of humanist intellectuals" (1.505), but *Utopia* is obviously meant to suggest by way of contrast that Europe, England in particular, stood in need of reform (discussed on pp. 43–44). More could not have foreseen the English Reformation, which would cost him his life and which gave England a new identity as the leading Protestant power in Europe. The Reformation initiated internal struggles between Catholic and Protestant and, then, among Protestants over which church best represented Englishness.

The cluster "Literature of the Sacred" (1.538) deals with several aspects of the Reformation. Among the most important was the translation of the Bible into English. Humanism stressed the revival of classical (as opposed to medieval) Latin and the study of Greek, but the new technology of printing also led to a widespread increase in literacy, which in turn created a demand for classical literature as well as modern French and Italian texts in translation. Wyatt introduced the Petrarchan or Italian sonnet to England, which Surrey adapted to the "English" or "Shakespearean" sonnet form. This would be a good occasion to discuss why the English language, in which stress normally falls on the initial syllable, is rich in alliteration but poor in rhyme compared to the Romance languages, thereby making the "English" sonnet easier to write. Wyatt and Surrey provided models for an explosion of aristocratic English lyric poetry, influenced by classical and Continental lyric genres.

All of these developments contributed to a consciousness of Englishness and pride in an English literary tradition of which Chaucer was seen as the fountainhead. Sidney's *The Defense of Poesy* is both a theoretical treatise, which displays a great deal of humanist learning, and a survey of "Poetry in England," which bestows somewhat patronizing praise on Chaucer and some of Sidney's contemporaries, notably Spenser's *Shepheardes Calender*, represented in *NAEL* by the tenth eclogue. The latter is a dialogue in praise of poetry and a complaint about the way it has been neglected in England. By making his poetic debut with a pastoral, Spenser was declaring, as would Milton in *Lycidas*, that he was working his way up to the epic, which classical genre criticism held to be the supreme in the hierarchy of literary forms. In the *Calender*, Spenser was already cultivating an archaic diction, drawn from Chaucer, which was supposed to highlight its native Englishness. The first book of *The Faerie Queene* is a key text because it is meant to be a national English epic (see pp. 51–53).

In the following century, the Church of England and the house of Stuart came into conflict with the English Puritans. Much of the literature that follows has to do directly or indirectly with which church most truly represents England and the English people. That conflict, of course, led to the establishment of a new England in the New World. The diffusion of English was also brought about by the voyages of exploration and the establishment of colonies, which were undertaken for economic reasons and for adventure. See Ralegh's *Discovery of . . . Guiana* (1.885), the texts included in the cluster "The Wider World" (1.889), and Bacon's *Of Plantations.* (On the topic of European versus Native American identity through contact between these cultures, see pp. 44–45.)

The nationalism of Milton's *Areopagitica* is especially pertinent in its invocation of England as a new Israel, the spearhead and bastion of the Reformation (1.1807; see also Milton's political sonnets, 1.1812–14). Dryden brilliantly satirizes that Puritan trope in *Absalom and Achitophel* (see p. 99).

The exile of Charles II and other royalists, under the protection of the French monarchy, would make English Protestants of all denominations suspicious of French and Catholic connections. Ascham's diatribe against "The Italianate Englishman" (1.567) is an early example of English prejudice at continental costume, manners, and morals. The vicious characters in *Volpone* and *The Duchess of Malfi*, as in many other Elizabethan and Jacobean plays, play upon the idea of Italy as a sink of vice and corruption that was infecting England. Jonson amusingly introduces Sir Politic and Lady Would-Be as a pair of English tourists in search of culture in Italy. In *Twelfth Night*, Shakespeare plays with nationality as well as with gender and class. The upstairs characters of the main plot have Italian names and converse with one another in courtly verse whereas the downstairs characters of the subplot (Sir Toby Belch, Sir Andrew Aguecheek, Maria, and—in spite of his Italian name—Malvolio) speak, for the most part, in racy English prose.

In the eighteenth century, the conception of a national character becomes explicit. In 1712 Pope's friend Dr. Arbuthnot invented the figure of John Bull, who was to become a satiric personification, in the language and in political cartoons, of England. Indeed one thinks about and responds to eighteenth-century characters, both men and women, with regard to their "Englishness," often in their reactions to characters, customs, and ideas that are not "English." The Spectator's Club is an assortment of different types of Englishmen exhibiting traits that have come to be identified in fiction and film as stereotypically "English." In many respects, the Dr. Johnson of Boswell's biography became to nineteenth-century readers a stereotype of outspoken, empirical, witty, judgmental, and conservative Englishness. To some extent Johnson promoted that persona in his conversation and writing (getting beyond the persona can be the subject of class discussion). In Boswell's *Life*, Johnson's prejudice against the Scots becomes a standing joke between him and Boswell (see 1.2763, 2776–77). Johnson's *Dictionary* was, of course, an important text in the development of the language (see "Dictionaries and Rules" [1 & 2.1i]; and Johnson's definition of OATS [1.2724]). His *Lives of the* [English] *Poets* was a milestone in the establishment of the English literary canon, as was his *Preface to Shakespeare* in the establishment of Shakespeare as the unofficial national poet.

Lemuel Gulliver, in his responses to Lilliput, which is of course a Tory version of England in miniature, Brobdingnag, and Houyhnhnmland, exhibits qualities that the Irish author regarded as quintessentially English. Swift's *A Modest Proposal* is a scathing satire of English treatment of what Bernard Shaw, like Swift an Irishman, would in the title of one of his plays call *John Bull's Other Island.*

If you can make time for it, an excellent addition to this course plan would be the inclusion of *Robinson Crusoe* (available in a Norton Critical Edition). Crusoe's "colonization" of his island and his relationship with Friday in many ways epitomize the inventiveness, self-reliance, practicality, evangelical piety, and racist assumptions with which the English would go about building their empire.

Historical events—the American and French revolutions, the rise and breakup of the British Empire, the Napoleonic wars, the industrial revolution, the two world wars, and the Easter Rebellion and the Irish "troubles"—have had a formative influence on questions of English, England, and Englishness in nineteenth- and twentieth-century literature(s). Much of that literature has been devoted to examining and redefining what England and Englishness stands for or ought to stand for. These are among the great social and moral questions addressed by Blake in the *Songs of Innocence, Songs of Experience*, and prophetic books like *Visions of the Daughters of Albion*. They dominate many of the *Lyrical Ballads* and Books 9–11 of Wordsworth's *The Prelude*. They are at the heart of Shelley's *Prometheus Unbound* and the choruses from *Hellas*. In the Victorian Age, they underlie Carlyle's *Past and Present*, Arnold's *Culture and Anarchy*, and the cluster of texts in "Industrialism: Progress or Decline?" The selections from Kipling (2.1865, 1892), Forster (2.2133), and Orwell (2.2457) deal with the British colonial experience, and the Forster, a newly added chapter from *A Passage to India*, deals also with the Indian experience of the British. Conrad's *Heart of Darkness* and Achebe's *Things Fall Apart* are classic novels about European colonialism in Africa, written from different points of view and spanning an era. The excerpt from Achebe's essay *Racism in Conrad's "Heart of Darkness"* provides perspective on both novels. For views of British imperialism, particularly for background on the struggle to establish the Irish Republic and the independence and partition of India, see selections under the "Rise and Fall of Empire" (2.2017), and on Norton Topics Online, see "Imperialism to Colonialism: Perspectives on the British Empire."

A basic question for non-English authors in volume 2 of *NAEL* is whether all literature in English should be designated as English literature. In Joyce's *The Dead*, Miss Ivors, an Irish nationalist, teases Gabriel Conroy as a "West Briton" because he writes literary criticism for *The Daily Express*, a politically pro-English journal (2.2247). The question of Irish identity is crucial for Joyce, writing in self-imposed exile about his native land, and for his alter-ego Stephen Dedalus. Leopold Bloom, an Irish Jew, is a wanderer and outsider in Dublin. Irish identity both directly and indirectly influences the writings of Swift, Goldsmith, Moore, Wilde, Shaw, Yeats, Beckett, O'Brien, Heaney, Boland, and Muldoon. Similar questions of nationality and identity arise for the Scottish writers Boswell, Burns, Scott, Carlyle, and MacDiarmid. Many native English authors in volume 2 have written about their experience as expatriates and about the political and artistic life of their host countries, among them Byron, Percy and Mary Shelley, Robert and Elizabeth Barrett Browning, Lawrence, and Auden (after World War II). Conrad and Eliot are expatriates from Poland and the United States, respectively.

The importance of commonwealth and postcolonial literature in English is evident from the fact that less than 20 percent of the pages in *NAEL* allotted to works published after 1950 are actually by writers born in England. The rest are by writers from the Irish Republic and Northern Ireland, South Africa, Australia, New Zealand, Canada, the West Indies, India, and Nigeria. Four of those writers (Beckett, Gordimer, Walcott, and Heaney) have received the Nobel Prize. The selections have both English and non-English settings; several deal with the clash between English and African, West Indian, and Asian cultures. Your course may well raise the question of nationalism in the making of languages, literature, literary histories, and literary anthologies as well as the creation of departments and curricula of language and literature.

Both volumes of *NAEL* contain essays and poems directly concerned with language, especially the language of poetry and prose, some of which you probably want to include in your syllabus. These include Donne, *Expostulation 19* ("The Language of God" [1.1278]); Jonson, *Timber* (1.1418); Bacon, *The Advancement of Learning* ("The Abuses of Language" [1.1542]); Herbert, *Jordan (1)* and *(2)* (1.1601, 1605); Carew, *An Elegy upon . . . Donne* (1.1656); Dryden (Criticism, 1.2114); Pope, *An Essay on Criticism* (1.2509); Johnson, *Rasselas* (Chapter 10), *Preface* to *A Dictionary of the English Language, The Preface to Shakespeare, Lives of the Poets* (1.2685, 2719, 2725, 2736); Wordsworth, Preface to *Lyrical Ballads* (2.238); Coleridge, *On Donne's Poetry* (2.466), *Biographia Literaria* (2.467); Byron, Letters (2.689, 693, 695, 697); Shelley, *A Defence of Poetry* (2.789); Keats, Letters (2.886–900); Arnold, *The Study of Poetry* (2.1534); Carroll, *Jabberwocky* and *"Humpty Dumpty's Explanation"* (2.1666–67); Eliot, *The Metaphysical Poets* (2.2401); and Orwell, *Politics and the English Language* (2.2462). You may also wish to include exercises or essay assignments using one or more of the "Poems in Process" (1.2889 and 2.2859). What considerations of language and style account for the revisions made to earlier drafts of these poems?

ENGLISH 2: Crossing Genres

Any historical approach to literature must at some time confront formal and generic questions. These can be dealt with for individual works as they come up in chronological order. But an instructor may choose to teach one or more genres as units, crossing period boundaries along the way to teach examples of epic, romance, pastoral, drama, and so on as separate groups and thereby trace the evolution of a genre in response to history, critical theory, and cultural background. Treatment of genre often brings into focus characteristics that define a period. At the same time, one comes to see the blurring of borderlines between genres and the authors' bending and breaking of the rules of genre to make something new. The extended example given below covers the epic, romance, and novel, three genres that participate and influence one another in the evolution of narrative poetry and prose.

Similarly, it is possible to devote a unit in either volume 1 or 2 of *NAEL* to the development of English drama. There are advantages to assigning *Everyman* and *Doctor Faustus* in tandem (see pp. 38–39). *King Lear*, although printed with the sixteenth-century selections, has more in common with the three other Jacobean plays in *NAEL* (see pp. 68–69). *The Way of the World* depicts a very different layer of society from that of *The Beggar's Opera*, but the wit of the dialogue in the latter depends greatly on the way characters of the criminal class think and talk like their superiors in Restoration comedy. Hogarth's *Marriage A-la-Mode* (1.2654), though not a play, looks like a series of scenes from a play staged by a master designer with an unlimited budget. One might study Byron's *Manfred* and Shelley's *Prometheus Unbound* as revolutionary "lyrical drama" (Shelley's term for the latter). The well-made plays of Wilde or Shaw make an excellent foil for the de-emphasizing of plot and breaking of dramatic illusion in the modernist plays of Beckett, Pinter, and Stoppard.

Poetry, too, can be assigned out of chronological order to compare and contrast the individual styles of poets yet, at the same time, to override categories such as "Metaphysical" and "Cavalier," which can be more misleading than helpful. By tracing a subgenre of poetry—ballad, sonnet, ode, pastoral, elegy—you can show your students that metrical and generic form are themselves a kind of language poets use to evoke a tradition. For example, the first two lines of Auden's *In Memory of W. B. Yeats*—"He disappeared in the dead of winter: / The brooks were frozen, the airports almost deserted" (2.2506)—both recall and break with conventional evocations of nature in pastoral elegy. Traditional examples would be the address to water nymphs and river gods in *Lycidas*, "O fountain Arethuse and thou honored flood, / Smooth-sliding Mincius" (1.1793, lines 85–86 and n. 6), or the return of spring in *Adonais*: "Through wood and stream and field and hill and Ocean / A quickening life from the Earth's heart has burst" (2.777, lines 163–64). That is not to say that Auden is condemning the form of pastoral elegy as Dr. Johnson did in a notorious attack on the genre (1.2738). On the contrary, the frozen brooks and the deserted airports evoke both the presence of an ancient literary tradition to which Auden's modern elegy attaches itself as well as the distance that separates this elegy from its predecessors.

Epic, Romance, Novel

> My poem's epic, and is meant to be
> Divided in twelve books; each book containing,
> With love, and war, a heavy gale at sea,
> A list of ships, and captains, and kings reigning,
> New characters; the episodes are three:
> A panoramic view of hell's in training,
> After the style of Virgil and of Homer,
> So that my name of Epic's no misnomer.
> (2.647, lines 1593–1600)

Byron is making fun of genre criticism but also quite seriously linking his work to literary tradition and telling us in what respect his poem is new and different. The *Odyssey*, the *Aeneid*, the *Divine Comedy*, and *Paradise Lost* treat readers to a "panoramic view of hell," which was to have been Juan's final destination in "canto twelfth" (2.648, lines 1655–56). At the same time, Byron is dissociating his poem from the heroic, the mythical, and the religious elements of both pagan and Christian epic. The hero of *Don Juan* is famous for his sexual, not his military, exploits. In Byron's poem there are no gods, no supernatural happenings, no attempts to justify the ways of god(s) to man. The difference between him and his "epic brethren," Byron declares, is that their poems are a "labyrinth of fables . . . / Whereas this story's actually true" (lines 1610–16). And so, in a sense it is. *Don Juan* is a story about modern life; in some respects, about Byron's own life.

Such statements assume an understanding, between the writer and the audience, of generic codes that set up certain expectations. What is interesting about the genre, however, is not that writers adhere to the code but that they use the code innovatively to surprise and, in this case, to amuse readers and to make them think. Thus Milton observes the classical rule of beginning with the invocation of a goddess or muse by addressing Urania, the muse of astronomy, but goes on to identify her with the Holy Spirit, through which God created the world and inspired Moses to write of the Creation and Fall in Genesis (1.1818). For pre-Miltonic examples from Homer, Virgil, and Tasso, go to "Epic Themes and Invocations," on the Web site under "*Paradise Lost* in Context." Wordsworth does not write a formal invocation, but he marks *The Prelude* as an epic poem and links it with Milton's Holy Spirit by beginning with a "gentle breeze," thus identifying his "muse" with nature—the divine energy that inspires him to begin his epic work (2.305, lines 1–45). Byron aggressively brushes aside epic formalities. "I want a hero," he begins abruptly and also rejects the "usual method" of beginning *in medias res*. Instead he adopts the biographer and novelist's practice of starting with the hero's family.

The classical epic conventions are already in place with Homer, were imitated by Virgil, and so were transmitted directly to Renaissance poets. We should not think of Germanic epic in terms of classical conventions. Little enough of the poetry survives, in any case, for us to deduce generic conventions with any assurance. The alliterative verse form and recurrent formulas indicate that there was a large body of heroic legends, which were performed by oral poets like the *scop* in *Beowulf* who performs the creation hymn, the Sigemund panegyric complimenting Beowulf, and the Finnsburg episode. The genealogy of the Danish kings, the ship burial, the attack on the hall, the sea crossings, the feasts, the dragon fight, the beasts of battle are probably all versions of set pieces common to Germanic epic. We modern readers have to piece together the tradition from a few fragments that have survived and from *Beowulf* itself, which is the most complete witness we have of early Germanic heroic poetry. Nor can we take for granted that this poet has passed on the stories in the form that they came down to him. The *Beowulf* poet has shaped his materials to show the world of pagan antiquity from the point of view of his own Christian culture.

The Battle of Maldon, though very late in the period, probably comes as close as any surviving heroic poem to the form of a short heroic lay. The contrast between the cowards who flee when their leader is slain and the brave men who fight to the death to avenge their lord is the heart of the tradition. Almost a third of the poem is given over to the loyal retainers who utter variations of the same speech, culminating in the eloquent lines of Birhtwold. Wiglaf makes the same kind of speech after Beowulf's other retainers have fled from the dragon fight. There is a strong ethical and hortatory imperative in these Old English epics, expressed in the formula "Swa sceal man don" (So must one do).

Epic always claims to be based on history—that is the point of the "We have heard" formula and the genealogy of the Danish kings with which *Beowulf* begins. The hero's fights with a man-eating monster, a troll-hag at the bottom of a tarn, and a flame-breathing dragon introduce epic motifs that *Beowulf* and the *Odyssey* share with later romance. The selections grouped together as "Legendary Histories of Britain" contain (1) a foundation myth told as a sequel to Virgil's *Aeneid*; (2) a court scene with an insulting challenge and heroic response followed by a counsel of war; and (3) a prophetic dream of disaster. All these are conventional epic motifs.

Romance heroes still occasionally fight in their kings' wars, but most of the fighting is done in the course of some rescue mission, often on behalf of a lady beset by a giant, a dragon, or some wicked knight. Popular romances are full of action, but in chivalric romances whatever action there may be is secondary to behavioral and psychological interests. How will the knight obtain the lady's love or regain it after offending her? Has he compromised his honor? A pattern in *Lanval* and *Sir Gawain and the*

Green Knight is temptation, fall, and redemption. Sir Lanval breaks his vow of silence to his fairy mistress. Sir Gawain unwittingly falls short of his own high standard of truth. It should be pointed out that neither of these romances is entirely typical because Marie de France and the English *Gawain* poet both treat romance conventions and pretensions with humor. In both these romances, as well as in *The Wife of Bath's Tale,* it is the knight who, in the end, has to be saved or spared and forgiven for his trespass.

Malory, on the other hand, treats his romance material with great seriousness. He believes strongly in the genuine historicity of the Arthurian legend, and his telling of the destruction of Arthur's kingdom recaptures the tragic and elegiac mood one feels at the death of *Beowulf* and in the lament of *The Wanderer*. In the civil war between Mordred and Arthur, Malory sees a prototype of the Wars of the Roses.

Spenser's *The Faerie Queene* is a hybrid of epic, romance, and personification allegory, the didactic purpose of which, he tells us in the prefatory "Letter of the Authors," "is to fashion a gentleman or noble person in vertuous and gentle discipline" (1.624–25). Like many medieval poems, however, the story is "a continued Allegory, or darke conceit"; but it follows "the antique Poets historicall," Homer and Virgil. The headings to each book, which begin with the formula "*Contayning / The Legende of* . . ." (1.628, 783), further identify the work as a series of saints' lives. You will probably want to focus on the historical and nationalistic aspects of Book One as an allegory of the English Reformation (see pp. 51–53), which is the chief thing that makes Book 1 a new departure for epic and romance. At the same time, Spenser, like Byron or the *Gawain* poet, enjoys playing with the conventions of his genre(s). A dragonlike serpent that vomits books and papers (1.633), Archimago's fake holiness and horrific spells (1.637, lines 307–15; 637, lines 316–42), the three Saracen brothers—these are caricatures of the monsters, enchanters, and "paynims" who are stock antagonists in medieval romance. We can take seriously the things they stand for (Error, False Holiness, Rival Religion) but at the same time enjoy them as comic variations of romance stereotypes. Book 3, canto 1, in which Malecasta (Unchastity), having mistaken Britomart for a man, creeps into bed with her, is almost pure farce. On the other hand, there is nothing comic about Spenser's powerful personifications of dangerous psychological states like Despaire. The "maske of Cupid" in the final canto of Book 3 brings out elements of cruelty (we could say sadomasochism) in courtly romance, the spell of which Spenser means to break. In these the allegorical component of the poem dominates.

Sidney's *Arcadia* is an example of a curious Renaissance crossing of pastoral and romance and also serves him as a frame for many of his lyrics. It is the source of the Gloucester-Edmund-Edgar plot of *Lear*. Sidney keeps up an elevated tone in the narrative and the rhetorical speeches and soliloquies of his characters. However, the plot of the *NAEL* selection (1.911) reads more like one of Shakespeare's romantic comedies. The king and queen both fall in love with the young man, who has disguised himself as an Amazon in order to woo their daughter.

In *The Reason of Church Government*, Milton speculates about the epic poem he has had to defer because "Time serves not now"; King Arthur had occurred to him as someone "in whom to lay the pattern of a Christian hero" (1.1798 and note 2). When after the Restoration he wrote *Paradise Lost*, however, he pointedly dismissed the traditional heroic subject matter of epic and romance, "fabled knights / In battles feigned," in favor of Christian virtues: "the better fortitude / Of patience and heroic martyrdom / Unsung" (1.1962, lines 30–33). The poem abounds in allusions to the epic poems of Homer and Virgil, but the epic posturing and speeches, the defiance of fate and refusal to admit defeat, are ironically reserved for Satan. Milton's models of true heroism instead are the first man and woman overcoming shame, guilt, and the certainty of death to accept the human condition they have brought into being.

Perhaps the aftermath of the Civil War and the towering achievement of Milton made it difficult for any major poet to attempt a serious heroic poem. Restoration playwrights, Dryden among them, cultivated a genre of heroic drama (the "heroic couplet" gets its name from the fact that these plays were written in pentameter couplets). Heroic drama featured exotic superheroes, lavish pageantry, and bombastic speeches. Dryden and Pope, eschewing Shakespearean or Miltonic blank verse, brilliantly translated Virgil and Homer into heroic couplets.

The one genuinely heroic work from the period is Aphra Behn's *Oroonoko, or the Royal Slave*. The story, as the headnote points out, belongs "in the still unshaped field of prose narrative," which prefigures the novel. It is a hybrid of a personal memoir of the author's, who presents herself as an "eyewitness"; a travel narrative; and a biography (1.2166). It is also a love story, a tragedy, and a powerful indictment of the slave trade.

The heroic couplet turned out to be an ideal verse form for satire and mock-epic, which in the Restoration and the eighteenth century served as a vehicle for political, social, and literary satire. When eighteenth-century satire takes the form of narrative, however, in poetry or prose, it begins to overlap with the novel, the new form that comes to replace epic and romance. In *The Rape of the Lock*, the satire does not degrade the characters or make them ridiculous as they are in burlesques like Butler's *Hudibras*. If one were to eliminate the epic machinery of the sylphs and gnomes, if the rape involved the sexual violence that Pope's imagery hints at instead of a lock, and if the couplets were turned into prose, then Belinda and the baron could easily turn into characters in an eighteenth-century novel of manners.

You may, therefore, wish to supplement *NAEL* with an eighteenth-century novel. (On the rise of the novel, see 1.2065.) If you want to make a point of connections between the epic and the novel, a logical choice would be Henry Fielding's *Joseph Andrews*. In a preface, Fielding presents his work—perhaps not altogether seriously—in terms of Aristotelian genre theory, as a "comic epic-poem in prose." *Joseph Andrews* starts out as a satire of Samuel Richardson's path-breaking novel *Pamela* (1.2066). Fielding had already written *Shamela*, a straight parody of *Pamela*. (*Joseph Andrews* with *Shamela* is available in a Norton Critical Edition.) *Joseph Andrews* is a more ambitious work; its hero is the benevolent, absent-minded, and innocent Parson Adams, a character influenced by *Don Quixote*. Romance continued to flourish in novels with titles like *The Reward of Constancy* and *The Tears of Sensibility*, novels that Lydia Languish, the heroine of Sheridan's play *The Rivals*, obtains from a circulating library, a newly established institution that played a part in making the novel the dominant literary form. Women not only provided the greater part of the readership for the new form but were also among its most prolific authors. Another good choice of a novel would be Frances Burney's *Evelina* (also available in a Norton Critical Edition). But you can at least give your students a taste of Burney's narrative style by assigning the selections from her *Journal and Letters*, which often read like a novel.

The Web site topic "Literary Gothicism" in the Romantic Period lets your students explore the Gothic novel and Romantic responses to Milton's Satan. That topic provides background for Charlotte Brontë's *Jane Eyre*, a novel that works equally well as a supplement to *NAEL* with questions of genre and gender. An excerpt is on the Web site. *Jane Eyre* is among the Norton Anthology Editions, which may be ordered packaged with *NAEL*.

Milton's invocations and comments at the beginnings of several books of *Paradise Lost* identify the narrator's personal experience with major events of his narrative. For example, the ascent out of Hell and the invocation to light at the beginning of Book 3 (1.1858) movingly remind us of the poet's blindness: "So much the rather thou celestial light, / Shine inward, and the mind through all her powers / Irradiate" (lines 50–52). There was precedent, therefore, for Wordsworth to write an epic in Miltonic blank verse about his own experience of loss and recovery. Wordsworth was, in fact, writing a poem that corresponds to one of the main types of the nineteenth-century novel, the so-called *Bildungsroman* or novel of education. Elizabeth Barrett Browning's *Aurora Leigh* is about the growth of the mind of a woman poet like herself, written like *The Prelude* in blank verse. It contains a sardonic description of the trivial and nonsensical contents of what passed for a fashionable education for Victorian young ladies (2.1180).

The title of Byron's *Childe Harold's Pilgrimage* associates its hero with the quests of a knight-errant in medieval romance for which the Spenserian stanza is an appropriate vehicle. In the persona of Harold, the disillusioned exile from England, Byron gloomily meditates on scenes of dead or "dying glory" (2.582, line 6)—the battlefield of Waterloo, the Bridge of Sighs, the ruins of the Coliseum. For *Don Juan*, Byron adopted the ottava rima of Ariosto's comic epic *Orlando Furioso*, which perfectly fits the free-wheeling discursive movement of his satire. Pronouncing his poetic credo, Byron dissociates himself from his fellow Romantic poets and attaches his new work to the poets he regards as his epic predecessors: "Thou shalt believe in Milton, Dryden, Pope; / Thou shalt not set up Wordsworth, Coleridge, Southey" (2.648, lines 1633–34).

Romance as a genre is a subject in Romantic poetry. For Keats romance was a kind of fairy mistress from whom he was often trying to break away to undertake an epic or tragic theme. In the sonnet *On Sitting Down to Read King Lear Once Again*, Romance is the "golden-tongued," the "Fair plumed syren, queen of far away" (2.833). In *The Eve of St. Agnes* and in *Ode to a Nightingale*, he associates romance with a dream-fantasy of the Middle Ages and with the view from the "magic casements," beautiful distractions from which he wakes "to my sole self" (2.851, line 72). The couplets and the satiric tone of *Lamia*, which was influenced by Dryden (2.857), are in stark contrast with the rich texture of the odes and *The Eve of St. Agnes*. The meaning of the poem is not altogether clear, but the choice between the beautiful mistress, who is really a serpent, and the "cold philosophy" from which "all charms fly" (2.870–71) could, among other things, hint at a generic choice between two forms, either of which proves fatal to the lover/poet. The two *Hyperion* fragments, of which *NAEL* prints the second, are attempts to write a Miltonic epic, which Keats abandoned. "Miltonic verse cannot be written," he wrote to his friend, "but in an artful or rather artist's humor" (2.874).

The plots of popular ballads—so called because ballads were thought to be poetry of the folk—are often like shortened versions of epic and romance. The Romantic poets saw in them a native idiom, purer and more natural than the poetic diction of the preceding century (See, for example, the Preface to *Lyrical Ballads*, 2.245). The ballads have been shifted in *NAEL7* from the end of the Middle Ages to the end of the eighteenth century because the great majority come from collections made in the eighteenth and nineteenth centuries, and ballads directly influenced the Romantic poets. Wordsworth's *Lucy Gray*, Scott's *Lochinvar*, Coleridge's *Ancient Mariner* and *Christabel*, Hemans's *Casabianca*, and Keats's *La Belle Dame sans Merci* are all products of the ballad revival.

Medieval romance, especially Malory's *Morte Darthur*, projected against a background of a social disorder and decay, captured the imagination of some Victorian writers and artists. They felt their time was out of joint and turned to Arthurian subjects as an escape from the tawdry England of the industrial revolution. Their Arthurian characters, however, especially the women, are pictured rebelling against the social and moral restrictions of *their* world. Tennyson's Lady of Shalott (2.1204), trying to escape her web and the shadows in her mirror, dies floating down the river. William Holman Hunt's engraving of the Lady, which represents her entangled in her own web, can be seen on the Web site ("Moxson's Illustrated Tennyson"); the oil painting made from the engraving is also on the Web and is used as the cover illustration for the *NAEL* volume of *The Victorian Age*. Rossetti's engraving of Lancelot bending over the body of the Lady is reproduced on 2.1208. In Morris's *Defense of*

Guenevere (2.1606), the queen, on trial for adultery, passionately denies the evidence against her, yet at the same time justifies her love as natural and good, something higher than her wedding vow to the cold king. The Web site shows Morris's painting of his wife Jane Morris, costumed as Guinevere, between a photograph of her and Rossetti's painting *Astarte Syriaca* (a Phoenician fertility goddess), for which Jane Morris was his model. The sensuality of this and other paintings of women by the Pre-Raphaelites (Rossetti's painting of the *The Blessed Damozel* is reproduced on 2.1575) reveals a freedom from restraint in Pre-Raphaelite poetry and art that shocked some of the Pre-Raphaelites' contemporaries.

Tennyson's *Idylls of the King* has a moralizing strain more commonly associated with Victorian literature. *The Coming of Arthur* has been added to the new edition to complement *The Passing of Arthur*. Tennyson's *Coming* completely revises Malory. It is centered on Arthur's marriage to Guinevere and the efforts of King Leodogran her father to make sure that Arthur really is King Uther's legitimate son. Merlin's magic is omitted; instead of coming to Ygerne in the shape of her husband, Uther forces her to marry him after her husband is already dead. Arthur and Guinevere swear a mutual vow of "deathless love." She is given only one line in this idyll, "King and my lord, I love thee to the death" (2.1292, line 469). In the *Passing*, before the final battle Sir Bedivere overhears Arthur lamenting in his tent, "all whereon I leaned in wife and friend / Is traitor to my peace, and all my realm / Reels back into the beast, and is no more" (2.1294, lines 24–26). Tennyson's conclusion of the *Idylls* implies a cyclical view of history, but not the apocalyptic one of Yeats's *The Second Coming*. "Things fall apart," but here the center still holds. In the passing of this Arthur, Tennyson continues to cling to the Christian faith he struggled to retain in *In Memoriam*. King Arthur doubts but does not despair. At the end, Bedivere watches Arthur's barge "vanish into light / And the sun rose bringing the new year" (2.1303).

For several important twentieth-century novels and narrative poems, ancient epic and romance provide an allusive framework upon which to structure plot and meaning. If you decide to teach any of these, questions arise about the purpose and function served by the frame. The most famous instance is James Joyce's *Ulysses*. Why should Joyce not just have called his novel *A Day in the Life of Leopold Bloom* and spared himself, and his readers, the trouble of working out the parallels with the *Odyssey*? Clearly these parallels are meant, in one sense, to be ironic, but Bloom cannot simply be described as a modern antihero. According to Aristotle, epic demands an elevated style. What seems to be happening in *Ulysses* is that the conception of what constitutes an epic subject matter and style has changed radically. The moment-by-moment sensations of sight, sound, smell, taste, and touch that Bloom and Stephen Dedalus experience as they wander through Dublin often seem trivial in themselves. But as they register in the character's consciousness, they undergo a momentous expansion in time and space through multiple allusions to literature, art, music, and history. To raise these large questions in a short time, even a small sampling of the text should suffice to demonstrate the complexities of modernist fiction.

Another long narrative poem with modern characters and themes drawn after Homer is Derek Walcott's *Omeros* (Homer's name in Greek), written in loosely rhymed terza rima, from which an excerpt is newly included in *NAEL* (2.2585). Walcott weaves together several plots based on events widely separated in time and place. The central character Achille, who is waking up from a dream about Africa on board a Caribbean fishing boat, is named for Achilles. He is one of several black characters who speak in Creole dialect. This excerpt focuses on a symbolic moment that lifts Achille's spirit: he watches a black frigate bird (also called man-o'-war) snatch a mackerel from a white seagull and soar away magnificently into the clouds. Achille identifies the bird with the chief of his ancestral tribe: "Afolabe . . . / The king going home."

Most of the poems and prose selections gathered under "Voices from World War I" and "Voices from World War II" (2.2048, 2525) deal with the traditional subject matter of epic. In their own way, these poems can be read as heroic statements about the horror, waste, and futility of war. What has become of Horace's *Dulce et Decorum Est pro Patria Mori* in Wilfrid Owen's poem, written shortly before he was killed in action (2.2069 and n. 1)? Compare this and other poems by Owen, Thomas, Sassoon, Gurney, and Rosenberg with Rupert Brooke's *The Soldier* (2.2050) or Tennyson's *The Charge of the Light Brigade* (2.1280) where Horace's "old lie" still seems to hold good. David Jones's *In Parenthesis* is about the annihilation of all but one of the members of an English platoon during the Battle of the Somme (2.2078). Jones directly forces the question by alluding to medieval epic and romance and Shakespeare's history plays so that the doomed soldiers move through a landscape of ancient epic and present no-man's-land.

Jones's technique, as pointed out in the headnote (2.2079), was influenced by Eliot's *The Waste Land*. That work, as Eliot indicated in his notes to it, was loosely based on an anthropological study of the relationship of the medieval grail romances to primitive fertility rites. Throughout the poem, figures in post-World War I Europe are identified by quotations from and allusions to earlier literature. The people flowing over London Bridge recall Dante's reaction to the souls of the damned crowding to the shore of Acheron in the *Inferno* ("I had not thought death had undone so many" [line 63]). The woman at her dressing table is ironically juxtaposed to the image of Cleopatra in her barge on the Nile going to welcome Mark Antony ("The chair she sat in like a burnished throne" [line 77]). The whole poem is made up of fragments of texts woven together in a mantra to restore some kind of order and life to a shattered civilization.

Kipling's *The Man Who Would Be King* and Conrad's *Heart of Darkness* are tales about the crumbling European dreams of empire. "I won't make a Nation," Daniel Dravot boasts, "I'll make an Empire!" (2.1881). Conrad sets Marlow's tale on the Thames, as night is falling, aboard the yacht of the Director of Companies, and evokes the voyages of exploration and commerce: "Hunters of gold or pursuers of fame, they had all gone out on that stream, bearing the sword and often the torch, messengers of the might within the land, bearers of the spark from that sacred fire. What greatness had not floated on the ebb of that river into the mystery of an unknown earth! . . . The dreams of men, the seed of commonwealths, the germs of empires" (2.1959). The grandiose language, which Marlow's narrative sustains, sets up his listeners on the *Nellie* and the reader for the knowledge waiting upstream on another river: "The horror! The horror!" (2.2010).

If you assign *Heart of Darkness*, you should also assign Chinua Achebe's essay *An Image of Africa: Racism in Conrad's "Heart of Darkness,"* which is new in *NAEL*, along with the other selections under "The Rise and Fall of Empire" (2.2035). You could then close out the semester with what is arguably the text closest to epic among the twentieth-century selections, Achebe's novel *Things Fall Apart*. Umuofia is the nearest thing in later literature to the warrior tribes in *Beowulf*, and Okonkwo is closest to an epic as well as to a tragic hero.

ENGLISH 3: Society in Literature

(*Volume 1 only*)

How does literature reflect the social history of English-speaking peoples? The answer of course changes as society changes. A problem for our students in dealing with many of the texts in volume 1 of *NAEL* is the unfamiliarity of the social order that the original audiences of these works took for granted. Until the early modern period, the great majority of all writings were addressed to members of the nobility, the church, and a minority of educated commoners who might be well-to-do landowners like Chaucer's Franklin, lawyers, merchants, administrators, and tradesmen. In the late Middle Ages, the old social order was changing, and many of the texts in *NAEL1* are responding to those changes. An important change was the increase in literacy, especially after the introduction of printing, and the growth and diversification of the reading public contributed to and intensified the changes taking place in society and in literature. By the end of the eighteenth century, one can see the emergence of what we now think of as a class system. Of course differences of degree, rank, or status exist in every society, but the earliest reference in the *OED* to *class* in the modern social sense is the title of a 1772 tract: "Observations on the Causes of the Dissoluteness which reigns among the lower classes of the people."

In much of the earlier literature, especially in poetry, class in this modern sense is not an issue because all the main characters belong to an aristocracy, and the rest of the world is largely ignored. But in later periods the others, who constitute the great majority of men and women, make their presence felt. In the fourteenth century, rebellions broke out against the feudal nobility in France and England, which were quickly suppressed but left their mark on history and literature. During the English "Uprising of 1381" (known to earlier historians as "The Peasants' Rebellion"), the rebels chanted, "When Adam delved and Eve span, / Who was then a gentleman?" On the Web site (in the Middle Ages, go to "Medieval Estates and Orders"), you can see letters circulated by leaders of the uprising to incite their followers and excerpts from a vitriolic satire (John Gower's *Vox Clamantis*) portraying the rebels as animals attacking their masters. In *Paradise Lost*, Adam and Eve make up a classless society of two; yet even there Satan's seduction of Eve, which begins "Wonder not, Sovran mistress" (1.1973, line 532), draws upon the rhetoric of romance and sonnets, which attributes power and mastery to courtly women. Milton's Heaven, too, it should be remembered, has its hierarchy of angels and was the site of the first revolution.

On medieval social theory of "three estates," go to "Medieval Estates and Orders" on the Web site, especially the English monk Aelfric's *Those Who Pray, Work, and Fight*. Practically everyone in *Beowulf* belongs to the warrior class (those who fight), if we exclude the monsters, and even Grendel and his mother are given a genealogy like those of the ruling families of Danes, the Geats, and the Swedes. That is not to say that an aristocracy resembling the Danish and Geatish nobility portrayed in heroic poetry ever existed any more than there had ever been a brotherhood of knights like those of King Arthur's Round Table. Although Heorot and Camelot are very different societies and reflect different cultures (see pp. 15–16, above), both are legendary places where those who fight, whether they fight against men, monsters, or the devil, are the only ones who matter in literature. "Protector," "Shield," "Shepherd" of the people are common formulaic expressions for a king, but one hears little about people outside of the retainers in the mead-hall and a few queens and princesses (an exception is the thief who steals the dragon's cup). The ideals of the warrior class are strength, courage, wisdom, generosity, fame, and loyalty to kin. Noble women like Wealtheow and Hygd attend the lord and his warriors. Like Hildeburg, Freawaru, and probably the speaker in *The Wife's Lament*, they serve as peace-weavers in marriages arranged to end tribal feuds, which the marriages only serve to exacerbate and of which the women become the helpless victims. *Beowulf* is about the preservation of the clan, and we know what fate awaits the Geats after the death of their king: "in the path of exile / they shall walk bereft, bowed under woe" (1.96, lines 3019–20).

The knights and ladies of medieval romance also inhabit an aristocratic world in which we rarely see anyone else who is not a servant, but it is a very different world in which the knights, instead of being served by their ladies, profess themselves to be the servants of those ladies and of all noble women. Strength, courage, wisdom, generosity, and loyalty to kin still define the noble hero, but a new badge of class in romance is courtesy. There are elaborate exchanges of courtesy in *Beowulf*, too, but nothing like "the polished pearls of impeccable speech" (1.177, line 917) that the company at Sir Bertilak's castle expect to fall from Sir Gawain's lips. Marie de France mentions Arthur's border wars in the opening lines of *Lanval*, but the rest of the romance is about social politics at Camelot and Lanval's affair with a fairy mistress, whose opulence makes Arthur's court seem shabby in comparison.

The social spectrum widens in *The Canterbury Tales*. Chaucer begins the *General Prologue* by telling his readers/listeners who the pilgrims are, specifically their "condicioun," "degree," and "eek in what array that they were inne" (1.216, lines 35–41). To Chaucer the pilgrim narrator, these categories all designate rank, profession, and what we now call class. The reader soon notices that the portraits describe not just the social and professional but also the moral and spiritual "condicioun" of the pilgrims. Their dress, opinions, speech, and behavior suggest that most are greatly concerned with status. For analogues to Chaucer's portraits go to "Estates Satire" on the Web site. The Host probably manipulates the drawing of straws, so that the Knight, the highest-ranking pilgrim, will tell the first tale. With *The Miller's Prologue*, however, the lower-ranking pilgrims begin to assert their social identities. We soon get into clashes—between the Host and the Miller, the Miller and the Reeve, the Host and the Parson, the Wife of Bath and the Pardoner, the Wife and the Friar, the Pardoner and the Host—which have been described as social comedy. Although Chaucer slyly pretends that the Miller's fabliau is "a cherles tale," the narrative voice is not that of the drunken Miller but that of the poet satirizing the courtly affectations of costume, manner, speech, and behavior of the petit bourgeois characters.

Marriage, money, and class are the crucial concerns for the Wife of Bath. Her *Prologue* deals with her stubborn refusal to let herself be exploited by a society where women have no education and few rights, and where rich old men acquire young girls as property. Like the fictional Wife of Bath, Margery Kempe has to negotiate with her husband, but, in her case, to obtain her freedom from the "marriage debt" in order to follow a religious vocation outside the cloister—a radically different life for a woman of her time that brings her into conflict with ecclesiastical authority.

Langland's *Prologue* to *Piers Plowman* depicts an acquisitive society on the move. Like Chaucer's *Prologue*, with which it overlaps and contrasts, you can teach it as an example of Estates Satire. The confession of Glutton is a superb tavern scene of London low life (1.323). The "Plowing of Piers's Half-Acre" reads like a parable about the breakdown of the feudal social order (1.328).

The mystery cycles, which were performed annually for the entire population, also portray the lives of medieval commoners. The biblical herdsmen in the Wakefield *Second Shepherds' Play* complain about cold winters, exploitation by servants of the gentry, and other hardships on the Yorkshire moors with which many of the spectators of these performances could identify. The trick of disguising the stolen sheep as a newborn baby is both comic and touching because the audience understands that Mak,

Jill, and their ever-increasing brood are poor and hungry. The tenderness of the shepherds presenting their symbolic gifts to their newborn king beautifully enacts the change that the birth of the savior, at least in the drama, has brought about in the human condition.

If Sir Thomas Malory of Newbold Revell is, as most scholars believe, the "knight prisoner" who wrote *Morte Darthur* (see headnote, 1.420), his criminal record may be a sign of the disruptions that the Wars of the Roses brought upon the feudal nobility in the late fifteenth century. The dying out of the old order helps to explain Malory's passionate nostalgia for chivalry, especially the chivalry of his hero Sir Lancelot. Sir Ector's eulogy for Lancelot (1.438) could be read as an elegy for chivalry itself.

The Tudors brought about centralization of the monarchy and with it changes in the feudal class system. Service at the Tudor court could lead to wealth and power but also to precipitate reversals of fortune. No career illustrates this better than Sir Thomas More's. A lawyer's son, More rose in the king's service to become Chancellor and, in consequence, a martyr to his faith. More is himself an outstanding example of the highly educated and accomplished courtier, a statesman and author, who supplants the ideal of knighthood described in Sir Ector's eulogy of Lancelot. Renaissance courtiership involves a code of conduct, an art, and a style to be learned, cultivated, and written about. According to Castiglione's famous treatise *Il Cortegiano* (1528), translated into English by Sir Thomas Hoby, the ideal courtier should have "sprezzatura" (1.577). A word difficult to define, "sprezzatura" refers to a studied social grace that comes across as though it were completely natural. More than charm in manners and conversation, such grace also assumed an appreciation of and some ability in music and literature—to perform on an instrument, sing a part in a madrigal, and to write verse. Queen Elizabeth herself wrote poems (1.594–95) as had her father Henry VIII. In many ways, one sees in this period the evolving of a culture of arts and manners shared by the nobility and educated commoners.

Many of the sixteenth-century English courtiers were fashioned by the humanist education that began to make its way from Italy to England toward the end of the fifteenth century (see "Renaissance Humanism," 1.472–74). The role of the universities in the Middle Ages was to educate men for the church; after the English Reformation, they would continue to produce clergymen for the Church of England. Now, however, sons of the upper nobility and well-to-do gentlemen began attending Oxford and Cambridge, and a university education became, as it still remains, an emblem of class and a stepping-stone not only to the church but also to government service. Sir Thomas Wyatt, Fulke Greville, and Edmund Spenser attended Cambridge. Sir Philip Sidney was at Oxford, although he did not take a degree, a superfluous distinction for someone of his rank. Humanist grammar schools gave an opportunity for boys of humbler origins to advance in the world. Spenser went to the Merchant Taylors' School (the name indicates that its founders were tradesmen). Christopher Marlowe, a shoemaker's son, was a scholarship student at the Kings School in Canterbury and at Corpus Christi College, Cambridge, from where he may have been recruited for the queen's secret service as a counterspy against Catholic conspirators.

We learn from Ascham's last visit to Lady Jane Grey (1.567) how greatly some women cherished the humanist education they received from private tutors. Sir Thomas More personally educated his daughter Elizabeth (in the film *A Man for All Seasons*, she puts Henry VIII to shame with the superiority of her conversational Latin). Sidney wrote the *Arcadia* (1.911–16), a pastoral romance, for his sister Mary Herbert, the countess of Pembroke, who was herself a poet (1.957–64) and patron of other poets. The sonnet sequence of Sidney's niece Mary Wroth (1.1428–32) may be read both as a tribute and as a response to her uncle's. The writings of Renaissance women represented in *NAEL*, some but not all of whom were of the aristocracy, are significant not only in their own right but because they are among our first records of intellectual and literary friendships between men and women.

Boys and a few girls studied Latin and Greek history, philosophy, and literature in the original languages; they would pick up French and, in many cases, Italian, through tutors and governesses, reading, and travels abroad. Thus the translation of classical, French, and Italian poetry and prose and the composition of original poems in English became an aristocratic pastime. Born aristocrats like Wyatt, Surrey, and Sidney circulated their works in manuscript, disdaining to submit them to the new printing trade. In 1557 Richard Tottel first printed, from pirated copies, samples of what he praised, in an address to the "gentle reader," as "the honorable style of the noble Earl of Surrey and the weightiness of the deep-witted Sir Thomas Wyatt." *Songs and Sonnets* or *Tottel's Miscellany*, as this famous volume came to be known, was a highly successful commercial venture designed for middle-class readers eager to appreciate and emulate the courtly manner and matter of such celebrated courtiers. That audience, most of whom would probably know little Latin, French, and Italian, also provided a market for such notable translations as Golding's Ovid (1.600), Florio's Montaigne (an excerpt is on the Web site), North's Plutarch, and Chapman's Homer (which inspired a famous sonnet by Keats). The same audience would also pay admission to the Elizabethan and Jacobean theaters to watch plays, many of which were adapted from French and Italian novellas.

On an intellectual and artistic level, friendship and even greater intimacy between a nobleman and a gifted actor, poet, and playwright were at least in the realm of possibility. The most powerful and convincing sonnet sequence is about the love of an older poet for a beautiful young nobleman. That sequence is, of course, Shakespeare's. The nature of that love, whether it is erotic or Platonic and whether it corresponds to an actual relationship in Shakespeare's life, has been the subject of endless debate. Whatever the truth is, no other poetry has expressed more poignantly and more ironically the pain caused by differences in rank, age, time, temperament, and commitment when love on one side is no longer reciprocated.

The Faerie Queene portrays an imaginary world or rather a number of imaginary worlds, but the many different courts, houses, bowers, and gardens, like *Utopia*, comment on aspects of the real world in which Spenser was making his way as a courtier and poet. The various places in Book 1 carry out the allegory of the conflict between Catholicism and the Church of England. Archimago and his hermitage are a satire of monasticism. The House of Pride and its maiden queen Lucifera (Pride) are the complementary opposite of Gloriana and her court; Lucifera's courtiers are the six other deadly sins. Although not specifically anti-Catholic, Pride's palace is a moral satire of courts in general.

Like cross-dressing, crossing class barriers provides some of the complications in Shakespeare's *Twelfth Night*. In a few Elizabethan comedies heroines marry up—a notable example is Thomas Dekker's *Shoemakers' Holiday*, where the Lord Mayor's daughter marries the nephew of the Earl of Lincoln in spite of her father's reservations and the earl's protests. In *Twelfth Night* there are ambiguities of rank as well as of gender. Olivia, a countess, rejects Duke Orsino but is eager to marry Viola disguised as the duke's servant Cesario. In the end she is happy to settle for Viola's identical twin brother, while Orsino gets Viola. The exact "estate" of Viola and Sebastian is never entirely clear, but Shakespeare takes pains to establish that they are wealthy gentlefolk. In Act 1, scene 2 (1.1047), Viola gives the Captain gold and tells him that she wishes to conceal her rank, promising to pay him "bountifully" to assist in her disguise. Furthermore, she addresses him by the familiar "thou" and he addresses her by the respectful "you." Thus she would seem to be, if not an equal, at least an eligible mate for Duke Orsino, and her brother, for Countess Olivia. Sir Andrew Aguecheek, whose chief claim to knighthood is "three thousand ducats a year," is, however, a ridiculous suitor for Olivia's hand. And the very notion of an unequal union is mocked in the subplot, where Malvolio falls into Maria's trap by believing that Olivia is in love with him. Malvolio is put in his place; still, the comedy suggests that such grand illusions are not outside the realm of possibility for less vain and more sophisticated suitors. Sir Toby, we learn in a line (1.1104, line 360), has married Maria in reward for her successful plot to humiliate Malvolio. Class barriers are growing permeable.

After her husband's death, the Duchess of Malfi falls in love with her virtuous steward Antonio and secretly marries him. The scene in which she dictates her "will" to him (Act 1.3) plays with verbal and social ambiguities. The marriage clearly has the blessing of playwright, audience, and all the decent characters in the play but precipitates the tragedy. When her brothers the Duke and the Cardinal discover the duchess's secret, they have her and her younger children strangled.

During the Elizabethan period, poets like Spenser, who depended on patronage in making their public and literary careers, did publish their works with dedications to noble personages. *The Shepheardes Calender*, Spenser's first publication, is dedicated on the title page "TO THE NOBLE AND VERTV- / *ous Gentleman most worthy of all titles* / both of learning and cheualrie M. / Philip Sidney." In spite of Spenser's celebration of Elizabeth as Gloriana, the Faerie Queene, she never paid him with the post in London that he desired. He spent the rest of his life working for the English colonial administration in Ireland (1.615; for Spenser on Ireland, see the excerpt from his dialogue *A View of the Present State of Ireland*, Norton Topics Online, under "Renaissance Exploration").

James I and Charles I used their patronage to promote the Church of England and to stage elaborate entertainments that made the Stuart court notorious for its luxury. One of the many ways to look at the extraordinary variety of poetry written during this period is to consider how the politics of court and church influenced the status and fortunes of some of the poets and what effect those politics may have had on the different kinds of verse they wrote. It is interesting, in this respect, to compare the effects of patronage on the careers and works of the first three poets represented in this period: Donne, Lanyer, and Jonson.

Students need to appreciate Donne's family history and the low tide Donne's fortunes had reached before the king's intervention. Born to a prominent and deeply committed middle-class Catholic family (an uncle and a brother died for their faith), he attended Oxford and Cambridge. But because he would not swear the required oath of allegiance to the Church of England, he was prevented from taking a degree or from following any career in which his remarkable gifts would have assured rapid advancement (1.1233–34). His conversion to the Church of England, whether for practical considerations or out of conviction, opened doors to him that were soon closed again after he eloped with the niece of his employer, Sir Thomas Egerton. The Egertons regarded Donne as totally unsuitable to be a member of their distinguished family. Donne's imprudent marriage for love was probably responsible for some of his finest poems such as *The Canonization*. Instead of being eternally separated like Astrophil and Stella, the lovers here are willing to die [with a sexual pun] as one person and to be preserved "in sonnets" through which they will be worshipped as saints by future lovers. In the poem at least, love triumphs over difference in class and wealth.

By withholding any other patronage, the king ultimately overcame Donne's reservations about taking holy orders and recruited him for the Church of England. In the pulpit, Donne found a true vocation. His dramatic sermons as dean of St. Paul's cathedral are said to have brought many of his aristocratic parishioners to tears. His emotional religious poetry and prose (1.1268–81) certainly sustain such a report. So does the excerpt "Donne on His Deathbed" from Isaac Walton's hagiographical *Life of Dr. John Donne* (1.1582–87). In Walton's biography, Donne did achieve quasi-sainthood, though not through sexual love. It's a good idea to teach "Donne on His Deathbed" (1.1583) alongside Donne's religious poetry; if possible, show your students a photograph of the image of

Donne in his winding sheet, described by Walton (you can find it in the Grierson edition of Donne).

Through his employment of Donne's talents, James shrewdly used patronage in the cause of the Church of England, a pillar of the monarchy under attack from the Puritan left for its hierarchy, liturgy, and rituals, which for many Protestants smacked too much of Roman Catholicism. James employed Jonson, a convert to Catholicism and an erudite classicist, to compose extravagant court entertainments for which the monarchy would also come under attack. *The Masque of Blackness*, the first of the twenty-four Jonson wrote, is not a work for which he is best remembered. But it is short and well worth assigning because the elaborate description of sets, makeup, costumes, and music and the preciosity of the dialogue will help students to understand what Puritans found objectionable about the Jacobean court. The appearance of the ladies of the court, at the queen's direction, in blackface as African beauties was doubtless intended to be exotic. Jonson gave this a mythological explanation out of Ovid: the Ethiopians were turned black when Phaëton drove the sun's chariot too close to the equator but now are instructed to seek out Britannia, where the more temperate sun (that is, King James) will restore their original whiteness. (For more on the masques, see Norton Topics Online, "Inigo Jones and Costumes of the Masques" under "Civil War of Ideas" in The Early Seventeenth Century.)

Jonson's plays for the public theater are derived from Roman comedy, and whereas the masques are operatic spectacles to entertain the court, the plays are sardonic satires of bourgeois greed and lust. In contrast to his satires of the city, *To Penshurst*, a country-house poem, praises the hospitality and way of life on the estate of the Sidney family and displays Jonson's fondness for the rural aristocracy and their acceptance of him.

The court apparently found no place for an accomplished woman like Aemilia Lanyer, who did, however, receive patronage and encouragement from the Countess of Cumberland. In *The Description of Cooke-ham* (1.1287), Lanyer recalls with gratitude and affection her reception there by the countess and her daughter. Like Jonson's poems, *Cooke-ham* is dotted with classical allusions. The fact that the poem is a nostalgic leave-taking of the place also gives it a feeling of sadness.

In *Affliction (1)* (1.1599), George Herbert traces a very different career course from those of Donne and Jonson. Like so many of his poems, this one is a dramatic monologue in which the poet's silent interlocutor is God. In contrast to Donne and Jonson, Herbert was born into a distinguished family and began life with brilliant prospects. A graduate of Trinity College, Cambridge, he obtained election to the Public Oratorship of the university, a post that, as the headnote points out, "would have been a step toward a career at court or in public service" (1.1596). The "service brave" Herbert originally anticipated (*Affliction* [1.1599, line 2]) was nominally dedicated to God and perhaps aimed at an ecclesiastical career; however, the "joys," "benefits," and "glorious household stuff" (lines 2, 6, 9) are a courtier's rewards. Herbert's complaints about the disappointment of his hopes and ambitions through illness and the death of patrons lead to a crisis and then a sudden reversal at the end, characteristic of his poems:

> Well I will change the service and go seek
> Some other master out.
> Ah, my dear God! though I am clean forgot,
> Let me not love thee, if I love thee not.

Like Donne, Herbert eventually took orders, but his career as an obscure country priest ministering to his flock was very different from Donne's in London as dean of St. Paul's. At university, Herbert had published poetry in Latin. His later religious verse, like music, was a recreation—a private conversation carried on with God; there is no evidence that it ever circulated in manuscript.

Milton's father was able to give him the economic freedom to acquire the most complete education possible not only by attending St. Paul's grammar school and Cambridge University but through private tutors, independent reading, and travel (1.1772). The opening lines of *Lycidas* (1.1791) declare that he is preparing himself to become a poet (in pastoral language to pluck the berries of the laurel); in *The Reasons for Church Government*, he digresses about his search for an epic subject. The outbreak of the Civil War put those plans on hold as Milton threw himself into the task of helping to create a free society. The key text is *Areopagitica*, which he wrote to oppose the censorship law enacted by Parliament. The argument is based on the premise of humankind's God-given freedom to seek truth and to choose right moral action. "[W]hen God gave [Adam] reason," Milton writes, "he gave him freedom to choose, for reason is but choosing; he had been else a mere artificial Adam, such an Adam as we see in the motions [puppet shows]" (1.1804). Censorship and hierarchy deprive people of the freedom to choose and, therefore, freedom of conscience and expression are essential if moral choices are to have any meaning. *Areopagitica* envisions a reformed utopian society—"a noble and puissant nation rousing herself like a strong man after sleep" (1.1809)—united "into one general and brotherly search after truth (1.1808).

The Restoration left Milton, as he wrote, "fall'n on evil days, / . . . In darkness, and with dangers compassed round" (1.1934, lines 25–27). For the epic he had been contemplating, he returned to first things, the book of Genesis, and the origins of the human condition in a fallen world. But freedom of the will to choose one's own destiny remained the essential theme. "Here at least we shall be free," Satan declares (1.1823, lines 258–59), without realizing that Hell is what he has freely chosen. Freedom of choice also brings about the fall of the first human couple. Milton elaborates the story of the fall in Genesis by inventing the scene in which Eve, to prove her independence, wants to leave Adam to work in the garden alone. Adam tries to persuade her to stay but cannot force her to remain at his side: "God left free the will; for what obeys / Reason is free" (lines 351–52). Unlike Lanyer in *Eve's Apology* (1.1285), Milton is unwilling to excuse Eve on grounds of her ignorance and the serpent's cunning and makes her reject Adam's warning. But he also makes her more generous than Adam in accepting responsibility for the fall. The quiet ending stresses once again their *mutual* freedom of choice:

> The world was all before them, where to choose
> Their place of rest, and Providence their guide:
> They hand in hand with wand'ring steps and slow,
> Through Eden took their solitary way.

For the royalist Hobbes, freedom of choice and justice are illusions. A state of nature is a state of war with every man against every other man, a war in which the stronger prevails rather than truth or justice. The only protection lies in surrendering one's freedom and submitting to the restraint of laws held in common in a society—"that great Leviathan called a Common-Wealth or State" (1.1588). Dryden, too, regarded liberty as a potential threat to the stability of the state. Capitalizing on a trope in which the English Puritans saw themselves as the new Zion or Israel, Dryden satirized them in *Absalom and Achitophel* as the Jews: "These Adam-wits, too fortunately free, / Began to dream they wanted liberty" (1.2078, lines 51–52). Achitophel's temptation of Absalom (1.2082, lines 230–302) is modeled on Satan's seduction of Eve in *Paradise Lost.*

The Restoration did not do away with the religious, political, and social divisions over which the Civil War had been fought, and literature of the period continued to be written in a partisan spirit. For the evangelical preacher John Bunyan, who had fought in the Puritan army, society is full temptations and detours on the way that leads from the City of Destruction to the Celestial City. "What are the things you seek," neighbor Obstinate asks Christian, "since you leave all the world to find them?" (1.2139). For Bunyan, the trials of dissenters in Restoration England are like the persecution suffered by Christian and his companion Faithful in Vanity Fair, who are mocked and locked in a cage like madmen for their strange dress, speech, and refusal to buy the goods in this consumer society.

The period saw a great increase in the number of women authors (see pp. 107–10). It also marked the popular success of authors like Bunyan and Defoe, who, as the headnote says of the latter, lacked "the refined tastes and classical learning that dominated polite literature during his lifetime." Both wrote for an increasingly literate class of readers who also did not have the classical education of Dryden, Swift, Pope, Addison, Steele, and Johnson. Moreover, they wrote about men and women from the same social strata as their own. Defoe's Robinson Crusoe is the ne'er-do-well son of a bourgeois family who runs away to sea and as a castaway finds God and learns to respect his parents' values.

Swift portrays Gulliver as a relatively humble and respectable English ship's doctor trying to find his bearings in the different social worlds where he is cast away. Lilliput, Brobdingnag, and Laputa, each in a different way, represent England or aspects of eighteenth-century society—its politics, its wars, and its new science. Unfamiliar with courts, Gulliver is eager to gain the respect and friendship of Lilliputian royalty. He is enormously proud of the title of *Nardac*, which he has received for his capture of the Blefuscudian fleet, only to be embittered by the articles of impeachment drawn up against him. Lilliput and Blefuscu are rival naval powers like Britain and France. Brobdingnag is a peaceful agricultural kingdom whose king is horrified by Gulliver's offer to enlighten and empower his backward country by introducing it to the technology of modern war. Whether Swift intended Houyhnhnmland to be an equine utopia of pure reason or a purely racist society remains a question. Gulliver tells us his master

> made me observe, that among the Houyhnhnms the white, the sorrel, and the iron grey were not so exactly shaped as the bay, the dapple grey, and the black; nor born with equal talents of mind, or a capacity to improve them; and therefore continued always in the condition of servants, without ever aspiring to match out of their own race, which in that country would be reckoned monstrous and unnatural. (2449)

Is Swift seriously endorsing the system of apartheid among the Houyhnhnms? Moreover, although one may be repelled by the Yahoos, it is difficult today to read of plans for the extermination of the Yahoos or about Gulliver's repairing of his shoes with Yahoo skins without being reminded of twentieth-century genocide.

The eighteenth century was fascinated by crime, about which a new literature developed. Executions were still public spectacles, and newspapers published sensational accounts of celebrated criminals. *The Beggar's Opera* traded on the notoriety of the London underworld to satirize, as the headnote explains, the Whig administration of Robert Walpole (2.2606). In many other respects, too, the language and mercenary values of Mr. and Mrs. Peachum reflect those of their social betters. Mrs. Peachum vents her indignation at Polly's marriage: "I knew she was always a proud slut; and now she hath played the fool and married, because forsooth she would do like the gentry. . . . If you must be married, could you introduce nobody into our family but a highwayman? Why, thou foolish jade, thou wilt be as ill-used, and as much neglected, as if thou hadst married a lord!" Hogarth's illustration (1.2646) brings out the resemblances between the characters in the *Opera* and the spectators. In one respect, however, the charm and success of the *Opera*, in its own day and in future generations, depend on the perennially popular character of the folk songs to which Gay's lyrics are set (three of them are performed on the Audio Companion).

As the century winds down, the hard and brilliant surface of so much earlier verse and prose seems to give way to a more tender feeling and style and a growing concern with the lot of the poor and oppressed. The dispossession of small farmers and the resulting growth of urban slums were changing the demography of England even before the industrial revolution got under way. The gap between the rich and the poor was widening. Goldsmith idealizes rural England and laments its decline in his sentimental poem *The Deserted Village* (1.2858). Crabbe's *The Village* (1.2867) should be read as a companion piece of Goldsmith's, to which it is in part a response, for it shows that village life had never been the way Goldsmith had pictured it but instead was an exhausting, demoralizing, and disease-ridden round of endless toil to eke out a bare subsistence, often terminated by early death. All the same, *The Deserted Village* expresses a strain of sympathy for the poor and oppressed and of protest against the conditions brought about by a changing economy, which carries over into the nineteenth century. (For a comparison of the common purpose but conflicting styles of Goldsmith and Crabbe, see pp. 112–13). The same sentiments fueled the abolitionist movement that would bring about the end of the British slave trade in 1807. That movement is documented by the selections in the cluster "Slavery and Freedom" (1.2806) and the Web site section "Slavery and the Slave Trade in Britain" (see also the discussion in Chapter 5, pp. 104–7).

Taken collectively, what all of these selections demonstrate is a gradual shift in literature away from the religious, political, and social concerns of the upper levels of society to concerns, on the one hand, "for the lives of common men and women" (1.2063) and, on the other hand, introspective concerns with personal and domestic life. Increasingly, the poet writes himself and his mood into the scenes he is describing. In this respect, one might compare formal and stately public odes, such as Jonson's *To the Immortal Memory and Friendship . . . of Sir Lucius Cary and Sir H. Morison* (1.1409) or Dryden's two odes for St. Cecilia's Day (1.2106, 2109) with Gray's *Ode on a Distant Prospect of Eton College* (1.2826). With the latter, the ode took a turn both outward and inward—that is, meditation upon a landscape or some phenomenon in nature inspires the poet to meditate within himself. Instead of feeling that the poet is participating in some public event, we sense that he is in solitary thought. Gray's use of landscape and of the schoolboys on the playing fields of Eton (1.2826) as a reminder of an earlier visit in his youth anticipates Wordsworth's *Tintern Abbey*. Or contrast Gray's *Elegy Written in a Country Churchyard* (1.2830) with Dryden's *To the Memory of Mr. Oldham* (2106) and Dr. Johnson's *On the Death of Dr. Robert Levet* (1.2672). Both of the latter are eloquent personal tributes to relatively obscure persons. The point of Gray's poem is that villagers buried in the churchyard are unknown but that "The short and simple annals of the poor" (32) remind us of our common fate in which they are equal with the great men of the world. The poem is not actually about them, but about the poet himself and his reflections upon nature and mortality and thus anticipates the concerns with the natural world and ordinary people and the poetic subjectivity of the Romantic Period.

CHAPTER 10

Examinations, Paper Topics, Study Questions

This chapter discusses the strategy of posing questions for students and setting topics for papers; it provides a variety of examples and also offers a few sample study questions to assist students in their reading assignments. The examples are not designed to cover the material in *NAEL* in a comprehensive way, nor do they include complete examinations. The purpose is merely to aid instructors in making up tests and paper topics suited to their own interests and class procedures.

We have arranged the sample questions in each part of the chapter in roughly chronological order, though comprehensive essay questions, of course, may range over two or more periods. Instructors will have no difficulty identifying the questions that apply to their course, but, because they are meant to provide "question ideas," many questions asked about the selections in one period could easily be adapted to another period as well.

Examinations

A few instructors base the course grade entirely on papers; most, however, use a combination of papers and examinations. In many courses that use *NAEL*, students are asked to write one or two hour-long exams and a two- or three-hour final. On any timed test, it is always difficult to cover a lot of material and also to ask questions that challenge students to write answers that show depth and understanding as well as evidence that they have done the reading. Outside essays, of course, provide such an opportunity. But one may also construct examinations, using a variety of questions, that test both the breadth and the depth of a student's knowledge.

Students greatly appreciate some instructions before the first test, telling them what to expect and giving them examples of the kinds of questions they will be asked. Such sample questions might even be accompanied by good answers, saved from previous tests, with comments by the instructor pointing out the qualities that made them good. It is also an excellent idea to return a set of exams with a handout of superior answers, selected from several bluebooks and reproduced anonymously (with perhaps minor editing). Although such a handout takes time to prepare, ultimately it can save a great deal of time in explaining to some unhappy students why they did poorly and how to improve their performance. No amount of comment on the deficiencies of a student's performance on an exam is likely to be as effective as the example of a good answer to the question. Students often cannot evaluate their own work because they have no standards by which to judge. They can, however, recognize good work when they see it, and the quality of their own work often improves dramatically as a result.

Identification Questions

This kind of question often appears first on a test and is meant to be brief (ten minutes at most), asking students to identify anywhere from five to ten items from a list, allowing them some choice. A problem is to get students to observe the time limit, for a few will tend to spill out everything they know about a single item. Therefore, it's a good idea to amplify the instruction to "identify" with wording such as "in *no more* than a sentence or two" or to state even more specifically: "Say *briefly* who, or what, the following are, and cite the author and title of the work in which they appear; you need not write complete sentences."

SAMPLE IDENTIFICATIONS

The Middle Ages: Heorot, a "book of wikked wivys," Bertilak de Hautdesert, the Harrowing of Hell, a stolen sheep, Lleuelys, Mordred.

Sixteenth Century: octave, Stella, Anne Askew, gold toilet bowls, "Venus' nun," Malvolio.

Early Seventeenth Century: carpe diem, "sweet swan of Avon," Bosola, Herod, *The Temple*. Pandemonium, Salomon's House.

Restoration and Eighteenth Century: Jebusites, the Slough of Despond, Glumdalclitch, the Spectator's Club, Atticus, Macheath, "Its form is that of a pastoral, easy, vulgar, and therefore disgusting."

Romantic Period: "spontaneous overflow of powerful feelings," Mary Wollstonecraft Godwin, Madeline and Porphyro, an albatross, *Adonais*, Robert Southey, Captain Walton.

Victorian Age: Teufelsdröckh, Arthur Hallam, Andrea del Sarto, Philistines, a windhover, Bunbury.

Twentieth Century: "The horror! The horror!," Maude Gonne, Shakespeare's sister, Leopold Bloom, *Little Gidding, Spain 1937*, Okonkwo.

Short-Answer Questions

Instead of simply asking students to identify items from a list, one can write a variety of questions that elicit different kinds of information. The latter requires a little more thought—from both the instructor and the students—than straight identifications.

SAMPLE SHORT-ANSWER QUESTIONS

The Middle Ages

1. Give one example each of a work in *NAEL* originally composed in (a) Latin, (b) a Germanic language, (c) a Celtic language, (d) a romance language.

2. Explain the differences between these three types of medieval religious life: (a) that of a monk or nun, (b) that of an anchorite or anchoress, (c) that of a mendicant friar.

3. What is a *pentangle*, who wore one, and what is one thing that it symbolized?

4. Identify Coll, Gib, Daw, and Good Deeds, and briefly explain how these characters illustrate a difference between a mystery and a morality play.

5. The following list contains pairs from three different works. Pick out the pairs, identify the works, and in a word or two say how the pairs are related: the Virgin Mary, Lancelot, Pertelot, Gill, Chauntecleer, Guinevere.

The Sixteenth Century

6. Identify two of these characters and explain the significance of their names: Raphael Hythloday, Astrophil, Duessa.

7. Briefly define *pastoral* and *epithalamion*, and give the author and title of one work in each genre.

8. Through what device on the Elizabethan stage might the following stage direction have been carried out? [Exeunt DEVILS with FAUSTUS.]

The Early Seventeenth Century

9. Identify the author and explain the double sense of the italicized words in the following quotations and title: (a) "When thou hast *done*, thou hast not *done*," (b) "Of man's first disobedience and the *fruit* / Of that forbidden tree," (c) *The Collar*.

10. Name the authors of two of the following works and say what the title refers to: *The Temple, L'Allegro, Novum Organum, Hydriotaphia*.

11. When Donne wrote that "new Philosophy calls all in doubt" what did he mean? Identify the poem in which Donne writes this, and briefly compare that poem's perspective on the new science with works by Bacon or Sir Thomas Browne.

12. Poets often write poems about other poets—e.g., Jonson and Milton on Shakespeare, Jonson on Donne, Carew on Donne and Jonson, Herrick on Jonson. Take one of these cases, and indicate how the poet-author treats his poet-subject.

13. Identify the authors who held the following positions: Dean of St. Paul's Cathedral, Latin Secretary to Cromwell's Council of State, Lord Chancellor of England.

The Restoration and the Eighteenth Century

14. Identify the author, the work, and the actual person represented by these figures: King David, Flimnap, Atticus.

15. What two passions motivate women, according to Pope, and how does Irwin criticize what he says?

16. What do Polly Peachum and Lucy Lockit have in common?

17. Who wrote that "the sound must seem an echo of the sense," and how do the following lines illustrate that principle?

> A Needless Alexandrine ends the song
> That, like a wounded snake, drags its slow length along.

18. In which two works do Clarissa and Imlac appear, and in what respects do they play similar roles?

The Romantic Period

19. In what way is shooting an albatross like eating an apple?

20. Arrange in chronological order the following events: the Peterloo Massacre, the Battle of Waterloo, publication of *The Prelude*, Wordsworth's first visit to France, publication of *Lyrical Ballads*.

21. What is literary Gothicism in the Romantic period? Name some defining examples.

22. With which Romantic writer do we associate each of the following?
   a. Negative Capability
   b. intellectual breeze
   c. Wedding Guest
   d. shaping spirit of Imagination
   e. invisible worm
   f. pleasure dome
   g. Cold Pastoral
   h. Beadsman

23. Who wrote each of the following lines, and what is being addressed in each? (a) "And all that mighty heart is lying still!" (b) "Oh! Lift me as a wave, a leaf, a cloud!" (c) "Thou still unravished bride of quietness."

The Victorian Age

24. Identify the historical event or situation that motivated the following works: *The Cry of the Children, Culture and Anarchy, De Profundis.*

25. Identify the work in which the following appear: a head in a bag, a manuscript in a handbag, a little girl in the snow.

26. Identify the author, speaker, and the person or persons addressed in two of these dramatic monologues: *Tithonus, My Last Duchess, The Bishop Orders His Tomb.*

27. Name the author and title of the following: a sonnet sequence addressed to her husband; a translation from the Persian; an edition of the papers of August Teufelsdröckh with commentary.

The Twentieth Century

28. What are the main geographical settings of the following works? *Heart of Darkness, Ulysses, The Waste Land, Things Fall Apart.*

29. What does Virginia Woolf suggest that a woman must have if she is to write fiction?

30. What is outside the interior which contains Nag, Nall, Hamm, and Clov?

31. Who killed the Angel in the House? Why did she do it?

32. Who wrote the following? "Poetry is not a turning loose of emotion, but an escape from emotion; it is not the expression of personality, but an escape from personality. But, of course, only those who have personality and emotions know what it means to want to escape from these things."

33. Identify the following:
    a. Shakespeare's sister
    b. The Easter Rising
    c. theater of the absurd
    d. the Great War
    e. stream of consciousness
    f. fatwa
    g. the British Commonwealth
    h. moments of being
    i. the partition of India
    j. Martian School of Poetry

For examples of short-answer questions on the historical introductions, see pp. 271–72.

A series of short-answer questions can be combined into a 15- to 20-minute question that tests the command of a particular author or work, as in the following example on Swift's *Gulliver's Travels:*

1. What are the main targets of satire in each of the four books of *Gulliver's Travels*?

2. How does the character of Gulliver contribute to the effect of the satire?

3. What aspect of human nature is chiefly criticized in the account of the *struldbruggs*?

4. In what ways does Part 4 sum up and conclude the themes of *Gulliver's Travels*?

Spot Passages

One of the most useful kinds of identification question asks the students to identify and also to comment on significant passages. The spot-passage examination has the virtue of focusing attention on the text and of developing the students' analytical skills. It is also relatively easy to make up, though selecting passages that are sufficiently prominent and distinctive and achieving a balance to cover the material of a course takes time. Disadvantages are that the exams tend to be long, and students, especially good students who have a lot to say, tend to get behind and feel considerable pressure.

There is almost always more to be said about a given passage than the allotted time permits. Therefore, one needs to decide how many passages the students can manage and to word the instructions so as to limit the parameters of the commentary. Only a minute or two are required to read a passage and to identify it by author, title, and speaker. Allowing six to seven minutes per passage, one might ask, in addition to identification: "In not more than a sentence or two, comment on whatever seems most significant or representative about the passage in context."

To prepare students for this type of question, one might advise them to avoid wasting time summarizing plot or simply paraphrasing the selected passage.

If one would like detailed commentary, and would be willing to reduce the number of passages so as to allow as much as eight to ten minutes each, one might direct the students to comment on the significance of specific details in the passage. The main reasons for asking students to elaborate on their comments is to train them to read closely and to give them a better chance to demonstrate imagination and originality.

Essay Exams Based on Passages

Answers to the latter type of question on passages border on brief analytical essays. One may give a sharper focus to such a question by arranging the passages in pairs and instructing the students to relate the members of a pair with respect to a specific topic, which may be stated simply as a word or phrase. The question could be worded as follows: "Relate the following passages on the topic suggested. Focus on the passages themselves and comment on the significance of specific details in them as they pertain to the topic. Avoid plot summary, paraphrase, and general interpretations except insofar as the latter bear directly on the passages. Make it clear in the course of your answer that you recognize and understand both passages." Writing about two passages in a single answer is a bit more economical than discussing them separately, and it creates opportunities for making connections within a larger work and comparisons between two writers and their works or between two works by the same writer. Thus students are actually writing short essays, grounded on the text, which may deal with characterization, structure, theme, tone, style, and so on. The three examples that follow illustrate how this method works. Note that in this question, identification, though still important, matters less than understanding. Students should have little difficulty in identifying these passages (for which they should get credit, of course), but the key to a really good answer is seeing how the passages fit together and using detail to support that relationship.

1. After the Fall

a. Farewell, happy fields,
Where joy forever dwells! Hail, horrors! hail,
Infernal world! and thou, profoundest Hell,
Receive thy new possessor, one who brings
A mind not to be changed by place or time.
The mind is its own place and in itself
Can make a Heaven of Hell, a Hell of Heaven.

b. Some natural tears they dropped, but wiped them soon;
The world was all before them, where to choose
Their place of rest, and Providence their guide.
They, hand in hand, with wandering steps and slow,
Through Eden took their solitary way.

2. Epic and mock-epic style

a. Thus Eve with countenance blithe her story told;
But in her cheek distemper flushing glowed.
On th' other side, Adam, soon as he heard
The fatal trespass done by Eve, amazed,
Astonied stood and blank, while horror chill
Ran through his veins, and all his joints relaxed;
From his slack hand the garland wreathed for Eve
Down dropped, and all the faded roses shed.

b. The meeting points the sacred hair dissever
From the fair head, forever, and forever!
Then flashed the living lightning from her eyes,
And screams of horror rend the affrighted skies.
Not louder shrieks to pitying heaven are cast,
When husbands, or when lapdogs breathe their last;
Or when rich china vessels fallen from high,
In glittering dust and painted fragments lie!

3. Treatments of the class system

a. I confess I feel somewhat bewildered by what you have just told me. To be born, or at any rate, bred in a handbag, whether it had handles or not, seems to me to display a contempt for the ordinary decencies of family life that reminds one of the worst excesses of the French Revolution. And I presume you know what that unfortunate movement led to? As for the particular locality in which the handbag was found, a cloak room at a railway station might serve to conceal a social indiscretion—has probably, indeed, been used for that purpose before now—but it could hardly be regarded as an assured basis for a recognized position in good society.

b. I hope you don't think I dirty my own hands with the work. Come! you wouldn't refuse the acquaintance of my mother's cousin the Duke of Belgravia because some of the rents he gets are earned in queer ways.

> You wouldn't cut the Archbishop of Canterbury, I suppose, because the Ecclesiastical Commissioners have a few publicans and sinners among their tenants. Do you remember your Crofts scholarship at Newnham? Well, that was founded by my brother the M.P. He gets his 22 per cent out of a factory with 600 girls in it, and not one of them getting wages enough to live on.

This kind of question can be made quite flexible by arranging the passages in pairs but placing the topics at the end and allowing students to write on them either individually or as pairs. This procedure gives them a chance to write on only one of a pair if they wish.

Exam Essays

In addition to brief identification or short-answer questions, a test might include one or more short essays, or it might consist of a single essay to take up almost the whole period for an hour-exam or a major part of a final. Some instructors like to word questions rather generally, letting students pick their own examples; others prefer to word questions specifically, limiting the choice to designated authors or texts. The possibilities are limitless. A few examples of both shorter and longer essays are given below.

TOPICS FOR 20- TO 30-MINUTE ESSAYS

Many of the sample short-answer questions listed above could easily be converted into brief essay questions. No. 4, for instance, is getting at the distinction that characters in the mystery plays are "historical," in the sense that they exist in the Bible, and that they are treated more or less realistically, while morality plays use allegorical figures. The same question could be expressed thus: "With reference to the mode of characterization in one of the mystery plays and in *Everyman*, explain the difference between the genres of the mystery and morality play." Writing on this topic, a good student could go further than in a short answer, pointing out that the difference between the genres is not altogether clear-cut: in the Nativity scene the shepherds become more symbolic; Everyman and his fairweather friends engage in some lively realistic dialogue.

On the other hand, longer essays that cover several writers can be scaled down to make a much shorter question. For example, in topic no. 19 below (p. 262), based on the quotation from *Don Juan*, "from Wollstonecraft to Woolf" might be changed to: "How would Wollstonecraft *or* Barrett Browning *or* Woolf respond to the quotation from Byron?" Many of the longer essay questions listed below can be broken up in the same way.

The advantage of short essays is that they allow time for other types of questions on the same test. They also tend to be fairly sharply focused, whereas long essays tend to elicit uneven writing and to become woollier as time runs out.

SAMPLE SHORT EXAM ESSAYS (20 TO 30 MINUTES)

1. Compare the role of women in one example of Old English or Old Irish epic or elegy (*Beowulf, The Wife's Lament, The Exile of the Sons of Uisliu*) and one example of medieval romance (*Lanval, Sir Gawain and the Green Knight, Morte Darthur*).

2. What does treasure signify in *Beowulf* and in *The Pardoner's Tales*, respectively, and in what ways do the attitudes toward treasure reflect the value system of a Christian poet in Anglo-Saxon England in late-fourteenth-century London?

3. In what ways is the Redcrosse Knight's encounter with Despair different from his previous encounters with villains in Book 1 of *The Faerie Queene*?

4. Compare the Redcrosse Knight with *either* Beowulf *or* Sir Gawain. How does the hero, faced with seemingly insuperable odds or in defeat, represent ideals of the heroic held by the author and his culture? You might focus your essay on the shields carried by these warriors and what these shields symbolize.

5. How does Chaucer's treatment of the Pardoner and Spenser's of Archimago reflect pre- and post-Reformation attitudes toward the Roman Catholic church?

6. Discuss the function of comedy in *The Second Shepherds' Play* and in *Dr. Faustus*. How does comedy contribute to the larger themes of these works. Does the comedy reinforce or problematize those themes?

7. Define in your own terms what is meant by a "metaphysical conceit," and give examples of two that seem to you to work well and of one that fails.

8. Compare the title characters of Cary's *Mariam* and Webster's *Duchess of Malfi* as rulers, wives, and heroines of tragedy.

9. Compare and contrast the country estates described in Jonson's *To Penshurst*, Lanyer's *A Description of Cooke-ham*, and Marvell's *Upon Appleton House*. Indicate how each of these estates relates to the resident community and to the society outside.

10. Briefly compare King David in Dryden's *Absalom and Achitophel* with the hero of Smart's *Song to David*.

11. Compare Boswell's and Burney's accounts of Johnson's conversation. Does Johnson's character seem to change when he talks to different people?

12. Briefly, what would Johnson have said about the Preface to *Lyrical Ballads* if he had been around to write a *Life of Wordsworth*?

13. Discuss the influence of the French Revolution on *two* of the following authors: Blake, Wollstonecraft, Wordsworth, Shelley.

14. Explain the different concepts of nature in Wordsworth's *Tintern Abbey*, Coleridge's *This Lime-Tree Bower My Prison*, and Percy Shelley's *Mont Blanc*.

15. What do *The Eve of St. Agnes* (a medieval romance narrative) and *Ode on a Grecian Urn* (a short meditation prompted by an antique artifact) have in common? Both were written by Keats. What else?

16. Briefly describe some differences between the Wordsworthian and the Keatsian odes, using the *Intimations Ode* and *Ode to a Nightingale* as your principal examples.

17. Compare the representation and concept of sensuality both in the poems *The Lady of Shalott* and *Goblin Market* and in the illustrations for both.

18. Compare the idea of comedy in *The Importance of Being Earnest* and *Mrs. Warren's Profession*.

19. Why does T. S. Eliot compare the Victorian poets Robert Browning and Tennyson so unfavorably to Donne in his essay *The Metaphysical Poets*?

20. In Mansfield's *The Garden Party*, the wealthy young protagonist Laura wishes to do away with the class distinctions that separate her from her poverty-stricken neighbors. Has Laura broken out of her class insularity by the end of the story?

21. Compare the diction, tone, and style of MacDiarmid's Scots dialect poetry and of his poems written in standard English.

22. How do two of the following writers portray the psychology of European colonialism? Conrad, Orwell, Gordimer, Achebe.

23. Who are the "barbarians" in Coetzee's *Waiting for the Barbarians*, Desai's *Scholar and Gypsy*, and Naipaul's *One Out of Many*?

24. Discuss the symbolic and narrative importance of the ritual sacrifice of Ikemefuna in Achebe's *Things Fall Apart*. How will the sacrifice affect Okonkwo's standing within the community and his relationship with Nwoye?

SAMPLE LONGER EXAM ESSAYS (45 TO 60 MINUTES)

1. Trace the Arthurian legend from the twelfth century through Malory's *Morte Darthur*. Specifically, what changes are there in the role of Arthur and in his relationship with his knights?

2. "What desireth God of me?" Everyman asks Death, and Death replies, "A reckoning." Discuss how *three* of the following characters or poets face their reckoning, and comment in each instance on how the reckoning is conceived in terms appropriate to the genre or type of the work in question: (a) Sir Gawain at the Green Chapel, (b) the Redcrosse Knight in the Cave of Despair, (c) John Donne on his deathbed or sickbed, (d) Herbert marveling at the Lord's "returns," (e) Milton as the "uncouth swain" in *Lycidas*, (f) Everyman in *Everyman*.

3. Identify and give an approximate date for three of the following quotations, and discuss how the conception of Jesus Christ in them is representative of the culture and the work from which each is taken:

a. "Then the young hero stripped himself—that was God Almighty."
b. "In the plate armor of Piers the Plowman, this jouster shall ride."
c. "All our mothers bear us to pain and to dying. But our very [true] mother Jesu, he alone beareth us to joy and to endless living."
d. "What is he, this lordling, that cometh from the fight / With blood-rede [garment] so grislich ydight [arrayed]?"

4. In the headnote to *Piers Plowman*, the editors note about Will the Dreamer, "But mere knowledge is not enough for him: he must learn by experience and feel in his heart what he learns." Show how this statement applies to Will and to two other medieval or Renaissance figures (possibilities include Julian of Norwich, the Redcrosse Knight, Astrophil, Faustus, King Lear, Adam and Eve).

5. The hero has been defined in a variety of ways in medieval and Renaissance literature. Write an essay that traces the changing conceptions of the hero in these periods. Be sure to focus on important attributes, physical descriptions, definitions of heroic action, and the forms the enemy takes in your assessment of this question. What different kinds of heroes have we seen? Why does the conception of the hero change over time?

6. Insofar as these can be inferred from *The Canterbury Tales*, compare Chaucer's notions about literature as an agent of moral education with those of Sidney and Spenser. What historical developments in the sixteenth century might explain differences in their literary theories?

7. Discuss the representation or metaphoric presence of other worlds and cultures in two or three texts (e.g., *Lanval*, *The Wife of Bath's Tale*, *Utopia*, *The Faerie Queene*, *Gulliver's Travels*, *Rasselas*). How do these "other worlds" serve to sustain *and/or* subvert the dominant ideological agendas of the works themselves?

8. How does Faustus represent the attractions and dangers inherent in sixteenth-century humanism when the goals and ideals of humanism are ignored?

9. Johnson famously complained that Milton's *Lycidas* is "a pastoral, easy, vulgar, and therefore disgusting." But pastoral was an important and valued literary mode in the sixteenth and seventeenth centuries. Define that mode and indicate how it is used and to what purposes in any three of the following: Spenser's *Shepheardes Calender*, Marlowe's *The Passionate Shepherd*, Marvell's Mower poems, Milton's *Lycidas*, Herrick's *Corinna's Going A-Maying*, Book 4 of Milton's *Paradise Lost*.

10. Is autobiography imagined as, in some special way, a "woman's" genre in the Middle Ages and Renaissance? Discuss how female authors and characters present their own lives and to what purposes they do so in three of the following texts: Chaucer's *The Wife of Bath's Prologue*; Speght's *Dream*; Moulsworth's *Memorandum*; Trapnel's *Report and Plea*; Milton's *Paradise Lost*, specifically the characters Sin and Eve; Cavendish's *True Relation of My Birth and Breeding*. Are there comparable self-analyses by male writers and characters?

11. "Thus is man that great and true amphibium whose nature is disposed to live not only like other creatures in diverse elements but in divided and distinguished worlds"—Sir Thomas Browne, *Religio Medici*. What are these "divided and distinguished worlds," and how is the tension between them experienced by characters in three works, including one from the early seventeenth century and one from the Restoration or eighteenth century?

12. In what ways is *Paradise Lost* also the story of Milton's life, and the Miltonic narrator a character who participates in the story as he tells it? Compare Milton's narrative self-portrait with those of two other writers we have studied. How does their fictive self as the speaker of their poems or as narrator or as a character in one of their fictions correspond to what we know about them from other sources, including their own writings?

13. Choose *three* of the following settings and discuss how, either directly or by implication, they reflect their authors' views about the social and political health of England: Faerielond (Spenser), Amalfi and Rome (Webster), Venice (Jonson), Jerusalem (Dryden), Vanity Fair (Bunyan), Hyde Park (Congreve), Hampton Court (Pope), Lilliput (Swift).

14. "The way of the world" stands for the principles that really drive society, not for high-minded ideals that nobody follows in practice. Compare those principles as they are acted out in Congreve's *The Way of the World* and Gay's *The Beggar's Opera.* What do people actually want, according to each of those works, and how do they get it?

15. Describe the various notions of wit that are offered by Addison, Pope, and Johnson, and show how those notions help to shed light on some witty passages in Restoration and eighteenth-century texts of your choice.

16. It is sometimes said that the Romantic period was one in which writers "rediscovered" nature. It could hardly be said, however, that eighteenth-century writers like Swift, Pope, Johnson, or Gray ignored the natural world and its images. It seems the case, rather, that writers from the earlier century looked on nature in somewhat different ways than the Romantics. Compare the work of *two* writers from the earlier period with that of *two* of the Romantics so as to discuss what seem to you the most important and revealing differences between them in their treatment of the natural world.

17. Compare Byron's Manfred and Mary Shelley's Frankenstein as Faustian overreachers (characters who attempt to go beyond human limitations to make use of supernatural power). Why do they suffer from remorse? Which character gets more sympathy from the reader (i.e., you)?

18. Discuss the Romantics' concern with communion (relatedness, connectedness, "togetherness," friendship, love, and so on). Name some writers and works treating the subject and explain (with selected examples) what they desire connection *with*.

19. "Man's love is of man's life a thing apart,
'Tis woman's whole existence."

Do you agree that this man's formulation (though attributed to a woman—it's from Donna Julia's letter to Don Juan) sums up "the woman question" from Wollstonecraft to Woolf? Discuss with reference to the situations of selected women authors and characters.

20. Why does Burns move in and out of Scots dialect in *To a Mouse*? In particular, trace the different effects of the language of the first stanza ("Thou need na start awa sae hasty, / Wi bickering brattle!") and the second ("I'm truly sorry man's dominion / Has broken nature's social union"). Think about the poet's choice of language (dialect vs. standard English) in the following paired works: Burns's *Auld Lang Syne* and *Afton Water*; Baillie's *Woo'd and married and a* and *Up! Quit thy bower*; Scott's *Jock of Hazeldean* and *Lochinvar*.

21. Can we read Robinson's *The Poor Singing Dame* as allegorical of the plight of the woman poet in a culture hostile to female authorship? Who does the Lord of the castle represent, and why is there such a pronounced class difference between this Lord and the old Dame in her poor little hovel? Explain why the Lord is haunted to death at the end of the ballad.

22. Dryden, Johnson, Wordsworth, Coleridge, Arnold, Pater, T. S. Eliot, and Woolf make up a distinguished line of critics, but they are critics working from different premises and preaching different aims and values to the publics they address. Compare and contrast the critical aims and methods of *three* critics, each from a different period.

23. A number of writers we have studied—Blake, Browning, Ruskin, Pater, Rossetti, and Yeats—were themselves either draftsmen and painters or strongly interested in the relationship between literature and the visual arts. Their interest in this relationship took for each of them, however, a variety of different preoccupations and forms. Compare and contrast the different interests of three or four writers in the visual arts and its effect on their work.

24. It is often said that the greatest influence on Victorian poetry was the novel. Argue for or against this proposition, discussing the work of at least five poets, including Tennyson, Browning, and Barrett Browning.

25. Choosing six women writers from *NAEL*, describe the way in which you think gender shapes their work.

26. Such writers as Milton, Pope, Johnson, Byron, Shelley, Arnold, Swinburne, Housman, and Eliot, among others, were all strongly influenced by the classics. However, they looked back to the civilizations of ancient Greece and Rome with quite different attitudes and values in mind. Compare and contrast three writers from at least two different periods with respect to the ways they drew on the spirit of the classics.

27. Identify the use of non-Standard English in any one or more twentieth-century text(s), and discuss the effects of features of the language such as words or word order which you do not associate with Standard English.

28. Write a response to *Achebe's An Image of Africa: Racism in Conrad's "Heart of Darkness,"* either defending *Heart of Darkness* on literary and/or historical grounds, or considering the broader question of the political content of literary texts and their relation to the "task of the artist."

29. How have writers in different periods responded to advances in "natural philosophy" or science—e.g., as a contributor to human progress, evidence of God's universal plan, a meaningless and often filthy investigation of trivia, a threat to religion and the humanities, an instrument of patriarchy? Discuss with reference to three writers from at least two different periods. They might be drawn from the following list: Bacon, Newton, Swift, Pope, Keats, Tennyson, Browning, Arnold, Huxley, Raine (*A Martian Sends a Postcard Home*), Adcock (*The Ex-Queen among the Astronomers*).

30. It has been said that ours is "the anti-heroic age," but if that is so, it has been in progress for a long time. When would you date its beginnings, and what do you think caused it? Discuss with reference to anti-heroes or anti-heroines by at least four writers. If you wish, you may argue that our age is as heroic as any, only our ideas of heroism have changed.

31. Read Heaney and Boland as specifically Irish poets. What is lost and what is gained by such an interpretive move?

32. "Going native" entails, among other things, losing one's own cultural identity as one becomes subsumed within a different culture, like Kurtz in Conrad's *Heart of Darkness*. For the Western imperialist, "going native" involves a movement into the seeming conditions of savagery or primitivism often associated by Westerners with non-Westerners. Discuss Desai's ironic, postcolonial use of the theme or motif of "going native" in *Scholar and Gypsy*.

Paper Topics

The following topics are designed for short essays of approximately three to four typewritten pages (750 to 1000 words). They cover a range of subjects in *NAEL*. A few of them are meant to develop techniques of analysis and close reading; most simply provide a chance to delve more deeply into works and into issues that can be dealt with only quite generally in class. It is a good idea to accompany the first paper assignment with some instructions about format, citations, and organization. If the object is to talk about the text, students might be warned away from long general introductions.

1. Compare the *Beowulf* poet's treatment of Grendel and the dragon. Do these monsters contribute to our understanding of the ethical/social values of Anglo-Saxon society? What purpose does the monster serve in the poem? Do Grendel and the dragon represent different kinds of evil?

2. Discuss the use of humor and satire by Marie de France in *Lanval* and by Chaucer and the Wife of Bath as the narrator of *The Wife's of Bath's Tale*. What is she/he making fun of—chivalry, romance, men, women? How can we differentiate Chaucer's comedy from Marie's and the Wife's?

3. How do clerks use scripture to attack the Wife of Bath and Margery Kempe? How does each woman use scripture in her defense?

4. In view of the striking differences between Old English and Middle English literature, is there any real justification in lumping these works together and referring to them as "medieval" literature? What, after all, do Chaucer and Langland have in common with the poets of *The Dream of the Rood*, *Beowulf*, and *The Wanderer* that sets them apart from later literature?

5. Choose and analyze a portrait from *The General Prologue* not discussed in class. Can you detect irony in the choice of details or in the tone? What is the pilgrim's "degree"—i.e., rank—and can you compare him with other pilgrims? Or discuss two portraits of pilgrims related in some way (e.g., Knight / Squire, Prioress / Monk, Sergeant of the Law / Franklin, Parson / Plowman, Miller / Reeve, Summoner / Pardoner). In what ways do the details in the pair complement one another?

6. Look up the story of Noah and the Great Flood in the Bible. How has the story been adapted for comic purposes by the author of *The Chester Play of Noah's Flood* and by Chaucer in *The Miller's Tale*?

7. The Green Knight says that he has only come to Arthur's court to ask "a Christmas game" (1.164, line 283). Much of the action in *Sir Gawain and the Green Knight* revolves around various kinds of games (including hunting games). How are all these games connected? What is the Green Knight's "game"? Is the poet also playing a game with the reader?

8. Look up Ephesians 6.12–16 and apply St. Paul's symbolism in this passage to *Sir Gawain and the Green Knight* and to *Passus 18* of *Piers Plowman* (the Crucifixion and Harrowing of Hell). What is the significance of armor and tournaments in these works?

9. Both *Everyman* and *The Second Shepherds' Play* attempt to deliver religious doctrine through a dramatic structure. Choose either the morality or the mystery play and discuss the strategies it employs to educate the audience about the truths of Christian experience. Be sure you think about these plays in dramatic terms. You might even want to discuss how to produce and stage it in order to bring out its doctrine.

10. Compare the treatment of the Crucifixion in *The Dream of the Rood* with that in either *Piers Plowman* or *Julian of Norwich's Showings*. Can you draw any conclusion about differences between Old and Middle English culture?

11. Write an analysis of a sixteenth-century sonnet. Consider such elements as structure, diction, imagery, figures of speech and symbols, tone, versification, and the sound of the language, though not all of these are equally important, and you should concentrate on only those aspects that are truly relevant and revealing. The object is to show the means by which the poem achieves its effects—whatever meaning and feeling it conveys. Consult the appendix on poetic forms, 1.2944–50. (Instructors will probably want to specify the sonnets the students may choose from.)

12. Discuss the character of Time (often personified) in Elizabethan sonnet sequences, especially Shakespeare's. Is the sense of time in Renaissance poetry in any way different from that in medieval works you have read (e.g., *Sir Gawain and the Green Knight*) or the mystery plays?

13. Explicate one of Shakespeare's sonnets both as a separate poem and as part of the sequence. You will want to read a few of the sonnets that precede and those that follow in *NAEL* or at the library. Do other poems in the sequence clarify the meaning? Instructors may want to specify the sonnet or provide a limited choice.

14. Write a comparative analysis of a pair of poems on a similar theme. Compare and contrast such aspects as (a) situation and point of view (what is stated or implied about the speaker, person(s) addressed, and circumstances), (b) figurative language (see 1.2934–37; 2.2950–53), (c) tone, (d) diction, (e) versification (see 1.2944–47; 2.2928–31), (f) rhyme scheme or stanza form (see 1.2948–50; 2.2932–34). You don't need to talk about all of these elements, though. Focus on those that lend themselves to a significant comparison. In conclusion, in what respects does each poem exhibit the individual style of its author; in what respects does it belong to a "school" (see 1.2953; 2.2937)? Possible pairs: Marlowe, *The Passionate Shepherd to His Love*, and Donne, *The Bait*; Herrick, *To the Virgins, to Make Much of Time*, and Marvell, *To His Coy Mistress*; Donne, *Sonnet 10* ("Death be not proud"), and Herbert, *Death*; Waller, *Song* ("Go, lovely rose!"), and Herbert, *Virtue*; Jonson, *Still to Be Neat*, and Herrick, *Delight in Disorder*.

15. Briefly, compare Spenser's representation of the Seven Deadly Sins in the House of Pride with Langland's portraits of Envy and Gluttony. In what ways does Spenser's procession resemble Renaissance painting (you might look at some books of Renaissance art at the library)? Is the procession just for show, or does it have a meaningful function in Book 1?

16. Lady Mary Wroth, the poetic heir of her famous uncle Sir Philip Sidney, exercised her own poetic strategies in her sonnet sequence *Pamphilia to Amphilanthus*. How does the language she uses about love and desire differ from that

used by Donne? Are the differences comprehensible in terms of gender ideologies about proper male and female social roles? Is female desire represented differently from male desire? Look carefully at the imagery and discuss several poems in detail.

17. Dryden claimed Milton told him that Spenser was his "original"—presumably a primary poetic influence. Where do you see Spenserian influences in Milton's poetry, and how important is that influence in *Paradise Lost*? In what ways does Milton depart radically from that "original"? Look beyond the allegorical characters to questions of moral choice, portrayals of character, verse form, subject matter, politics, conceptions of history, and so on.

18. How does Milton use imagery (both literal and figurative description) to manipulate the reader's response to Satan? Discuss examples from the first two books and some of the later books. Can you trace an emerging pattern?

19. How do the treatments of Cromwell by Milton, Lilburne, Winstanley, and Hyde display different factions during the Civil War? Does a close reading of Marvell's *Horatian Ode* reveal any partisanship? Can you as a modern reader construct a true portrait of Cromwell from these documents, and to what degree must your construction take into account your personal twentieth-century biases?

20. In classical epic the gods play an active role in determining the fates of people. This is often referred to as "celestial machinery," defined as "the supernatural agents in epic action" (1.2526). How has Milton adapted celestial machinery in *Paradise Lost*; how has Pope, following Milton, used it in *The Rape of the Lock*?

21. Compare and contrast any two of the following as religious poets: Donne, Herbert, Vaughan, Crashaw. How do they represent themselves, their relationships to God, and the special responsibilities of the religious poet? Consider how their choices of subject, verse form, genre, and imagery bear on these issues.

22. What cultural differences emerge from a comparison of the treatments of madness in *King Lear* and *A Tale of a Tub*?

23. "Unhappy woman's but a slave at large," according to Mary Leapor. Discuss several Restoration and eighteenth-century works—for instance, *Oroonoko, Marriage A-la-Mode*, and *The Life of Olaudah Equiano*—that deal with the situation of women and/or slaves. How well does Leapor's analogy hold? Where might it break down?

24. Many eighteenth-century poems, including Pope's *Epistle to Dr. Arbuthnot*, Swift's *Verses on the Death of Dr. Swift*, and Gray's *Elegy*, conclude by drawing an idealized portrait of the poet's own character. Compare such portraits in three poems (at least one by a woman). What aspects of the self are singled out for praise?

25. Does the last book of *Gulliver's Travels* prove what we have suspected all along—that Swift is both a misanthrope and a misogynist?

26. To what extent is "P" in Pope's *Epistle to Dr. Arbuthnot* a projection of the poet himself? To what extent is he a dramatic persona, a mask assumed to project several different and changing views of himself in what amounts to a brilliant self-defense?

27. Compare Dr. Johnson's self-portraits as "Sober" (*Idler* No. 31) and Imlac (*Rasselas*) with the images of him in Boswell's biography and Burney's journals. How well do they complement one another?

28. Select one of the complementary pairs of poems in *Songs of Innocence and of Experience* (e.g., *Lamb / Tyger*; the two *Chimney Sweeper* poems; the two *Nurse's Song* poems). How do they illustrate Blake's thesis that they show "Two Contrary States of the Human Soul"? Study the Blake illustrations in *NAEL*, and find in the library an edition of Blake's engravings; discuss this artwork in relation to the thesis mentioned above.

29. Discuss Coleridge's "conversation" poems as a genre. The two best are *This Lime-Tree Bower My Prison* and *Frost at Midnight*. Analyze one of them, focusing on some but not all of the following:

a. the structure—how the poem is organized, and whether or not it holds together
b. nature description (and the relation of the description to the ideas of the poem)
c. the philosophical/religious content

A variant of this general topic would be to compare *Frost at Midnight* with Wordsworth's *Tintern Abbey* (the latter written a few months after the former).

30. Consider the causality in *The Rime of the Ancient Mariner*. Wordsworth criticized the plot as "having no necessary connection." Discuss connection and lack of connection in the poem. Where do we know why things happen, and where do we not know? Is it a fault not to be told why something happens?

31. Compare Percy Shelley's *Alastor*, Mary Shelley's *Frankenstein*, and Byron's *Manfred*. The three authors were in close association during 1815–16, the years in which they composed the poem, novel, and play, respectively. List and discuss some of the concerns that the three works have in common.

32. Compare ideas of nature and natural process in Percy Shelley's *Ode to the West Wind* and Keats's *To Autumn*. Other poems (and poets, both male and female) can be added or substituted from the course reading list, and they don't have to mention seasons!

33. Discuss causes of melancholy or dejection in poems by Smith (the sonnets), Wordsworth (e.g., *Tintern Abbey, Resolution and Independence, Ode: Intimations of Immortality*), Coleridge (e.g., introductory note and poetic text of *Kubla Khan, Dejection: An Ode*), and Keats (e.g., *La Belle Dame, Ode to a Nightingale, Ode on Melancholy*). Choose two or three poems and consider both causes and solutions to the problems.

34. What arguments and rhetorical strategies do Wollstonecraft's *A Vindication of the Rights of Men* and *A Vindication of the Rights of Woman* share? Given the concerns of the former text, is it surprising that two years later Wollstonecraft compared the situation of women to that of the poor, brought up in ignorance? What do you make of her assertion that women are also like the rich of both sexes, trained in folly and vice, and soldiers, instructed in gallantry, prejudice, and blind submission to authority? What is the effect of her making such a trio of comparisons?

35. Consider Robinson's two poems of the city, *London's Summer Morning* and *January, 1795*, as seasonal poems. You might find it useful to contrast Blake's

lyrics *To Spring* and *To Autumn*, which use the conventions of apostrophe, personification of the season, and imagery drawn from the natural world. How does Robinson convey the essence of the season of summer or winter using only the cityscape and its human inhabitants? Given that Robinson's poems, written in the same year, share certain strategies—both proceed by means of itemization and addition, both use figurative language sparingly—how do they manage to achieve such different effects?

36. Discuss the historical context of any one of Browning's dramatic monologues. What relationship does the poem have to problems and issues of the Victorian period? Why has Browning chosen to present them in a historical setting?

37. *In Memoriam* and *Thysis* are both elegies for close college friends of the authors. What differences in form are there between these poems? Despite differences in form, do you find similarities in dealing with grief and similarities in the resolutions?

38. A literary "source" is material a writer has adapted and reworked for his own ends. Nearly all of Chaucer's tales and Shakespeare's plays are based on sources. Comparing a work with its source to see what has been added, changed, or left out can tell us a lot about an author's intentions and methods. Compare Tennyson's *Ulysses* with its source in Canto 26 of Dante's *Inferno* or compare *The Passing of Arthur* with its source in Malory's *Morte Darthur* (1.430–35).

39. Compare the representation of English civilization in Arnold's *Culture and Anarchy* and Kipling's *The Man Who Would Be King*.

40. Compare the use of the supernatural in Coleridge's *Christabel* and Gaskell's *The Old Nurse's Story*.

41. Discuss the ways in which singing birds—Hardy's aged thrush and Yeats's creature of hammered gold—are figurations of the poet in *The Darking Thrush* and *Sailing to Byzantium*. In general, how is nature represented in these poems?

42. "Irish is not my language. . . . I'm sick of my own country, sick of it!" In Joyce's *The Dead*, the protagonist Gabriel reveals a great deal of ambivalence about Irish culture, Irish history, Irish nationalism, and his own Irish identity. Compare Yeats's ambivalence about Ireland, particularly Irish nationalist politics, in *No Second Troy, September 1913*, and *To a Shade*.

43. Most of the great modernist writers (e.g., Conrad, Joyce, Yeats, Eliot, Woolf) are closer in time to the Victorian age than they are to us. *The Waste Land* and *Ulysses* (1922) are chronologically closer to *Idylls of the King* than they are to the early twenty-first century. Choose a pair of nineteenth- and early-twentieth-century works and write an essay pointing out what continuities and what differences you find. In what respects, if any, is the twentieth-century work closer to your own time than the corresponding nineteenth-century work? If in some respects you feel more attracted to the earlier work, explain why you feel that way. Some possible pairings: Burns's *To a Mouse* and Lawrence's *Snake*; Keats's *Ode to a Nightingale* and Hardy's *Darkling Thrush*; Arnold's *Thyrsis* and Auden's *In Memory of W. B. Yeats*; Wordsworth's *Ode: Intimations of Immortality* and Yeats's *Among School Children*; Wollstonecraft's *A Vindication of the Rights of Woman* and Woolf's *A Room of One's Own* and *Professions for Women*; a pair of your own choice.

44. Compare the District Commissioner's scholarly treatise, The Pacification of the Primitive Tribes of the Lower Niger (Achebe, *Things Fall Apart*), with Kurtz's pamphlet for the International Society for the Suppression of Savage Customs (Conrad, *Heart of Darkness*). Why is each man writing his document, and how does his document elucidate his other work as a colonizer? How does each understand or classify the native peoples? Would Kurtz approve of the District Commissioner's methods, and vice versa?

45. Compare treatments of sexuality in one of the following pairs of works: *The Rape of the Lock* / *Visions of the Daughters of Albion, Christabel* / *Goblin Market, The Eve of St. Agnes* / *Don Juan, The Waste Land* / *The Horse-Dealer's Daughter*.

46. Discuss the intersecting representations of sexuality and class in Lawrence's *Odour of Chrysanthemums* and Munro's *Walker Brothers Cowboy*. How do class-based aspirations and class differences between marital partners cause or aggravate domestic tension in each of these stories?

47. Compare and contrast Gordimer's *The Moment Before the Gun Went Off* and Coetzee's *Waiting for the Barbarians* as both explore the psychology of colonialism—that is, the ways in which one group explains, justifies, and perpetuates its systematic dominance over another.

48. Walcott's *The Glory Trumpeter* sounds a lament for all whom race and exile have defeated. Discuss the treatment of race and exile in this and one other Walcott poem and in Naipaul's *One Out of Many*.

49. Irony is sometimes described as "the English disease." Analyze the different uses of irony in works by any of the following: Woolf, Lawrence, Smith, Larkin, MacNeice.

50. Discuss the parallels and differences between any of the following pairs of texts: Housman's *Epitaph on an Army of Mercenaries* and MacDiarmid's *Another Epitaph on an Army of Mercenaries*; Brooke's *The Soldier* and Owen's *Anthem for Doomed Youth*; Woolf's *Modern Fiction* and Lawrence's *Why the Novel Matters*; Joyce's *The Dead* and Mansfield's *The Garden Party*. Your answer should refer to form, structure, and style, as well as to subject matter.

51. Pick out a work of some length (at least as long as one of Keats's odes) that you found strange or difficult but finally liked a lot. Explain why you found the work difficult, and devise a plan for teaching it either to high school students or to undergraduates (state who your audience is). What sort of information do the students need beyond what the introductions and notes provide? How would you get across the historical importance of the work; how would you explain to students what it means to you and help them to find personal meaning and significance in the work today?

Creative Assignments

1. Write a sonnet in imitation of Elizabethan sonnets. Use the English form of three quatrains ending with a couplet, and be careful to observe the meter and rhyme scheme. It need not be a good poem, but it should at least be technically correct. If you want to try this but can't think of anything to say, find a prose translation of Petrarch's or Ronsard's sonnets in the library and translate one of these as freely as you like into an English sonnet.

2. Write a satire in verse or prose, imitating either Pope's mock-heroic couplets or Swift's creation of a persona, as in the *Abolishing of Christianity in England* or *A Modest Proposal*. For your subject, choose any aspect of contemporary life in America. For example, following Swift, you might make an argument that abolishing grades might, as things now stand, be attended with some inconveniences, and perhaps not produce those many good effects proposed thereby. If you choose Pope, use his technique of treating the trivial as though it were of immense importance, though you needn't employ all sorts of classical rhetoric. If you imitate Swift, make your persona consistent and convincing. Keep the target of your satire constantly in view.

3. It is often said that Pope mastered the heroic couplet in his translations of Homer. Imitating Pope's style, translate some earlier passage in *NAEL* into heroic couplets. Some possible subjects might be a portrait from Chaucer's *General Prologue*, a famous speech from one of Shakespeare's plays, a passage from *Paradise Lost*, Surrey's blank verse translation of Virgil (1.576), Golding's translation of Ovid in "fourteeners" (1.601). In the latter cases, look up the prose translations of the originals in the Loeb Classics at the library. Do at least twenty-five couplets; then write a two-page essay on the art of the heroic couplet and the problems you encountered in your imitation.

4. In the manner of Browning, write a dramatic monologue in blank verse, spoken by one of the authors or characters in *NAEL* (e.g., Hazlitt on an outing with Coleridge and Wordsworth, the Wedding Guest telling someone about his encounter with the Ancient Mariner).

5. Write a parody of a student paper, using for your title " 'Who killed Simon Gascoyne? And why?': Appearance and Reality in *The Real Inspector Hound*."

Study Questions

Study questions can be a great help to the students, especially at the beginning of the course. Study questions, however, are no substitute for the texts, and, after a time, the texts should certainly begin to generate their own questions and incentives. Instructors will have to decide for themselves for how long such handouts are profitable and at what point they become a form of well-meaning pedagogic interference. Students might be advised to use the questions as long as they seem to help with the reading and to discard them when they get in the way. It would be too bad to take away a student's pleasure and initiative by asking the very questions that he or she might well have thought of unassisted.

Study questions can take many forms. There may be a whole battery of them to guide students through a text. Or there may be just one or two to start students thinking along the right track. We provide sample questions for the Middle Ages and the Romantic period introductions and a long (A) and a short (B) form of study questions for three assignments.

Sample Study Questions

1. HISTORICAL INTRODUCTIONS

A. The Middle Ages

1. Into what three periods is medieval English literature divided?

2. To what family of tribes did the Angles and Saxons belong?

3. Why was most of the poetry of these tribes lost?

4. How was King Alfred indirectly responsible for the preservation of some of this poetry?

5. What is the form (i.e., the organizing principle of versification) in which Old English poetry was composed?

6. How did Old English poets represent biblical figures like Moses or Christ in terms of their own literary tradition?

7. What was the ancestry of the Norman conquerors of Britain? What language did they speak?

8. What language would have been used by a monk writing a theological treatise? During the period from 1066 to approximately 1200, what language would have been used by a poet writing a romance for the English court?

9. Point out one major difference between the subject matter of Old English and Middle English literature.

10. What pseudo-historical figure is Layamon's Brut named for, and what did he do?

11. In the Middle Ages, what distinction was there between the Britons and the English peoples? Which was King Arthur's nationality, and who were the invaders against whom he fought?

12. What is the name of the genre under which we classify adventure stories in the later Middle Ages? In what country was that genre chiefly developed?

13. What is the predominant subject matter of extant medieval literature?

14. Who were the three major authors of Middle English literature and during what quarter-century were they writing?

15. Name the first English printer and a major work he published.

B. The Romantic Period

1. Name two events of the French Revolution that alienated its English supporters.

2. What were the consequences of the Napoleonic wars for political life in England?

3. What did Disraeli mean by the "Two Nations"?

4. What was the Peterloo Massacre?

5. What reforms were instituted by the 1832 Reform Bill?

6. According to neoclassic poetic theory, art is "imitation." What key word would define the nature of art in Romantic theory?

7. According to neoclassic poetic theory, art should be produced according to rules. According to Romantic theory, how should art be produced?

8. Are Shelley's *Ode to the West Wind* and Keats's *Ode to a Nightingale* simply nature poems about the wind and a nightingale?

9. What quality in the experience of children was prized by the Romantic poets?

10. What qualities in medieval literature appealed to Romantic poets?

11. In what sense, according to Romantic theory, might an imperfect work of art be better than a perfect one?

12. What changes in journalism were instituted by the *Edinburgh Review*?

13. Name the three best-known essayists of the period.

14. Name the two major novelists of the period.

1. THE GENERAL PROLOGUE TO THE CANTERBURY TALES

A.

1. Focus on the first eighteen lines. What does the description of spring have to do with going on pilgrimage? Why does Chaucer begin in this way? How does he define the motives for going on pilgrimage? What do you know about pilgrimages? Who was Becket, and why did people seek him out?

2. Do you find your feelings about the Prioress (lines 118–62) changing as you read her portrait? In the end, do you like her or do you have some reservations?

3. Now look at the portrait of the Monk (lines 165–207). What was the idea of entering a monastery? What would you expect a monk to be like? Does this monk meet your expectations? Do you approve of him or not?

4. What can you conclude from the narrator's observations about the Monk (look especially at lines 183–88). Is he very perceptive? Judgmental?

5. Examine the Friar (lines 208–71) in the same way. Is there any discrepancy between what we are being told about him and the way we react to him?

6. The narrator tells us that he has tried to arrange the pilgrims in order of their "degree," i.e., their social rank, but he's not sure he has succeeded (lines 745–48). Are there other ways of ranking the pilgrims, and how might that change the order?

7. What is the narrator apologizing for in lines 727–48? How does he present himself to his audience?

8. What agreement does the Host make with the pilgrims? What are his motives in proposing it?

9. Chaucer says he doesn't know whether it was "aventure, or sort, or cas" (luck, fate, or chance) that the Knight drew the short straw to determine that he would tell the first tale. What do you think it was?

B.

What is the principle of order behind the arrangement of the portraits? Is there any irony in that order? Would you agree that the Prioress, Monk, and Friar are outstanding members of their religious orders?

2. THE RIME OF THE ANCIENT MARINER

A.

1. Is the Mariner released from the curse at the end or not? Though he is allowed to return to port, why is he compelled to pass "from land to land" telling his story? Can this be understood as a punishment or a redemptive act? (His blessing of the water snakes is usually taken to be the act that redeems him.) Is the Hermit, a representative of orthodox religion, of any help to him?

2. Is the simple moral (lines 614–17) adequate to the poem as a whole, or does it characterize the Mariner, who is a simple man? Is it of any relevance or comfort to the Mariner or to the Wedding Guest? Coleridge once said of the poem that it should have next to no moral.

3. Robert Penn Warren interprets the poem by noting which parts take place by moonlight and which by sunlight. In his reading, the moon symbolizes the imagination. Does this make sense, and does the scheme work out consistently?

4. Another critic, E. E. Bostetter, interprets the poem as symbolic of alienation, especially relevant to Coleridge's life but also of more general application. He compares the Mariner's final situation to that of the inspired poet at the end of *Kubla Khan*. The poem stimulates such interpretations because it seems so obviously symbolical. Many nineteenth-century critics, however, insisted it was only an imitation of a medieval ballad. Which way of looking at the poem do you prefer, and why?

5. Why *did* the Mariner shoot the albatross? Is it a symbolic action, or is it completely inexplicable, the way things in ballads sometimes are?

B.

The Ancient Mariner seems to belong to the archetype of a figure who is forced to wander the earth in order to expiate a curse. Think about the symbolism of the story: Why does the Mariner's action have such enormous consequences not only for himself but for the crew? Has he expiated the curse or does it continue? Why might the Wedding Guest be a "sadder" and a "wiser" man? What has he learned, and does wisdom make one sad?

3. THE LADY OF SHALOTT

A.

1. One can read this story literally, but it is strongly evocative of allegory. What is its subject? What is the poem about? Could you connect it in any way with the young Tennyson? Can you connect it in any way with yourself?

2. What do mirrors represent generally as symbols? What does this mirror represent?

3. What might the destruction of the mirror represent?

4. What are the basic differences between the Lady's island and the surrounding countryside?

5. Can you find color symbolism in the poem?

6. How does the use of repetition, especially of the rhymes *Shalott, Lancelot, Camelot,* affect one's response to the poem? In medieval poetry such identical sounds were called "rich rhymes," but later poets avoided them. Why would Tennyson insist on them in this poem?

B.

Try to devise an allegorical interpretation of the poem that accounts for the Lady of Shalott's confinement to her tower, her weaving, her mirror, the breaking of the mirror, and her death.

APPENDIX A

Special Problems in Teaching Poetry and Drama

We want to address two general problems: teaching lyric poetry and teaching the staging of drama. The first involves strategies of reading; the second involves imagining plays in performance on the stages for which they were written. We provide general questions about poetry that have proved helpful to students in the past and a brief history of English stages that amplifies the discussions of pre-nineteenth-century staging in *NAEL* with information about the evolution of theaters, scenery, costuming, and acting styles.

Teaching Lyrics

Lyrics are generally the hardest of all assignments to teach because students often come into a course in literary history with very little training in reading poems that contain no narrative thread. Most students have enjoyed reading fiction and watching drama on the stage, on television, or at the movies, and they feel comparatively at ease with those forms even when they happen to be written in verse. Faced with a lyric that doesn't obviously tell a story, however, students feel at a loss because they don't know what to look for.

Even though a historical approach is not the same as an introduction to poetry, the two are not incompatible. While one would want to avoid giving the impression that there is a "method" for anatomizing all poems, some instructors may wish to provide their students with a set of preliminary questions, with the caution that these are just a way to begin thinking about poems, especially difficult poems.

Exploratory Questions for the Analysis of Poetry

1. What is the meter, rhyme scheme, and stanza form, if the poem has these features? (Old-fashioned as this approach may be, it remains a useful way to classify and to identify poems, an inducement in a class where the exams will require the identification of passages. More important, this question may become part of a program to get students to listen to poems and to identify their characteristics by ear, not just by the way they look on the page.) Students may be referred to the appendix on poetic forms in *NAEL*. See also Appendix B in this *Guide*, which contains a scansion exercise and suggestions for reading poetry aloud.
2. Does the poem have a relevant historical or generic context? Is it an occasional poem? Is it addressed to a private or to a public audience; or are we meant to be overhearing the poet's solitary meditation? Supposing yourself to be the poet's contemporary, would you already be familiar with similar poems; and, if so, does this poem resemble the others or is it in any respects different or original?
3. Does the poem contain any particular setting or circumstances: a place, a time of day, a season, a situation?
4. Does the poem advance an idea or a line of argument?
5. What is the poem's structure? Can you divide it into parts, based on stanzaic or other divisions; breaks in the syntax, the subject matter, the thought; changes of tone? Is there any progression of thought or feeling, or is the poem repetitive or circular, ending where it began?
6. Examine the images, including any figures of speech. Do they form any patterns? Does the poem contain any unusual metrical effects, contrasts, irony, understatement, hyperbole, and so forth?
7. Does the poem say anything to you personally? Can you relate it to your own thoughts, feelings, or experiences, or is its interest, as far as you are concerned, mainly historical?

A very useful aid in teaching lyric poetry is the section "Poems in Process" at the back of each volume. It is interesting in itself to see how poets go about their work. And, by comparing earlier drafts with the final versions as printed in the anthology, the students can themselves enter into the poetic process and come to see the reasons behind the revisions.

The Staging of the NAEL Plays

Most of our students have it some time been exposed to innovative staging that makes the audience rely on language and imagination instead of on scenery, lighting, and a curtain to locate them in dramatic space and time, and one may refer to such experience in explaining early English stages. Analogues might be drawn with the communal aspects of outdoor rock concerts, with performances at "Renaissance fairs," or with street theater. Some present-day street-theater companies perform on the backs of trucks—very much like the wagons used by the medieval guilds for the mystery plays, as noted on 1.379.

A contemporary recount describes the wagon on which the mystery plays were presented as a "Theater . . . very large and high, placed upon wheels," while mother calls it "a high place made like a house with two rooms, being open at the top: [in] the lower room they apparelled and dressed themselves; and in the upper room they played." The spectators stood (or milled around) on all four sides of the wagon, which meant that actors were always aware of their audiences. The actors did not confine themselves to playing on the wagon: they acted scenes or entire plays in front of it. This playing space, the *platea*, was unlocalized. There was no realistic scenery of the sort we are used to; the wagons were, however, rather elaborately decorated, and some had machinery for God or angels to ascend or descend. A favorite wagon decoration was the "hell mouth," into which Satan and his fellow devils gleefully shoved lost souls. Costumes were rich, according to surviving financial records.

NAEL cannot include every kind of drama between the medieval plays and the plays of Marlowe and Shakespeare, so students may wonder how stages developed from the pageant wagons to the solid structure in the generalized illustration of a playhouse of Shakespeare's time on 1.2962. In the years between the mysteries and the golden age of English theater, itinerant professional acting troupes performed brief dramas or interludes (see 1.491), often on and in front of a wagon which they set up in innyards or noble houses. Thus the upper stage and windows ("B" in the drawing) and the curtained recess ("C") were logical extensions of windows in the innyards. Another influence was that of the big Tudor halls, where dramatic entertainments might follow a dinner party. A screen traversed the lower end of the hall, flanked by two doors into the kitchen; compare the doors in the drawing. But note that whether in front of a wagon, in an innyard or on the floor of the hall, there is always a *platea* space.

When students look at the drawing and read 1.490–95, you may want to emphasize that James Burbage was not an architect but a carpenter: he did not invent the structure, but adapted elements from the innyards and halls. You may also want to stress that almost all the acting was done on the big thrust stage, projecting out into the audience, which (as we know from the contract, which has survived, to build the Fortune Theater) might measure as large as forty-three by twenty-seven feet. This thrust stage was the *platea*, which authors could turn into whatever locale they wanted: see, for example, *Twelfth Night* 4.2 (1.1092–95), where the clown Feste, disguised as Sir Topas the curate, visits Malvolio, who is in "prison" in Olivia's house. Malvolio speaks from "within" his offstage prison, where he will later be found "in a dark room and bound" (3.4).

Earlier twentieth-century reproductions of Elizabethan stages erred in emphasizing the recess and the upper gallery as playing areas. Indeed, modern scholarship questions whether earlier theaters even had the recess (the one surviving contemporary drawing of an Elizabethan theater shows none). In any case, the recess was, if employed, a "discovery space," in which Dr. Faustus or Volpone might be revealed. He would then immediately come out to the main acting area, where he would be surrounded by an audience standing on all three sides, wealthier spectators in boxes, and gallants actually sitting on the stage.

Very little is known about Elizabethan modes of acting, but we can infer from the plays themselves that physical agility was important. We can also infer, from a contemporary letter which states that performances averaged about two and a half hours, that speeches must have been delivered in a fast, bravura style. The Elizabethans were no doubt better listeners than we are.

The Elizabethans enjoyed spectacle as well as language. Philip Henslowe's inventory of his property room lists, for example, "i [*sic*] rock, i cage, i tomb, i Hell mouth . . . i tomb of Dido, i bedstead . . . i tree of golden apples"—that is, painted set pieces that could be moved onto the stage as needed; the hell mouth was a legacy from the mystery and morality plays. Essential also, for tragedies and histories, was the "state," or throne. Another aspect of spectacle was provided by bladders of pig's blood, which produced a gory realism in battle scenes. Finally, one must not forget the trapdoor ("D" in the drawing), which played its part in the last scene of Dr. Faustus, and, in some theaters, the flying throne that descended from the painted ceiling (under the roof). But as with every other aspect of Elizabethan staging, our knowledge is tantalizingly fragmentary and Henslowe's Admiral's Men may have been richer in props than other companies. Peter Thomson notes ("Playhouses and Players" in *The Cambridge Companion to Shakespeare Studies*, Cambridge, England, 1986, p. 81) that "we must assume that the platform on to which the Elizabethan actor walked was fairly empty. It was he who had to fill it."

Thomson also notes that, as we say on p. 1.411, costuming was "sumptuous." Leading actors were expected to provide their own costumes, and paid highly for them; for example, one actor, who perhaps had in annual income of £30, paid a tenth of that for "a man's gown of Peachcolour grain."

Dr. Faustus, Twelfth Night, King Lear, Volpone, and *The Duchess of Malfi* were all written to be performed on the public stage. It might be a useful exercise to ask students to direct a scene from one of these plays—either with other students as actors or in a short paper giving the "blocking moves"—so that they can experience for themselves the freedom of a big, unlocalized acting area.

Later in the period the public theaters were in competition with the more exclusive private theaters, such as the Blackfriars (see 1.494), which were indoors and artificially lighted. These were the prototypes of the Restoration theaters In this connection, students might read the description of masques (1.1294–95). These costly productions with innovations such as sliding wings, invented by Inigo Jones, also influenced staging during the Restoration During the Commonwealth the theaters were officially closed, but a few "underground" performances were also produced indoors. Some of the latter were quite elaborate, such as the operas staged by William D'Avenant, who subsequently received one of two royal licenses to operate a theater after the Restoration.

The new Restoration theaters were more intimate than the Elizabethan and Stuart private playhouses, though still larger than many college theaters today. Spectators now sat on benches in the pit (or, as we would say, the orchestra) instead of standing, or in the more expensive boxes, and they now faced a proscenium arch with its curtain. Prologues and epilogues were spoken on the forestage, and the curtain was drawn to reveal the "scenes." Most entrances and exits, however, were still made through the doors on either side of the proscenium arch. That, despite other changes in theater architecture, these doors remained as a holdover from the Tudor halls is a reminder that theater design is often conservative and ad hoc.

Restoration scenery was not three-dimensional but flat, facing the audience. The painted "flats" were set in grooves and were moved, for changes of scene, in full view of the audience; performances relied, as well, on stage machinery for impressive spectacles. Lighting was provided by the light in the auditorium, by footlights, and by hanging chandeliers.

The most important innovation was perhaps the substitution of actresses for the boy actors of the earlier theater. Many spectators in the new audiences had seen actresses in France during Charles's exile there, and, after the restrictions of the Puritan Commonwealth, the new sense of freedom seemed to apply to women as well. At first the recruitment of actresses was a problem because women had no tradition of acting; this is one reason why quick-witted women such as Nell Gwyn found early favor Together with young male actors, they were trained in the licensed theaters' acting schools, or "nurseries," to learn the manners and deportment of the gentry they were to play in the comedies.

With an indoor theater, a proscenium separating the audience from the stage, and scenery on that stage, we are within hailing distance of the "fourth-wall" theater familiar to students from their high schools. Indeed, the history of nineteenth-century staging might be very loosely summed up as the ongoing building-up of that fourth wall.

After the two licensed theaters—Covent Garden and Drury Lane—burned down in 1808, they were replaced by two "vast and ill-lighted" buildings (2.18), capable of housing the increasingly spectacular scenic effects demanded by growing audiences. Special effects obviously require distancing. By the 1820s most theaters were lit by gas, enabling the auditorium to be darkened, thereby, of course, separating the audience from the stage even more.

In 1848 licensing was repealed, and many new theaters were built, housing the varied fare described on 2.1063. Many of the elaborate productions were done by actor-managers such as Henry Irving, who ran their own companies and also starred. Toward the end of the nineteenth century, however, some playwrights were making attempts at realistic drama and were served by companies working at a quieter and more natural style of acting. *The Importance of Being Earnest*, though lavishly produced, was performed in this more subdued and realistic style. In the productions of the Gilbert and Sullivan operettas, Gilbert and his producer, Richard D'Oyly Carte, also strove for realism in costuming and sets. Gilbert was one of the first directors: he worked out the blocking moves of his actors and actresses before rehearsals, and coached their readings of lines. Shaw reviewed many elaborate productions of bad plays before he began writing his own plays. Moreover, his earlier plays, too controversial for the commercial theater, had simple productions in lecture halls; hence he, too, was a force for theatrical realism.

The contemporary plays in *NAEL* could be, and have been, produced very satisfactorily on proscenium stages. But if the direction of the nineteenth-century theater was to build the fourth wall, one major direction of recent staging has been to demolish it. There is no space here to describe all the innovations of twentieth-century theater; suffice it to note the popularity of open stages or theaters in the round. The audience coming in to see *Endgame*, for example, might sit around the sheet-covered ashbins Clov examines in the opening tableau. Or the drama critics in *The Real Inspector Hound* might perform in or near the audience. From the epic theater of Bertolt Brecht and the music hall, among others, directors are now able to choose a variety of acting styles for their productions. To bring us full circle, in 1985 the poet Tony Harrison, in collaboration with the Cottesloe Company of the National Theatre, combined many of the medieval mystery plays into three evening-long productions, wherein all the action took place *among* the audience.

APPENDIX B

Scansion Exercise for Volume 1 and Suggestions for Reading Poetry Aloud

Scansion Exercise

Read about rhythm and meter in *NAEL*, at the start of "Poetic Forms and Literary Terminology," pages 2944–47, and then follow the instructions below. Within the rhythm and meter section, on page 2946, you are given two scansions for the first time of Shakespeare's *Sonnet 116*. The first is strictly according to meter. The second is according to a rhythmical reading of the line. In metrical verse the rhythm is superimposed on the underlying regular meter, and there are often several ways of reading a line rhythmically, depending on where you place the stress. The formal meter, however, is quite regular. In this exercise, you are being asked to pick out the regular metrical beat. This means that an iambic pentameter should have five feet of two syllables, in each of which the second syllable receives the stress. Some lines end with an eleventh unstressed syllable (called a "feminine ending"). Never mind that some of these syllables may be very lightly stressed compared to others. For example, *to* and *of* are not important words in the first line of *Sonnet 116,* and *true*, in the last foot, is rhythmically more heavily stressed than *of*. However, within the foot, *of* is stressed relative to the last syllable of *marriage*, and *true* is slightly less stressed than the rhyming word *minds* (always stress the rhyming syllable). There is one metrical variation that you can indicate. In many feet, especially in the first foot of a line, the stress is inverted. Thus in the first foot of the sonnet, *Let* takes both metrical and rhythmical stress.

1. Identify the meter and verse length (the number of feet) in the following lines:

When I do count the clock that tells the time

Simple Simon met a Pieman

This is the forest primeval the murmuring pines and the hemlocks

'Tis the voice of the lobster I heard him declare

2. Scan the first stanza of Wyatt's *My Lute, Awake!* (1.530)

3. On 1.529–30, there are two versions of the same poem by Wyatt (*They Flee From Me*). The first is from a manuscript. The second is from a famous edition of poetry by Richard Tottel (*Tottel's Miscellany*)—see 1.526). Compare the scansion of lines 2, 3, 4, 5, and 16. What is the difference? Which do you prefer and why?

Suggestions for Reading Poetry Aloud

1. *Understand the meaning of the poem as best you can.*
If you know what the poet is saying and the poet's attitude to what is being said, you can then find an appropriate tone of voice and give the correct emphasis to each part of the poem.

2. *Read the poem silently to yourself before trying to read it aloud.*
Think of yourself as an actor with a script. Prepare your reading in advance (if you don't know how to pronounce a word, look it up in a dictionary). Mark the text for yourself, to indicate what to emphasize, where to pause (and how long), where to raise and lower your voice, etc.

3. *Read deliberately, as slowly as you can without exaggeration.*
You will almost invariably read faster in your audience's opinion than you imagine. You want the audience to appreciate your reading, not to be always conscious that you're in a hurry to get it over with.

4. *Don't recite in a mechanical way.*
The poem may have a definite and strong rhythm, but don't let your reading emphasize this at the expense of the sense. Watch the punctuation, making slight pauses for commas, a bit longer for semicolons and colons, and longer for full stops (periods, question marks, exclamation points). If your ear tells you the printed poem has a punctuation that is incorrect, change it.

5. *If the poem has rhymes, don't make the rhymes stand out by overemphasizing them.*
A brief pause at the end of the line will be sufficient for the listener to get the point. This may cause some trouble with run-on lines, but it is more important for the listener to hear the rhymes.

Index

This index covers authors and works discussed or listed in chapters 2–9 of this Guide.